Local Interests

Local Interests

*Politics, Policy, and Interest Groups
in US City Governments*

SARAH F. ANZIA

THE UNIVERSITY OF CHICAGO PRESS   CHICAGO AND LONDON

The University of Chicago Press, Chicago 60637
The University of Chicago Press, Ltd., London
© 2022 by The University of Chicago
All rights reserved. No part of this book may be used or reproduced in any manner
whatsoever without written permission, except in the case of brief quotations in critical
articles and reviews. For more information, contact the University of Chicago Press,
1427 E. 60th St., Chicago, IL 60637.
Published 2022
Printed in the United States of America

31 30 29 28 27 26 25 24 23 22   1 2 3 4 5

ISBN-13: 978-0-226-81927-3 (cloth)
ISBN-13: 978-0-226-81929-7 (paper)
ISBN-13: 978-0-226-81928-0 (e-book)
DOI: https://doi.org/10.7208/chicago/9780226819280.001.0001

Library of Congress Cataloging-in-Publication Data

Names: Anzia, Sarah F., author.
Title: Local interests : politics, policy, and interest groups in US city governments /
    Sarah F. Anzia.
Description: Chicago : University of Chicago Press, 2022. | Includes index.
Identifiers: LCCN 2021041769 | ISBN 9780226819273 (cloth) | ISBN 9780226819297
    (paperback) | ISBN 9780226819280 (ebook)
Subjects: LCSH: Local government—United States—Citizen participation. |
    Public interest groups—United States. | Police administration—United States—
    Citizen participation. | Economic development—United States—Citizen participation. |
    Housing policy—United States—Citizen participation.
Classification: LCC JS303.5 .A69 2022 | DDC 320.80973—dc23
LC record available at https://lccn.loc.gov/2021041769

TO EMMA AND NORAH

Contents

CHAPTER 1.   Interest Groups and Public Policy in US Local Government   1

CHAPTER 2.   The Policy-Focused Approach to Studying Interest Groups   20

CHAPTER 3.   How Active Are Interest Groups in Local Politics?   55

CHAPTER 4.   What Kinds of Interest Groups Are Most Active?   81

CHAPTER 5.   Political Parties in Local Politics   114

CHAPTER 6.   Influence: Issues, Approach, and Expectations   135

CHAPTER 7.   Business and Growth   163

CHAPTER 8.   Unions, Public Safety, and Local Government Spending   201

CHAPTER 9.   Interest Group Influence in Local Elections   240

CHAPTER 10. Local Interests and Power   264

Acknowledgments   279

Notes   283

Index   327

CHAPTER ONE

Interest Groups and Public Policy
in US Local Government

For a long time, local politics in the United States seemed tranquil compared to that of Washington, DC. Even as divisiveness and dysfunction were on full display in national politics, local governance appeared relatively uneventful. Other than the occasional scandal or crisis, usually in the largest cities, it seemed like most local government was well-functioning government: effective policies, responsive elected officials, and political consensus.

The past few years have shattered that illusion. Multiple wide-ranging crises have thrust America's local governments into the spotlight, exposing policy failures and problems that have been mounting for years. High housing prices in many metropolitan areas—fueled in part by a shortage in supply—have become a drag on growth, decreased mobility, and contributed to racial segregation.[1] Police misconduct is now known to be widespread, not confined to a few cities or a few officers as it once may have seemed.[2] Two recessions have exposed vulnerabilities in local government revenue structures and patterns of inefficient spending, which have combined to force cuts in public service provision.[3] All is not well in local government, and it hasn't been for some time.

Growing awareness of these kinds of problems has inspired a groundswell of reform efforts, including a YIMBY (Yes in My Backyard) movement,[4] calls to defund and reimagine policing,[5] and pushes to curb growth in public employee retirement costs.[6] But reform momentum often seems to rise and fall without major policy changes of note. Housing development continues to be delayed, efforts to densify snuffed out.[7] Even after the massive protests against police brutality and systemic racism during the summer of 2020, few cities were quick to make significant changes to policing or police budgets.[8] And in local governments around the country, growth in public employee retirement costs shows little sign of abating, and local governments continue to feel the crunch.[9]

Why does it seem like so little changes even as public recognition of these problems grows? A look at a few cities helps to illustrate. Consider Albuquerque, New Mexico, where a developer, Gamma Development, recently proposed a 23-acre, 76-unit, single-family housing development on the west side of the city. After the city's Environmental Planning Commission approved the plan, the Taylor Ranch Neighborhood Association and nearby neighbors appealed the decision,[10] arguing that the development failed to provide sufficient open space and would threaten the nearby Oxbow wetlands. In response to these objections, the city council sent the decision back to the commission for reconsideration, delaying the development of new housing.[11] More than a year later, the proposed housing development had been downsized, the city was planning to purchase some of the land to preserve as open space, and none of the housing had been built.[12]

Consider also Seattle, Washington, where efforts to reform the police department have met strong resistance from the city's labor unions. In 2010, community organizations wrote to the US Department of Justice (DOJ) requesting an investigation of excessive use of force by officers in the Seattle Police Department. The city entered into a consent decree with DOJ in 2012 that required that the city implement reforms, and the city did eventually pass a new police accountability law. But just a few months later, collective bargaining agreements reached with the Seattle Police Officers Guild (SPOG) rolled back some of the reforms, imposing new restrictions on how police officers can be investigated and disciplined.[13] Community activists were outraged, but the city's labor unions defended the sanctity of collective bargaining and due process for city employees.[14] As Kenny Stuart, president of the Seattle Fire Fighters Union, told the city council, "Collective bargaining is a fundamental element of labor relations and the progressive movement."[15] The *Seattle Times* wrote that Seattle mayor Jenny Durkan "is almost certain to be aggressively lobbied to seek sweeping changes" to the contract but "also will face the sway of the labor community, one of her biggest backers, which has fiercely supported SPOG's collective bargaining rights."[16]

Then there is Redwood City, California, where the pandemic-induced economic downturn in 2020 collided with the city's structural deficit problem to produce a $7 million hole in the city budget.[17] To deal with the shortfall, the city proposed widespread budget cuts, including a 5.6% total cut to the fire department and temporary replacement of one of the two engines in the downtown fire station with a smaller, less expensive vehicle. But that proposal met resistance from the city's firefighters and the Farm Hill Neighborhood Association,[18] which warned of increased emergency response times and the endangerment of city residents. In response to the pressure, the city council walked back its proposal, agreeing to dig deeper into reserves and contemplate other cuts so that the second downtown engine could remain in service.[19]

These are just a few examples, but they share something in common: in each case, interest groups appear to play a prominent role. If we were to sit back and reflect on how to characterize policy making and political representation in these cases, we would certainly build in a role for real estate developers, neighborhood associations, and labor unions. It is simple and obvious. In Albuquerque, Seattle, and Redwood City, interest groups seem to be involved in shaping public policy.

Yet research on local politics has tended to ignore interest groups, and research on interest groups has tended to ignore local government. In studying American cities, most political scientists have focused on elected officials, the mass public, and active subsets of local residents, such as homeowners or voters.[20] Recent scholarship on political representation in local government conceives of representation as a relationship between elected officials and citizens—and barely mentions interest groups.[21] Meanwhile, the research literature on interest groups is almost entirely about national politics,[22] and its theories offer few insights into what to expect of interest group activity in the local arena. It also offers little guidance on how to evaluate interest group influence, whether in the local context or any other. As it stands, we know stunningly little about the role of interest groups in local politics.

This book is a step toward remedying that. It is a book about interest groups in local government: how active interest groups are, what they do in local politics, and how they shape a wide range of local public policies, including the use of business tax incentives, housing development, spending on the police, and the size of local government budgets. It shows that interest groups are politically active in many cities and that they often do have influence. A major payoff of this in-depth look at local interest groups is a clearer account of why cities have the policies they do—and how it has a lot to do with forces that are hard at work even when it appears as though not much is happening. But by putting the spotlight on interest groups in local politics, this book also accomplishes something else: an approach to studying interest groups that is a departure from the way they have been studied for the past several decades.

The core of my argument is that to understand what interest groups do in politics, and what influence they have, we need to put the focus on what interest groups care most about: public policy.[23] To explain the constellations of interest groups active in a government, we should start by thinking about what the government actually *does*—the policies it makes. And public policy is also the key to detecting interest group influence. Scholars focused on interest groups have long recognized that public policy is the place to look for the fingerprints of their influence, but they have gotten bogged down by a variety of conceptual, measurement, design, and inferential problems and have deviated from analyzing public policy as the dependent variable. In my analysis of local politics, I keep the focus on public policy as the dependent variable when testing for interest group influence, and I find that interest groups often *do* make a difference.

This fresh theoretical approach allows us to see things differently—and more clearly. For instance, we might think, from what we know about national politics, that local politics would be intensely partisan, that business would clash head-on with labor, or that the clout of groups with abundant resources would far outweigh that of groups with members of lesser means. Alternatively, from what has been said about local politics, we might guess that local government would involve few interest groups and little regular political conflict. None of that would be right. In this book, I apply a policy-focused approach to questions about interest groups in US municipal governments, and the result is a more comprehensive and more accurate view of the political dynamics of American local governments.

A Different Perspective on Local Politics

In recent decades, "American politics" has mostly been taken to mean national politics, and to the extent that political scientists have branched out to study other American governments, they have mainly looked at states—not local governments like counties, municipalities, and school districts. Yet local governments are and always have been an important part of American government. The nearly ninety thousand local governments in the United States spend roughly a quarter of the nation's public money. They are responsible for public education, infrastructure, housing, public safety, public health, and other important services. The policies they make touch the day-to-day lives of virtually everyone living in the United States, and they play a significant role in shaping broader social outcomes, including the size of government and economic, political, and racial (in)equality. In all of the examples above—housing, policing, and fire protection—the issues at stake are nationally important, but the decision makers and the politics are primarily local.

Researchers and political observers have recently started to pay much more attention to local government—a positive development—but with that shift has come new debate about how best to characterize the dynamics of local politics.[24] Within the relatively small group of political scientists who have continued to study local politics over the years, a prominent view is that local politics is distinctive—and perhaps even less "political" than state and national politics. By one account, the ease of mobility of taxpaying residents and businesses forces city officials to have a laserlike focus on economic development; and since all city residents benefit from a strong local economy (the argument goes), there simply isn't much for them to disagree about—and little room for traditional politics.[25] Another perspective depicts local elections as managerial in nature: instead of being defined by partisanship, ideology, or regular issues that divide local residents, they are decided on the basis of custodial performance, that is, whether incumbents successfully maintain satisfactory levels of taxes and services. According to this account, the issue divisions that do arise in local government are idiosyncratic, such as scandals afflicting particular places at particular times, and regular political conflict is rare.[26]

Recently, a newer wave of research has challenged that perspective and given rise to a very different account—one that depicts local politics as not only political but also similar to national politics in fundamental ways. Studies of the ideologies and party affiliations of city residents have found that cities with liberal and Democratic residents tend to produce different policies from those with conservative and Republican residents: for example, they spend more overall per capita and have more liberal environmental policies.[27] Others have demonstrated that cities and counties with Democratic elected officials have greater expenditures than those whose elected officials are Republican.[28] The conclusion to be drawn, according to some scholars, is that local politics is *not* that distinctive. Like national politics, it is divided along partisan and ideological lines.

While there are elements of truth in both of these accounts, both are off-target in key respects, as I show throughout this book. Accounts of local politics as partisan and ideological have not been sufficiently attentive to the fact that local governments are quite different from the federal government. They are smaller. Their institutions are usually different: most hold nonpartisan elections on days other than state and national elections and do not have independently elected executives or districted legislatures.[29] Even more important, however, are the differences in what local governments *do*. It is not just that the range of policies they can make is more limited or that they are constrained by state and national government, as some have discussed.[30] The actual substance of what they do is mostly different from the federal government as well, and the implications for their politics are hugely important.

What, then, do US local governments do? It varies, of course, but some generalizations help set the stage. The nation's single-purpose governments are easiest to characterize because by definition they each do only one thing: school districts provide public education, library districts provide library services, and so on.[31] The responsibilities of municipal governments vary both across and within states, but at the heart of what they do are economic development, regulation of land use (such as housing development), and the provision of services like police protection, fire protection, street repair, parks and recreation, and sewers and water.[32] As figure 1.1 shows, in 2017, 17% of all municipal government expenditures in the United States went to utilities (water, electric, gas supply, and transit), 10% to police protection, 8% to sanitation (sewerage and solid waste management), 6% to highways and roads, 5% to both fire protection and health and hospitals, and 4% to parks and recreation. The functions of county governments vary more widely than those of municipal governments, but the ones that account for the largest shares of total county expenditures are health and hospitals (18%), public welfare (9%), police protection (7%), corrections (6%), and highways and roads (6%).[33] A few of these local policies have parallels to the issues that divide the parties and define ideology in national politics, but many of them do not.

Instead of starting with partisanship and ideology, we should start with these core functions of local government and consider the kinds of interests they generate. In attempting to assess the forces that shape local politics and policy, we should put the focus on the issue areas that are

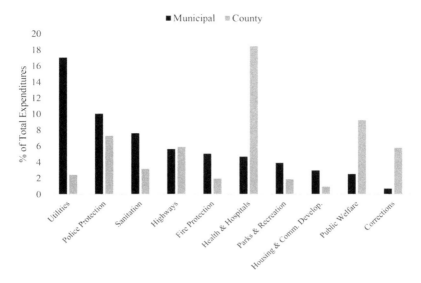

FIGURE 1.1 Local government expenditures, 2017

at the heart of what local governments do. That is my approach in this book, and the picture that emerges is clear: Local politics *is* distinctive. In most places, most of the time, it is not strongly defined by national partisan and ideological alignments. Instead, local interest groups' activities and alignments—and thus political conflict—are shaped by what the governments do. Moreover, local residents' national-level partisanship and ideology are often weak predictors of local policy. One of the main reasons for this, again, is policy: most local governments handle different kinds of issues from those of the federal government.

But that does not mean that local policy making and governments are apolitical. Far from it. Local politics is often intensely political but in ways that are different from national politics. Moreover, a lot of the politics in local government is regular and predictable. There are issues that come up again and again, and there are constituencies with vested interests in them.[34] Open, visible conflict is less common in local politics than in other arenas, so it can be easy to miss this—and easy to think that local residents must be in agreement on local policy matters. But there can be conflict without an active fight. Local policy making still has winners and losers, even when policies are made in the shadows, out of public view. It is by putting the focus on interest groups and public policy that we gain this perspective and see that underlying conflict. Local governments have their own unique brand of politics, but it is politics nonetheless.

A Broader Conceptualization of Political Representation

Putting interest groups and policy front and center in the study of local politics makes clear the need for a broader conceptualization of political representation. Regardless of whether the case being examined is national, state, or local government, research on political representation has up to this point been largely about how well public policies (or political elites' positions on policies) align with the preferences of the mass public.[35] The general setup is one in which the policy preferences of the mass public are measured with public opinion data, as seems sensible. The problem, however, is that there are many issues that have profound impacts on citizens that typically aren't the subjects of active debate and don't get asked about in public opinion polls. The lack of public opinion data on such issues doesn't mean they are unimportant or that citizens agree on them. Yet those issues are excluded from assessments of political representation because the mechanics of the dominant paradigm require public opinion data. The result is a highly filtered view of whose interests get represented in American policy making.

Policing is a case in point. Before 2020, there were relatively few public opinion polls on police reform or the funding of police departments. Then, when policing became much more salient in 2020, public opinion polls on the topic increased dramatically.[36] But it is not as though the policies that contributed to the crisis were made in 2020. The reality, rather, is that for years and decades before policing problems attracted widespread public attention, cities and counties were regularly making policies governing police practices. They were making rules for how officers could be evaluated and disciplined. They were crafting budgets that allocated certain resources to local police agencies. For those trained to look for public opinion data and active policy fights, it would have seemed like there was little there to study until 2020. But of course there was. The policies made during quieter times have profound and nonuniform impacts on American citizens. That those impacts came into fuller view in 2020 does not mean that the policies being made in previous years were any less important.

If we start with what governments do—the policies they make—instead of the special set of issues for which there are public opinion data, we see the importance of including issues like these in assessments of political representation, regardless of whether they generate open conflict. In the study of local politics, the focus of this book, that means examining policies that seem technical and perhaps uninteresting but are in fact crucial to broader outcomes of interest, such as minimum lot size requirements for new housing development, rules governing how local government employees provide public services, and the myriad budgetary decisions that can ultimately lead to fiscal distress. But the implications of this shift in perspective are relevant beyond the local context. It means we should consider whose interests are represented when state governments underfund pensions, put caps on the number of charter schools allowed, or provide rebates for home solar power systems. It extends to national politics as well, where policies like the tax rate on carried interest and financial deregulation deserve to be part of accounts of political representation.[37]

Extending the study of political representation to issues without public opinion data naturally makes it harder to assess whether policy is responsive to mass publics. But that raises the question of why pride of place has been given to mass publics.[38] Why, in the study of political representation, have interest groups been treated as a peripheral matter, as though questions about interest group influence are somehow separate?[39] The reason is not that political scientists at some point decided that interest groups were unimportant. Instead, it has to do with the challenges of studying interest groups and the way the field of political science evolved.[40]

The unresolved debates about community power during the 1960s played a significant role in pushing interest groups to the sidelines. At that time, interest groups were at the center of how political scientists understood American politics, especially in the pluralist research tradition.[41] One especially famous study—Robert Dahl's analysis of key policy decisions in New Haven, Connecticut—found that different individuals and groups appeared to be influential on different issues.[42] A conclusion drawn from this was that group power must be broadly distributed in American society. But that approach and conclusion prompted a sharp critique: namely, that group activities during active decision making only represent the "first face" of power, the one that is easiest for researchers to observe.[43] Groups might also exercise considerable power by *prevent-*

ing debate and *blocking* issues from being placed on the agenda. Moreover, groups that expect to lose a potential fight might not bother to contest the policy in question in the first place. In such cases, power is being exercised, but there is little for the researcher to see.[44] What becomes clear, then, is that one cannot draw general conclusions about power by looking only at issues that are being actively debated.

The inability to see or measure the "second face" of power was a problem for the study of groups, and it became an even bigger problem as rational choice and behavioralist approaches to studying politics gained prominence.[45] These approaches put the emphasis on individual choice and quantitative analysis, and the study of groups did not fit comfortably within them.[46] Tracking and quantifying the behavior of voters and legislators proved simpler.[47] The later turn to causal inference and "big data" made it even more difficult for interest group scholarship to find a foothold in the mainstream. Much of what interest groups do to try to exercise influence is difficult to measure and quantify, and a lot of it is also strategic: endogenous to outcomes of interest and rooted in calculations about anticipated reactions. With all of these challenges, it is no wonder that research on political representation evolved to be mainly about the linkages between elected officials and the mass public.

There is one big problem with this, however. Interest groups appear to be quite important in American politics. As we will see, in the local arena, if we tried to explain the politics of business tax incentives, policing, or even city spending without considering the role of interest groups, we would be missing a big piece of the puzzle—and in some cases drawing the wrong conclusions.

Thus, if the pluralists foundered by trying to draw general conclusions about group power by looking only at active decision making, then the modern study of political representation has done something similar by focusing primarily on mass publics and issues for which there are public opinion data. My approach in this book offers a broader take on local political representation—one that considers a wider range of local policies and prioritizes interest groups as potential influencers.

A Policy-Focused Approach to Research on Interest Groups

In turning attention to interest groups in local politics, we are confronted with a host of basic, unanswered questions: How active are interest groups in local government? What kinds of interest groups are politically active, and what do they do? Do interest groups have influence in local politics? If so, under what conditions, and what does that influence look like? Are local policies different from what they otherwise would be because of interest groups?

Given that these are all questions about interest groups, it is only natural to look to scholarship on interest groups for insights. There is, after all, research literature on interest groups, even if it has developed separately from research on political representation. And while research on interest groups has focused almost exclusively on national politics, one would think it would still contain theories and frameworks relevant to the local context.

Unfortunately, though, it does not. Because of its focus on the federal government, which is awash in a wide variety of interest groups, interest group scholarship hasn't developed theories of how active interest groups will be in different kinds of governments or the conditions under which interest groups will be more or less politically active. In attempting to explain which types of groups will be most active, it has stressed the importance of resources—a theoretical lens that does not shed light on which groups will be most active in local politics. Moreover, research on interest group influence has produced mixed, inconclusive findings. Some studies have uncovered evidence of influence, but just as many have turned up little or none.[48] The interest group scholar Beth Leech sums up the situation well: "For those who try to quantify and systematically measure [interest group] influence . . . it has proved illusive. . . . Almost everyone believes that interest groups are influential, and yet systematic studies have as often pointed to the limits on interest group influence as have concluded that strong influence exists."[49]

Thus, to explain patterns of interest group activity in local politics and to evaluate the extent of interest groups' influence on local politics and policy, I cannot rely on existing theoretical frameworks and empirical strategies in the interest group literature. I have to build them from the ground up. I do that by putting public policy at the foundation.

This provides a way to move forward on basic questions about local interest groups, but it also generates a new approach to studying interest group activity more generally. By emphasizing interest groups' need to survive and need for resources, existing theoretical frameworks have deprioritized their interests. As I show, however, we cannot get very far in explaining patterns of local interest group activity without consideration of what groups are trying to achieve in terms of policy. Actually, one of the first steps toward understanding whether interest groups will be active in local government, how active they will be, and which ones will be active should be to consider the policies the government makes—and groups' interests in them. Importantly, moreover, not all interests are equally motivating. What I argue in this book is that the most politically active interest groups tend to be those with a large, direct, regular, and economic interest in what that government does.

The policy-focused approach also forges a link between two parts of the interest group literature that have developed in a disconnected way: research on interest group activity, which has deprioritized interest groups' policy goals, and research on interest group influence, which has not—at least in principle. On the influence side of the interest group literature, scholars have long viewed public policy as the main goal of interest groups and the outcome they are trying to influence. Yet in designing quantitative empirical tests of interest group influence, they have deviated from modeling public policy as the dependent variable. Instead, they have analyzed roll-call votes or indicators for policy change. These deviations may seem minor, but they have been consequential and have very likely limited scholars' ability to detect interest group influence. And the main reason they have done this is that they have gone looking for cross-sectional variation within a single government: the federal government. The near-exclusive focus on the federal government has thus done more than hinder progress on learning about other parts of American government; it has also meant that the enterprise of testing for interest group influence has been developed and pursued in a setting where it is perhaps most difficult to detect.

The beauty of diagnosing the problem is that it points to a path forward. It shows us that when testing for interest group influence, we should try to model public policy as the dependent variable. Historical analysis of policy is one way of doing that, but another—perhaps more appealing to quantitatively inclined researchers—is to compare public policies across subnational governments, including local governments. Local governments feature thousands of versions of housing policy, thousands of approaches to policing, and thousands of local education policies. When the subject matter is local government, the dependent variable can actually be public policy. And because the content of public policy embeds the influence of interest groups that has accrued over a long period of time, analyzing public policy as the dependent variable sets things up to detect interest group influence when it exists.

My approach also opens the door to more theoretical clarity on questions about the conditions under which we should expect an interest group to have influence on policy. The key, I argue, is to consider the nature of a group's interest in a particular policy, such as whether to move forward with a high-density housing development or whether to deploy body cameras for the city's police officers. Are the interest group's preferences on that policy homogeneous? Does the group have interests in the policy that differ from those of other political actors, such as elected officials? And is the interest group politically focused on that particular policy? I argue that these three considerations will shape whether an interest group's political activity in a city—conceptualized broadly—will result in public policies that are different from what they otherwise would have been.

In the end, then, local politics is both the puzzle and a solution of sorts. To gain a better understanding of local political representation and public policy, I set out to learn about local interest groups. In the process, I uncovered deeper layers of problems in existing research on interest groups. And, as it turns out, putting the focus on local government helps unpack and address those deeper problems. The more limited policy scope of local government allows us to see clearly how policy shapes interest group activity. The cross-sectional variation in local public policies enables tests of whether and under what conditions interest group activity makes a difference to public policy. And because public policies are everywhere, this is relevant beyond interest groups in local government. Once we see and appreciate that policies are a linchpin for understanding interest group activity and influence at the local level, that helps us to understand what interest groups do—and to what effect—in contexts beyond the local arena. By moving the study of interest groups to this new context, we gain fresh perspectives that transcend the local government setting.

Plan of the Book

I begin in chapter 2 with an in-depth discussion of the theoretical, conceptual, and design matters outlined above. I lay out the policy-focused approach and explain how it connects to and departs from existing scholarship on interest groups and political representation. Because I build on multiple research literatures, there is a lot of ground to cover, and readers not wishing to wade deeper into the scholarly literature on these topics can focus on the later, data-oriented chapters on local interest groups and local policies. But, importantly, chapter 2 sets up the theoretical scaffolding for the empirical analysis to follow and is essential for fully understanding how my approach helps reorient the study of interest groups and broaden the study of political representation.

The empirical portion of the book begins in chapters 3, 4, and 5 with an assessment of the activity of groups in municipal governments throughout the United States. This is a crucial first step, but even this first step is difficult and messy because of the various challenges of data collection, measurement, and inference. These challenges are confronted by all social science researchers, but they are especially acute for those studying interest groups, and the local context is the most challenging of all. Unlike the cases of state governments and the federal government, there are no data bases of registered lobbying groups or campaign contributions for the nation's local governments.[50] Most of the data on local interest groups that we might want aren't even stored somewhere waiting for an enterprising researcher to collect them. This alone is a major barrier—*the* major barrier—to studying local interest groups.

Still, the examples from Albuquerque, Seattle, and Redwood City tell us that there *are* local groups to be studied and that formal lobbying and campaign contributions are not the only—and perhaps not even the most important—ways that they get active in local politics. In order to clear this hurdle and make progress, I surveyed elected officials and candidates in hundreds of municipal governments across the United States. The first survey, fielded in early spring 2015, asked city council members and mayors to rate the overall activity of interest groups in their cities as well as the political activity of several different types of groups. The second survey, fielded in two waves in 2016 and 2017, asked city council and mayoral candidates to rate the activity of different interest groups and political parties in their most recent elections. The resulting data are the basis of my main measures of interest group activity in this book.

They are by no means perfect, and I round out my analysis using campaign contribution data and case studies, but the survey-based measures have notable strengths. First, and most simply, they are data on local interest group activity, which are difficult if not impossible to collect in other ways. Second, they allow for broader, more inclusive measures of interest group activity than do data on campaign contributions or hypothetical measures of formal lobbying. Third, they are good measures of who the *regular* players are in local politics. Some groups get involved only when there is a scandal or a contentious decision, and unless my surveys happened to coincide with such an event it is likely that I missed most of them. But the surveys are well positioned to pick up the groups that are regularly and consistently involved in local politics—"normal" local politics. For a first study of local interest groups, and one ultimately focused on understanding their influence, that is what we most want to know.

Chapters 3 and 4 thus give the lay of the land, describing the amount of interest group activity in American cities (chap. 3) and showing what types of interest groups are most politically active and how that varies across cities (chap. 4). My analysis in these chapters presents the first assessment of the policy-focused approach and illustrates how the amount and the type of interest group activity are shaped by the policies cities make. Larger cities that make policy on a wider range of issues have more interest groups. And the types of interest groups that are most politically engaged are the ones with large, direct, regular, and material interests in what the city does. Chambers of commerce, developers, and neighborhood associations are some of the most politically active interest groups; they have large stakes in policies related to economic development and land use, including housing. But just as active in most cities are unions of police officers and firefighters, which likewise have a lot at stake in city decisions, in their case, decisions on public safety provision and spending. This local mix of interest groups does not look like that of Washington, DC, nor do the data show that unions everywhere are less active than business. The main reason is that most local policy issues are different from those that dominate national politics, and the issues are a prime motivator of interest group activity.

Anyone accustomed to following national politics in the United States might expect political parties to be the most important groups in local politics, so in chapter 5 I examine political party activity in municipal elections. I find that political parties are active in many local elections but not as active as interest groups. Moreover, when parties are engaged, it looks as though they are operating as just another group alongside interest groups—not coordinating or structuring local interest group activity. As one illustration of this, labor unions and business- and growth-oriented interest groups like chambers of commerce and developers devote most of their energy in local politics to different issues, and even when labor and business are interested in the same local issues, often their interests do not conflict. The explanation, again, is that policies shape interest group activity. Group alignments vary according to the issues—not necessarily according to the partisan and ideological alignments we are used to seeing in national politics.

In the second half of the book, I turn to interest group influence—to what difference all of this interest group activity makes. This, in many ways, is the hardest part. Venturing into a study of interest group influence means wading into a thicket. But this is also the most important part. The main reason we want to understand interest group activity in the first place is so that we can assess whether it affects outcomes we care about. That is what connects the study of interest groups to the study of political representation, governance, and democracy.

And so I move forward, without letting the inevitable measurement, endogeneity, and inferential challenges deter the whole endeavor. My approach is not without shortcomings, but it improves on the ways interest group influence has been evaluated before, in three ways. First, my survey-based measures of interest group activity—here the key independent variables—are broader than measures of any single form of interest group activity and therefore set things up better for detecting interest group influence. Second, I insert interest groups into the familiar structure of research on political responsiveness: I evaluate whether greater activity by particular interest groups is associated with different outcomes, controlling for other variables that have been emphasized in the local politics literature, including city size, local demographics, citizen partisanship and ideology, and political institutions. Third, and most important, I analyze local policies as dependent variables.

Chapter 6 describes the broad local issue areas I focus on: economic development and growth (including housing development) and public safety policies (including local government spending). I use the framework developed in chapter 2 to set expectations about the conditions under which interest group activity will affect specific policies in these two areas, and in so doing I draw on insights from research on the politics of economic development, housing, and public-sector unions. In addition, chapter 6 explains how my analysis contends with other forces that might shape local policies, including homeowners and the partisan and ideological commitments of city residents.

Chapter 7 dives into a wide-ranging analysis of local policies related to economic development and growth, and the findings showcase both the importance of interest group influence and the constraints on that influence. In general, cities with more active business groups have local policies that are friendlier to business and growth, but this plays out in different ways depending on the particular policy examined—and the extent of open conflict.

I start with an analysis of which cities rely more heavily on business tax incentives and lose greater revenue to tax abatement. The role of interest groups there is clear: cities with more politically active chambers of commerce rely more heavily on business tax incentives and lose more revenue per capita to tax abatement than cities with less active chambers of commerce. There is little sign that city residents' political leanings have much to do with it.

Housing development policies are another matter. Business group activity is still associated with pro-growth policies: cities with more active chambers of commerce have regulations and processes that make it easier to develop new housing, and cities with more politically engaged developers permit more units of new housing construction. But the bigger picture is hardly one of cities as "growth machines" dominated by development and growth interests as some have asserted.[51] In fact, this is an area where the mass public (or at least a subset of it) appears to be quite influential—and is pushing in the direction of less development. Consistent with what others have theorized and found,[52] cities with more homeowners permit less housing development—in particular, less high-density, multifamily housing development. This, then, is a policy area with an unusual amount of open contestation and politically active opposition, in part because the costs imposed on the "losers" are so direct and visible.

In chapter 8, I put the spotlight on police and firefighters' unions and the local policies they care most about, including spending on compensation and policies governing how police officers do their jobs. These kinds of policies have received far less attention from researchers—probably because under normal circumstances they don't generate open political conflict—but are incredibly important to how local governments operate and to local residents. Consistent with research on public-sector unions,[53] I show that greater political activity by police and firefighters' unions in city politics is associated with more spending per capita on police and firefighter compensation. In addition, I find that when police unions have collective bargaining and are more politically active, cities are more likely to compensate police officers with certain forms of "extra pay," such as shift differential pay, and are less likely to offer compensation policies unions are likely to oppose, specifically, merit or performance pay. As of 2016, they also appear to have been less likely to have deployed body cameras.

This much is important for anyone interested in local policing or public-sector unions, but it is also directly relevant to our understanding of political representation. As I discussed earlier, research has found that cities with more liberal residents tend to have greater overall expenditures and concludes that this is because local city officials are being responsive to their citizens.[54] But I show that the influence of public-sector unions through both traditional politics and collective bargaining pushes up total police and fire protection spending. Having collective bargaining, in turn, increases overall municipal government spending. Once I account for this, it becomes clear that the reason more liberal cities tend to have higher expenditures is not necessarily that they are being responsive to their citizens' preferences. They are also being responsive to their unions, which are more politically active and more likely to have collective bargaining in more liberal, Democratic places.

Finally, in chapter 9, I examine one potentially important stage at which interest groups might have influence: local elections. Using new data on local candidates' positions on economic development and public safety, I show that preferences in the two issue areas are only weakly correlated, adding to evidence that local politics in many places is not structured by a single ideological dimension.[55] I also find that in cities where police and firefighters' unions are more active in local elections, the winning candidates express more favorable views toward spending on fire departments and stronger support for collective bargaining for police officers and firefighters. While these findings are preliminary, they suggest that the electoral activity of some interest groups is associated with winning candidates having policy positions more favorable to them.

By examining local interest groups with this policy-focused lens, then, what emerges is a clearer and more comprehensive picture of local politics: one that is more accurate about who is being represented and how and one that helps us understand the political dynamics behind why local governments have the public policies they do. In addition, we gain a new theoretical framework for studying interest groups. Developing it and putting it to use shows that interest groups often do have influence. But to see that influence, we have to focus on it, prioritize it, and break out of the standard ways of doing things. We have to look beyond the federal government. We have to consider public policies that don't come with public opinion data. We have to let go of the presupposition that everything is structured by national partisanship and ideology. And we have to look beyond the open conflict to the quieter corners of public policy making—where power is exercised out of the spotlight in ways that profoundly affect everyone in the United States.

CHAPTER TWO

The Policy-Focused Approach to Studying Interest Groups

If we allow ourselves to step back and ask why it is important to study interest groups, the answer comes easily: because interest groups might influence politics and policy. We know that political and policy outcomes don't always align with citizens' preferences.[1] Some major policy enactments are wildly unpopular, and some proposals that are popular don't get enacted. There are also important policy and political economic shifts that cannot be explained by shifts in public opinion.[2] Interest groups are important to study because they might contribute to these phenomena. They are important to understand because they might have influence.

Whether stated explicitly or not, research on political representation is also about influence. It is just that it has mainly focused on the influence of mass publics, conceiving of the potential "influencers" as individual citizens and their preferences. But while interest groups have played a secondary role in such models—if they are considered at all—there are strong reasons to think that interest groups have even greater potential for influence than individuals operating autonomously. The sole political activity of most individuals is voting. By itself, casting a vote for a candidate does not clearly communicate policy preferences. How, then, do policy makers know what their constituencies want, so that they can be responsive to them should they wish? Often they learn from *other* political activities that more effectively convey policy preferences, such as communicating with officials, testifying at hearings, and lobbying. Crucially, moreover, those activities are often executed and coordinated by organized groups. Then there is the question of how individuals come to

THE POLICY-FOCUSED APPROACH TO STUDYING INTEREST GROUPS   21

have certain policy preferences in the first place, how they know which policy proposals are in their interests, and how they become mobilized into political action on the basis of those preferences. Typically individuals don't do all of this on their own, in isolation. Groups are critical in this regard [3] Interest groups therefore not only deserve to be incorporated into models of political representation; they deserve to be prioritized in them.

Doing that requires moving beyond public opinion as the only benchmark against which representation can be evaluated. As I said earlier, there are important issues that are not included in public opinion polls. There are also policies about which the public doesn't have meaningful opinions.[4] Most Americans, for example, probably don't have crystallized views on the details of the Volcker Rule—a key provision of the 2010 Dodd-Frank reform—even though large banks have been arguing with government agencies over the particulars for a decade. Citizens often have opinions on outcomes, such as preventing another major economic crisis, but not on the specific policies that produce those outcomes.[5] There are still important questions to be answered about whether policies in these cases are in the public interest—even if the public isn't paying close attention. These may even be the issues on which interest groups are in the best position to push policy in their favor, because they are in the "electoral blind spot."[6]

Highlighting the centrality of influence therefore points to the need for broadening the study of political representation, but it also helps to ground the study of interest groups. If we care about interest groups because we care about whether outcomes are in the public interest, or whether interest group influence results in policy that is different from what it otherwise would have been, then influence is what motivates—or should motivate—the enterprise of studying interest groups. This may seem basic and uncontroversial, but it is important. It helps clarify what we should prioritize in the study of interest group activity: we should study interest group activity in a way that is a stepping-stone to studying their influence. Moreover, if we are looking for evidence of interest group influence, we should be focused on the kinds of outcomes interest groups care about and most want to influence.

What interest groups care about, ultimately, is public policy.[7] For example, large banks want favorable provisions put into the Volcker Rule and a less regulated environment. Teachers' unions want to limit the number of charter schools and enact other policies that protect public school teachers' jobs and compensation. Environmental groups want stricter auto emissions standards and policies that promote clean air and clean water and preserve national parks and hiking areas. These groups may not fully achieve those goals in the next roll-call vote, after the next election, or even in the next few years, but that is what they are seeking in the long run: public policies they favor.

The most productive first step toward answering questions about interest groups in any government is therefore to adopt what Jacob Hacker and Paul Pierson call a "policy-focused approach."[8] When governments create policies, those policies generate incentives for interest groups that benefit from them to try to keep them in place.[9] And when governments are capable of making policies on a particular issue, interest groups that care about that issue try to influence the decision makers in the hope of steering policy in the direction they favor. In a policy-focused approach, then, the starting point for thinking about interest groups is policy. That is what they are ultimately trying to influence. It is the key to understanding interest group activity as well: if we want to know how active interest groups will be in a government and which interest groups will be active, we should start by considering the policies the government makes and the particular issues it considers.

This policy-focused approach is by no means new—in fact, it is a guiding insight of the policy feedback literature—but by prioritizing interest groups, it departs from the mainstream American politics approach to studying representation.[10] It is also a departure from the American politics subfield's prioritization of causal inference in that it is explicit about the endogeneity of interest group activity and public policy. But most important for my discussion in this chapter is that it is even a significant departure from the literature on interest groups. The literature on interest groups is substantial though fragmented. But whether viewed in segments or as a whole, it tends to deprioritize interest groups' policy goals. Most of it does not study interest groups with a strong policy focus. And as I explain, this is a major reason that this literature offers little guidance on important questions of interest group activity and influence.

My approach puts policy at the center of the study of interest groups. Once we focus on interest groups' *interests*, theoretical expectations about local interest group activity come somewhat naturally. And rather than develop separate theories of interest group activity and interest group influence, as much of the existing literature does, my approach conceives of these aspects as parts of the same whole. It promotes studying interest group activity as a stepping-stone to studying group influence, with public policy being the linchpin that connects the two. Moreover, by keeping the focus on public policy and by studying local government, I am able to diagnose and address some of the main problems that have hindered the study of interest group influence. And by making improvements in the area of empirical design, I am able to make progress on the theoretical dimension as well.

Interest Group Activity

Because my goal is to understand interest groups in local governments, an obvious way to begin is to try to answer some basic questions about interest group activity in local politics. How active are interest groups in local politics? Does it vary across local governments, and if it does, what explains that variation? What *kinds* of interest groups are active? And how does *that* vary across the United States?

There are strands of research on interest group activity in the existing literature, but almost all of that research is about the federal government. Most research on lobbying and campaign finance is about lobbying and campaign finance in the federal government and national elections. The literature on interest group systems, which attempts to characterize the broad contours of the set of interest groups present in a government, is mostly about the population of interest groups in Washington, DC.

It is still possible that these literatures could offer theories of relevance to the local context, but they are actually quite limited in that respect. Much of the research on interest group systems is descriptive. The more theoretical work does not ask whether interest groups are active at all or about the conditions under which interest groups are active in a government. And it makes sense that they wouldn't: they are focused on the federal government, and it is well established that there are thousands of interest groups active in Washington, DC. In local governments, by contrast, there could be areas with no interest group activity at all, but this is something we just don't know yet.[11] For the local context, these questions are precisely where we want to begin.

What is more, even if we try to apply the theories that are developed in these literatures to the local context—to say something about what interest group activity in local politics should look like—they do not carry us very far. Consider the well-known arguments of Mancur Olson, that small groups should be more successful than large groups in overcoming the collective action problem and that if large groups do manage to get organized, it is because they offer selective benefits.[12] These have been some of the most influential insights in the past several decades of scholarly research on interest groups, but by themselves they don't really help us understand what kinds of interest groups will be active in local politics. There is also a sizable body of literature on lobbying, but most of it starts from the basic premise that groups do lobby and then proceeds to ask questions about how and why they lobby.[13] In the literature on campaign contributions, moreover, the primary research questions are about interest group strategy, such as whether groups give money to buy legislators' support on key votes, to buy access to legislators, or to support ideologically compatible candidates, not about how active groups will be as contributors in different contexts.[14] While interesting, this research is not helpful for explaining patterns of interest group activity across governments.

In principle, the literature on interest group systems is more directly relevant because it is about types of groups that have greater and lesser presence. For example, a popular approach in this line of work is to use lists of lobbying groups with Washington offices or lists of registered lobbyists, categorize the groups on several dimensions (such as whether they are membership groups or institutions), and then use counts of the groups in different categories to draw conclusions about whether the interest group system is biased in favor of certain interests.[15] These studies find that occupationally based groups are more numerous than citizen groups and that business interests and corporations far outnumber unions and groups representing the less privileged.[16] But while some scholars argue that these patterns arise because of inequality in group resources—specifically, constituencies with higher incomes are better able to pay the costs of organizing and advocacy—the literature is focused on describing the national interest group system rather than developing a general theory of interest group activity.[17]

Virginia Gray and David Lowery offer a more theoretical account of interest group systems,[18] but it does not yield predictions about the amount or type of interest group activity in a government. Their central idea is that an interest organization is akin to a species: its main objective is to survive, and it competes for scarce resources with other interest organizations (other species) that live off the same resources in the same environment. In addition, they define guilds as "sets of species

THE POLICY-FOCUSED APPROACH TO STUDYING INTEREST GROUPS 25

'that make their living in the same way,'" for example, all farming organizations in a state.[19] Just as some species compete with one another for resources like food, they argue, interest organizations in the same guild compete with one another for resources like members and government benefits, and thus resource availability shapes interest group system "density." But because their theory does not account for which guilds we should expect to find in a state,[20] it does not generate expectations about the overall number or types of interest groups either. It is therefore unclear how one would use this population ecology framework to understand patterns of interest groups in local politics.[21]

The Disconnect

Why, with all the literature on lobbying, campaign finance, and interest group systems, are we left with little theoretical guidance on basic questions about interest group activity in local politics—other than the proposal that groups with more resources will perhaps have greater presence? The main reason is that interest group scholars have been focused on other questions, such as interest group strategy. But there is something bigger going on here too, which is that across the board much of this scholarship has lost sight of the importance of interest groups' *interests*.

For all the faults of the pluralist approach, which assumed that groups with shared interests will be organized, its strength was that it put groups' interests at the heart of the inquiry.[22] The modern literature does not do this. It largely divorces the study of interest group activity from their interests. And that is one of the reasons we get stuck when we try to use it to answer basic questions about interest group activity in local politics. Moreover, because of this shift away from groups' interests, research on interest group activity has become disconnected from the study of interest group influence—even though the potential for influence is the main motivation for studying interest group activity in the first place.

Olson's theory is both an example of this and one of the reasons it happened.[23] The major strength of Olson's individual-based account is that it presents a clearer logic of collective action. Yet a key implication is that groups' collective interests aren't all that important. Moreover, it raises the theoretical puzzle of how interest groups manage to form at all. Over the years, this puzzle has distracted political scientists from developing theoretical answers to other questions about interest groups, such as which groups will be most politically active and when. It is important to try to explain why and how groups form, but that has proven to be a stumbling block, and meanwhile there are undeniable empirical regularities that should inspire other avenues of inquiry. Interest groups *do* form—many of them. In national and state politics, groups *are* politically active. As Jack Walker writes:

> The work of Olson largely undermined David Truman's theory of the spontaneous generation of groups, yet, despite the power of Olson's analysis, the recent increases in the number of groups suggest that Truman has the data on his side. . . . The political system is beset by a swarm of organizational bumblebees that are busily flying about in spite of the fact that political scientists cannot explain how they manage it.[24]

Note that even though scholars have yet to agree on the "solution" to the rational choice puzzle of why people vote, research on voting has proceeded without much difficulty. The same needs to happen with interest group activity: we should go about trying to explain patterns of interest group activity without requiring that we first settle the matter of why individuals join groups.[25]

Gray and Lowery's theory of interest group populations tries to move forward in this direction but remains chained to the Olsonian predicament of how groups manage to form. Recall that the starting premise of Gray and Lowery's theory is that the main goal of interest groups is to *survive*.[26] An example serves to show how different this is from an approach focused on interest groups' policy interests. Consider environmental groups and polluting industries. The policy-focused approach would view them as adversaries, locked in competition over their conflicting policy goals. Gray and Lowery, however, are explicit about deprioritizing groups' policy goals. In a telling statement, they write, "The population ecology approach is concerned less with policy outcomes . . . than it is in understanding how populations of interest organizations are constructed. . . . [T]he primary competitors of an environmental organization are other environmental organizations, not polluters."[27] This is a theoretical move with real consequence. By prioritizing groups' goal of survival, not what groups are trying to achieve in policy, their theory is not set up to be a launching pad for studying interest group influence.

This is not meant to dismiss problems of collective action and group maintenance—they are still important, as I discuss later—but rather to

THE POLICY-FOCUSED APPROACH TO STUDYING INTEREST GROUPS   27

say that they are not the way to begin to understand patterns of interest group activity. The way to begin is with groups' policy goals. Common sense suggests this is right. Even the best-organized, most robust pro-life organization will probably not be active in a government that does not make any decisions about abortion policy. Group activity flows from what governments actually do.

This same critique applies to accounts of interest group activity that focus first and foremost on *resources*. From one perspective, the focus on group resources makes sense. Groups with more affluent members may be better able to overcome the collective action problem and maintain their organization. Once organized, moreover, privileged groups argu-ably have more money to dedicate to activities like lobbying and cam-paign finance. But in thinking about which groups will be most politi-cally active, groups' policy interests are just as important as resources. Interest groups' main goal—the reason they *need* resources (and access and to survive)—is to influence certain policies.[28] Holding groups' pol-icy interests constant, it may be true that well-resourced groups are more politically active than less well-resourced groups. But groups' policy in-terests are *not* constant across governments or across issues—and that matters. Even the best-resourced business group may not be active in a local government that does not make decisions that affect that business. And a different group whose members are less privileged might manage to be quite politically active if it has a great deal at stake in the local gov-ernment's decisions.

Adopting a policy-focused approach also makes clear the importance of categorizing and thinking about interest groups in terms of their pol-icy goals—in terms of what they are trying to achieve. In part because of its focus on inequality of resources, scholarship on interest group systems does something different: it categorizes groups according to whether they are membership groups or institutions, whether their mem-bers are individuals or businesses, or whether their members are privi-leged or not. This approach can be helpful for answering certain kinds of questions, but it is not directly useful if the ultimate goal is to test for interest group influence. Categories like privileged versus nonprivileged do not tell us what those groups want to have influence *on*; they are not based on what the groups are trying to achieve policy-wise.

In addition, the way scholars conceive of and operationalize inter-est group activity in the various literatures makes for a weak setup for the study of group influence. In the interest group systems literature, for example, researchers use counts of the groups in different categories (such as privileged or nonprivileged) to draw conclusions about whether the interest group system is biased in favor of certain interests.[29] When the starting point of the research endeavor is a list of registered lobbying groups, as it often is in work on interest group systems, counting groups of different types is one of the only ways of analyzing the data. The problem, though, is that it is not clear why the count of groups matters for influence. It may not matter much whether there are one, two, or ten organizations of a particular type (such as environmental groups) that are active in politics. After all, some interest groups are enormous; others are very small. Some are extremely active; others only occasionally dabble in politics. By looking only at the number of groups, we do not learn much about how large or active certain interests are—even though surely that matters for influence. If the ultimate goal is to study influence, we should also track what groups do in pursuit of those goals.

In doing that, moreover, it makes sense to study activities like campaign contributions and lobbying together, not in isolation. A moment's reflection suggests that lobbying and campaign finance are probably pillars of group influence that reinforce each other.[30] While there are many possible reasons for why a policy maker would be responsive to a lobbyist's requests, certainly one is that the policy maker recognizes that the lobbyist or group has clout in funding campaigns and thus might affect their reelection.

Furthermore, interest group "activity" need not be limited to formal lobbying and campaign contributions. If the goal is to understand interest group influence, then we want to study all the activities interest groups engage in in their attempts to exert influence—not just the ones that come with readily available quantitative data. This includes electoral activities such as endorsing candidates and on-the-ground campaigning for candidates and issues. It includes testifying at hearings, attending public meetings, and encouraging members to contact or donate to officials. It includes sitting on boards and commissions or forms of engagement in which interest groups are in positions of advisory or even decision-making authority.[31] And it includes less conventional activities as well. For public-sector unions, it includes engaging in collective bargaining and threats to strike.[32] For businesses, it includes mobilizing employees to engage in politics.[33] And as the pluralists' critics have explained, it includes efforts to set the agenda and block change. An approach to interest group activity that is focused on understanding their influence should conceive of interest group activity broadly: anything a group does to try to shape policy in its favor.

Putting Policy Interests First

To study interest group activity in the way that is most useful for studying influence, we have to put interest groups' policy interests first. In terms of theory, this means that to understand whether interest groups will be active in local government, how active they will be, and which interest groups will be active, we should start by considering what the local governments do. It also implies that the conceptualization and measurement of interest group activity should be done in a way that sets the stage for studying interest group influence. The group categories we use should be based to the extent possible on the groups' policy goals. And beginning with a broad, influence-oriented conception of interest group activity is important—especially for local politics, where it is not clear that formal lobbying and campaign finance are the most important forms of activity. While I tackle the measurement challenge in chapter 3, here I want to lay out some broad theoretical parameters.

The first questions to be answered are the most basic. Are interest groups active in municipal government? If so, how much interest group activity should we expect to find in a particular city? The policy-focused approach suggests that it will depend on how much the government does—how much is at stake in its policy making. Compared to the federal government, cities are much more limited in the types of policies they can pursue, so as Paul Peterson argues, there is relatively less reason for interest groups to get involved.[34] But cities do make policies, and that means there is reason for interest groups to be active. And the overall amount of interest group activity in a city should depend on how much that city does.

As Eric Oliver, Shang Ha, and Zachary Callen emphasize in their theory of local elections, local governments vary greatly in scope, meaning how much power and authority they have, and their capacity for action. Some cities make policy on a large number of issues, while others are limited to zoning, land use, police protection, and other basic municipal concerns. Oliver, Ha, and Callen theorize that this is one of the three main features of local governments that shape their electoral politics.[35] I argue that it matters for interest group activity as well, because interest groups are motivated by policy. Governments that make decisions on a wide range of issues should tend to attract more interest group activity, whereas governments that make decisions in only a few policy areas will tend to attract less. And it is not just whether a city makes policy in a given area but also how big the stakes are. As others have argued, large costs and benefits are more likely to motivate political activity than small costs and benefits.[36] As a general rule, larger cities with more at stake—larger budgets, more expansive regulatory authority— should tend to attract greater interest group activity.

This much should help explain the overall amount of interest group activity in cities and how it varies, but more important for the study of interest group influence are questions about which interest groups are most active in local politics. Again, the key is to start with what policies the local governments make and consider the nature of groups' interests in those policies. The most important questions to ask are as follows: Which interest groups have an interest in the policies the government makes? What kinds of policy interests are most likely to motivate political activity? And which groups have alternative ways of pursuing those interests?

We can begin by asking whether a certain group has an interest in what a particular local government does. If we cannot answer affirmatively, then we should not expect that group to be active in that local government's politics. This might seem like a trivial distinction but only because most American politics scholars are accustomed to thinking about interest groups in the context of the federal government, which has far-reaching authority on a virtually limitless set of issues. In such a context, it is difficult to identify any group that has no stake whatsoever in government decision making. For local government, however, the distinction is useful. Local governments cannot do everything, and their actions (even if expansive) do not affect every potential interest group. There are therefore probably many interest groups—including those that are very active in national and state politics—that would have little to no interest in policy making in Sunnyvale, California, or Oak Park, Illinois. We should not expect to find widespread activity by abortion rights groups in local politics, for example, because most local governments do not regularly make decisions on the issues that motivate them.[37]

The kinds of policies local governments do make vary dramatically— the City of Miami, Florida, grapples with a much larger set of issues and has greater policy-making authority than Spencer, Iowa—but a few policy areas are especially common in large and small cities alike. Municipal elections usually revolve around economic development, property development, zoning, taxes and budgets, and city services.[38] As for the services most commonly provided by city governments, they are police protection, fire protection, street repair, public parks, and water and sewers.[39]

The list of groups that might have some stake in city land use, economic development, and service provision could be long, of course. Yet having some interest is a necessary but not a sufficient condition for group activity.[40] Of all the potentially active groups with some interest in city decisions, which ones are the most likely to be active, and why? To move forward, we also have to think about the nature of a group's interest in a policy or issue. While there are a number of dimensions that could matter, I propose a few that should be especially important: the size of the group's stake in local policy, whether the group's interests are economic, the directness and regularity of the group's interests, and whether the group has means of pursuing those interests other than engaging in politics in a particular city. Some of these policy features have been shown in the policy feedback literature to shape the participation of mass publics,[41] and here I propose that they should shape the political activity of interest groups as well.

The assertion that the size of a group's interest is important grows out of both the logic developed above and existing theoretical insights about what motivates political activity generally. Many scholars have noted that individuals and groups that stand to reap large benefits and costs from a policy are more likely to be politically engaged than those confronting smaller benefits and costs.[42] The policy feedback literature identifies two reasons for this: larger government benefits confer greater resources on beneficiaries, which enhances their capacity for political participation, and "larger benefits fuel . . . a greater sense that a benefit is worth fighting for."[43]

In addition, we should expect that groups with an economic or material stake in local government policy making are more active than groups with noneconomic interests. This idea of material interests as an important motivator for political action has deep roots in social science. In political science, it dates to at least E. E. Schattschneider's 1935 study on the Smoot-Hawley tariff that noted that the most influential groups were those that had a material stake in the policy.[44] Olson's model of collective action assumes that individuals are motivated by economic benefits and costs.[45] In more recent work, Terry Moe has argued that material benefits are essential to the emergence of "vested interests": interests that grow out of the creation of government programs.[46] This is just the tip of the iceberg: many social scientists have argued—explicitly or implicitly—that economic interests are a primary motivator for interest group political activity.[47]

The directness of a benefit or cost matters as well. Citizens who are directly affected by a government policy are more likely to be politically attentive than citizens who are indirectly affected.[48] Directness can be defined in different ways, and I mean to include all of them. It can refer to whether the policy's benefits (or costs) accrue mainly to the group or also to a broader array of constituencies—the concentration of the benefits and costs. It can describe how important a policy or benefit is to the daily needs of a group's members. Preserving a public park, for example, might be quite important to a local environmental group whose members visit the park regularly. Directness can also refer to the strength, clarity, and visibility of the link between the policy the government makes and the outcome as experienced by the group. As Douglas Arnold discusses, for some policies, the causal chain between a policy decision and an outcome is short and highly visible. For others, it involves multiple stages or is difficult to perceive, such as the link between increased spending on education and economic growth.[49] For citizens, this affects whether an outcome is visible and traceable to government action, but it also affects the certainty with which the policy leads to the outcome—and all of this might shape group activity. To keep things simple, I refer to these considerations as directness. We should expect interest groups to be more active when a policy's effects on the group are direct, that is, clearly visible and attributable to government policy making, concentrated among group members, and important to group members' daily lives.

The regularity or frequency of a group's stake in government decision making has received less attention in the literature but is also potentially quite important. Groups that regularly and dependably have interests in local decision making should be more active in local politics than groups that only occasionally have interests in local decision making—even if the latter's interests (when they do arise) are large, economic, and direct. Arnold captures this nicely: "The strongest coalitions are those in support of programs that deliver large and regular funds to the same citizens year after year. . . . Coalitions are considerably weaker when programs deliver benefits to an ever-changing cast of recipients."[50] Very generally, we should expect the most active interest groups in local

THE POLICY-FOCUSED APPROACH TO STUDYING INTEREST GROUPS   33

politics to be those with a regular stake in the policies municipal governments make.

One other general consideration is worth highlighting given the focus on local government. Even if interest groups have large, direct, regular, and economic interests in government policy, they vary in their dependence on politics in a particular city for pursuing those interests. The idea that citizens and businesses can "vote with their feet" is central to the local political economy literature.[51] Most famously, in Charles Tiebout's model of local governance, it is the competition among governments for mobile, taxpaying citizens that induces government responsiveness—not political activity.[52] In reality, of course, the transaction costs of moving can be substantial, and when they are, political activity (or "voice") becomes an attractive option.[53] Moreover, as I discuss later, some interest groups are locked into their communities and cannot pick up and move elsewhere. Thus, I expect that interest group activity in a particular city's politics will depend on whether a given group has alternative ways of pursuing its interests.

What this all looks like more concretely—empirically—is the subject of chapter 4. But laying this theoretical groundwork is an important first step. It establishes some baseline expectations for how the overall level of interest group activity will vary across governments. It proposes that the nature of a particular group's interests in a city's policies will shape the extent of that group's activity in the city's politics. Collective action, survival, and resources are surely important, but explaining patterns of local interest group activity demands that we first consider who has a large, economic, direct, and regular stake in city policy making and which of those groups have little choice but to engage in local politics to meet their needs. By studying interest group activity in this way, with a clear focus on what they are trying to achieve, the stage will be properly set for evaluating interest group influence.

Interest Group Influence

There is a research literature on interest group influence spanning decades and using various approaches, but overall its conclusions have been very mixed.[54] Tellingly, in the most comprehensive interest group study of the past twenty years, Frank Baumgartner and colleagues studied over a thousand groups active on ninety-eight national policy issues,

34   CHAPTER TWO

and in the end, they found that interest groups' resources have little to
no relationship with whether the groups get what they want.[55] Experts
working in this area have long noted that there seems to be some kind
of trouble with existing approaches to evaluating interest group influence.[56] But so far, no clear diagnosis has been made, nor has a remedy
been proposed.

While I do not wish to repeat others' efforts to provide a comprehensive review of this literature,[57] it is important to reflect on its main features with the policy-focused perspective as a guiding framework. That is
my next step here. What this reflection reveals is that many of the strug-
gles of the quantitative literature on interest group influence stem from a
variety of problems with the dependent variable.[58] Moreover, one major
reason scholars have not yet overcome these dependent variable problems is that they are looking for variation within a single government—
almost always the federal government. It is certainly understandable
that one would want to understand interest group influence in Washington, DC, but by looking beyond the federal government, we begin to see
why it is relatively difficult to detect interest group influence in that context or by analyzing any single government in isolation.

Once we diagnose the most important underlying problem, a different path emerges. Not only do we begin to see how we should go about
testing interest group influence in local politics, but we also begin to see
how studying local politics helps us understand interest group influence
more generally.

"Policy as Prize" and the Dependent Variable

The policy-focused approach conceives of interest groups as seeking favorable public policies. That's what Hacker and Pierson are referring to
when they discuss "policy as prize" and organized interests as important
actors pursuing that prize. As they write, "[T]he battle to control public
authority is fierce, ongoing, and highly consequential. . . . [F]or important players, especially the most knowledgeable, well-resourced, and enduring, elections are just one means to the greater end of exercising co-
ercive authority. For these actors, policies are not a sideshow; they are
often the main show."[59] Two points here are key. First, the main goal of
interest groups is to seek favorable public policy. Second, interest groups
are playing a long-term game. They of course care about the next roll-

call vote and the next election, but those are just steps in their broader agenda.[60]

The literature on interest group influence shows that scholars are—at least in principle—focused on public policy as the place to look for signs of influence. There seems to be agreement that public policy should be the dependent variable in these studies. And yet in quantitative research on interest group influence, in the turn to empirical analysis, nearly all scholars have used dependent variables that are not public policy. These dependent variables are related to public policy, but they are not the same, and the difference has major implications for how we should interpret the findings. There are at least two major manifestations of this: using *roll-call votes* as the dependent variable and using a binary indicator for *policy change* as the dependent variable.

As a starting point, it is worth highlighting that this is a matter on which the older case study–based literature got things right: it set out to explain public policy. For example, some of these studies focused on specific policy areas or industries, such as national water policy or sugar production, and used case studies to evaluate the influence of various "policy subsystem" actors.[61] In trying to understand the effects of organized interests, they considered a range of ways that interest groups might influence public policy.[62] Much of the work in this older research tradition did conclude that interest groups have influence on public policy, often in ways that can be difficult to see and track.[63] The qualitative nature of this work made it difficult to isolate the effect of any one group relative to other actors and influences, but to its credit, it used public policy as a dependent variable.

The shift to quantitative analysis seemed to hold great promise for isolating the influence of particular groups. Naturally, though, in moving from a qualitative approach to quantitative modeling, analysts had to simplify: one cannot bring as much detail to quantitative analysis as, for example, Schattschneider did to his account of the Smoot-Hawley tariff. As Baumgartner and Leech explain, "The trick is to simplify in such a way that the model distills reality rather than distorts it."[64] And that is where the problem arose. The way quantitative studies of lobbying simplified *did* distort reality. In shifting to quantitative analysis, scholars removed the content of public policy from the dependent variable.

Consider the most common type of empirical analysis on this topic: quantitative analysis of congressional roll-call votes.[65] Analyzing roll-call votes can certainly be productive and informative. But there are three major limitations to using this approach to learn about the extent of interest group influence. First, it is not always clear how legislators' votes and positions are connected to actual policy outcomes, even in the short run.[66] Second, as mentioned previously, interest groups care most about policy outcomes in the longer run. When researchers analyze roll-call votes, they are analyzing whether an interest group won a particular battle—not necessarily whether they are winning the war. This is true not just of roll-call vote analysis, but any analysis in which the dependent variable represents one stage in the long, multistage process of public policy making. It is true of analysis of an election outcome, for instance. This is not to say that we cannot or should never evaluate interest group influence on a particular roll-call vote or in a particular election, but we must be aware that these short-term outcomes are precisely that. They are parts of the whole of what interest groups are trying to achieve.

Third, roll-call votes may well be the stage at which we are least likely to see interest group influence—because of selection bias.[67] Just as the pluralists' critics argued decades ago, policy is shaped by both decisions and nondecisions.[68] While interest groups can exercise influence by persuading legislators to vote a certain way, they can also exercise influence by *blocking* issues from reaching the agenda.[69] As Baumgartner and Leech point out, "Most quantitative assessments of group influence tend to overlook a well-documented truth about policymaking: most action takes place long before the floor vote."[70] Pierson clearly explains an implication of this: the special sets of issues that actually come to a roll-call vote are probably the most salient, contentious ones—the ones in which interest group influence tends to be limited.[71]

The first and second concerns I laid out above are relevant for any analysis that focuses on one stage of the policy-making process, but the third concern is particularly acute for analysis of roll-call votes. As we know well from the literature on agenda setting, many issues are not considered by Congress at all, and most of the bills that are introduced are modified in committee or blocked by committees or party leaders.[72] The issues that come to a roll-call vote are a special set. By comparison, we can worry less about analysis of election results; in the United States, most elections occur at regular intervals and cannot easily be blocked in the same way. Thus, of the potential studies that analyze one stage of the policy-making process, studies of roll-call votes may be the most problematic if the goal is to evaluate whether interest groups have influence.

Baumgartner and colleagues' influential study, *Lobbying and Policy Change*, takes a different approach and confronts two of these concerns head-on: it moves beyond roll-call votes as the action being analyzed, and it looks beyond policy making at a single point in time.[73] The sheer size and scope of the Baumgartner et al. study is truly impressive. The researchers selected ninety-eight national policy issues, both conflictual and nonconflictual, and documented all the groups that actively lobbied on those issues over a period of a few years. Then they tracked what happened on those policy issues for another few years after that. Despite such an enormous undertaking, however, they uncovered little evidence that interest group lobbying made any difference to policy outcomes on these ninety-eight issues.

It is possible that the explanation for this finding is that interest groups do not influence policy in Washington, DC, but more likely this is the dependent variable problem in a different form. Baumgartner and colleagues set out to test interest group influence in the federal government—a single government. The comparisons they make to understand the effect of interest group lobbying are across the ninety-eight different issues. So far, so good. It sounds like the dependent variable is public policy.

The problem, however, is that policy outcomes are usually not comparable across issue areas: there is no easy way to say, for example, whether a policy on auto emissions standards is friendlier to interest groups than an abortion policy. Thus, even if Baumgartner and colleagues ultimately wanted to adopt policy as a dependent variable, because they are making comparisons across issue areas, they are instead forced to shift from studying policy to studying *policy change*, asking—for each issue—whether the policy changed or the status quo persisted. Then, by coding whether interest groups prefer policy change or the status quo, they can test whether interest groups that are more active, or that have more resources, are more likely to get the outcome they prefer—in a way that is comparable across issues. The shift to policy change is what enables the quantitative analysis.

The main problem with this maneuver is one that the researchers themselves identify: if an interest group is influential, it is quite likely that the status quo policy already embeds that influence. In fact, perhaps the interest group is so influential that it has *already succeeded* in getting most of what it wants, such that further changes in its direction—even if the group prefers it—are unlikely. In this scenario, we would certainly

38   CHAPTER TWO

not want to conclude that the interest group is uninfluential just because the policy did not change in the current time period. Instead, we would want to somehow measure the friendliness of the status quo policy to the interest group. But with this approach, we cannot do that, because again we cannot compare the interest group friendliness of auto emissions policy and abortion policy. So in an effort to find variation in a single government, they have to treat all status quo policies as equivalent, regardless of how much interest groups may have influenced the status quo.

What at first seem like minor, innocuous moves to enable quantitative comparisons actually have big implications for inference. There appears to be agreement that we should be looking to public policy to find signs of interest group influence. And yet most quantitative studies are not doing that. They are analyzing other dependent variables. Because of that, it is hard to know what to infer about interest group influence from this research.

There is also a certain irony to all of this. As I discussed earlier, the main reason scholars should care about interest groups—even scholars of political representation—is that interest groups might influence policy. Policy may well be different from what it otherwise would have been because of interest groups. Policy is therefore the obvious place to look for the fingerprints of interest group influence. Yet to make possible quantitative studies of interest group influence, scholars have removed the substance of policy from their outcome variables. The result is a body of work that does not say much about how public policy is different (or not) because of interest groups—even though presumably that was the primary motivation for the inquiry.

The Focus on the Federal Government: A Cause of the Problem

Diagnosing the problem is an important step, but just as important is understanding why this has happened. Why has interest group scholarship, which recognizes that policy is the prize, turned away from policy as the dependent variable?

The answer, as I see it, is simple: virtually all the literature is about the federal government, the vast majority about Congress.[74] Designing a quantitative analysis of a single government leaves researchers with few options other than moving away from public policy as the dependent variable. In a single government, at a given point in time, the content of public policy is fixed. This is a problem because researchers studying causal questions—such as whether an interest group's efforts influenced policy—are in the business of making comparisons. To make comparisons, one needs variation. And to find variation in a single government, where overall public policy is fixed at any given point in time, scholars have either turned to variation in policy makers' *positions* on issues or they have made comparisons *across issues.*

While roll-call votes and indicators of policy change do offer solutions to the design problem of limited policy variation in the federal government, they are solutions that lead scholars to look for influence in places where they are less likely to find it. Both maneuvers have the effect of removing the content of public policy from the dependent variable. And harkening back to the pluralists' dilemma, analysis of roll-call votes alone is a great example of focusing only on the first face of power, ignoring the influence that interest groups may have through agenda setting and blocking and keeping things quiet—the second face of power.[75]

The second maneuver—comparing across issues and analyzing policy change—can solve one problem but raises another. Specifically, it can solve the single-stage problem; Baumgartner and colleagues moved in the right direction by allowing for the effects of lobbying to happen over a period of a few years. But this does not eliminate their need for a dependent variable that varies within the single government they are studying. And the solution they adopt—to analyze policy change over a few years—still does not fully capture the essence of what interest group success looks like.[76]

Much of the development of public policy happens gradually, incrementally. There is therefore good reason to think that interest group influence on policy often happens slowly, gradually, and incrementally. It is probably best characterized as what Pierson calls a "slow-moving process" rather than as something that happens at a moment in time or even over a period of a few years.[77] Capturing the full essence of interest group influence therefore demands that we consider this gradual accumulation—and that we adopt a dependent variable that reflects that.

That is why so much is lost once the policy content is removed from the dependent variable: it is within that content where we can see the accumulation of interest groups' effects in the past. Analyzing an indicator of whether policy changed over a four-year period is better than analyzing whether change happened in a single year. But regardless of the time period studied, there is still the issue that the status quo policy in the starting year reflects the accumulation of interest group success in earlier years. Actually capturing that policy content in the dependent variable is therefore crucial, as it contains the effects of interest groups in the past. And yet the quantitative literature on interest group influence has not done this.

"Bringing Policy Back In": Solutions to the Dependent Variable Problem

What, then, should we do to test for interest group influence? One thing is clear: we should—to the extent possible—use public policy as a dependent variable. When we cannot, we must be clear-headed about the inferential limitations, and about what the analysis can and cannot tell us about interest group influence.

One way of "bringing policy back in" to the dependent variable is the approach Pierson recommends: historical analysis, or analysis of particular policy issues over a long period of time.[78] For those interested in finding variation within the federal government without losing policy content, this may be the best option. Why interest group scholars have not relied more heavily on this approach is something of a puzzle, but the reason may be the one Pierson identifies in *Politics in Time*: quantitatively oriented political scientists are inclined to conceive of political interactions as "snapshots" rather than as "moving pictures."[79] Further, there are the difficulties of historical data collection, separating out the effect of an interest group from other potential influences, as well as the pesky issue of what to choose as the starting point—especially given the potential for influence to be embedded in the status quo. Still, historical research is one way to study interest group influence without deviating from public policy as the dependent variable.

There is another way, however, one that has been underappreciated and underutilized: we can compare policies across subnational governments. In studying subnational policy, including local policy, we do not have to compare across issues, nor do we have to look to roll-call votes for evidence of interest group influence. Consider that states are fifty units that make policy on many of the same issues, for example, fifty policies on auto emissions and fifty policies on abortion. Across local governments, the focus of this book, there are thousands of versions of land use policy, thousands of approaches to law enforcement and policing, and thousands of local education policies. In principle, we can measure policies of the same type across many units, and we can compare

THE POLICY-FOCUSED APPROACH TO STUDYING INTEREST GROUPS   41

them on the basis of how friendly they are to various interest groups. In an analysis of subnational government, then, the dependent variable can actually be policy.

Moreover, in taking this approach, some of the most interesting and useful variation for testing interest group influence is *cross-sectional*: the variation in policies across different governments at a particular point in time. This warrants explanation as cross-sectional data analysis is often heavily criticized—and in some circles may be sufficient grounds for rejecting the credibility of an analysis. For the question at hand, however, we need to think hard about the advantages and disadvantages of different approaches and recognize that there is no perfect way. And for the study of interest group influence—an important topic that needs to be studied—cross-sectional analysis may be the least problematic approach of those available.

The problems with cross-sectional analysis of observational data are of course real and well known. Scholars focused on causal inference rightfully point out that with cross-sectional data, it is difficult or impossible to pin down where the variation in the independent variable comes from—and thus to deal convincingly with the threat of selection bias. Panel data at least allow the researcher to analyze change over time within units, such as with difference in differences, which can help reduce that threat. Cross-sectional data do not allow that. For those using a historical approach, moreover, cross-sectional data are problematic for a different reason: "snapshots" do a poor job of explaining slow-moving processes.[80] Based on these considerations alone, then, studying interest group influence with cross-sectional data would seem to be doubly problematic; it is a study of a causal process and a slow-moving one at that.

In fact, though, cross-sectional analysis is an extremely useful approach for testing interest group influence, because a snapshot of local government policies at any point in time reflects the accumulation of interest group influence up to that point—which, here, is precisely what we want to know about. An example is useful. As of 2010, states' public-sector labor laws varied a great deal. Some, such as those in Wisconsin and Ohio, were friendly to public-sector labor: they gave virtually all state and local government employees full collective bargaining rights on a wide range of issues, and they allowed unions to charge agency fees to workers who did not want to become union members. Other states, like South Carolina, were very unfriendly to labor: South Carolina not only was a right-to-work state (no agency fees allowed) but also prohibited collective bargaining for government employees entirely. The cross-sectional variation in state labor policy was therefore substantial.

Then, in 2011, state Republican majorities—backed by conservative groups and opposed by public-sector unions—passed laws in Ohio and Wisconsin that weakened collective bargaining rights, making those states' policies less friendly to labor than they had been before.[81] No such policy change was passed in South Carolina.

Note that if we were to adopt the policy change approach and analyze, for each state, whether policy changed or not and in which direction, we might infer that public-sector unions were more influential in South Carolina than in Wisconsin and Ohio, because policy changed against labor's interests in Wisconsin and Ohio but not in South Carolina. That would of course be wrong. It would be wrong for precisely the reason I have explained: the status quo policies (as of 2010) in Wisconsin and Ohio were much friendlier to labor than in South Carolina. They were friendlier to labor in large part because for decades, public-sector unions had been much stronger in Wisconsin and Ohio than in South Carolina. The policy change variable would not capture that. A measure of the content of state labor policies would.

What is more, even after 2011, state labor policies were friendlier to labor in Wisconsin and Ohio than in South Carolina. Although 2011 saw a shift in the labor-friendliness of policy in Wisconsin and Ohio, the magnitude of the within-state shifts in Wisconsin and Ohio pales in comparison to the cross-sectional difference between the midwestern states and South Carolina. Depending on the research question, both kinds of variation are important. But if the goal is to understand the extent of interest group influence in the United States and how policy is or is not different as a result, the cross-sectional variation is a huge part of the picture. Whether measured in 2010 or 2011, before or after the change, state labor policies across the United States reflect decades of wins and losses by both public-sector unions and conservative groups.

This is not to say that state labor policies—or any cross-sectional variation in policy—*only* reflect the accumulation of interest group influence. Numerous scholars have pointed out that public policy and institutions have considerable status quo bias and that that bias probably arises from different sources.[82] Importantly, some or perhaps even much of that status quo bias probably does reflect interest group power: often the groups that benefit from the current arrangement—the ones that stand to lose if it is changed and want to keep things the way they are—

are the best organized and the most politically engaged.[83] But even beyond any imbalances in group power, American political institutions are designed so that enacting change is politically more difficult than blocking it, and that further advantages the status quo.[84] My argument is not that policies at a given point in time *only* reflect the accumulation of interest group influence but that they contain it, and it is important to recognize this when the goal is assessing interest group influence.

Neither do I intend to suggest that methods like difference in differences should not be used for testing interest group influence; the point I want to make is that we must be aware of their limitations. Difference in differences is often helpful for reducing omitted variable bias, but for the study of interest group influence, to the extent that it necessitates shifting away from policy as the dependent variable (to within-unit *change* in policy), the cure may be worse than the disease. Turning back to the state labor policy example: If we were to, say, analyze change in state labor policy over a period of a few years, we would be missing the previous decades of important interest group influence. We might even conclude that public-sector union activity caused policy to change in their opponents' favor, because there was very likely a surge in union activity in Wisconsin and Ohio once public-sector unions were threatened. Sometimes such an analysis is called for, but for understanding interest group influence—the big picture—there are advantages to focusing on the cross-sectional variation.

What about the argument that snapshots are often unhelpful for explaining slow-moving processes? Interest group influence, I argue, is an exception to that. In touting the merits of cross-sectional data analysis in this case, it is true that I am arguing in favor of using a snapshot to understand a slow-moving process. But here the snapshot is incredibly informative. The snapshot of state labor policies in 2010 *or* 2011 reflects decades of interest group successes and failures—not just their successes and failures in one year. It reflects the accumulation of the slow-moving, gradual causal effects of the past. Would it be preferable to have decades of over-time data for each state? Absolutely. But often that is not feasible for state and local governments, most of which do not have the same kinds of historical records as the federal government. And the relatively easier collection of over-time data at the federal level does not mean that we should disregard state and local governments either. For the study of interest group influence on policy, there are tremendous gains to be realized from analyzing cross-sectional variation in subnational policy.

The Policy-Focused Approach to Evaluating Interest Group Influence

That, then, is my approach in this book. Once we have studied interest group activity in a policy-focused way—explaining variation in interest group activity across local governments—we can move on to the harder and more important task of evaluating interest group influence. The policy-focused approach helps clarify how we should do that: how to set up the empirical analysis and what kinds of variables to use. In addition, I make progress on the theoretical dimension by laying out some conditions for when interest groups will be more or less influential. As Leech writes, "Many of the contradictory findings throughout the interest group literature may be attributable to [the] contingent nature of influence."[85] With a better setup in place for testing interest group influence, it is a good time to begin developing and evaluating some of those contingencies.

Importantly, the basic empirical setup I adopt for testing interest group influence is the same as the general structure of empirical research on political responsiveness and local political economy.[86] The standard approach in those literatures is to start with some independent variable of interest, such as voter turnout, public opinion, or partisanship, and then model dependent variables that are expected to be affected by them, such as incumbent vote share. The estimate of "influence" is then the estimated effect of the independent variable on the dependent variable, such as the coefficient on voter turnout, or public opinion, or partisanship. My approach here is structurally the same. The main independent variables are measures of interest group activity (discussed more fully below and in chapters 3 and 4), and the dependent variables are public policies. The question being asked, then, is whether more activity by an interest group causes policy to be different from what it otherwise would have been. The estimate of "influence" in this setup is the estimated effect of interest group activity on policy.

Lest this seem like the obvious thing to do, it is important to point out that some research takes a different approach, treating influence as the dependent variable—something to be measured—rather than as the estimated effect of an independent variable. For example, in some of the few existing quantitative studies of local interest groups, a common approach is to ask local officials to rate the influence of different kinds of groups and adopt that measure as the dependent variable. The analysis then revolves around comparisons of influence across different types of groups—such as privileged or nonprivileged groups—or under different kinds of institutions—such as in environmental or planning agencies.[87] That approach can be useful for understanding the relative influence of different groups in different settings, but because influence itself is the dependent variable, it does not allow for assessment of how interest groups shape key political or policy outcomes.

As an approach, moreover, it creates an unnecessary separation between the study of interest group influence and the study of the influence of other political phenomena, such as public opinion, ideology, and institutions. Few scholars would propose studying the influence of political institutions by asking elected officials how influential they think council-manager government is. Similarly, responsiveness scholars do not ask local policy makers how important residents' ideology is to local decisions; they *measure* ideology and then *estimate its effect* on policy. An advantage of my approach is that it puts interest groups on the same playing field as the other political actors and phenomena that get more attention from political scientists, such as voters, political parties, and political institutions. In studying how these other actors and institutions matter, researchers study their effects on outcomes. That is their "influence." Interest groups can be productively studied in the same way. By putting interest groups into the same kinds of models as voters, residents' ideology, and institutions, my approach inserts interest groups directly into the study of political representation, which is where they should be.[88]

This also allows me to *compare* and *control for* the influence of these other political actors. One obvious potential force is residents, or voters, in particular, their partisan and ideological leanings.[89] Also, particular *subsets* of residents, such as homeowners, are especially active in local politics and may have preferences that differ from those of other residents on some issues.[90] Elected officials presumably have their own preferences and goals as well, those that stem from their personal convictions and experiences as well as those induced by a desire to be reelected. Also, the effectiveness of any one organized group might be shaped by the activity of other, potentially competing groups.[91] And political institutions might shape the incentives and effects of all these actors. Given the potential complexity of the local political economy, it is important to be able to assess the influence of these political phenomena on the same terrain. That is possible with my approach.[92]

For scholars closest to the literatures on local political representation and political economy, then, my general approach should be familiar; it is the focus on interest groups that is new. Situated within the literature on interest group influence, however, my focus on interest groups is familiar, but the empirical setup and approach are new—in two important ways. First, I retain the policy content of the dependent variables by analyzing variation in municipal government policies. Second, having laid new groundwork in the study of interest group activity (outlined above), the independent variables—which describe interest group activity—are broader than measures of lobbying or campaign contributions alone, and they have some relationship to what the groups are trying to achieve in terms of policy. My approach therefore brings some of the strengths of the older, qualitative tradition into a quantitative analytical framework.

A final advantage of this design setup is that it is more precise in its operationalization of interest group influence: an interest group has influence to the extent that its *activity* results in policies that are *different from what they otherwise would have been*. One can quibble with this definition, just as one can quibble with virtually any conceptualization of interest group influence. I do not propose that this is the only or best definition. It does, however, have significant strengths, and it is a good jumping-off point for making progress. The first strength is the one I have already explained: this is how political representation research generally conceives of the influence of other phenomena, such as public opinion, so my approach puts interest group activity on the same playing field. That is an important linkage. The second and third strengths have to do with the relative clarity of the counterfactual and the independent variable—activity—both of which require more explanation.

The relative clarity of the counterfactual—what policy would have been otherwise—has the potential to generate productive discussions about prominent theories of interest groups and their connections to questions of influence. Consider Richard Hall and Alan Deardorff's theory of lobbying as legislative subsidy,[93] wherein the group provides policy and political information to elected officials who lack it. Is this a channel of interest group influence? The answer, based on my conceptualization, depends on what would have occurred otherwise. If the legislative subsidy allows legislators to introduce or pass more bills, as Hall and Deardorff suggest, and if that increase in productivity changes the content of policy from what it otherwise would have been, then by my definition we should think of that as influence. But if an interest group providing information simply gets the legislator to do what they would have done otherwise, it would just be neutral information provision—and not

THE POLICY-FOCUSED APPROACH TO STUDYING INTEREST GROUPS   47

necessarily influence. Again, this approach pushes us to think about the policy implications of what interest groups do.

Perhaps more controversial is my decision to study interest group influence as the effect of interest group *activity*. No doubt some will see this as falling into the same trap that ensnared Dahl in *Who Governs?*: ignoring the second face of power.[94] It is true that my approach does not and cannot capture the entirety of the second face of power.[95] But it does dip further into the second face of power than most other approaches that have been used in the interest groups literature. By studying public policy as the dependent variable, I am not looking only at decisions. This is important, because policies are the accumulation of decisions *and* nondecisions[96] and because it is possible to study important policies with low levels of open conflict—the kinds of issues where policy is made with little fanfare but great consequence. (I return to this point below.) As for the independent variable—interest group activity—I am proposing a broad theoretical conceptualization of interest group activity, one that includes *all* the actions interest groups take to push for policy in their favor.

To see how a broad conceptualization of interest group activity does or does not account for the second face of power, we need to be clear about what the second face of power means. At its core, the debate about community power was about how a great deal of power is not visible to the researcher. But that can mean two different things; it is important to distinguish between the total absence of activity and activity that is difficult to observe. The latter is still activity. When interest groups have informal meetings with legislators, participate on advisory boards or commissions, and engage in public relations campaigns, those are activities. They may not be tied to a particular decision or event, and they can be very difficult to study, but they are actions that in theory could be observed. It is also not wildly unrealistic to propose that they could be measured. Qualitative research is one option. Consider also the strides political scientists have made in recent years in examining how businesses encourage their employees to be politically active and how interest groups in state politics give legislators model bills and even secure positions of policy-making authority in government agencies.[97] A large part of what is meant by the second face of power refers to these kinds of activities that are hard to observe but are activities nonetheless. As a theoretical definition, "interest group activity" includes them.

Of course, no matter how broadly interest group activity is defined, it cannot include actions not taken. And policy makers could be responsive to an interest group—leading to policies different from what they otherwise would have been—because they know that the group *would* and *could* take action if need be. If the interest group does not have to take action, there is nothing for the researcher to see.

This is perhaps the most problematic aspect of studying interest group influence, and it explains why some researchers have chosen to adopt interest group resources as the independent variable instead of activity. Resources, according to this logic, are a measure of an interest group's *potential* activity, and it is potential activity that is the source of power and influence.

This is a reasonable position, but given the problems involved in operationalizing resources as the independent variable, it is often better and more feasible to focus on activity. As Dahl writes in *Who Governs?*, "The idea of potential influence, which seems transparently clear, proves on examination to be one of the most troublesome topics in social theory. . . . [I]t is clear that if individuals do vary in the extent to which they *use* their resources to gain influence, this variation might be fully as important in accounting for differences in influence as variations in the resources themselves."[98] The problem with resources as an independent variable—even as a theoretical matter—is that it is not clear what counts as resources relevant to political influence. I am not referring to the difficulty of defining what forms resources can take. Regardless of whether a group's resources are money or members or something else, it is difficult to say which resources could or would be effectively channeled into political action. It is problematic to consider a corporation's total net worth as its political resources or potential activity, just as it would be misleading to consider all the teachers in Mississippi as the resources of a Mississippi teachers' union: the corporation won't exhaust its net worth on politics (especially in one local government), and not all Mississippi teachers are in the union or would participate in the union's political efforts. How, then, does a business or a union credibly signal that it could and would use its resources to push for its way in policy? By actually *doing* something in politics. Through activity.[99]

It is also worth asking: If an interest group never did anything at all in a city's politics—never gave money, never talked to legislators, never attended a meeting—would it continue to have influence? As a practical matter, I would say probably not. The interest group has to keep its hand in the game, make its presence known, and show force. It has to make

THE POLICY-FOCUSED APPROACH TO STUDYING INTEREST GROUPS   49

sure that policy makers—who turn over—know and remember its policy preferences. It is true that an interest group might be able to shape institutions or societal values, and then sit back and watch the policy-making wheels turn in its favor. That is a problem with using activity as the theoretical independent variable of interest. But we have to draw the line somewhere. As a general rule, a group that never speaks to city officials and never gives a dollar to elections would probably be forgotten. *Some* political activity is necessary. Activity is what demonstrates that a group is able and willing to effectively use its resources in politics.

Making interest group activity the independent variable in the study of influence is therefore not a move that ignores the second face of power. It cannot possibly cover the entirety of it, even as a theoretical variable, and the slippage will of course be greater once it comes to measuring interest group activity quantitatively. But there are many forms of interest group activity that buttress the second face of power, and the alternative—measuring resources as potential activity—often leads to a dead end. We must confront the trade-offs and make a choice. And for this endeavor, using interest group activity is a good one.

Conditions of Influence

With this setup in place, I can begin to lay out some theoretical expectations for when—that is, under what conditions—an interest group's activity in a city will make a difference in policy. The key, as earlier, is to focus on the particulars of the policy in question and the nature of a group's interest in it. Influence thus depends on the characteristics of the group-policy pair in question. Three features of those pairs are especially important.

First, for an interest group's political activity in a city to result in a policy that is different from what it otherwise would have been, presumably the group has to have relatively homogeneous within-group preferences on that policy. For example, police unions probably have fairly homogeneous preferences in favor of better police officer compensation. A local environmental group, however, might have mixed preferences on a proposed multifamily housing development: some members might be in favor because the density could reduce the need for cars; others might be opposed because the development threatens green space where they like to hike and bird-watch. The environmental group might be quite active in city politics in general, but we would not expect its activity to have much impact on the progress of the development. That, then, is the first general condition: there should be a clearer relationship between the political activity of a group and the policy when the group's preferences on the policy are more homogeneous.[100]

Second, there is a greater chance that a group's political activity will make a difference in a policy when the group's preferences on that policy are distinct from those of other political actors. For example, if virtually everyone in a city is in favor of some pro-business policy, or if elected officials tend to favor such a policy, it may not matter how politically active the local chamber of commerce is, because other local actors would push for such a policy regardless. The situation is different when a group's preferences diverge from those of other important actors. Consider an environmental group that is homogeneously opposed to a proposed multifamily housing development: its position may be in alignment with the preferences of other groups and individuals, such as nearby homeowners and neighborhood associations, but its interests may also be distinct from the preferences of developers, the local chamber of commerce, and elected officials who want the development to move forward. It is that division—the distinctiveness of group preferences—that generates more potential for a group's political activity to make a difference to policy outcomes. That, then, is the second condition: a group's political activity should make a clearer difference to policy when its interests run counter to those of other actors in the polity.

These first two conditions are about groups' interests in a policy, but it is equally important for influence that a group's political activity be *focused* on that policy. It is not enough for a group to want something; it has to ensure that decision makers know what it wants on that issue, to be active and vocal on that issue, and to convince elected officials that it is willing to use its political clout to get its way on that issue. As I said earlier, this is largely what differentiates the activities of interest groups from the individual act of voting: interest groups have greater ability to communicate their preferences and back them up with politically meaningful actions like giving money, mobilizing voters, and giving endorsements. To have influence, then, a group's political activity has to be focused on that issue, meaning that it communicates its preferences to policy makers and demonstrates its willingness to expend political resources on it.[101]

When will a particular interest group be focused on an issue? To answer that, we can return to the earlier discussion of the kinds of inter-

THE POLICY-FOCUSED APPROACH TO STUDYING INTEREST GROUPS 51

ests that are most likely to motivate group activity. In general, an interest group's political activity in a city will be focused on policies that affect the group in a large, economic, direct, and regular way and on policies for which it has little alternative to politics for getting its way. A group's activity is less likely to be focused on issues that affect it in smaller, less direct, and nonmaterial ways. It should also be less focused on policies that do not affect it regularly or if it can get what it wants outside of politics.

These are the broad theoretical guidelines I use in studying interest group influence—three features of group-policy pairs that should matter for the extent to which a group's activity will shape policy. There is of course much work to be done in moving from the broad and theoretical to the specific and empirical, and that's the job for the rest of the book. But this approach does have some implications for what interest group influence looks like in general. It is contingent, as interest group scholars such as Leech have suggested.[102] The nature of influence—who has it—varies by issue area, just as Dahl concluded in his studies of urban redevelopment, public education, and party nominations in New Haven.[103] But my approach suggests that influence may be even more policy-specific than that. There could be different degrees of interest group influence not just across groups, or across broad issue areas like the ones Dahl explores, but also within groups and within broad categories of policy. For example, as I will discuss, in the broad area of local economic development and growth, the group politics of business tax incentives is not the same as the group politics of property development, and business interests are not all alike on either issue. What this policy-focused approach suggests is that the degree to which interest groups matter to policy depends on the specifics of the policy and the specifics of the group's interests in it.

Pluralism Resurrected? Representation and Influence in Local Politics

It would seem natural to close the discussion of my approach with a commentary about the overall distribution of power or about whose interests get represented in American democracy. I leave most of my discussion of those topics to the end—after the data and the analysis. But to be clear from the outset, my end goal is not to make grand statements about who governs, or even about who governs in local politics. In fact, the trajectory of this approach is in the direction of "it depends." It depends on the city, on the issue, on the policy particulars. And I am not aiming to add up what I learn across issues and groups and cities to say something general about power. The goal instead is to say something about policy: why we get the policies we do and whether interest groups have something to do with that. (They do.) If we were to find one group influential in one policy area and a different group influential in another, the important takeaway would not be that power is distributed. It would be that interest groups are influencing policies in two different areas.

That said, my approach does get us closer to a more complete account of representation, power, and influence in local politics. Dahl's classic study on these questions was based on decisions on three broad issues in a single city. The literature on political representation in local, state, and national politics is focused on public opinion—and thus also the kinds of issues for which there are public opinion data. My analysis broadens the inquiry by incorporating interest groups and examining policies in hundreds of cities. Just as important, I do not look only at issues that are in the spotlight—the ones where open contestation is common. And the theoretical framework I have laid out in this chapter helps us see what kinds of local issues those will be—and which ones will tend to be quieter and more one-sided.

One of the implications of the theoretical framework is that the amount of contestation by groups will vary by policy issue, depending on whether groups on opposing sides of the issue are mobilized into action. For reasons I will explain, most of the policies I explore in my empirical analysis of influence feature a mobilized beneficiary: an interest group with a large, economic, regular stake in the policy—usually a direct stake—and often a group that is locked into city politics to get what it wants. What varies across the policies I explore is whether the costs of the policy affect any potential opposing groups in these same ways. As in James Q. Wilson's typology,[104] some policies pit concentrated interest against concentrated interest and other policies tend to be one-sided; the difference has to do with the benefits and the costs.

In cities in particular, many policies have costs in the form of land use. Land use costs are often very direct: they are concentrated, highly visible, and easily attributable to policy makers' actions. Everyone can see or at least envision the building going up across the street, and if they experience decreased utility because of shade on their property, increased difficulty parking, or reduced green space, there is little ambiguity about the role of that new building in causing that decreased utility. Just as Arnold says that costs of this type are likely to activate the inattentive publics of congressional action,[105] the concentration and visibility of land use costs make them especially likely to generate active opposition. Based on my framework, then, land use policies should be some of those most likely in municipal government to erupt in open conflict.

It is probably not a coincidence that urban and local politics research focuses heavily on land use. The overwhelming emphasis of the urban politics literature is the politics of local economic development and growth.[106] Peterson writes that "urban politics is above all the politics of land use."[107] When John Logan and Harvey Molotch write about the negative consequences of the "growth machine," they talk mainly about the "intensification of land use."[108] Studying land use is important, but a reading of the urban politics literature could leave one with the impression that land use is most of what municipal governments do, or what local politics is mostly about. That would be a mistake. Openly contested policies are not the only policies of importance. And our studies of influence in local politics need to go beyond the high-conflict area of land use.

For many local policies, the costs are primarily budgetary. When government officials grant a salary increase to public employees or agree to pay the employees' share of their pension contributions, the effects appear in the government budget. There is no physically visible change, and the costs are often diffuse—perhaps in the form of higher sales taxes, lower public-sector employment, or public parks maintained less well. These policies may be less likely to generate active and targeted opposition. Even less studied are policies governing how local government employees do their jobs and how their managers manage them, such as rules for when police officers can use force or what managers can and cannot do to discipline them. These kinds of policies do have costs, but most of the time those costs are not readily visible and are difficult to attribute to the actions of policy makers. They are less likely to engender targeted, active political opposition.

As a result, these other policies are less likely to generate open conflict. But they are hugely important to what local governments do—and to citizens—and there are interest groups trying to influence them. These kinds of policies need to be included in accounts of local politics, political representation, power, and influence. We need to try to study interest group actions that are hard to see, as I have discussed, but we also have to try to study the issues where it seems like nothing is happening. I do not claim to give these matters the full treatment they deserve in this book. But by discussing them and by bringing them into the study of interest groups in local politics, I get a step closer to a fuller picture of local politics and a step closer to a more comprehensive understanding of power, influence, and representation in American politics.

CHAPTER THREE

How Active Are Interest Groups in Local Politics?

In his classic account of politics and power in New Haven, Dahl writes, "The important constituents were of two kinds. One consisted of the organized and often institutional interest groups in New Haven, the other of the voters."[1] Local politics researchers have already done a great deal of work to try to understand voters in American cities. This chapter begins an empirical investigation of the other "important constituents": interest groups.

It is easy enough to find examples of active interest groups in local politics. For example, when Northland Investment Corporation proposed a mixed-use development in Newton, Massachusetts, a suburban city of 89,000 residents, it ignited a flurry of political activity, with an organization called RightSize Newton lining up in firm opposition and a pro-housing group called Engine 6 siding with the developer. The proposed development was a prominent issue in its city council election in fall 2019, with council candidates receiving endorsements depending on whether they were in favor of or opposed to more housing and growth.[2]

Meanwhile, on the other side of the country, in the Moraga-Orinda Fire District—a special district serving 38,500 residents in the small California cities of Moraga and Orinda—firefighters' union PACs spent over $30,000 in support of three candidates during the district's contentious 2018 election campaign. All three of the supported candidates were former firefighters or employees of fire districts. As the incumbent, Steve Anderson, said after his loss to the union-backed challenger, Steve Danziger, "It's clear that money talks. . . . I never realized that on the local level."[3]

But is this kind of activity common or unusual?[4] How active are interest groups in local politics, and how does that vary from place to place?

In this chapter, I describe how I measure interest group activity in a large, diverse set of US municipal governments. Equipped with these new data, I then provide a bird's-eye view of interest group activity in different types of cities. In addition to its descriptive value, my empirical analysis serves as an initial evaluation of the policy-focused approach. As I explained in chapter 2, the amount of interest group activity in a city should depend on how much the government does, meaning how much is at stake in its policy making. In what follows, I test that expectation in an analysis of how overall interest group activity varies across cities, accounting for other city characteristics that have been shown to be important for local politics and policy. The findings begin to demonstrate the usefulness of the policy-focused approach for understanding the behavior of interest groups—and also contain some surprises of relevance to the literature on local political representation.

The Data Hurdle: Measuring Interest Group Activity

By far the biggest obstacle to studying interest groups in local government is the scarcity of data. It is true that all scholars studying interest groups confront a number of challenges, but those studying state and national interest groups at least have data bases of registered lobbying groups and their campaign donations.[5] Such data bases do not exist on any large scale for local governments. Aside from a few large cities that track lobbying activity, and some scattered campaign finance data, there are no data on interest groups in local government. Even if such data were available, formal lobbying and campaign giving may not be the most important forms of interest group activity in local politics anyway.

To get over this hurdle, I fielded a survey of city council members and mayors in early 2015. The survey asked city officials about the overall amount of interest group activity in their cities, the intensity of activity by several categories of interest groups, the activity of those interest groups in different settings and on different local issues, and some characteristics of the cities. The data from this City Interest Groups Survey are my main source of information about interest group activity in this book.

While there are advantages and disadvantages of using a survey to measure interest group activity, the most important advantage is that it makes this study possible. This is one of the only ways of obtaining data on interest group activity in a large number of local governments.[6] Surveying local officials also allows me to ask about interest group activity in a broader, more inclusive way than would be possible in a study of campaign finance records or a study of registered lobbyists in a single city, for example. The main downside of using survey data to measure interest group activity is that it relies on respondents' perceptions of that activity. Local officials' perceptions could be inaccurate—and possibly even influenced by local policies. Still, on the whole, surveying local officials is a reasonable approach given that they probably know more than most people about interest group activity in their cities.

I supplemented this main data source with two other quantitative datasets. The first is a dataset of groups' campaign contributions in municipal elections in two states: Washington and South Carolina. Local campaign finance data are very difficult to collect, and they have their own limitations: not all politically active interest groups give money, and money may not necessarily be the most important form of interest group activity in many local governments. That said, the campaign finance data measure actual group activity rather than perceptions of activity, so they help to round out the analysis.

The third dataset came from a two-wave survey of candidates for municipal government offices in nine states, the City Elections Survey. All the respondents to this elections survey ran for office in either November 2015 or November 2016—some in partisan elections, others in nonpartisan elections. I use this second survey to ask about the types of interest groups that were active during those elections in their cities, what specific kinds of activities those groups engaged in, and also to measure the activity of political parties in city elections. I discuss the election survey data in greater detail in chapters 4 and 5.

Survey Design

In designing the main survey, there were a number of competing priorities to weigh, but given that I was starting from something close to a blank slate, it was most important for it to be comprehensive, simple, and flexible. Because my interest here is local politics, moreover—an area in which data are scarce in general—I wanted to focus on local governments for which I had some preexisting information and data.

Selecting a sample was also not as simple as trying to get a random sample of units, as is typically the case in studies of individuals.[7] Drawing a simple random sample in this case would result in a dataset dominated by very small local governments, because there are far more small local governments than large ones in the United States. One common alternative approach in local politics research is to collect data on the full population of larger local governments, such as all big cities, but that was not desirable here either given my interest in how interest group activity varies across different kinds of local governments. Even if either of those approaches were desirable, moreover, the resulting dataset would not be representative because of non-response.

As a way of balancing all these considerations, I began with a sample of 1,004 municipal governments across the United States, stratified by size. I focused on municipal governments because they are the most frequently studied in local politics research, and thus the current state of knowledge about their politics is higher than for other general-purpose governments (counties). It was also important to have a large number of other variables for the analysis, so I leveraged the rich data on city institutions that already existed: the data from the International City/County Management Association's (ICMA) Municipal Form of Government (FOG) Survey. My initial sample therefore included all US cities with a population of more than 250,000 (78 cities) and all 326 cities with a population between 50,000 and 250,000 that responded to the 2011 ICMA FOG Survey. (The overall response rate to that survey was 41%.) For the smallest cities—those with fewer than 50,000 people—I selected a random sample of 600 cities, stratified by size, from among those in the ICMA dataset.

For these 1,004 municipal governments, I set out to collect the individual email addresses of their city council members and (where applicable) mayors. This was straightforward for most cities: 74% listed all the individual email addresses on their websites. Most of the remaining cities provided a web form or the email address of a staff person, in which case I requested the individual emails.[8] In the end, I was unable to obtain any individual email addresses for elected officials in 173 cities. For 48 of those, I still invited elected officials to complete the survey: I sent personalized survey invitations through staff contacts, asking that they be routed to the appropriate official. The remaining 125 cities were dropped from the sample.[9] In late February 2015, I sent out a total of

TABLE 3.1 **Survey response rates by city size**

Population	Number of Cities in Sample	Number of Emailed Invitations	Number of Cities in Dataset	Number of Respondents in Dataset	% of Cities with at Least One Response	Response Rate, % of Individuals
500,000 or more	32	458	25	42	78	9
250,000–499,999	36	321	22	41	61	13
100,000–249,999	94	676	62	120	66	18
50,000–99,999	207	1423	127	229	61	16
25,000–49,999	186	1277	109	167	59	13
10,000–24,999	180	1101	102	183	57	17
Less than 10,000	144	830	68	120	47	14
Total	879	6086	515	902	59	15

6,086 invitations with a link to the questionnaire, following up with three reminders to individuals who had not responded.[10]

In total, 902 elected officials provided at least partial responses to the survey, yielding a 15% individual response rate—comparable to that of other elite surveys.[11] Notably, 515 cities—59% of those in my sample— had at least one respondent. (Table 3.1 provides the response rates by city size.) Again, although this dataset is not a representative sample of any population of municipal governments, it offers a picture of interest group activity in a large, diverse set of American municipal governments. As I discuss below, it also includes variation on city characteristics relevant to the policy-focused approach.

Another important issue that had to be considered in designing the survey was how to ask city officials about interest group activity. First there is the matter of defining "interest group" even as a theoretical concept, as well as the fact that some scholars dislike the term "interest group" because it is usually meant to include entities that are not membership organizations.[12] Regardless, I use "interest group" in this book because it is commonly used and familiar to most readers. As for how to define an interest group, there would be some fuzziness to just about any definition, but there is something approaching a common understanding of this in the literature: an interest group includes a variety of organizations and groups active in politics, including businesses, institutions, and membership groups (regardless of whether their members are individuals or institutions). For Dahl in *Who Governs?*, for example, interest groups in New Haven include banks, a university, and labor organi-

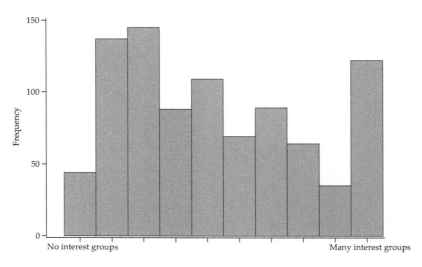

FIGURE 3.1 Overall interest group activity

zations—a variety of entities, all of which are something more than just individuals acting as individuals in politics.[13]

For similar reasons, I used the term "interest groups" in the survey itself, beginning with a broad question about interest group activity in the respondents' cities. Specifically, I asked, "In some cities, there are many interest groups that try to influence city politics. In other cities, there are no interest groups that try to influence city politics. What about in your city? Using the 10-point scale below, how would you rate the number of interest groups that try to influence politics in your city?" Respondents selected a point on a scale from 1 ("There are no interest groups") to 10 ("There are many interest groups"), which I adjust to a 0–9 measure for analysis.

Figure 3.1 shows the distribution of the 902 individual responses. Fewer than 5% of the respondents indicated that there are "no interest groups" active in their cities. However, the two most common responses were at the low end of the spectrum, suggesting that there are many cities in which elected officials perceive there to be few interest groups active in politics. Still, 14% of the respondents chose the maximum option, and 42% of the respondents placed their city on the upper half of the scale. Thus, almost all respondents perceive that there are at least some interest groups active in their cities, and a sizable proportion indicate that there are many. This is the first strong signal that there are interest groups active in local politics—and that they are more active in some cities than in others.

I intentionally did not provide respondents with a definition of interest group or activity because I did not want to start by priming them to think about certain kinds of groups or certain forms of activity. It is therefore reasonable to wonder whether this approach picks up meaningful information about city interest group activity and whether respondents tended to interpret the question in similar ways. There are different ways to try to assess this, but two preliminary ones suggest that the answer is yes.

First, on the question of whether respondents interpret the term "interest group" in similar ways: It is possible that some respondents would be thinking mainly about formally organized, permanent groups, whereas others—perhaps those in smaller cities—would also be thinking about less formal groups of citizens who organize on a temporary basis and then disband. Those different definitions could make this a noisy measure.

As one way to evaluate this possibility, I also asked respondents about the overall nature of interest group activity in their cities. Specifically, I asked, "In some cities, the groups active in local politics tend to be informal and organized on a temporary basis. In other cities, the groups active in local politics tend to be formal and organized on a permanent basis. What about the groups in your city? Using the 10-point scale below, how would you rate the nature of groups in your city?"[14] Note that it is entirely possible that a city could have very few active interest groups that are permanent and formally organized, just as it is possible a city could have many groups that tend to be loosely organized. But the correlation between this formality-of-organization variable and my main interest group activity variable is 0.57. That at least suggests that in answering the question about the overall amount of interest group activity, respondents were thinking mainly of formal, permanent organizations.

In addition, 47% of the cities in the dataset had more than one respondent, and for those, I examined whether respondents in the same city gave similar answers to the question about the overall amount of interest group activity. Specifically, for this subset of cities, I calculate the difference between the maximum and the minimum response. Those ranges for each city are plotted in figure 3.2. The range was either zero or one for a third of the cities, and it was within two points for more than

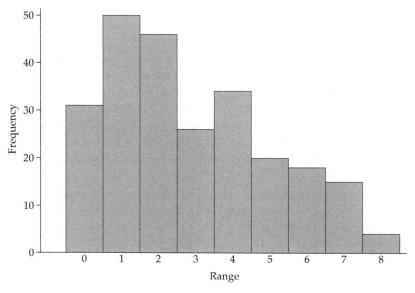

FIGURE 3.2 Range of responses in the same city, overall interest group activity

half the cities. Less than a quarter of the cities with multiple respondents had a difference greater than four points.[15] I do additional within-city analysis of the responses later on, but as a preliminary matter, this suggests that most of the time, respondents in the same city answered in similar ways.

Policy Stakes and Interest Group Activity

The next step is to analyze the variation in interest group activity across cities—and to assess whether it varies in systematic ways. In chapter 2, I proposed some possibilities for what might influence the amount of interest group activity in a local government. First, there is the argument from the interest group systems literature that groups whose members have more resources may be more likely to overcome the collective action problem and be active in politics.[16] It may be, therefore, that interest group activity is higher in cities where residents have more resources. The policy-focused approach instead points to the policy stakes of a city as the key consideration: if interest groups' motivation to be active in politics stems from the policies the governments make, then interest groups should be more active in places where the governments' policy stakes are greater.

Operationalizing the "policy stakes" of a city is not entirely straightforward, however, and it raises important questions about how and why the policy stakes of cities might vary and whether and how those sources of variation are causally related to interest group activity. To illustrate with an example, the size of a city's budget, or its total expenditures, would be one fairly clear measure of the policy stakes of a city (although admittedly one that does not factor in a city's regulatory authority): cities with greater expenditures presumably do more, and thus there is more to attract interest group activity. Theoretically, and as a descriptive matter, it seems quite reasonable to examine the relationship between interest group activity and city expenditures, and the expectation is that that relationship would be positive.

Figure 3.3 shows that it is. There, I average the interest group activity variable from figure 3.1 by city and show its relationship to the log of total city expenditures in 2012 (in thousands of dollars), using data from the Census of Governments. It is clear that cities with larger expenditures tend to have more interest group activity than cities with smaller expenditures.

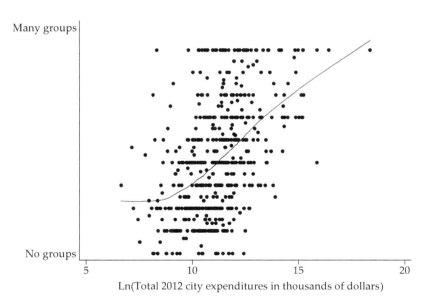

FIGURE 3.3 Interest group activity and city expenditures

But taking this beyond a descriptive exercise runs into problems. On the one hand, as a broad theoretical matter, the policy-focused approach is explicit about the endogeneity of public policy and interest group activity: an association between interest group activity and the policy stakes could arise because governments with greater policy stakes attract greater interest group activity, or it could be that interest groups that are more active successfully persuade government officials to expand the policy stakes. But the immediate empirical question here is whether the policy stakes shape the amount of interest group activity. And for measures of city spending, it seems quite likely that greater interest group activity could lead to higher government spending, perhaps more than the other way around.

For the task at hand, then, it helps to instead focus on characteristics of cities that are less malleable than city government expenditures—characteristics that are either measures of or correlated with their policy stakes. Consider, for example, the range of issues on which a city makes policy. Cities that make decisions on a larger number of issues should tend to have more interest group activity. It is of course possible that interest group activity could also lead a government to take up policy authority on a larger number of issues, but that is somewhat less likely, especially for local government. As Peterson argues, cities are limited in their ability to pursue a wide range of policies, such as redistributive policies, because of the competitive pressure generated by the mobility of taxpaying residents and businesses.[17] They are also constrained in what they can do by rules and restrictions imposed by the states.[18] This does not rule out the possibility that local interest groups persuade local governments to take on more issues, but most local governments are not free to do just anything. In any case, compared to the city's expenditures, the number of issues on which a city makes policy is probably less prone to influence by interest groups.

The same is true for city population as a measure of its size and thus its policy stakes. The policy stakes of a city that serves 100,000 people are almost certainly greater than those in a city with 1,000 people. And while it is not impossible that interest group activity could affect city population—for example, certain city policies pushed by interest groups could lead to more population growth, and cities could pursue annexation in response to interest groups—the more likely scenario is one in which interest groups are more active in larger cities because of the greater policy gains to be had there.[19] Furthermore, population seems less likely to change because of interest group activity than city expenditures.

Focusing on these relatively more fixed characteristics of cities does not fully address concerns about causality and the direction of the causal arrow, of course, but it does provide a sturdier foothold for this analysis. In addition, it creates an opportunity to advance conceptual clarity about what "policy" in "policy-focused" means, in ways that will prove useful throughout the book. Given that the central idea of the policy-focused approach is that policy affects interest group activity and interest group activity also affects policy, there is a more general question here about how to gain traction on questions of causality. In this shift from the theoretical to the empirical, therefore, it helps to recognize that there are different sources of variation in "the policies governments make."

Central to my approach in this book is the distinction between (1) whether or not a city makes any policy on an issue, or more fixed characteristics of cities; and (2) the particular details of the policies in a city. The factors I have just laid out—city government scope and population— are in the first category. They probably shape the amount of interest group activity that emerges in a city, but because they are relatively more fixed, they are somewhat less likely to be shaped by interest group activity. The second category refers to the particular policies a city government makes in an issue area, such as the size of the required minimum lot for new housing or whether police officers are required to wear body cameras. These are different from the first set; they are specific policies (conditional on a city making policies in that issue area). Compared to the first set of city characteristics, they are more susceptible to being influenced by the amount and nature of interest group activity in a city.

In drawing this distinction, I am not making a bright-line statement about the direction of the causal arrow when policy particulars are under consideration. As the policy feedback literature makes clear, policies more generous to a group of individuals can increase the political activity of those individuals,[20] just as threats to benefits and policies that are bad for groups can be powerful motivators as well. There is therefore potential for the particulars of policy to influence interest group activity, just as there is potential for interest group activity to influence the policy particulars. But how this all works likely varies by issue and by group, as I discuss later. And in the meantime, it helps to cordon off the first set of factors—the relatively more fixed features of cities—as policy-relevant

66   CHAPTER THREE

characteristics that likely shape the amount of interest group activity in a city and the factors that I focus on for the analysis here.[21]

Explaining Variation in City Interest Group Activity

In figure 3.4, I average the interest group activity responses by city and evaluate that variable's relationship to three city-level characteristics. The first is logged per capita income in the city using the 2009–13 estimates from the American Community Survey (ACS). Notably, figure 3.4 shows that there is no clear bivariate relationship between this measure of city affluence and the overall amount of interest group activity. Based on this initial assessment, the link between citizens' material resources and the overall amount of interest group activity is not as straightforward as some have suggested.

In the middle plot of figure 3.4, I look at a second independent variable: city government scope. To create this measure, I identified twenty-four categories of spending in the 2012 Census of Governments' city finance reports and created an index equal to the number of categories in which a city had positive direct expenditures.[22] The figure shows that this variable has a clear positive relationship with city interest group activity. Thus, consistent with the policy-focused approach, cities that make policy on a larger number of issues tend to have more active interest groups.

The same is true for the log of city population (as of 2010), as I show in the bottom plot of figure 3.4. The relationship there is strong and positive. Municipalities with the smallest populations are an exception to this pattern: for them, the slope of log population is flat or even negative,[23] which might suggest that below a certain threshold, variation in population size does not matter for the amount of interest group activity.[24] But beyond these smallest towns, larger population is associated with more interest group activity, as expected.

I next use ordinary least squares (OLS) to model interest group activity in the city using city scope, population, and per capita income as explanatory variables, clustering the standard errors by state. The results are given in column 1 of table 3.2.[25] The estimates show that there is a positive, statistically significant relationship between government scope and interest group activity. The coefficient on scope is 0.156, which implies that shifting from a city that has five functions (the 5th percentile) to one that has 15 functions (the 95th percentile) is associated with a

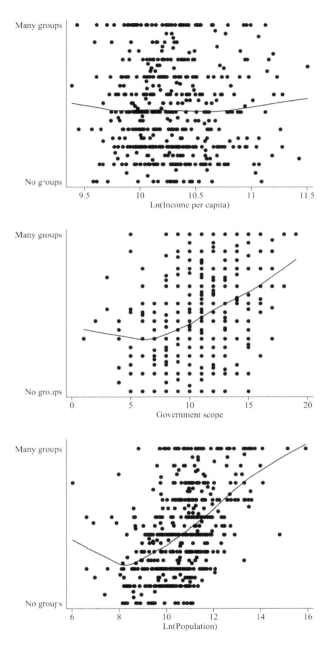

FIGURE 3.4 Interest group activity by city characteristics

68 CHAPTER THREE

TABLE 3.2 **Interest group activity in US municipal governments**

	(1)	(2)	(3)	(4)	(5)
Scope of government	0.156***	0.109**	0.159**	0.117*	0.176**
	(0.041)	(0.046)	(0.076)	(0.067)	(0.072)
Ln(Population)	0.728***	0.55***	0.478***	0.517***	0.448***
	(0.094)	(0.089)	(0.089)	(0.088)	(0.090)
Ln(Income per capita)	0.578	1.567***	0.817**	0.451	0.473
	(0.507)	(0.446)	(0.396)	(0.338)	(0.521)
Democratic presidential vote		2.119***	4.278***	3.374***	
		(0.653)	(0.796)	(0.858)	
Conservative citizen ideology					−1.748***
					(0.323)
Percent homeowner		−4.454***	−2.076**	−1.009	−2.261**
		(1.072)	(0.994)	(0.968)	(1.081)
Percent Black		0.364	−0.751	−1.402	0.563
		(0.803)	(1.241)	(1.386)	(1.458)
Percent Latino		0.684	−1.735	−2.427**	−1.61
		(1.040)	(1.441)	(0.964)	(1.683)
Percent rural		1.078	1.313*	1.216**	0.991
		(0.661)	(0.742)	(0.595)	(0.717)
Off−cycle elections		0.154	0.402**	0.05	0.407*
		(0.159)	(0.176)	(0.212)	(0.208)
Nonpartisan elections		0.771***	0.4	0.177	0.485
		(0.253)	(0.435)	(0.493)	(0.436)
District elections		0.138	0.218	0.255	0.189
		(0.259)	(0.271)	(0.239)	(0.277)
Mayor−council government		−0.22	−0.096	0.081	−0.078
		(0.228)	(0.285)	(0.212)	(0.270)
R−squared	0.25	0.34	0.41	0.39	0.4
Observations	515	512	512	501	512

Notes: Standard errors clustered by state in parentheses. Models 3–5 include state fixed effects. Dependent variable in column 4 is an index of interest group activity.

*p < 0.10, **p < 0.05, ***p < 0.01 (two-tailed).

shift of 1.56 units up the interest group scale—about 60% of a standard deviation. Population size also has a strong relationship with interest group activity, with city officials from larger cities reporting more interest group activity than officials from smaller cities. The coefficient on log per capita income, however, is statistically indistinguishable from zero.

There are several other characteristics of cities that research has shown to be associated with city politics and policies, and while it is not theoretically clear how some of those city characteristics would be related to the overall level of interest group activity, I include them in the next set of models. The first is city partisanship or, alternatively, ideology. Researchers have found that local government spending outcomes vary with both the ideology and partisanship of city residents,[26] but it is not obvious how either would be related to overall city interest group activity. As I discuss in the next chapter, it does seem as though certain *types* of interest groups would be more active in more Republican or Democratic cities, but that is getting ahead of the discussion here. Purely based on the partisanship or ideology of city residents, there is little reason to anticipate that cities with certain partisan or ideological leanings would have more groups—at least there is not much in the literature to suggest it.

Throughout the book, my main measure of city residents' partisan and ideological leanings is the share of the city's two-party vote that went to the Democratic presidential candidate, Barack Obama, in 2012. For most cities, this variable is measured at the city level, but in a small number of cases, I had to use presidential vote share data from the city's parent county because city-level figures were not available. As a secondary measure, I use Chris Tausanovitch and Christopher Warshaw's multilevel regression and post-stratification (MRP) measures of citizen ideology.[27] For many of the cities in my dataset, these ideology estimates are available at the city level; for those for which they are not available, I use the county-level estimates.

The second set of independent variables I add are city demographics from the US Census. I include the share of the city population living in owner-occupied housing units (percent homeowner), because homeowners have been argued to be a highly engaged, politically influential force in local politics.[28] I also account for the racial composition of cities—the share of city residents who are Black and Latino—because race and ethnicity have been shown to be important for explaining political behavior and outcomes in US city politics.[29] To account for the possibility that more rural municipalities operate differently from heavily urban ones, I include the share of city residents living in rural areas (percent rural). While the literature does not point to ways in which these variables would be correlated with the amount of interest group activity in a city, I include them because of their demonstrated importance in research on local politics.

Third, the local politics literature has examined the effects of political institutions,[30] so I include indicators of four primary ones here: mayor-council form of government, off-cycle elections, nonpartisan elections, and district (as opposed to at-large) elections. Most of the data on political institutions come from the ICMA 2011 Municipal FOG Survey, with the exception of the election timing variable, which I collected as part of my survey.[31]

For all but nonpartisan elections, the theoretical link to the overall amount of interest group activity seems tenuous at best. And while nonpartisan elections might be associated with interest group activity, theory suggests that relationship could go in either direction. Holding nonpartisan elections might reduce the activity of political parties in elections.[32] If so, and if political parties can be thought of as coalitions of interest groups,[33] then perhaps interest group activity should be lower in cities with nonpartisan elections. An alternative account is that interest groups are substitutes for political parties in organizing elections.[34] If that is the case, then perhaps we should find *more* interest group activity in cities with nonpartisan elections. I explore this more directly in chapter 5, but for now, as a preliminary investigation, I include an indicator for whether the city has nonpartisan elections.

There is also some justification for adding state fixed effects to the model. Local governments are creatures of the states, and the states set different limits on their local governments—including rules about the kinds of policies municipal governments can pursue. States and regions also have different political cultures, which may shape the overall amount of interest group activity in cities. By including state fixed effects, I partial out the effects of any such variables that are constant within states. However, two of the political institutions variables—off-cycle elections and nonpartisan elections—have little within-state variation in this dataset. In order to evaluate their relationships to interest group activity, I therefore estimate these models both without and with state fixed effects.

The estimates are presented in columns 2 and 3 of table 3.2. As before, the coefficients on government scope are positive. In column 2, the coefficient is smaller than that in column 1, but in column 3, where state fixed effects are included, it is roughly the same size as before. City size is positively associated with interest group activity as well in both models. This much is largely the same as in the basic model in column 1 and is consistent with expectations that flow from the policy-focused approach: on average, cities with greater policy stakes have more interest group activity.

In column 4, I switch out my main dependent variable for an index of interest group activity composed of the average city responses to three separate survey questions. The first is the question analyzed above, but the second two ask respondents how active interest groups are in trying to influence outcomes in their cities at two different political stages: during city elections and when the city government makes decisions and policies. Responses to the three questions are highly correlated—the main dependent variable has a correlation of 0.68 with election activity and 0.76 with activity on decisions and policies—so I average them and model the resulting index with the same variables as in column 3.[35] The takeaway is again that interest group activity increases with the size and the scope of city government.

Interestingly, in these models with additional city characteristics as controls, logged per capita income has a stronger relationship with city interest group activity than in column 1. In columns 2 and 3 in particular, the estimated coefficients on per capita income are positive and significant (although not in column 4). The estimate in column 3 suggests that going from the 5th to the 95th percentile of logged per capita income is associated with approximately a one-point shift up the interest group activity scale. Thus, in the models with the full set of controls, there is some indication that more affluent cities have more interest group activity.

Of the other demographic variables, the only one showing a clear pattern is percent homeowner: the coefficient in column 3, for example, shows that a shift from the 5th percentile (43% homeowners) to the 95th percentile (90% homeowners) is associated with about a one-point decrease in the overall level of interest group activity in the city.[36] The share of city residents who are Black does not appear to be associated with the amount of interest group activity, and the coefficients on percent Latino and percent rural do not show consistent patterns either.

Of the political institutions variables, moreover, the only two that seem to have a relationship with overall interest group activity are nonpartisan elections and off-cycle election timing.[37] The coefficient on off-cycle election timing is only statistically significant when state fixed effects are added (see column 3), however, and it suggests that within states, cities with off-cycle elections have a higher average rate of interest group activity. In column 2, the results show that having nonpartisan elections is associated with more interest group activity as well, which I explore more in chapter 5.[38]

Of all of these additional variables, perhaps most surprising are the strong positive coefficients on Democratic presidential vote. Focusing on the estimate in column 3, moving from a city with 26% Democratic presidential vote (the 5th percentile in these data) to one with 82% Democratic presidential vote (the 95th percentile) is associated with well over a two-point shift up the interest group activity scale. Moreover, as I show in column 5, this relationship persists when I replace the Democratic presidential vote share variable with the MRP estimates of citizen ideology (for which higher values mean more conservative): cities with more liberal residents tend to have higher levels of interest group activity.

That there is such a strong correlation between the amount of interest group activity in a city and partisanship and ideology demands further investigation. It is possible that this implies that Democrats are more likely than Republicans to form and be active in interest groups, but I think that is unlikely given that Republicans and conservatives seem quite willing and able to join and be active in interest groups in state and national politics.[39] Another interpretation, which I explore in the next chapter, is that this relationship is generated by patterns in the *types* of interest groups that are active. In particular, certain types of groups are more active in Democratic cities, whereas others are active regardless of city ideology and partisanship.

For the moment, though, simply finding these relationships between city interest group activity and local partisanship and ideology is important. Research on local political representation finds an empirical link between local government spending and city residents' partisanship and ideology and interprets that link as a sign that local governments are being responsive to the preferences of their residents.[40] My findings here suggest that it might not be as simple as that. Those local political representation studies do not consider the role of interest groups. And yet in this initial investigation of how interest group activity varies across cities, I find that more Democratic and liberal cities have more interest group activity.

Of course, it could just be that survey respondents who are Democrats—and who are more likely to be found in Democratic-leaning cities—are more inclined to report more interest group activity, but the data suggest that this is not the explanation. As part of the survey, I asked the city officials for their party identification and ideology.[41] In table 3.3, I turn back to the individual-level survey data and model the ratings of interest group activity with city government scope, size, and per capita income and the demographic variables from table 3.2, plus either their self-reported partisanship (column 1) or ideology (column 2). In

HOW ACTIVE ARE INTEREST GROUPS IN LOCAL POLITICS? 73

TABLE 3.3 **Interest group activity and respondent party ID and ideology**

	(1)	(2)	(3)	(4)
Scope of government	0.187**	0.197***		
	(0.071)	(0.066)		
Ln(Population)	0.441***	0.402***		
	(0.125)	(0.125)		
Ln(Income per capita)	0.897**	0.508		
	(0.394)	(0.465)		
Respondent party ID	0.072		0.023	
	(0.051)		(0.095)	
Democratic presidential vote	4.007***			
	(1.014)			
Respondent ideology		0.216**		−0.076
		(0.091)		(0.181)
Conservative citizen ideology		−1.494***		
		(0.511)		
R-squared	0.36	0.36	0.79	0.8
Observations	707	721	707	721

Notes: Standard errors clustered by state in parentheses. Models include demographic controls from table 3.2. Models 1 and 2 include state fixed effects; models 3 and 4 include city fixed effects.

*p < 0.10, **p < 0.05, ***p < 0.01 (two-tailed).

column 1, city-level Democratic presidential vote is positive and significant, but the respondents' party ID is not significant. In column 2, I find that more liberal respondents report more interest group activity, but that does not fully explain why liberal cities have more interest groups: the coefficient on city-level conservative citizen ideology is still negative and statistically significant. Moreover, in columns 3 and 4, where I add city fixed effects and leverage within-city variation in respondents' self-reported party ID and liberalism, I find that neither respondent party ID nor respondent ideology is a significant predictor of the amount of interest group activity. Thus, it seems that more Democratic and liberal *cities* have more interest group activity—not that more Democratic city officials *report* more interest group activity.

Insights from Local Campaign Finance Data

The analysis thus far shows that interest group activity is not at all unusual in US municipal governments but also that it varies across cities in some predictable ways. Larger cities and cities that make policy on a larger number of issues have significantly more interest group activity, as do cities with more Democratic and liberal residents. But up to this point the analysis has focused on survey-based measures of interest group activity. It is also worth evaluating whether the same patterns hold when I analyze other data on local interest group activity: interest group campaign contributions.

As I have said, local campaign finance data are very hard to collect. Most states do not assemble campaign finance data for their local governments. And most local governments do not make it easy to acquire and use such data. Even in the best scenario, determining which contributions come from individuals as opposed to interest groups can be tedious and time consuming. Fortunately, though, there at least two states that provide relatively accessible online data bases of campaign contributions in their local elections: Washington and South Carolina.

The Washington cities data come from the Washington Public Disclosure Commission. I downloaded the itemized campaign contribution data for its November 2015 local elections, which include candidates running for city council or mayor in 64 municipal governments.[42] For South Carolina, I collected data from the South Carolina State Ethics Commission's Public Disclosure and Accountability Reporting system; for the November 2015 local election cycle, the data base includes individual campaign contribution data for 26 cities. For both states, I hand-coded whether each contribution was made by an individual or a nonindividual, such as a business, union, or association. For Washington, the result was campaign finance data for candidates in 78 unique races, 18 mayoral races and 60 city council races (including one race for city council president in Spokane). In South Carolina, I have campaign finance data for 38 unique races: 23 city council races and 15 mayoral races.

To evaluate how the overall amount of interest group activity varies by city using this dataset, I sum all the campaign contributions by city and type of race (city council vs. mayor). In the resulting dataset of 116 unique races, the median total contribution amount is \$12,416, and the median amount contributed by interest groups (not individuals) is \$3,245. As expected, however, there is considerable variation in these amounts across cities. The question is whether the key variables from table 3.2 help explain patterns of local interest group campaign giving as well as they do the survey-based measures of interest group activity.

I evaluate this in table 3.4 by regressing the log of total interest group campaign contributions in the city race on city government scope, size, income per capita, Democratic presidential vote, and the city demographics from table 3.2.[43] I also include indicators for whether the city

HOW ACTIVE ARE INTEREST GROUPS IN LOCAL POLITICS? 75

TABLE 3.4 **Municipal campaign contributions in South Carolina and Washington, 2015**

	Ln(Interest group contributions) (1)	Ln(Individual contributions) (2)
Scope of government	0.272**	0.157*
	(0.124)	(0.090)
Ln(Population)	0.842**	0.857***
	(0.405)	(0.278)
Ln(Income per capita)	−1.382	1.423*
	(1.496)	(0.773)
Democratic presidential vote	6.792**	2.004
	(3.246)	(1.665)
Percent homeowner	12.875***	1.625
	(4.412)	(1.831)
Percent Black	4.059	2.104
	(4.651)	(2.283)
Percent Latino	7.14*	3.344
	(3.617)	(2.722)
Percent rural	−2.989**	−0.543
	(1.470)	(0.856)
City council race	0.323	−0.586*
	(0.605)	(0.322)
R-squared	0.42	0.45
Observations	116	116

Notes: Standard errors clustered by city in parentheses. Models include an indicator for Washington.
*p < 0.1, **p < 0.05, ***p < 0.01 (two-tailed).

is in Washington (not shown) and whether it is a city council or a mayoral race.

The estimates in column 1 of table 3.4 are similar to those in table 3.2. First, the coefficients on city government scope and log city population are positive and statistically significant, showing that the total amount of money given by interest groups to city candidates grows with the number of city functions and city size. Also mirroring the results from the survey data, more Democratic cities tend to have more interest group campaign contributions.[44] These findings are important, because they show that even when I use the campaign contribution data, there is clear evidence that interest group activity increases with city size, scope, and residents who lean Democratic.

A few features of these results are different from those in table 3.2, however. First, in this model, cities with higher percentages of Latino residents tend to have more interest group campaign contributions. Second, the coefficient on log per capita income is again statistically insignificant, and the coefficient on percent homeowner is positive (whereas it was negative in table 3.2). These differences could be due to the different sample, or it could just be that the patterns are different when the focus is on one particular form of interest group activity.

Importantly, however, I find that per capita income *is* a positive predictor of total campaign contributions by *individuals*. I show this in column 2 of table 3.4, where I regress the log of total individual contributions on the same set of predictors. Thus, the affluence of the community does seem to matter for individual local campaign giving; however, it is not clear that it is an important factor in explaining the amount of interest group campaign contributions. Moreover, it is not the case that individuals give more money to local candidates in more Democratic cities; the coefficient on Democratic presidential vote in column 2 is statistically insignificant. This suggests that interest group activity is greater in more Democratic cities but not campaign giving by individuals.

The most important takeaway, however, is that the estimates from the model of local interest group campaign contributions are similar to those in table 3.2. The same policy-relevant city characteristics that predict the survey-based measure of city interest group activity also predict total city campaign contributions by interest groups. That the survey data and the campaign finance data tell the same general story indicates that the survey data provide good measures of interest group activity and that the campaign contribution data can be relied on for helpful information as well.

"Normal" Interest Group Politics

As a final step in laying out this initial picture of the amount of interest group activity in American cities, it is important to ask whether these datasets tell us something general about interest group activity or if they are just capturing the dynamics in these cities at a particular moment in time (which, for both the survey data and the campaign finance data, is 2015). The answer is probably both. But if it is both—and not just what was happening in 2015—this is important to acknowledge for the data analysis ahead. That means that to some degree, these data are showing us what "normal" interest group politics looks like in these cities in the years before and after and including 2015.

There are of course idiosyncratic components of politics in every place and political cycle,[45] and I expect it is no different with these data. City interest group activity is almost certainly shaped by particular features of cities and time periods, such as a city's culture, or national crises like the Great Recession, or the birth of the Black Lives Matter movement, or a scandal affecting a city in a given year. It is possible, for example, that I happened to survey a particular city at a moment when interest group activity was especially high or low, and if local officials answered the survey with those most proximate conditions in mind, the data for that city would not really be reflective of its "normal" politics.

Yet the fact that relatively fixed, slow-changing features of cities can explain a lot of the variation in interest group activity across cities suggests that what I am capturing here is much more than idiosyncratic variation. It suggests that this is a measure of what interest group activity normally looks like in most of these cities.

A closer look at two cities in California—Dana Point and West Sacramento—is illustrative. Dana Point is a beach city of just over 33,000 residents in Orange County, and West Sacramento is a city of roughly 50,000 just across the river from the larger city of Sacramento. Both cities have about the same rate of homeownership, but they are different in important ways. In addition to being larger in population, the city of West Sacramento does more: it has a score of 11 on the measure of government scope, compared to 4 for Dana Point. West Sacramento also leans Democratic—its 2012 two-party vote share for Obama was 62.9%—whereas Dana Point residents lean Republican (40.8% vote share for Obama in 2012). Dana Point is also a more affluent community: its per capita income according to the 2009–13 ACS was double that of West Sacramento. And consistent with the account I have provided, the survey data show that West Sacramento has more interest group activity than Dana Point. A local official in West Sacramento rated the city's interest group activity as a 7 on the 0–9 scale. A local official in Dana Point, by contrast, rated that city as a 4. Consistent with what I found in my analysis of the larger dataset, then, the larger, more Democratic city with more city government functions has more interest group activity.

But was this just for 2015, or does it represent something close to "normal" politics? To evaluate these two cities over a longer period, I collected detailed campaign contribution data for the cities' elections from 2008 to 2014. This is difficult to do for most California cities: it requires requesting individual candidates' disclosure forms from the city, which typically come as PDFs (often scans), and then I had to hand-code individual contributions as either coming from individuals or groups and organizations. But going through this exercise for these two cities helps

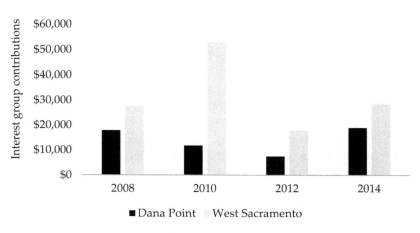

FIGURE 3.5 Over-time comparisons in two cities

shed light not only on how interest group contributions compare to each other across cities—and whether that aligns with the survey data—but also on whether local campaign contributions (and thus interest group activity) fluctuate greatly within cities from year to year.

In figure 3.5, I present the sum of all interest group (non-individual) contributions made to city council and mayoral candidates in each of the cities and years. Two patterns stand out. First, consistent with my survey data and the results in table 3.2, West Sacramento had more interest group campaign contributions than Dana Point in all four of these election years. Second, while there is some fluctuation in interest group campaign giving year to year—for example, relatively high contributions in West Sacramento in 2010 and lower contributions in 2012 for both—there is some consistency in the amounts contributed each year. In Dana Point, the yearly interest group totals ranged from $7,530 to $18,935, and in West Sacramento, they ranged from $17,824 to $52,850. What this at least suggests is that there is some normal pattern of interest group activity in these cities and that that is a big part of what my data on interest group activity are picking up.

This is important to keep in mind for the analysis going forward: the main survey data from 2015 are a measure of what interest group activity normally looks like in most of these cities. That is not to deny that my survey might have been fielded at a particularly turbulent or peaceful point for some of them. But on the whole, we can expect that the survey (and the campaign contribution data) does a fairly good job of capturing the regular interest group dynamics of these cities—not just what was happening that year.

Conclusion

In this chapter, I have taken the important step of moving from the broad and theoretical to the empirical and have confronted some of the data, measurement, and conceptual challenges involved in analyzing interest group activity in local politics. I have introduced the three datasets on interest group activity that I use throughout the book and used two of them to paint a general picture of the overall amount of interest group activity in a large, diverse set of US municipal governments. The results show that interest groups are active in many municipal governments and that the overall amount of activity varies from city to city.

Moreover, much of that cross-city variation in interest group activity can be explained by city characteristics that measure or are correlated with the policy stakes of the city: the number of issues on which the city makes policy and the size of the city. I also found that a city's per capita income—a measure of its citizens' resources—is not an especially strong or consistent predictor of overall interest group activity. And in a finding that has special significance for the literature on local political representation, my analysis shows that cities with more Democratic and liberal residents have more interest group activity than cities with mostly Republican and conservative residents.

This much lays important groundwork for the empirical analysis to come. With these data in hand and the big picture of local interest group activity presented, I can move on to questions about the types of interest groups that are most active in local politics and why interest group activity is higher in more Democratic, liberal cities. All this will help fill out the account of local interest group activity, but it will also prove essential for the shift to the study of interest group influence in later chapters.

This chapter has also begun to specify some of the different ways in which the policy stakes of a city can vary. The crux of the policy-focused approach to studying interest groups is the notion that the causal arrow between policy and interest group activity runs both ways: policy affects interest group activity, and interest group activity affects policy. As a theoretical matter, this is fine, but it raises thorny issues for any attempt to empirically evaluate one side of the question or the other. I do not provide a perfect solution to these issues in this book—there is no experiment here in which I randomly assign cities different policy stakes or levels of interest group activity—but I do gain some traction on them. I began that effort in this chapter by drawing a conceptual distinction between (1) whether a city makes policy on a given issue (or, alternatively, relatively less malleable characteristics of cities) and (2) the specifics of the policies a city makes on the issue. The analysis in this chapter has been focused on how the policy stakes of a city influence the overall activity of interest groups, so I have looked at the first set of factors: measures of cities' policy stakes that are less likely than some alternatives to be influenced by interest group activity. In the analysis that follows, I revisit this issue and this distinction, both in the further analysis of how policy affects interest group activity and in the later analysis of how interest group activity affects policy.

CHAPTER FOUR

What Kinds of Interest Groups Are Most Active?

Now that we know interest groups are usually active in city politics, there are many more questions to answer. What kinds of interest groups are involved? When and how do they get active in city politics? And why does the political activity of any particular type of interest group vary from city to city?

In national politics, researchers have shown that business interests and privileged groups dominate the lobbying scene and that unions and groups representing the less privileged are severely underrepresented. The standard explanation offered is that businesses and groups with affluent members have the resources needed to overcome the collective action problem and engage heavily in politics. Some such groups may not even have a collective action problem because they organized for some other purpose (such as business) and simply put that organization to use in politics. In contrast, unions and less privileged groups are stymied by limited resources, which—by this account—is why they have a lesser presence in the nation's capital.

But if resources are the only or the primary driver of interest group activity, then the same general pattern should appear in every government, including municipal governments. Business should dominate. Unions and groups representing those of lesser means should have a much smaller presence.[1] Inequality in representation should look the same in local government as in the federal government.

The policy-focused approach, however, suggests a different emphasis—with different implications. It suggests that collective action problems and variation in group organization are not necessarily the place to begin, even though they are important to consider. It instead points to patterns of interest group activity being shaped by the kinds of policies the government makes and groups' interests in those policies. And because municipal governments have mostly different policy responsibilities from those of the federal government, the kinds of interest groups that are politically active in municipal government should be mostly different as well.

In this chapter, I continue to evaluate these accounts by presenting and analyzing new data on the political activity of different types of interest groups in local politics. I begin with an overview of the kinds of interest groups that are most active in city politics. The patterns I find are very much in line with what the policy-focused approach suggests and deviate from the resource-based expectation of weak unions and business dominance. I then provide details on *when* and *how* different types of interest groups get active in city politics, examining patterns of their activity on specific policy issues and in local elections. I find that different groups tend to be active on different issues and that some local issues involve much less contestation than others. Finally, I evaluate how the political activity of particular types of interest groups varies across cities. For certain types of groups, political activity depends heavily on the state and local context and whether that context is favorable to their organization. But once those contextual differences are taken into account, it is very clear that their political activity depends on what is at stake for them in a city.

Expectations: Using Issues and Interests to Predict Groups

Using the policy-focused approach means starting with city policies: the most common and most active interest groups should be those with a stake in what cities most commonly do. And to devise expectations about what kinds of interest groups will be active in city politics, it makes sense to begin with the issues of economic development, property development, and land use. These are some of the core functions of municipal governments everywhere. Nearly all cities have the authority to regulate what can be built and where. As Peterson argues, cities have to be focused on economic success, because a strong local economy is key to a healthy local fiscal base.[2] Economic development and growth are also the overwhelming focus of studies in the urban politics literature.[3]

In studying the politics of growth and development, moreover, urban politics scholars have underscored the importance of one type of interest group in particular: business. According to Logan and Molotch, the reason cities operate like "growth machines," pushing them toward the "intensification of land use,"[4] is that city officials and businesses are complicit in their desires to line the pockets of capitalists. Regime theory emphasizes the importance of business as well: how the business community influences city politics through informal, collaborative, and symbiotic relationships with city officials.[5]

As a starting point, then, the emphasis on business is sensible. There are strong reasons to expect that business interests play a prominent role in city politics. But from a policy-focused perspective, the main reason for that is not (or is at least not primarily) because of business resources or organization. Rather, it is because of the potential for businesses to have a large, direct, regular, and economic stake in city policies—especially city policies related to economic development, property development, and land use. Moreover, with the policy-focused approach, we can make more precise and conditional statements about the activity of business in local politics. Certain types of businesses and business groups should be more active than others, and their activity should vary across cities depending on the policy stakes.

For instance, we can make distinctions between different types of businesses and business groups. Some businesses depend in a large, direct, economic way on city policies on economic development and property development, whereas for others, the interests are smaller or less direct. In particular, for real estate developers, contractors, construction firms, realtors, and other growth-oriented businesses, profits depend directly on what a city allows to be built and whether and how it pursues growth. This sets them apart from other types of businesses. The profits of retail businesses, for example, depend on city government decisions but in a smaller and less direct way. They benefit financially when a city keeps the streets clean and has low crime, low taxes, and ample parking. But these are collective goods for retail businesses. The ways city policies affect them are smaller and less direct than how a city's decision on a development affects the developer. Compared to developers and growth-oriented businesses, then, there is good reason to expect retail businesses to be less politically active in municipal government.

In addition, businesses vary in how dependent they are on the decisions of a particular city government. Some have other means of pursuing their interests; others have fewer outside options. Consider the difference between a local business and a national corporation that has a presence in a city. A local Target store and a locally based retailer may be similarly affected by city parking, crime, street cleaning, and taxes. Moreover, Target may have greater resources to get involved in a city's politics than a locally based retailer. But their incentives to get involved in the city's politics may be different, because Target may have a greater ability to move out of the city if its policies become too inhospitable. By comparison, the local retailer may be confined to operating within that particular city—and therefore may be more likely to engage in local politics.[6]

Business mobility might also limit the extent to which even developers and other growth-oriented businesses get active in city politics. Most developers are probably not locked into doing business in a particular city; a development firm might pursue business in any number of municipalities. Because of this, developers may not feel the need to get deeply involved in the institutions and inner workings of a particular city government. We can expect that developers get involved when they are trying to get one of their own projects approved, but it is not obvious that they would be an active force pushing for the city to be a more pro-growth, pro-business place in general. The developer's interest in getting its own project approved is large and direct, although this may come up infrequently for a particular developer in a particular city. By comparison, the developer's interest in one city having a pro-business, pro-growth climate is less direct.

This makes it sound as though business interests in local politics are isolated and uncoordinated, but that is because I have not yet considered the main way local businesses are coordinated to pursue business-friendly policies in a city: the local chamber of commerce. A tie-in to Olson's theory of collective action is helpful here.[7] Individual businesses can have their own private interests in city policies; for example, a developer wants the city to approve a project, or a local business wants a tax break. But both the developer and the local business are also better off when the city provides collective goods like low crime, low taxes, and clean and attractive streets that draw in customers. There may be cases in which a single large business pushes for these collective goods itself, but typically collective action will require businesses to contribute to an organization that advances their collective interests. This is where local chambers of commerce come in.

There are many reasons to expect local chambers to be highly active in local politics. Olson says that they can overcome the collective action problem because their potential membership is small. Others might point to member resources: local businesses can afford to pay dues to an organization to represent their collective interests. They are also occupational groups, because a condition of membership is being a local business. But perhaps more important are two characteristics of their interests. First, even though low taxes and clean streets are collective goods for local businesses, they affect businesses' profits—a core economic interest. Second, unlike individual businesses that may be able to move to a different community, a local chamber of commerce is locked into its city. The El Cerrito Chamber of Commerce cannot simply move to nearby Berkeley if conditions in El Cerrito are inhospitable. Its whole purpose is to support business in El Cerrito, so it will stay there and focus on its politics.

For all these reasons, we should expect local chambers of commerce to be highly active in municipal governments. However, the pattern of their activity is likely broader and more spread out across issues than that of developers. As a general rule, I expect that developers and growth-oriented businesses are intensely active on issues related to growth and development—especially when it involves their own projects. Chambers of commerce, however, are more generalist organizations with interests in multiple city policies related to business and therefore are probably more moderately active on a wider portfolio of issues.

Starting with these considerations of business interests makes good sense, but businesses and chambers of commerce are not the only groups that may have a stake in city policies related to economic development, property development, and land use, although there is reason to expect that, on average, other groups will be less active than developers and chambers of commerce. First, consider carpenters, electricians, plumbers, and other workers in the building trades, which in some parts of the United States are well organized in unions. They, too, have large, economic interests in what cities allow to be built and developed. Similar to developers, a carpenters' local is only sometimes directly affected by a city's development decision, such as if a development project in question has a contractor committed to using that union local's carpenters. But just as chambers of commerce pursue collective goods for local businesses, local labor councils may help coordinate the interests of union locals, pushing for more building and more pro-labor local policies generally. On the basis of policy interests, then, we would expect to see building trade unions and local labor councils active in local politics.

But here is where the issue of organization enters the equation. Unlike business, which is ubiquitous, workers in the building trades are only unionized in some parts of the United States. In a state like Washington, for example, 25% of private-sector construction workers are members of unions, whereas in South Carolina, only 1% are.[8] This is an important contextual constraint, and it implies that, on average, building trade unions will be less active in local politics than businesses and business groups. If a city does not have building trade unions, we certainly cannot expect to see much political activity by them in city politics.[9]

But noting this pattern and factoring it into expectations of local interest group activity does not mean that we have to explain the pattern in order to move forward. That would take me far afield; labor experts continue to debate and puzzle over why private-sector union membership varies across the country and why it has declined over time.[10] Besides, the primary cause of variation in group organization does not necessarily have to be differences in potential group members across places or something about the local political economy. Collective action problems are often solved from the top down. Laws and public policies can incentivize or even require group membership.[11] In interest groups with a federated structure, moreover, a national or state entity might assist with organization and advocacy at the local level.[12] And many groups organize for nonpolitical reasons and then become active in politics after the fact. When private-sector workers unionize, for example, presumably they do so mainly to engage in collective bargaining with their private-sector employers—not primarily for the purpose of getting involved in local politics.[13] Thus, while the local political activity of groups like building trade unions does depend on whether they are organized in a particular place, the explanation for why they are organized in a particular place does not necessarily boil down to some characteristic of local politics or the people in it.

There may also be non-occupational groups with interests in city policies related to growth, economic development, and land use. Affordable housing groups are one example, and their interests are easy to discern: they seek affordable housing. Still, characterizing those interests is more difficult than it seems, because it depends on who their members are. If the members of affordable housing groups are the people who stand to get affordable housing as a result of cities' decisions, then the link between the groups and city policy would be large, direct, and economic—even if not regular. More likely, however, these groups are driven by people who are passionate about the issue of affordable housing and are not its direct beneficiaries. If so, then their interests are noneconomic and indirect, and I would expect them to be less politically active than developers and chambers of commerce.

Urban politics scholars have also mentioned environmental groups and neighborhood associations as active in many cities—and possibly in opposition to the growth and development impulses of businesses and developers.[14] But it is difficult to say in advance how active these groups will be in local politics. On the one hand, we cannot dismiss them as inactive simply because they are citizen groups. Walker proposes that citizen groups are less active because "their fundamental purpose is to procure broad public goods such as world peace or clean air," because their "members are usually geographically dispersed," and because "the activities of the groups are marginal to the daily needs and responsibilities of the members."[15] But Walker is focused on interest groups in national politics, and all these features hold with lesser force for environmental groups and neighborhood associations in local politics: they may not be large and geographically dispersed, and they may even interact with each other on a regular basis. On the other hand, characterizing their interests is complicated, which makes it hard to move from the theoretical framework to concrete expectations.

Consider local environmental groups. They could prioritize issues like reducing carbon emissions, in which case group members' interests in city policies would be noneconomic and indirect. They could also prioritize the preservation of green space and hiking trails in the city area, which might affect their members more directly. We could even imagine that environmental groups' interests are economic if members are mostly homeowners whose property values depend on the preservation of nearby parks and hiking trails. Which characterization is most accurate? At this point, it is unclear. Most likely there is heterogeneity of interests and goals both across and within local environmental groups. This heterogeneity could mean that environmental groups will be less consistently active in local politics than the developers and chambers of commerce whose interests in city policy are clearer.

The interests of neighborhood associations are also difficult to characterize. One study of neighborhood associations finds that most are spurred into existence by opposition to a planned development,[16] but some of those that persist become engaged in other local issues as well, such as public safety. They may therefore be generalist organizations interested in multiple issues, similar to chambers of commerce. They are also locked into the politics of a particular city, because a neighborhood association in one city is not going to move its operations to another city. But are their interests economic? They could be if a goal is to protect local property values. Are they direct? They could be if the people driving the organization into action are the ones whose property values stand to be directly affected by a proposed development. But the truth is that there isn't a sufficiently strong theoretical (or empirical) basis to say how common these patterns are within neighborhood associations. There is likely heterogeneity in both neighborhood association membership and goals, and as a general rule, I expect that means they will be less active than the interest groups with the clearer local policy focus: developers and chambers of commerce.

The discussion of expectations so far has focused on potential interest groups with stakes in city policies on economic development, property development, and land use, because those are important city functions that have been the main focus of the urban politics literature. And clearly there are a lot of groups to consider on the basis of those issues alone. But cities do more than economic development and growth. One of the main reasons city officials feel pressure to maintain the fiscal base is that they need revenue to pay for a variety of public services, including police and fire protection, sewers, street cleaning, and public parks.

Are there potential groups that have large, direct, regular, economic interests in city decisions about public service provision? Indeed there are: the employees and organizations that provide those services. Most city services are highly labor-intensive. As Redwood City's interim fire chief put it, "Our biggest cost is the people."[17] Municipal governments depend on their employees for law enforcement, fire protection, street cleaning, maintaining public spaces, and more. In most parts of the United States, moreover, city employees are organized in unions. And when municipal governments make decisions about these services—which they do on a regular basis—the decisions affect those unions' members in a large, direct, and economic way, because they are fundamentally decisions about their jobs, salaries, benefits, and working conditions. Moreover, these unions are locked into pushing for favorable policies in that city; a city employee union cannot depart for another city if its home city becomes inhospitable. Strangely, these interests of employee organizations in city policy are rarely raised or discussed in the urban politics literature—even in the very small number of studies that discuss local interest groups.[18] That is a glaring omission. On the basis of their policy interests, we should expect municipal employee unions to be highly active in city politics.

As with building trade unions, city employees are not well organized everywhere, but there are two good reasons to expect public-sector unions to be more prominent in city politics than the private-sector unions I discussed earlier. First, unionization rates are higher, on average, in the public sector than in the private sector. Barry Hirsch and David Macpherson have compiled annual union membership statistics using data from the Current Population Survey (CPS),[19] and according to their figures, 35.2% of government employees in the United States were in unions as of 2015, compared to 6.7% of all private-sector workers and 13.2% of construction workers. The 35.2% national average also masks significant variation across the states. Public-sector labor-management relations are mainly governed by state laws (unlike the private sector, which is governed by national law), and those state laws profoundly shape the extent of unionization among government employees.[20] In states that require governments to engage in collective bargaining with their employees, local government employees tend to be heavily unionized.[21] In most states without mandatory collective bargaining, public-sector union membership is much lower. For example, Hirsch and Macpherson report that as of 2015, 7% of government workers in South Carolina were in unions, compared to 52% in the state of Washington.

Second, city employee unions have a more direct and regular economic stake in city policies than private-sector unions.[22] Private-sector unions might occasionally depend on city government for a job or a contract, but for city employee unions, the municipal government is quite directly the provider of the union members' jobs. Virtually everything about city employees' jobs and compensation is decided by the city government. Moreover, many of those decisions are made through collective bargaining with city employee unions, which means that union engagement is built into the policy-making process. It is difficult to imagine a larger, more direct, and more regular economic interest in city policy.

Still, just as the policy-focused approach suggests that not all businesses are the same—and that business's political activity in cities will vary depending on the nature of their interest—the stakes of public-sector unions in city politics are not uniform either. What underpins the expectation of high city employee union involvement in city politics is that the municipal government is the provider of the union members' jobs. Teachers' unions have also been found to be highly organized and active in politics,[23] including local politics, but teachers are typically not employed by municipal governments. In some rare cases they are, but usually teachers are employed by independent school districts, which are separate governments. I therefore expect that, on average, municipal government employees will be more active in municipal governments than teachers' unions.

In addition, both because of what cities do and how local employees are organized, I expect that unions of police officers and firefighters will be more politically active than other groups of municipal government employees. The range of services cities provide varies, but almost all cities provide police and fire protection, and those two functions make up a large share of the typical city budget. Public safety provision has long been a municipal government staple. What is more, police and firefighters in some states have mandatory collective bargaining laws even when other local government employees do not. Within cities, moreover, they usually have their own bargaining units and unions—unions for employees of that type—whereas nonpublic safety employees are usually grouped into more heterogeneous "miscellaneous" unions. All these differences affect their organization. Based on my own estimates from the CPS data,[24] for example, 69% of all full-time local government employees in Washington State are members of unions, but 90% of police officers and firefighters are. We should therefore expect to see high rates of city political activity by police and firefighters' unions—higher than for other local employees.

Finally, I focus on municipal employee unions because most cities provide core services using city employees, but the same general logic should apply to businesses with regular contracts with the city and nonprofits that provide city services or rely on city funds. For them, too, livelihoods depend on city decisions about service provision. We should expect them to be politically active as a result, especially if the city regularly makes decisions that affect them. However, the extent of contracting and reliance on nonprofit service provision probably varies a great deal across cities, in ways that are difficult to measure. Some cities may contract a lot of city services, whereas some contract very little. Because of this heterogeneity, I generally expect the political activity of these businesses and nonprofits to be somewhat lower, on average, than police unions and firefighters' unions.

Are there any other groups that are likely to have a large, direct, economic stake in city service provision, in particular, in public safety provision? Ethnic and racial minority organizations are one possibility: in cities where minority communities are greatly and economically affected by police activity, one might expect such organizations to be quite politically active. That said, some research shows that interactions with the criminal justice system tend to dampen political efficacy and participation rather than enhance it.[25] Moreover, only a small proportion of municipalities in the United States have sizable minority communities, and that may also be an important condition for such groups to become active. Collective action is also likely to be more difficult for such groups than for police, who (like other local employees) have been aided by state collective bargaining laws. And because my data collection was done in 2015 and 2016, in the early years of the Black Lives Matter movement and well before the 2020 protests against police misconduct, I expect racial and ethnic minority organizations to be less active in local politics than police unions and firefighters' unions.

Another type of group that may have a stake in city service provision is taxpayer groups, which presumably come together based on a common interest in keeping local taxes low and ensuring that local government funds are spent efficiently. Such groups might become active on a variety of local issues that involve the use of public funds or changes to the tax base, including local development projects. But given that public service provision involves public spending by definition, it seems especially likely that taxpayer groups would be focused on it. Still, these groups almost certainly face considerable collective action problems, and their interests in city policy on taxes and spending—while economic and regular—are indirect. We should therefore expect them to be less active overall than public employees, who, in most places, are already organized and have larger and more direct interests in city taxing and spending policies.

There may be other groups drawn into city politics on the basis of economic development, property development, and city service provision, but these are the most likely candidates. And because these broad categories of policy making are major functions of city governments almost everywhere, casting a net for interest groups on the basis of these issues should do a good job of reeling in the main interest groups that are active in city politics. Naturally, cities with a broader set of functions should attract interest groups beyond those considered here. But this is a good start. As a first attempt to characterize the interest group systems in US municipal government, it makes sense to focus on the big picture and the most common and most active players.[26]

Political Activity by Type of Group

I first turn to data from the City Interest Groups Survey for information on the types of interest groups active in city politics. As part of that survey, I asked city officials to rate the political activity of all the types of interest groups mentioned in the discussion above; respondents placed each group on a five-point scale ranging from "not at all active" to "extremely active."[27] Because my analysis in the previous chapter showed that overall interest group activity increases with city population, I start by focusing on cities with a population of more than 50,000—the smallest population category within which one of the individual groups is rated, on average, as at least "somewhat active." Figure 4.1 plots the average

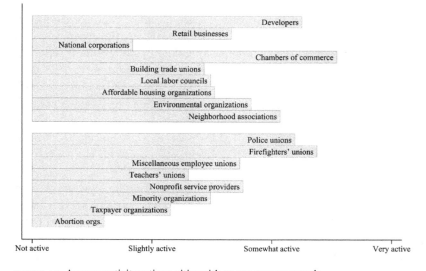

FIGURE 4.1 Average activity ratings, cities with 50,000 or more people

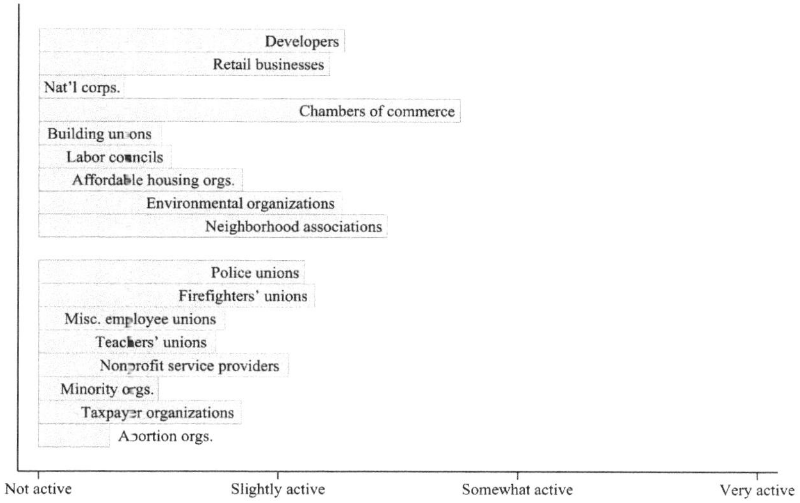

WHAT KINDS OF INTEREST GROUPS ARE MOST ACTIVE?

FIGURE 4.2 Average activity ratings, cities with fewer than 50,000 people

political activity ratings for seventeen types of interest groups in cities of that size.

At the top of figure 4.1, I compare the average activity ratings of nine types of interest groups that came up in my discussion of economic development and growth: real estate development firms and their associations ("developers"), retail businesses, national and multinational corporations, chambers of commerce, building trade unions, local labor councils, affordable housing organizations, environmental organizations, and neighborhood associations.

Clearly, officials in the average city perceive developers to be more politically active than retail businesses. The average rating for development firms is 2.25 on a scale of 0 to 4, placing them between "somewhat active" and "very active." The average activity rating of retail businesses is 1.66, between "slightly" and "somewhat" active and significantly lower than developers. Retail businesses, in turn, are significantly more active than national and multinational corporations, whose activity rating is only 0.84. On average, then, in these cities, the businesses with the largest and most direct economic stake in city policy are more active than those with a less direct stake, and businesses that are less tied to doing business in a particular city tend to be less active in local politics

But chambers of commerce stand out as having the highest average political activity rating of all these groups.[28] That average is 2.54, significantly higher than the rating for developers. What is more, in cities with a population of less than 50,000—shown in figure 4.2—all the groups are perceived as less active, but chambers of commerce are still the most politically active of all. It is therefore very clear from these ratings that chambers of commerce are prominent interest group actors in local politics.

By comparison, building trade unions and local labor councils are less active, on average, even in cities with more than 50,000 people. Figure 4.1 shows that the average activity rating for building trade unions is 1.43 and for labor councils, 1.49, both of which are lower than all the business group categories except for national corporations. In the larger cities, moreover, affordable housing organizations and environmental groups average between "slightly" and "somewhat" active: the average for affordable housing groups is 1.52; for environmental groups it is higher, at 1.83. Both of these are significantly lower than the average activity ratings of developers and chambers of commerce, consistent with an account in which homogeneously economic interests are strong motivators for political action.

Strikingly, I find that neighborhood associations are quite politically active. For the cities in the dataset with more than 50,000 residents, the average political activity rating is 2.07, or "somewhat active," which puts them close to developers and chambers of commerce. And while neighborhood associations are less active in the smaller cities, figure 4.2 shows that neighborhood associations are the group with the second highest average activity rating in these smaller places, second only to chambers of commerce and higher than developers.

The next set of bars in figures 4.1 and 4.2 present the average political activity ratings of the groups mentioned in my discussion of city service provision: police unions, firefighters' unions, miscellaneous employee unions, teachers' unions, nonprofit service providers, racial and ethnic minority organizations, and taxpayer organizations.[29] Here, too, patterns align with expectations. The average rating of police unions is 2.19; for firefighters' unions, 2.38. Notably, both of these averages are statistically indistinguishable from the average rating of developers, even though the averages include cities in states with low public-sector unionization rates. The ratings of both are also higher than the average activity of miscellaneous employee unions, which is rated at 1.73. And all three of the municipal employee union averages are significantly higher than the 1.3 average rating of teachers' unions.

Figure 4.1 shows that the average activity rating of nonprofit service providers—1.76—is lower than those of police and firefighters' unions but about the same as miscellaneous employees. It is also the case that the average activity of ethnic and racial minority organizations is rated lower than that of police unions: 1.49, compared to the average of 2.19 for police. Taxpayer groups are the least active of this set, with an average rating of 1.16. Clearly, then, there can be different types of groups involved in the politics of city service provision, but this suggests that the most consistently active are police unions and firefighters' unions.

A final observation regarding figures 4.1 and 4.2 is that the overall picture of local interest group activity does not have much in common with the national interest group scene and does not appear to be overwhelmingly dominated by business interests. Unions—particularly the unions of police officers and firefighters—are highly politically active in many places. Citizen groups like neighborhood associations and environmental groups are somewhat active as well. As I show at the bottom of figures 4.1 and 4.2, moreover, abortion groups—which are highly active in state and national politics—are barely active at all in local politics. This makes sense as local governments do not usually make policies on abortion. Thus, from this initial look at average interest group activity ratings, it appears that the policy-focused approach can be quite helpful for thinking about the types of interest groups that will be active, and the picture that emerges is quite different from the national interest group system.

When and How Are Interest Groups Active?

The average activity ratings are informative, but the activity levels of these groups should also depend on the issue at hand. The policy-focused approach suggests that developers and other growth-related businesses should have a sharp focus on matters related to development. Police unions and firefighters' unions should have a sharp focus on matters related to police protection and fire protection. And if chambers of commerce and neighborhood associations are generalist organizations, as I have suggested, they should focus on many different issues, with a more moderate level of activity on each one.

To test these expectations, I presented survey respondents with two simple vignettes about city decisions and asked them to indicate which interest groups (from a list) would likely try to influence those decisions. In the first vignette, I asked respondents to imagine that their city is charged with figuring out how to use a vacant plot of land. In the second, the hypothetical decision was about the staffing levels and budget for the police department.

Figures 4.3 and 4.4 present the proportion of cities (of those with more than 50,000 people) in which respondents indicated that a particular interest group would be active, first for the land use vignette and then for the police department vignette. The patterns that emerge are striking. It is clear, first, that development firms and police unions focus their political efforts on the issues in which they have a large, direct, economic interest: city officials report that developers would be active on the land use issue (67%) but not on the police issue (14%), whereas they expect that police unions would be active on the police issue (82%) but not on the land use issue (7%). By contrast, local officials anticipate that chambers of commerce and neighborhood associations would be somewhat active on *both* issues. Moreover, chambers of commerce are expected to be less active than developers on the land use issue (57% vs. 67%),

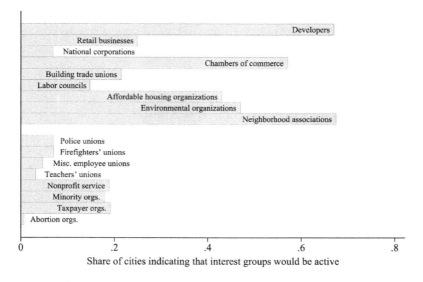

FIGURE 4.3 Interest groups active on land use, cities with 50,000 or more people

WHAT KINDS OF INTEREST GROUPS ARE MOST ACTIVE? 97

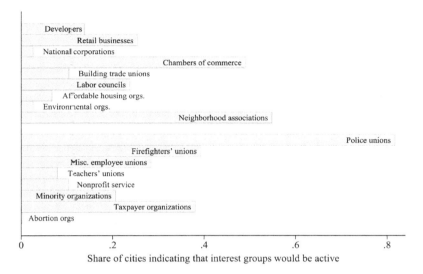

FIGURE 4.4 Interest groups active on police budget, cities with 50,000 or more people

and they are also expected to be much less active than police unions on the police issue (49% vs. 82%). All these patterns are consistent with my expectations.

The pattern is interesting for neighborhood associations as well. As expected, city officials report that neighborhood associations would only sometimes be active on the police department issue: they are cited only 55% of the time. Interestingly, however, city officials also anticipate that neighborhood associations would be just as active as developers on the land use issue. This may suggest something important about neighborhood associations: as a set of groups, they tend to be more focused on land use issues than other local issues, such as public safety or budgets. It also raises questions about what generates this high rate of activity on land use issues. Are neighborhood associations economically motivated, perhaps with the members with the clearest economic stakes in a decision driving the organization? Or is neighborhood association involvement in land use politics driven by something other than material interests? I suspect the former, but it is a topic that deserves more research. For now, it is a finding worth noting: city officials think that neighborhood associations would be as active as developers on land use issues.[30]

The bigger picture, however, is that different interest groups are active on different policy issues, with some exceptions for the more generalist organizations. Just because an interest group is active in city politics does not mean it gets involved in every matter of city government. Consistent with the policy-focused approach, interest groups tend to be more active on the issues in which they have a larger and more direct economic stake. And figures 4.3 and 4.4 also suggest that the amount of competition varies across issues. The land use issue features more active groups, including some that might be opposed to growth and development, such as neighborhood associations and environmental groups. The police issue, by contrast, features one group that is much more consistently active than all the rest—police unions—and low average political activity from groups that might plausibly be opposed to its efforts. It thus seems that some local issues typically feature little active conflict, whereas others have quite a bit.

What, then, of city elections? Elections are another stage at which interest groups are potentially active—and potentially an important one for influence. Not only do interest groups want to elect candidates who are friendly to their policy goals, but they also need to demonstrate their presence and clout to the current and future elected officials who will be making policy decisions that affect them. This is especially true for the interest groups with a regular stake in city policy making. Even if an issue is not salient in a particular election, with candidates actively debating it, an interest group that knows the issue will come up in future city policy making still has incentive to be active in the election.

This is important to recognize as not all issues are equally likely to come up in city elections. To see this, I turn to data from the City Elections Survey—a survey of city council and mayoral candidates that I fielded in two waves. The first wave, fielded in spring 2016 and focused on the November 2015 elections, included city candidates in Indiana, South Carolina, Washington, Ohio, and some cities in California. The second, fielded in spring 2017 and focused on the November 2016 elections, included city candidates in Arkansas, Oregon, Kentucky, Rhode Island, and other cities in California. For some states, such as Washington, California, and South Carolina, the data include responses from a large number of both winning and losing city candidates, whereas for others, such as Indiana, Oregon, and Kentucky, most of the responses are from winning candidates. I provide more detail about the City Elections Survey in the appendix to this chapter.

As part of the City Elections Survey, I asked city candidates to

WHAT KINDS OF INTEREST GROUPS ARE MOST ACTIVE?

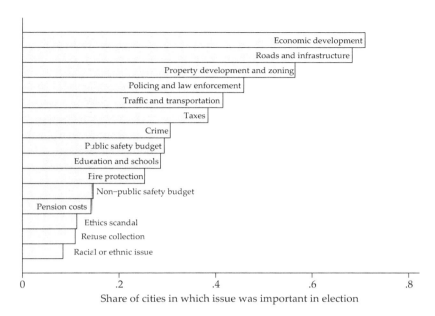

FIGURE 4.5 Issues in city elections

indicate which of a list of common local political issues were important in their city's most recent election. Figure 4.5 shows the results. (I average the responses for cities with more than one respondent.) Economic development, property development and zoning, and roads and infrastructure are the most common issues in local elections. Notably, all of these are about economic development, land use, and space. The second most common set of issues—although less common than development and land use—is policing, crime, public safety, and taxes. But certain topics come up very rarely in city elections, such as fire protection, pensions, ethics, refuse collection, and issues of race and ethnicity. These are still important issues in city governance, but fire protection, pensions, and race and ethnicity are much less likely to be live issues during municipal elections than matters of growth and land use.[31]

Importantly, however, this does not mean that it is only groups with a stake in growth and land use that are active in city elections. Patterns of interest group activity in city elections look a lot like the general pattern of interest group activity shown earlier. As part of the City Elections Survey, I asked city candidates to rate the activity of interest groups in their city's most recent election. The results are summarized in figure 4.6. They are very similar to what is shown in figures 4.1 and 4.2, even though figure 4.6 concerns election activity specifically and with a different sample of municipalities. In the larger cities (the bottom panel), the most active interest groups are chambers of commerce, developers, firefighters' unions, and police unions. In the smaller cities and towns (the top panel), all the groups are less active, and chambers of commerce are the most active of the set. The only substantive difference when the focus is on elections is that neighborhood associations are somewhat less active. In general, though, the interest groups with the greatest presence in city politics are the same ones that are most active in city elections.

Still, interest groups get involved in city elections in different ways. To solicit more detail on the form interest group electoral activity takes, I asked the candidates in the City Elections Survey to indicate what particular interest groups did in their most recent city elections, from a list of six activities: recruiting candidates, giving money to candidates, endorsing candidates, mobilizing citizens to vote, providing publicity (such as mailings and yard signs), and campaigning (such as door-to-door canvassing and phone calls).[32] Figure 4.7 shows the proportion of cities with more than 50,000 residents in which each interest group engaged in a given activity. The candidates report that it is rare for any of these

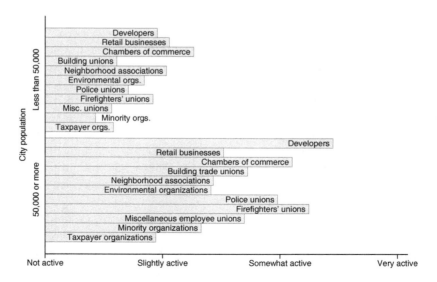

FIGURE 4.6 Interest group activity in city elections

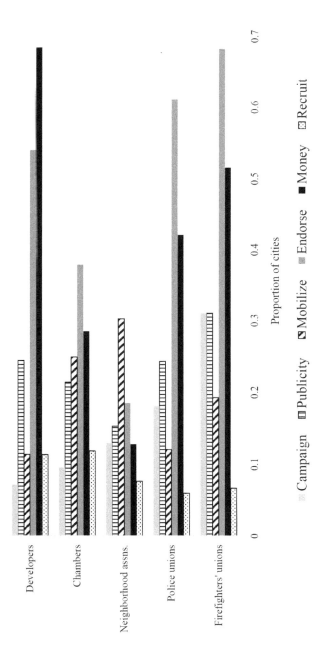

FIGURE 4.7 Types of interest group electoral activity

groups to be involved in recruiting candidates for city offices. By far the most common forms of electoral activity are giving money and endorsing candidates. Developers most often get involved by giving money, but they also commonly endorse candidates. Police and firefighters' unions most often get involved by endorsing candidates, but they also frequently give money. Neighborhood associations are less involved, but when they do get involved, it is usually by mobilizing voters. And compared to the other groups, firefighters' unions are among the most involved in almost all the activities: they are second only to developers in giving money and are the most likely of the groups to endorse candidates, provide publicity, and campaign.

Interest groups therefore get active in city politics on different issues and in different ways, and this is an important part of the picture of interest group activity in American cities. If we were to focus only on economic development and property development, we would miss the high levels of political activity by police and firefighters' unions. If we were to focus only on campaign donations during city elections, we might overstate the importance of developers and understate the role of neighborhood associations. By looking at city interest group activity from all these different angles—at different stages, on different issues, and with an inclusive conceptualization of activity—the bigger picture emerges. And it is a picture of city interest group activity in which the activity follows from the groups' policy interests.

Within-Group Variation in Activity across Cities

Interest group activity also varies within group types across cities, for the same reasons I have discussed. First, as a general rule, interest groups are more politically active in larger cities, and some groups may also be more active in cities that do more (although some focus on a single issue). Second, groups will be more active in a city when they have a large, direct, and regular economic interest in that city's policies and when they have few other options than city politics for pursuing their interests. And third, some types of groups vary in the extent of their organization across the United States. Business is present in every city, but some groups like labor unions are not. And that means that the interest group environment in cities will depend on the context and whether particular groups are organized.

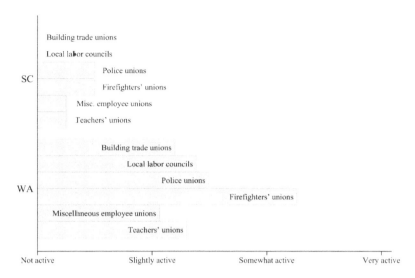

FIGURE 4.8 Labor groups in South Carolina and Washington

A comparison of Washington State and South Carolina illustrates this last point. South Carolina cities lean more Republican than those in Washington, but South Carolina also has some of the lowest union membership rates in the country, in both the public sector and the private sector, whereas union membership in Washington is relatively high. Interest group activity varies accordingly. In figure 4.8, using data from the City Interest Groups Survey, I plot the average political activity ratings of the labor groups in both states, focusing on cities of more than 50,000 people. The figure shows that there are major differences in the city interest group environments in these two states. Labor unions have very little political presence in South Carolina's local politics. In Washington, however, there is a considerable union presence, especially public-sector unions and especially firefighters' unions.

The same pattern emerges in the 2015 city campaign finance data. Using each state's city campaign finance records, I coded every nonindividual contributor using a detailed list of possible contributor types. Table 4.1 summarizes the contributions from three main groups of contributors: growth-oriented businesses (e.g., real estate developers, contractors, construction companies, real estate agents, and architects), other businesses (e.g., financial services, waste treatment companies, law offices, and restaurants), and labor groups, including public- and

TABLE 4.1 **City campaign contributions in Washington and South Carolina, 2015**

Contributor Type	Total Races	Races in Which Group Contributed	% of Races in Which Group Contributed	Contributions from Non-Individuals ($)	Total Contributions from Group ($)	% of Non-Individual Contributions from Group
Growth-oriented businesses						
Washington	75	48	64	1,376,375	276,720	20.1
South Carolina	38	17	45	1,649,200	645,928	39.2
Other businesses						
Washington	75	46	61	1,376,375	324,704	23.6
South Carolina	38	20	53	1,649,200	869,674	52.7
Labor						
Washington	75	45	60	1,376,375	469,209	34.1
South Carolina	38	4	11	1,649,200	11,000	0.7

private-sector unions. The first column shows the total number of races represented in the dataset in each state,[33] the second column shows the number of races in which each category of group contributor gave money, and the third column shows the percentage of all races in which the group gave money. Columns 4 through 6 do the same for the contribution amounts: column 4 shows the total amount of money donated in these races by non-individuals (approximately $1.4 million in Washington, and $1.6 million in South Carolina), column 5 shows the total amount donated by each group, and column 6 shows the percentage of the total non-individual contribution amount that came from the group.

The biggest difference between Washington and South Carolina, as shown in table 4.1, is the role of labor groups. In South Carolina, labor groups gave money in only 4 of the 38 municipal races and only $11,000 in total—less than 1% of the total contributions from non-individuals to city candidates in the state. In Washington, by contrast, labor groups gave money in 45 of the 75 municipal races, almost $470,000 in total and making up more than a third of all interest group contributions to municipal races throughout the state. Clearly, labor unions have a much greater presence in city elections in Washington than in South Carolina.

Moreover, businesses and business groups are major contributors to municipal races in both states. In Washington, businesses with an interest in growth and development (developers, construction companies, realtors) gave money in 64% of the races, and other businesses without an obvious stake in growth—such as local retailers and restaurants—contributed in 61% of the races. In South Carolina, growth-oriented businesses gave money in 45% of the municipal races, and other businesses gave in 53% of them. The difference between the two states is that in South Carolina, the business contributions (summed together) make up 92% of all money from non-individuals. In Washington, business contributions are only 43.7% of all interest group contributions—mostly because labor groups gave substantial amounts as well.[34] The takeaway is that the shape of city interest group systems is very different in Washington compared to South Carolina.

Could these differences in the interest group environments of states like Washington and South Carolina help explain the puzzling pattern I discovered in chapter 3—that cities with more Democratic residents tend to have greater interest group activity than cities whose residents lean Republican? Could it be that having more Democratic citizens happens to be correlated with greater activity from certain types of groups, like labor groups? I explore these questions in figure 4.9. There, I regress each of the interest group activity variables from figures 4.1 and 4.2 on the scope of city government, log city population, log per capita income, and Democratic presidential vote, and I present the estimated coefficients on Democratic presidential vote from each of those models, with 95% confidence intervals. Notably, local residents' partisanship is not significantly associated with the political activity of any of the business

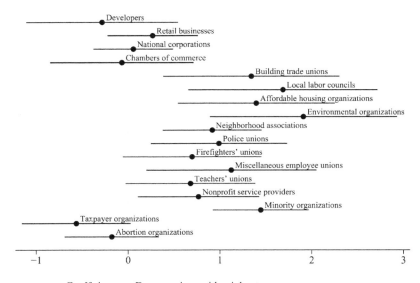

FIGURE 4.9 Coefficients on Democratic presidential vote

interest groups. But it is positively associated with the activity of building trade unions, local labor councils, and public-sector unions. Thus, the greater activity of labor unions in more Democratic cities is in part why more Democratic cities have more interest group activity overall. Democratic presidential vote is also positively associated with greater activity by affordable housing groups, environmental groups, neighborhood associations, nonprofit service providers, and racial and ethnic minority groups. Only one of the interest groups depicted here—taxpayer groups—is more active in more Republican cities. Thus, it appears that interest group activity is greater in more Democratic cities because there are several types of groups that are more politically active in them.

A thorough explanation of why this is would require in-depth studies of each of these interest group types (which is beyond the scope of my endeavor here), because the reasons probably vary by group. It may be that some groups, such as environmental groups, are more active in Democratic places *because* Democrats tend to have more pro-environment policy views. But at least for some of the groups—in particular, the local public-sector unions—the preferences of citizens probably do not account for the variation in group activity.[35] As I said earlier, public-sector unionization rates are heavily shaped by state labor-management relations laws, and, on average, more Democratic states have laws that are friendlier to unions. To show this, in table 4.2, I model the local political activity of the public-sector unions using the same variables as those in figure 4.9 but add the relevant state-level unionization rates.[36] The result is that for all these unions, the coefficients on Democratic presidential vote shrink in size and are no longer statistically significant. This suggests that local public-sector union activity is better explained by state-level union organization (which is correlated with local partisanship) than city residents' partisanship itself.

Especially for labor groups, then, the context is important. But even within different types of interest groups, including but not limited to labor groups, interest group activity should depend on whether the group has a large, direct, regular, and economic interest in a city's policies and whether it has alternatives to local politics for achieving its goals.

Consider business groups. I expect developers to be more active in cities where there is greater opportunity for development. Chambers of commerce, by contrast, are probably not entirely focused on development, so their activity should not necessarily be associated with a city's development opportunity. However, the political activity of businesses

WHAT KINDS OF INTEREST GROUPS ARE MOST ACTIVE? 107

TABLE 4.2 **State public-sector union membership and local political activity**

	Police Unions (1)	Firefighters' Unions (2)	Misc. Employee Unions (3)	Teachers' Unions (4)
Scope of government	−0.006	0.032	−0.011	0.051**
	(0.021)	(0.019)	(0.023)	(0.023)
Ln(Population)	0.457***	0.419***	0.417***	0.197***
	(0.046)	(0.045)	(0.051)	(0.041)
Ln(Income per capita)	−0.298**	−0.37**	−0.385***	−0.069
	(0.126)	(0.163)	(0.117)	(0.132)
Democratic presidential vote	0.437	0.338	0.324	0.163
	(0.338)	(0.371)	(0.402)	(0.371)
% Police in unions	0.854***			
	(0.248)			
% Firefighters in unions		0.768***		
		(0.256)		
% Local employees in unions			1.382***	
			(0.332)	
% Teachers in unions				0.925***
				(0.299)
R-squared	0.35	0.3	0.32	0.18
Observations	465	465	466	466

Notes: Standard errors clustered by state in parentheses.

*p < 0.10, **p < 0.05, ***p < 0.01 (two-tailed).

and business groups, including chambers of commerce, should be greater in cities where it is more difficult for business to leave. In places where businesses cannot credibly commit to the threat to exit, they may find that political activity is their main avenue for exerting influence.

To test these expectations, I continue with the data from the City Interest Groups Survey and model the political activity of developers and chambers of commerce, using OLS with standard errors clustered by state. I measured city development potential with a survey question that asked officials to rate the amount of land available for development in their city (on a 4-point scale). Higher values mean there is more developable land. To measure businesses' exit options, I asked respondents to evaluate how difficult it would be for businesses in their city to move to another city (again on a 4-point scale). In all models, I include the full set of city-level variables from chapter 3, including the scope of government, log population, city demographics, city political institutions, and Democratic presidential vote. I run and report models with and without state fixed effects.

The coefficient estimates and standard errors are summarized in table 4.3. Both developers and chambers of commerce are more

TABLE 4.3 **Business activity in city politics**

	Developers		Chambers of Commerce	
	(1)	(2)	(3)	(4)
Land available	0.197***	0.226***	0.104	0.047
	(0.064)	(0.075)	(0.076)	(0.084)
Difficult for business to move	0.138*	0.159*	0.143**	0.152**
	(0.082)	(0.086)	(0.067)	(0.069)
Scope of government	0.017	0.061**	0.024	0.044*
	(0.022)	(0.026)	(0.019)	(0.025)
Ln(Population)	0.363***	0.275***	0.259***	0.244***
	(0.057)	(0.066)	(0.047)	(0.060)
Ln(Income per capita)	0.615***	0.52**	0.344**	0.201
	(0.178)	(0.221)	(0.153)	(0.201)
Democratic presidential vote	−0.348	0.161	−0.114	0.303
	(0.319)	(0.480)	(0.339)	(0.389)
R-squared	0.31	0.44	0.26	0.36
Observations	433	433	433	433

Notes: Standard errors clustered by state in parentheses. Models 2 and 4 include state fixed effects. All models include city demographic and political institution variables (not shown).

*p < 0.10, **p < 0.05, ***p < 0.01 (two-tailed).

politically active in larger, more affluent cities, and their activity does not vary significantly with the partisanship of city residents, as I have already shown. In columns 1 and 2, however, I find clear evidence that the political activity of developers is associated with the amount of opportunity for development: the coefficient on the land availability variable is positive and statistically significant. This is not the case for chambers of commerce: in columns 3 and 4, land availability is not significantly associated with the political activity of chambers of commerce. For both of these main business interest groups, however, political activity is higher in cities where it is more difficult for businesses to leave. Thus, in cities where leaving is more difficult, business interest groups are more likely to pursue their interests through political action.[37]

While these associations are consistent with my expectations, I cannot say whether they are causal effects. It remains possible, for example, that more active developers push city officials to allow more development and that that is why officials in those cities say they have more land available to be developed. As a final step, however, I apply this same policy-focused logic to public-sector unions, and for them, there is less reason to be concerned about endogeneity.

For public-sector unions, the key consideration is whether their members have job interests in the city. When a union's members are employed by the city, the union has a large, direct, economic interest in the city's decisions about members' jobs, salaries, and benefits. In addition, when it comes to these job interests, public-sector unions do not have alternatives to political action; the only way to pursue higher compensation for their members, for example, is through political activity (broadly construed). When a union's members are not employed by the city, by contrast, the union may still have some interest in city decision making (e.g., housing policy), but those interests are smaller and less direct, and I would expect lesser political activity as a result. Moreover, compared to developers and the availability of developable land, it seems less likely that police and firefighters' unions would lobby city officials to create a police department or a fire department (although they might try to prevent the elimination of such departments once created).

In table 4.4, I model the political activity of police unions, firefighters' unions, and teachers' unions. In each of the three models, the main

TABLE 4.4 **Public-sector union activity in city politics**

	Police Unions (1)	Firefighters' Unions (2)	Teachers' Unions (3)
City provides police	0.729***		
	(0.132)		
% Police in unions	0.741***		
	(0.266)		
City provides fire protection		0.651**	
		(0.247)	
% Firefighters in unions		0.703***	
		(0.255)	
City provides education			1.122***
			(0.196)
% Teachers in unions			0.711***
			(0.227)
Scope of government	−0.027	−0.023	−0.013
	(0.021)	(0.022)	(0.026)
Ln(Population)	0.467***	0.483***	0.273***
	(0.044)	(0.045)	(0.034)
Ln(Income per capita)	−0.101	−0.288	−0.145
	(0.164)	(0.186)	(0.179)
Democratic presidential vote	0.308	0.591	0.012
	(0.402)	(0.414)	(0.433)
R-squared	0.37	0.35	0.29
Observations	462	462	463

Notes: Standard errors clustered by state in parentheses. All models include city demographic and political institution variables (not shown).

*p < 0.10, **p < 0.05, ***p < 0.01 (two-tailed).

independent variable is an indicator for whether the city had positive direct expenditures on police protection (92% did), fire protection (82% did), or elementary and secondary education (9% did) as of the 2012 Census of Governments. As before, I control for the state-level percentage of workers in each occupation that are members of unions and the full set of covariates discussed in chapter 3.

In all three columns, I find that the public-sector unions are more politically active in cities where the city government is a provider of their members' jobs. While almost all cities provide police protection, column 1 shows that in the cases where they do not, police unions are significantly less active in city politics. Similarly, in column 2, I find that the perceived political activity of firefighters' unions drops by 0.651—half of a standard deviation—when the city does not have direct expenditures on fire protection. And while the vast majority of cities do not provide public education, in the cities that do, the activity of teachers' unions in city politics is more than a standard deviation higher. Thus, the political activity of public-sector unions is significantly greater when those unions stand to reap large, direct, economic benefits from city decisions. When I add state fixed effects, moreover, these findings persist (not shown).

Conclusion

This chapter has come a long way from what seemed to be a truism about interest group activity in the United States: namely, that business interests dominate interest group systems and that unions are weak. That pattern does appear to hold in local politics in states like South Carolina. But as a general rule, unions have a sizable political presence in city governments across the United States. Business interests do feature prominently, and developers are especially engaged on questions of land use. But particular types of unions—especially those whose members are employed by the city government and especially police and firefighters— are also highly active in city politics. Of all the interest groups, they are the most politically engaged on questions about the city budget that affect them, and they actively participate in municipal elections as well.

But this chapter also shows that the overall shape of local interest group systems is contingent in important ways. Several types of interest groups are more politically active in cities whose residents lean Democratic. There are likely many different reasons for this, and the explanations probably vary depending on the particular group in question. But for one set of highly active local groups—public-sector unions—it has more to do with the labor environment of the state than residents' Democratic partisanship per se. An important takeaway from this analysis is that business groups are more consistently present in local politics, whereas the engagement of labor groups depends on the context. Yet this contingency notwithstanding, police unions and firefighters' unions are among the most active interest groups in city politics, on average, in the United States.

Finally, my analysis in this chapter demonstrates the usefulness of the policy-focused approach. The reason most local interest group systems don't look like that of Washington, DC, is that city governments and the federal government for the most part make decisions on different issues—and interest group activity follows from the issues. Whether I look at average interest group activity or within-group variation across cities, I find that groups are more politically active when they have a large, direct, regular, economic interest in the government's policies and when they have few alternatives to politics for pursuing their interests. We have seen in this chapter that organization certainly matters. But interest groups' interests are also central, and it would be hard to account for these patterns without considering them.

Appendix: City Elections Survey

The City Elections Survey is an internet survey of city council and mayoral candidates who ran for office in November 2015 or November 2016. The survey asked candidates about the interest groups and political parties active in their recent elections, and it also asked the candidates for their opinions on common local policy matters.[38]

I designed the City Elections Survey to include candidates from different regions of the United States, variation in city size, and cities with both partisan and nonpartisan elections as well as off-cycle and on-cycle elections. The main practical challenges were identifying local governments that were having elections, obtaining the names of candidates running in those elections, and finding email addresses for those candidates. Municipal elections are held at many times throughout the year, and states often do not track when they are held. Therefore, I focused this survey on states where I knew that a large number of municipal elections are held either in November of odd-numbered years or in November of even-numbered years. Of those, I placed priority on the states where state or county governments provided lists of the candidates and election results.

Of the nine states, the only one that provided email addresses for most of its municipal candidates was Washington. In five others—Arkansas, California, Ohio, Oregon, and South Carolina—the official candidate lists only sometimes provided candidate email addresses, and in the remaining three (Indiana, Kentucky, and Rhode Island), no email addresses were provided. For all candidates without email addresses provided on the official lists, I had a team of research assistants visit the cities' websites after the elections to collect the email addresses of the candidates who won. The research assistants also conducted simple internet searches for existing candidate campaign websites that might include emails.

I sent the survey to 6,811 individual candidates in 1,414 unique municipal governments. See table A4.1 for details. The individual response rate for both waves of the survey was 15%, and I received at least one re-

TABLE A4.1 **Number of individual respondents and cities, City Elections Survey**

	Candidates	Cities	Cities, <10K	Cities, 10–25K	Cities, 25–50K	Cities, 50–100K	Cities, >100K
Number contacted	6811	1414	767	278	172	130	67
2015 election	3745	785	497	152	80	40	16
2016 election	3066	629	270	126	92	90	51
Number responded	1040	696	301	150	115	84	46
(complete and partial)							
2015 election	573	375	194	85	59	22	15
2016 election	467	321	107	65	56	62	31
Arkansas	30	23	11	5	4	3	0
California	343	218	28	44	49	63	34
Indiana	103	62	28	14	13	4	3
Kentucky	50	41	31	7	3	0	0
Ohio	208	138	65	44	23	4	2
Oregon	54	41	32	3	4	2	0
Rhode Island	44	27	8	13	4	2	0
South Carolina	58	38	24	7	3	2	2
Washington	150	107	74	13	12	4	4
Total response rate	15%	49%	39%	54%	67%	65%	69%
(complete and partial)							
2015 election	15%	48%	39%	56%	74%	55%	94%
2016 election	15%	51%	40%	52%	61%	69%	61%

sponse from 49% of the cities in the sample. The number of small municipal governments in the United States is much larger than the number of large municipal governments, and the same is true in this dataset. Finally, because California has many more large cities than the other states, the set of larger cities in the dataset is heavily weighted toward California.

CHAPTER FIVE

Political Parties in Local Politics

The emphasis thus far has been on interest groups. In this chapter, I turn to political parties.[1] Political parties are clearly important in US national and state politics and a major topic of American politics research. Some might even say that parties—not interest groups—should be the main focus of a study of groups and organizations in local politics.

As it stands, however, we know almost nothing about how involved political parties are in local elections and local policy making. While researchers have recently studied whether the partisanship and ideology of local *residents* make a difference to certain local policy outcomes[2] and whether the party affiliations of local *elected officials* matter,[3] the activity of party organizations in local politics has hardly been studied at all in the past few decades. Are political parties even active in most cities around the country? We simply don't know.

As important as political parties are in national and state politics, moreover, there are good reasons to think they do not loom nearly as large in local politics. We know from existing research on political parties, for example, that political institutions shape the party systems that emerge in different contexts.[4] Notably, political institutions in US local governments are mostly different from those of the federal and state governments: most local elections in the United States are formally nonpartisan, meaning that the party affiliations of candidates do not appear on the ballot, and most are held on days other than national elections. Given what we know about parties, it would be surprising if those institutions did not make a difference. In addition, existing theories emphasize the importance of history and elite strategy for how the US party system evolved,[5] and local governments have their own interesting history with political parties: Progressive Era municipal reformers pushed to weaken the activity and influence of political parties in local government and seem to have had some success in that endeavor.[6] We therefore cannot assume that parties play a dominant role in local politics. In fact, it seems quite likely that they play a lesser role in local government than in federal and state government.

But I would be remiss to not consider political parties before moving forward, both because American politics scholars consider them very important and because an influential theory of political parties conceptualizes them as coalitions of interest groups. That theory—the theory of parties associated with scholars affiliated with the University of California, Los Angeles (UCLA) (hereafter called the UCLA Theory of Parties)—argues that interest groups and policy demanders need to create party coalitions in order to secure the requisite majorities for making policies.[7] Like other theories of American political parties, it was developed to explain parties in national politics, in particular, presidential elections. But if its core logic is extended to the local context, it could mean that the interest groups I have focused on so far—and focus on going forward—are working within political parties. That could mean that political parties rather than interest groups are the primary movers.

My goals in this chapter are therefore modest but important: I aim to shed light on the activity of political parties in local elections and to evaluate the possibility that local interest groups are operating within political parties. I start with a descriptive analysis that shows that political parties are engaged in many of the cities' elections but also that their presence is far from universal. I then combine theory and snippets of data to build a case for an alternative, locally based account of how interest groups and political parties are related to each other: I propose that when political parties are engaged in local elections, they are mainly working *alongside* interest groups, not as umbrella groups steered by coalitions of local interest groups, but rather as just another kind of group trying to influence local elections. Furthermore, I find that of the two types of groups, interest groups are more involved. In the chapters that follow, it is therefore not only reasonable but also warranted to focus on whether and how interest groups influence local public policies.

My analysis in this chapter also highlights the need for a theory of political parties in local politics, and while I cannot take that on fully here, as my focus is interest groups, I make a start for others to build on. Such a theory necessarily has to be more complex than a theory of interest group activity, because unlike interest groups—which can be thought of as primarily seeking favorable policies—political parties are amorphous: scholars continue to debate what they are, why they form and change, and how they navigate their many competing goals.[8] In an analysis at the end of this chapter, I begin to show that complexity. I find that many different factors are associated with the amount of political party activity in local politics, including interest group activity, political institutions, party competition in national elections, and the state's history of political parties. Once again, turning our gaze away from national politics to explore the very different local context helps us see things differently. Here, it helps produce new insights about political parties in the United States.

Political Parties in City Elections

An account of political parties in city politics has to start with the basics. As part of the City Elections Survey, I asked city council and mayoral candidates in nine states a series of questions about political party involvement in their most recent elections (either November 2015 or November 2016). First I asked them to rate how active the Republican Party, the Democratic Party, and any other political parties were in their most recent election. Responses were on a five-point scale ranging from "not at all active" (coded 0) to "extremely active" (coded 4). Then I asked them to indicate whether the Republican Party and the Democratic Party engaged in the specific political activities I discussed in chapter 4: recruiting candidates, giving money to candidates, endorsing candidates, mobilizing citizens to vote, providing publicity (such as mailings or yard signs), and campaigning (such as door-to-door canvassing or phone calls). In what follows, unless I note otherwise, I handle cities with multiple responses by averaging the survey responses within the city.

Table 5.1 summarizes the responses to these questions for all cities for which respondents rated the activity of political parties. In rows 1 through 3, I present figures that describe the activity levels of the Republican Party (row 1), the Democratic Party (row 2), and other political parties (row 3) in the elections of all the cities in the dataset. The first figure for each is the party's average activity rating across all cities. The second is the percentage of cities in which the party is rated "not at all active" or "slightly active," meaning an average activity rating between

POLITICAL PARTIES IN LOCAL POLITICS

TABLE 5.1 **Political party activity in municipal elections**

	Average		% Not Active or Slightly Active	% Very Active or Extremely Active
(1)	Republican Party (0–4)	1.40	58	22
(2)	Democratic Party (0–4)	1.53	52	26
(3)	Other party (0–4)	0.18	96	2
(4)	Most active party (0–4)	1.95	38	38
(5)	Party activities index (0–6)	2.6	28	29

Notes: In row 5, % Not active or slightly active is the percentage of cities in which parties were engaged in 0 of the 6 specific electoral activities, and % Very active or extremely active is the percentage of cities in which parties were engaged in at least 5 of the 6 electoral activities.

0 and 1.5. The third is the percentage of cities where the party is rated as either "very active" or "extremely active," meaning an activity rating of over 2.5.

Focusing first on the top two rows, the average activity ratings for the Republican Party and the Democratic Party—1.40 and 1.53, respectively—suggest that as a general rule parties in these cities are between slightly and somewhat active. More important, though, there is considerable variation in party activity across cities. In 22% of the cities, the Republican Party is highly active in local elections, and for the Democratic Party, that figure is 26%. Yet respondents in 52% of these cities say that the Democratic Party is not at all active or only slightly active in their city elections, and that figure is even higher—58%—for the Republican Party. Moreover, when parties *are* active in municipal elections in these nine states, it is almost always the Democratic or Republican Party (or both): in row 3, I show that the average activity rating for other parties is a mere 0.18 and that nearly all respondents indicated that other parties are not active in their cities.[9]

Most local constituencies are more homogeneous than state and national constituencies, so many cities might feature far more activity by one party than the other. To get a sense of whether at least *some* party is active in each of these cities, I present (in row 4 of table 5.1) the same three statistics for whichever party is rated as most active in each city. In 38% of the cities in this dataset, at least one party was rated very or extremely active in the November 2015 and 2016 elections. But 38% of the cities' elections featured little to no party engagement. Moreover, when I focus on the cities with at least some political party activity—defined as an average Democratic Party or Republican Party activity score greater than 1.5—only 22% of the cities report having equal activity by both parties (not shown). In 34%, the Republican Party is more active, and in the remaining 44%, the Democratic Party is more active.

Finally, in row 5 of table 5.1, I summarize candidates' responses to the questions about whether the major parties engaged in six specific activities in their cities' November 2015 and 2016 elections. For each of the six activities, I coded a city as 1 if at least one respondent in the city indicated that some party engaged in that activity. I find that parties recruited candidates in 35% of the cities and that in 41% they contributed money to candidates. Moreover, parties endorsed candidates in 58% of the cities, mobilized voters in 45%, provided publicity in 42%, and campaigned in 41%. When I add these six indicators, creating an index ranging from 0 to 6, I find that parties engaged in an average of 2.6 activities per city (see table 5.1). But again I find considerable variation in this index across cities. In 172 cities—29% of the sample—parties were heavily engaged, participating in five or six activities. By contrast, in 28% of the cities, political parties were not engaged in any of the electoral activities.

In this set of local governments, then, the amount of party electoral activity varies widely. We cannot assume that just because most cities have Progressive Era institutions like nonpartisan and off-cycle elections that party organizations are absent from city elections. But we also cannot assume that parties will always be involved. There isn't a simple "yes" or "no" answer to the question of whether party organizations are active in municipal elections. The answer, based on this sample, is that it depends.

The Relationship between Political Parties and Interest Groups

With these basics established, the crucial next step is to evaluate whether and how interest groups and political parties are related to each other in the local context. The UCLA Theory of Parties can be read as implying that interest group activity and political party activity should generally "go together," because interest groups have to work within political parties to achieve policy success. If that is the case, then the cities where interest groups are most active should also be the cities where political parties are most active.

To explore this, I use data from the City Elections Survey to create a summary measure of the level of interest group activity in each city's elections: the average of all the city's 0–4 interest group ratings.[10] Strikingly, this interest group activity variable is positively correlated with the measures of political party activity presented in table 5.1. Its correlation with Democratic Party electoral activity, for example, is 0.50. For Republican Party activity, it is 0.41. When I instead look at the maximum political party activity variable, the correlation with overall interest group activity is 0.55. Thus, political party and interest group activity do tend to go together: parties are more active in the cities where interest groups are more active.

This could mean that the local interest groups are forming and working within political parties, as the UCLA Theory of Parties suggests. Another possibility, however, is that interest groups and political parties just happen to be active in the same kinds of cities for some other reason—and that the two types of organizations operate somewhat independently in local politics. While the former may seem like the default interpretation given prevailing theories of parties in national politics, in what follows, I make a case for why the latter is actually the more plausible one for the local context.

The Major National Parties Are a Bad Fit for Local Interest Groups

It is useful to once again start with what local governments actually do—with the policies local governments make. We have seen so far that interest group activity in local politics follows in large part from the issues at stake in local government. Moreover, because many of the important issues in local politics are different from the issues that define parties and ideology in national politics, local interest group systems look different from those in national politics. If we take the next logical step, what we should expect is that any coalitions and divisions that form between interest groups in local politics should *also* be different from those that form in national politics. And political parties are defined by issues.[11] Why, then, would we expect local interest group coalitions and divisions to be the same as those of the major national political parties, which are defined by very different (national) issues? If the political parties that are active in local politics are formed by local interest groups, then why would the parties formed be Democratic and Republican? As a general rule, the two major national political parties seem to be a poor fit for local interest groups seeking to have influence on local policies.[12]

A look at the relationship between business and labor in local politics illustrates this point. In national politics, business and labor are usually adversaries: they compete over policy, and they are at home in different political parties. Moreover, in the previous chapter, we saw that both business and labor groups feature prominently in local politics—they are in fact among the *most* prominent interest groups—and that labor groups (along with some other groups) have a greater presence in cities whose residents lean Democratic. It would be tempting to take this as a sign that local politics mirrors national politics or that local politics is nationalized. But drawing such a conclusion from these patterns alone would be a mistake, because it does not take into account what these interest groups care about and want in *local* government where the issues are different. Even though business and labor groups are both active in local politics, it does not necessarily follow that they would conflict in the same way they do in national politics.

Consider data from the City Interest Groups Survey, in which I asked city officials, "Which of the following statements best describes the relationship between business and public-sector labor (such as municipal employee unions) in your city's politics?" Figure 5.1 summarizes the individual-level responses for all cities. Only 16% of the city officials said that business and public-sector unions tend to care about the same local issues and that their interests usually conflict. Forty-three percent said that they care about the same local issues but that their interests usually *don't* conflict. And 41% said they care about different issues. A similar pattern emerged when I asked city officials about the relationship between business and private-sector unions (such as building trade unions) in their cities. Most local officials report that business and private-sector unions care about the same issues but that their interests do not conflict. Thus, in some of these major local interest groups, interests do not clash in the same way that they do in national politics.

Another way of exploring the relationship between business and labor in local politics is to look at patterns of campaign contributions in Washington State, where, as I have shown, both business and labor groups are highly active in municipal elections. If unions and businesses tend to back different candidates in local races, that might suggest that their interests conflict and that they are political adversaries in local politics. But if they often back the same candidates, that would suggest that their interests in local politics are often not in direct conflict.

Here I focus on the 103 contested municipal races in the Washington campaign finance dataset in which either businesses or labor groups

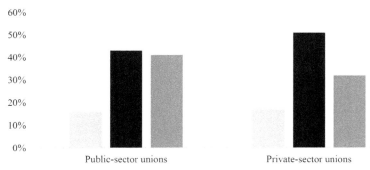

- They tend to care about the same local issues, and their interests usually conflict.
- They tend to care about the same local issues, but their interests usually don't conflict.
- They usually care about different issues.

FIGURE 5.1 Relationship between business and labor in city politics

made campaign contributions to at least one candidate.[13] Notably, both labor groups and growth-oriented businesses (e.g., real estate development firms and construction companies) tend to target their giving to particular candidates. Labor groups made contributions in 78 of these 103 races, and in 60 of those, the labor contributions went to only a single candidate in the race. Similarly, growth-oriented businesses made contributions in 71 of the 103 races, and the money went to only a single candidate in all but 18 of them. This suggests that there is usually a candidate viewed by labor groups as pro-labor as well as a candidate viewed by growth-oriented businesses as pro-growth.[14]

In the races in which both labor groups and growth-oriented businesses gave money, did that money go toward backing opposing candidates? More often than not, the answer is no. There are 50 such races in the dataset, and of those, there were only 5 in which all the labor money went to candidates different from those backed by growth-oriented businesses. In the remaining 45 races, at least some—and often all—of the labor and growth-oriented business contributions went to the same candidates. This suggests that municipal candidates are very often viewed as both pro-labor and pro-growth and that in local politics, the two most active segments of labor and business are usually not in direct conflict with one another.

There is therefore nothing fixed or set about how groups such as business and labor relate to each other.[15] It depends on the issue. In local politics, we can see this more clearly because there are issues on which their interests do not conflict, and they can even be on the same side. The way these interest groups come together and conflict in local politics is based on local issues, not necessarily according to the partisan and ideological alignments we are accustomed to seeing in national politics. And that raises doubts about the proposal that local interest groups are working within political parties to achieve their policy goals.

Interest Groups May Not Need Political Parties

It is worth taking this line of thought a step further to ask whether interest groups actually do need to form political parties to achieve their policy goals. The argument that they do comes from a theory of parties, not a theory of interest groups. And because that theory of parties was developed with a focus on national politics, it starts with the notion that parties exist—because in national politics they do—and then explains how to think about them. I am instead starting from the vantage point of interest groups and local politics—a context where parties are not always active. And looking at parties from this angle, it becomes clear that interest groups might sometimes choose to *not* work within parties.

That interest groups might work alone is not a new idea, just an underappreciated one. In his 1967 textbook, for example, Dahl explained that political movements have four broad options for trying to influence policy: a movement can "organize a separate political party of its own"; it can "form a new coalition party by combining with another group or movement that has similar, overlapping, but not identical objectives"; it can enter "into one of the existing parties"; or it can "remain neutral between the two major parties" and "act as a pressure group to secure favorable legislation and the nomination and election of sympathetic candidates."[16] The scholars associated with the UCLA Theory of Parties mention this possibility as well: "Few if any groups of intense policy demanders are big enough to get what they want working alone. So they seek allies. But in joining party coalitions, groups do not put the good of the party ahead of their own goals. Parties are a means to an end, and the end is the group's own policy agenda. Groups cooperate in party business only insofar as cooperation serves their interests."[17] Interest groups can therefore reasonably choose to work outside party coalitions, but we do not yet have a theory of the conditions under which they would do so.

Developing a full-fledged theory along these lines is more than I can accomplish here, but it is worth noting that interest groups are probably less inclined to work within political parties in local politics than in national or state politics. For an interest group to join forces with a party, it has to be worth its while. The policy benefits of joining have to outweigh the costs. And if the group anticipates that it will be just as likely or more likely to secure the policies it favors working outside of parties, then we should not expect to find it working with a party. For a few reasons, this scenario is more likely in local politics. Local governments are smaller. Groups and individuals can gain access to policy makers much more easily in local government than in national government.[18] The resource requirements for having an impact on policy are lower. And as a general rule, because of the kinds of issues at stake and the smaller number of groups overall, it is probably more common for interest groups to face lower levels of direct competition over the policies they care about in local politics than in state and national politics. This is not to say that interest groups would never work within parties in local politics—just that it is probably less likely in local politics than in national politics.

Moreover, the assertion that interest groups would usually want to work within political parties stems from the UCLA Theory's emphasis on nominations. If interest groups' only path to influence in elections was nomination of candidates, then there would be strong incentives for them to form coalitions. When it comes to nominations, an interest group has only two choices: it can cooperate with other groups (and join forces to nominate a single, mutually acceptable slate of candidates), or it can compete with them (and nominate its own slate of candidates that will compete with that of other groups). Unless the group can mobilize large numbers of votes for its own slate, it has incentives to combine forces with other groups to find acceptable candidates.[19]

But nominating candidates is only one of the ways interest groups (and political parties) can influence elections; they can also endorse candidates, contribute money, mobilize voters, provide publicity, and campaign. For these electoral activities, an interest group's choice set is not limited to cooperating with other groups or directly competing with them. It can also wait to see which candidates emerge and then independently put its resources behind the candidate it deems most likely to support its policy goals. This might sometimes put it in indirect competition with other groups; for example, developers and the local police union might choose to support different candidates, pitting the two groups against each other. But the developers and the local police union could also decide to support the same candidate—not because they coordinated their decisions about whom to support, but because their independent decision making happened to lead them to the same candidate. For these postnomination electoral activities, the incentives for interest group coordination are weaker.

There is therefore a theoretical rationale for a model in which interest groups operate mostly independently of political parties—one that seems especially plausible for the local context. To the extent that parties and interest groups are active in the same cities, it may just be that both happen to have something at stake—not that one type of group is the engine of the other. More than sixty years ago, Charles Adrian observed patterns consistent with this model in his research on nonpartisan municipal elections: often there were interest groups operating in the absence of political parties, and many local governments featured a mix of parties and interest groups—all nominating slates of candidates, operating alongside each other rather than as a hierarchy of groups.[20] The same may well be the case today.

While the data I have do not allow for a thorough evaluation of why there is a positive correlation between interest group activity and political party activity in cities, a few empirical patterns suggest that this alternative model may be on target. First, as part of the City Elections Survey, I asked respondents to evaluate the importance of six specific group activities in influencing elections in their cities; the response options for each activity ranged from "not at all important" (coded 0) to "extremely important" (coded 4). As before, the first activity is recruiting candidates, an activity at the nomination stage. The other five activities come later in the electoral process: giving money to candidates, endorsing candidates, mobilizing citizens to vote, providing publicity, and campaigning. The candidates' responses show that group efforts to recruit candidates are indeed somewhat important in influencing local elections; the average is 1.9 on the 0–4 scale. But they also show that four of the five postnomination electoral activities are even more important: the average for endorsing candidates is 2.18, for mobilizing voters is 2.55, for providing publicity is 2.45, and for campaigning is 2.66. Only giving money (1.92) is rated similarly to recruiting candidates. If it is the case that interest groups have weaker incentives to form party coalitions after the nomination stage, then this finding that the nomination stage is relatively

POLITICAL PARTIES IN LOCAL POLITICS

less impor:ant could mean that interest groups do not have strong incentives to work within party coalitions in local politics.

The second empirical pattern worth highlighting is that there are many cities where candidates say that interest groups are active but political parties are not. To see this, I create an indicator called *Some party activity* equal to 1 if the city's average overall party activity rating (on a scale from 0 to 4) was greater than 1; it equals 0 if the rating is less than or equal to 1. Then I create a variable called *Some interest group activity* equal to 1 if the maximum activity rating given to the interest groups in each city is greater than 1, 0 otherwise. Table 5.2 presents a cross-tabulation of these two binary indicators. There, we can see that 81 cities report no interest groups or political parties, and 387 cities report having both types of groups. A select few—21 cities—have active parties but no interest groups. But the remaining 133—over 20% of the sample—report at least one active interest group but no active political parties. In a non-negligible number of cities, then, interest groups are active in the absence of parties.

A third set of patterns that lends support to the alternative account comes from the campaign finance data from Washington and South Carolina. In table 5.3, I present information on the frequency with which

TABLE 5.2 **Number of cities by interest group and political party activity**

	No Party Activity	Some Party Activity	Total
No interest group activity	81	21	102
Some interest group activity	133	387	520
Total	214	408	622

TABLE 5.3 **Campaign contributions by political parties, 2015**

Contributor Type	Total Races	Races in Which Group Contributed	% of Races in Which Group Contributed	Contributions from Non-Individuals ($)	Total Contributions from Group ($)	% of Non-Individual Contributions from Group
Republican Party						
Washington	75	8	11	1,376,375	4,700	0.3
South Carolina	38	2	5	1,649,200	1,250	0.1
Democratic Party						
Washington	75	27	36	1,376,375	30,994	2.3
South Carolina	38	1	3	1,649,200	622	0.04

126   CHAPTER FIVE

political party organizations gave money in municipal races in the two states in 2015 as well as the amounts they gave. The structure of the table is the same as that of table 4.1 (see chap. 4) but this time with the focus on political parties.

Table 5.3 shows that political parties are far less active in giving money than the main types of interest groups highlighted in chapter 4. Republican Party groups gave in only 8 of the 75 races in Washington and 2 of the 38 races in South Carolina, 11% and 5%, respectively. Moreover, the contributions from the Republican Party amounted to only 0.3% of all non-individual money contributed in Washington and 0.1% of the non-individual money in South Carolina. The Republican Party, it seems, is far from a major force in supporting municipal candidates financially in these two states.

The Democratic Party is somewhat more active in Washington: it gave to candidates in 36% of the races and accounted for 2.3% of all the non-individual money in municipal races in the state. But compared to the giving habits of the major interest groups active in these elections (as we saw in detail in chap. 4), even these contributions from the Democratic Party are quite small. Recall that in Washington State, businesses with an interest in growth and development (developers, construction companies, realtors) gave in 64% of the races and contributed a fifth of all non-individual money. Other businesses without an obvious stake in growth—such as local retailers and restaurants—contributed in 61% of the races and gave 24% of the non-individual money. And in Washington State, labor groups gave in 60% of the races and accounted for 34% of all local campaign money from non-individuals. The 2.3% from the Democratic Party is minuscule by comparison.

In South Carolina, as we saw in chapter 4, the picture is very different: labor groups are barely active in local races. Table 5.3 shows that political parties are definitely not making up the difference. The share from the Democratic Party is a mere 0.04% of non-individual campaign contributions in South Carolina. Thus, the most active types of interest groups in local elections are far more active than political parties in these two states.

National Party Incentives to Be Involved in City Elections

If parties are not serving as coalitions of interest groups in local politics and most local issues do not map well onto the issues that define and divide the two major national political parties, then that raises the question, why would the Democratic and Republican Parties bother to get involved in city elections in some places?

One possibility is that the national parties have nonpolicy reasons for doing so. Party leaders presumably have to groom candidates to run in future state and national elections, and perhaps helping their up-and-comers win local elections plays an important role in that effort. Moreover, parties have to maintain their organizational infrastructure at the state and local levels, even between national elections. It may be that encouraging and nurturing the engagement of local party clubs and committees are essential for maintaining networks of volunteers and keeping data bases of supporters up to date. More generally, parties might derive a number of organizational advantages from staying active in local politics—which could help explain why the major parties would be active in local elections even if local interest groups are not coordinating with them.

A second possibility is that the local clubs and committees of the two major national parties sometimes have genuine policy interests in local elections, driven by the interests of the policy demanders that make up their national coalitions. For example, the Democratic coalition includes unions and environmental groups, and those interest groups might push local Democratic clubs and committees to take part in local elections where there are labor and environmental issues at stake. Likewise, the Republican coalition at the national level includes business associations and taxpayer groups, which might push local Republican Party committees to intervene in local elections where the business climate and taxes are salient issues. By this account, parties get active in local elections at the urging of some of their national-level coalition members who see their own high-priority issues in play at the local level.

Table 5.4 provides some evidence consistent with that account: when the major parties do give money to city candidates, they tend to give to candidates with other group donors that look somewhat typical of the larger party profile. For each of the 47 candidates in Washington State who received contributions from either the Republican or the Democratic Party, I provide information about who their other non-individual donors were and how much they gave.[21]

Toward the top of the table, I show that of the 11 candidates in Washington municipal races in 2015 who received contributions from the Republican Party, 8 received money from growth businesses, 9 received

128   CHAPTER FIVE

TABLE 5.4 **Interest group contributions to candidates who received contributions from political parties, Washington municipal elections**

	Number of Candidates	Total Contributions (\$)	Median Contribution (\$)
Republican Party	11	4,700	200
Growth-oriented businesses	8	69,375	3,100
Non-growth businesses	9	60,332	1,050
Labor	1	450	0
Democratic Party	36	30,994	275
Growth-oriented businesses	16	18,401	0
Non-growth businesses	24	34,412	400
Labor	29	156,500	1,350

money from non-growth businesses, and only 1 received a donation from labor groups. Still, even though all 11 received Republican Party money, the total contributed by the party was only \$4,700. For growth and non-growth businesses, the totals were much higher: \$69,375 and \$60,332, respectively. Thus, where the Republican Party is active in giving money to Washington local candidates, it gives to candidates who receive larger amounts from businesses and almost never receive money from labor groups.

Of the 36 candidates who received contributions from the Democratic Party, moreover, 29 also received contributions from labor groups, typically in large amounts. For these 36 candidates receiving money from the Democratic Party, the median amount they received from labor groups was \$1,350—quite large compared to the median of \$275 they received from the Democratic Party. In total, these 36 candidates received \$156,500 from labor groups. And while these Democratic Party–supported candidates did often receive some contributions from businesses—16 candidates received money from growth businesses and 24 received money from non-growth businesses—the typical amounts are smaller than for the Republican-supported candidates. For candidates backed by the Democratic Party, the median contribution from growth-oriented businesses is \$0. For non-growth businesses, it is \$400—much smaller than the \$1,050 for Republican-supported candidates.

Therefore, there is some sign that when the two major parties put money into municipal races, they do so to support candidates who have donors that look like the parties' respective donor bases: business for Republicans and labor for Democrats. But the importance of this pattern for understanding local politics should not be overstated. Most of the candidates who got money from labor or business (or both) did not get money from parties. For example, while there are 29 candidates in Washington local races who received money from both labor and the Democratic Party, there are 86 who received money from labor but not from either party, and those 86 received significant contributions from businesses as well. The same is the case for the business side. Eighty-seven candidates received money from pro-growth businesses but no money from political parties. And half of those 87 candidates also received labor contributions. It is true, then, that parties give to candidates whose donor bases generally look like the party profile, but it is much more common for candidates to receive interest group money in the absence of party money. And in those cases, the patterns of giving do not look like a standard Democratic and Republican account of interest group giving. Instead, the picture that emerges is one of candidates who get money from labor groups, from pro-growth businesses, and from non-growth businesses without coordination by the political parties.

In sum, we cannot conclude that, just because interest groups and political parties tend to be active in the same cities, interest groups are forming and working through party coalitions. There is also a theoretical logic and some empirical support for an alternative explanation: namely, that both interest groups and political parties just get active in local elections for their own reasons. Political parties are engaged in some cities but generally less than interest groups. And importantly, it does not look as though parties are coalitions of local interest groups.

Why Does Political Party Activity Vary across Cities?

All of my findings suggest that it is reasonable to give interest groups pride of place in a study of groups and organizations in local politics and that doing so does not require that I also develop and test a comprehensive theory of local political parties. For interest groups, there is a rationale for what they are doing in local politics and why. For political parties, it is harder to pin down what they are or what they are trying to achieve in local politics.

Still, because political parties are quite important in American politics more broadly and because others may want to take up these questions, I move that agenda forward by using the data I have to explain variation in political party activity across cities. Specifically, I use OLS to regress three of the measures of local political party activity—maximum party activity, Republican Party activity, and Democratic Party activity—on a set of variables describing characteristics of the cities and their states.

The first two sets of independent variables capture the amount of interest group activity in the city and the most relevant electoral institutions. I include the summary measure of city interest group activity that I introduced earlier in the chapter, which should again be positively associated with party activity. I include indicators for whether the city has nonpartisan or partisan elections and whether the city's elections are on-cycle or off-cycle, because Progressive Era municipal reformers advocated nonpartisan and off-cycle elections as institutional ways of weakening political parties in local politics.

Furthermore, because most of the party activity in local elections is activity by the two major national political parties, the amount of party activity in local politics probably also depends on how competitive those two parties are within the city in national politics.[22] For this reason, in the models of maximum party activity, I control for the competitiveness of the two parties. The competitiveness variable ranges from 0 to 0.5, where 0.5 would be a city where the 2012 two-party presidential vote was evenly divided between Barack Obama and Mitt Romney. When I turn to modeling the activity of the Democratic Party and the Republican Party separately, I instead control for the percentage of the city's two-party presidential vote that went to Barack Obama in 2012, expecting it to be positively associated with Democratic Party activity and negatively associated with Republican Party activity.

In addition to these variables, I control for log city population, because political parties may have a larger role to play in organizing elections in bigger cities.[23] I also include an indicator equal to 1 for the cities in the dataset where all survey respondents ran unopposed, because political parties might be less active in noncompetitive races. To account for the possibility that states that David Mayhew identifies as having had "traditional party organizations" (TPOs) during the 1960s feature political parties that are more active in local elections,[24] I first estimate a model that includes a binary indicator variable equal to 1 for Ohio, Rhode Island, Indiana, and Kentucky (all strong TPO states) and 0 for the other five states. However, there may be other characteristics of states, such as political culture, that shape the local electoral rules, inter-

POLITICAL PARTIES IN LOCAL POLITICS   131

TABLE 5.5 **Correlates of political party activity in municipal elections**

	Most Active Party		Republican Party	Democratic Party	Most Active Party
	(1)	(2)	(3)	(4)	(5)
Interest group activity	0.943***	0.941***	0.775***	0.817***	0.946***
	(0.111)	(0.109)	(0.102)	(0.086)	(0.110)
Partisan elections	1.096***	1.151***	1.048***	1.023***	0.983***
	(0.104)	(0.116)	(0.101)	(0.044)	(0.193)
On-cycle	0.177	0.421***	0.434***	0.216***	0.416***
	(0.114)	(0.023)	(0.038)	(0.017)	(0.023)
Ln(Population)	0.173***	0.158***	0.143***	0.084**	0.156***
	(0.025)	(0.031)	(0.034)	(0.035)	(0.031)
National party competitiveness	0.958*	1.014**			0.822
	(0.416)	(0.424)			(0.476)
Partisan elections * National party competitiveness					1.588
					(0.881)
Democratic presidential vote			−2.326***	2.173***	
			(0.553)	(0.475)	
Race unopposed	−0.026	−0.075	−0.182	−0.033	−0.077
	(0.073)	(0.080)	(0.133)	(0.057)	(0.078)
TPO state	0.254*				
	(0.130)				
R-squared	0.46	0.47	0.41	0.42	0.47
Observations	570	570	570	569	570

Notes: Standard errors clustered by state in parentheses. Models 2–5 include state fixed effects.

*p < 0.10, **p < 0.05, ***p < 0.01 (two-tailed).

est group activity, and the activity of political parties, so I also estimate
models that include fixed effects for individual states.

The results of these models are presented in table 5.5. I start with the
model of the 0–4 activity rating of the most active party in the city. Column 1 presents the estimates from the model that includes the indicator for historical TPOs and no state fixed effects, and column 2 shows
the results of the model that includes state fixed effects. Throughout, I
find that greater political party activity tends to go with greater interest
group activity, as shown by the positive coefficients on the interest group
activity variable in all the models. Focusing on columns 1 and 2, I estimate that a one-unit increase in this 0–4 interest group activity variable
is associated with nearly a one-unit increase in the activity of the most
active political party.

I also find that there is a strong association between the appearance
of party labels on the ballot and party activity: the coefficient estimate
on partisan elections is positive and statistically significant. In terms of
magnitude, this coefficient suggests that party activity is more than a

point higher on the 0–4 activity scale in partisan elections than in nonpartisan elections—which we can think of as being the difference between "somewhat" and "very" active. And in columns 3 and 4, where I look at the relationship between partisan elections and Republican and Democratic Party activity separately in models that include state fixed effects, I find a strong positive association for both.

The coefficient on the indicator for on-cycle election timing is also positive in all the models, but it is smaller in magnitude than the coefficients on partisan elections and only sometimes statistically significant. Focusing first on the model without state fixed effects, in column 1, where the dependent variable is the 0–4 activity rating of the most active party, I find that having elections in November 2016, as opposed to November 2015, is not significantly associated with higher party activity ratings. The models that include state fixed effects show stronger positive relationships between on-cycle timing and party activity, but California is the only state in this sample with within-state variation in city election timing. What I can conclude, then, is that within California, the cities with November 2016 elections saw greater party activity than the cities with November 2015 elections.

The findings for the other independent variables are also mostly as expected. Throughout, the relationship between city size and party activity is positive. Also, cities that lean Democratic see more local electoral activity by the Democratic Party and less activity by the Republican Party. And in column 1, where I include the indicator for TPO states, I find evidence that states with strong TPOs in the 1960s have more active parties in local elections today.

One final finding of note in columns 1 and 2 is that cities where the two parties are more competitive in national politics have more political party activity in local elections, on average. This finding is broadly consistent with Peter Bucchianeri's recent study of city council roll-call votes: he finds that city council decision making is only structured by a single dimension in cities with competitive parties and partisan elections—and that otherwise local roll-call votes are much more unstructured.[25] While I am focused here on the activity of political parties in local elections rather than council roll-call votes, in column 5, I evaluate whether these same two conditions work together to shape the amount of party activity in a city. Specifically, I model the activity of the most active party in the city with the same set of variables as before but this time adding the interaction of partisan elections with party competitiveness. The results show that partisan elections are associated with significantly more party activity even when the two parties are not competitive in the city, and it does look as though national-level party competition is associated with more party activity even in the absence of partisan elections ($p = 0.123$). However, based on the positive interaction term ($p = 0.109$), political party activity in city politics is greatest when the parties are competitive in national elections and when the city has partisan elections.

In terms of the bigger picture, what we learn from this analysis is that there is no single, simple explanation for why the activity of political parties varies from city to city. It depends on many different factors. It is true that political parties are more active in places with more active interest groups. But several other local conditions are also important: whether city elections are partisan, whether they are held at the same time as national elections, the amount of support for the two major parties in the electorate, and whether there were strong party organizations in the state in the 1960s. In local politics, there is nothing inevitable about party competition.

Conclusion

As an account of political parties, the analysis in this chapter yields more questions than answers, but considerable progress has been made nonetheless, and the focus on local politics and interest groups deserves much of the credit for that. Major theories of American politics start with national politics and political parties as the entities to be explained, and with that as the starting point, it is all too easy to assume (1) that local politics conforms to the national model and (2) that interest groups must be subsumed within political parties. By instead starting with local politics and interest groups as the entities to be explained, I cast doubt on both of those assumptions. Local interest group alignments do not appear to mirror national ones, and thus a major component of local politics does not fit the national model. Moreover, it does not look like interest groups are working within political parties in most cities. And why would they have to? Interest groups can perform many of the same functions as political parties. As Chicago mayor, Lori Lightfoot, said of one set of interest groups in her city, unions "have other aspirations beyond being a union and maybe being something akin to a political party."[26]

Political parties do not have a monopoly on endorsements, campaign giving, lobbying, campaigning, or even nominations. Interest groups can do these things too and, as I discuss later, sometimes more.

Acknowledging as much throws wide open questions of what role political parties play in local politics and why they are active in some places but not others. I have offered up some theoretical logic and empirical evidence here, but I leave it to others to fully flesh out a theory of parties that fits the local context. For my purposes, the most important takeaway of what I have argued and shown in this chapter is that an evaluation of interest group influence in local politics can move forward, even if there are still unanswered questions about political parties. We do not have to worry much that the activity of local unions or businesses is subsidiary to some national partisan or ideological structure and that it is that structure that really matters. We can instead take local interest group activity at face value and move on to an investigation of whether and how interest group activity makes a difference to public policy.

CHAPTER SIX

Influence

Issues, Approach, and Expectations

We have seen so far that interest group activity is different in local and national politics, that group activity varies across municipal governments, and that a policy-focused approach helps make sense of the types of interest groups that are most involved. Explaining patterns of interest group activity is the easier part, however. Evaluating what difference it makes to politics and public policy is more difficult. For decades, efforts to assess whether interest groups have influence have run into a host of conceptual, design, and inferential problems. As a result, we still do not have a clear answer as to whether interest groups have any effect—in the local context or any other. And yet if we want to understand political representation and why we get the policies we do, evaluating interest group influence is crucial. It is high time for a fresh approach.

The key elements of my approach, as I explained in chapter 2, are that the dependent variables are public policies—meaning the particulars of the policies a city makes—and that the independent variables are measures of interest group activity. The question to be asked in the analysis is whether greater political activity by a group leads to policies that are different from what they otherwise would have been. While this approach does not and cannot fully capture all elements of the second face of power, it avoids the pitfalls of looking only at political decisions, and it recognizes that public policies are the accumulation of decisions and nondecisions over a long time. Moreover, the measures of interest group activity I use are more inclusive than measures of campaign contributions or formal lobbying alone. Finally, by setting up tests of interest group influence in this way, my approach aligns with the general approach in the study of political representation, which means I can also account for other forces that might shape public policies, such as residents' partisan and ideological leanings.

My theoretical approach also implies that there is no way to carry out an all-encompassing test of how much interest groups influence local politics. The goal is not to make a blanket statement about municipal government responsiveness to interest groups or, for that matter, to mass publics, or homeowners, or residents' partisanship. Instead, I expect interest group influence to be conditional. It should depend on both the interest group and the public policy in question. And in chapter 2, I proposed three conditions that should matter: an interest group's political activity should make a bigger difference to a policy when its preferences on that policy are relatively homogeneous, when its preferences are distinct from those of other important actors, and when the group is politically focused on the issue—meaning that it communicates its preferences to policy makers and demonstrates its willingness to expend political resources on it.[1] Notably, these conditions are specific to policy-group pairs.

In order to pursue an empirical analysis of interest group influence, then, I have to choose which policies (and groups) to focus on. That is my first task in this chapter: to provide a rationale for the policies I focus on in my empirical tests in chapters 7, 8, and 9, all of which fall within the broad issue areas of economic development and growth (including housing development) and public safety policies (including local government spending). Because I am now moving into an analysis of local public policies, it is important to take stock of what we already know and understand about the politics of those policies, especially any role of interest groups. My second aim in this chapter, then, is to review the key ideas and findings of research literatures that are especially relevant. Drawing and building on insights from each and applying my theoretical framework, I develop expectations about the conditions under which interest group activity would affect outcomes in these two broad areas. Those expectations are then the basis of the empirical tests in the following chapters.

Finally, after laying out my expectations for interest group influence and discussing some of the inferential issues involved, I turn to a discussion of the role of mass publics. My focus, it must be stressed, is on the extent to which interest groups influence policies, a topic that has been neglected in local politics research. But by moving forward with a study of influence, I am also jumping into a large pool of political representation research that has heavily emphasized how voters, public opinion, party, and ideology influence political and policy outcomes. Their potential role in shaping local policies therefore cannot be ignored. In this chapter I explain how I incorporate these other constituencies and factors into my empirical analyses. However, I do not expect them to make much difference to the local policies I explore. At the end of the chapter, I explain why.

The Policies

In evaluating interest group influence, I cannot possibly consider all the kinds of policies municipal governments make, but I do cover a lot of ground. First, within the area of economic growth and development, I evaluate the extent to which city governments rely on tax incentives and tax abatement, and then I examine processes, regulations, and outcomes related to housing development. When I turn to local public service provision, I focus on police protection and fire protection, analyzing variation in police and firefighter compensation, patterns of overall city spending, trends in community policing, and decisions about whether to require police officers to wear body cameras. Because all these policies are central to what most municipal governments do almost everywhere, focusing on them will shed light on key elements of local politics.

Moreover, analyzing this set of policies helps reduce concerns about whether an interest group's activity prompts local governments to take up an issue or whether a local government taking up an issue prompts the interest group activity. Again, these are issues on which most municipal governments make decisions, so there is less need to worry that any relationship between group activity and policy is explained by differences in the basic policy functions of local government.

There is also theoretical justification for focusing on these policies. As I explain when I get into the specifics of each policy, these are issue areas and policies for which I can make reasonable assumptions about the goals and interest homogeneity of the groups that I have found are most active in municipal government: chambers of commerce, developers, firefighters' unions, and police unions. Moreover, both across and within the two broad issue areas, sometimes these groups' preferences are distinct from those of other actors in local politics, whereas in other situations they are not. The homogeneity and distinctiveness of potentially opposing groups' preferences likely vary as well. And perhaps most important, there is almost certainly variation in the focus of potential opposition groups. Examining this wide range of local policies therefore allows me to evaluate my expectations about how these distinctions matter for groups' influence.

One final advantage of focusing on these two broad issue areas is that they have already been the subject of research. Economic development and growth have been a major focus of the urban politics literature for decades, and in recent years there has also been excellent research on the politics of housing. There is relatively less work on the politics of public service provision or public safety specifically, but the small literature on public-sector unions establishes some key theoretical foundations and empirical patterns that prove useful. Targeted discussion of these research literatures therefore helps set the stage for my analyses of interest group influence in later chapters.

Local Economic Development and Growth

Local economic development and growth has long been a major emphasis of urban politics and local political economy research, and Paul Peterson's book, *City Limits*, played an important role in setting the agenda.[2] By Peterson's account, city politics is heavily shaped by the constraints cities face, the most important being their relatively small geographic size and the ease with which taxpaying individuals and businesses can move from one municipality to the next. Because cities are locked into competition with one another for these taxpayers, local government officials have to be intensely focused on their cities' economic success. After all, a large share of local government revenue comes from taxes and charges for services, so economic prosperity means a larger fiscal base and more city revenue with which to provide services. Moreover, local officials are rewarded politically for successfully pursuing economic prosperity and for securing the widespread community benefits that come with it. And many local officials simply care about the communities they come from and seek local economic prosperity because it helps those communities. The upshot, Peterson argues, is that city policies are in everyone's interest when they strengthen the city's economic position and improve its "attractiveness as a locale for economic activity."[3] Cities

INFLUENCE: ISSUES, APPROACH, AND EXPECTATIONS

therefore have a powerful interest in building and sustaining a strong local economy.

While Peterson's argument is perhaps best known for its implication that cities will generally not pursue large programs of redistribution, it is most useful here for what it implies about the importance of local economic prosperity, the incentives of local elected officials, and the role of voters, interest groups, and elections in shaping local policy. Peterson suggests that economic development and growth is of first-order importance to city politics and that it is a valence issue: a stronger local economy is in everyone's interest, including and especially local elected officials. He also concludes that the politics of economic development and growth will be consensual and thus that the activities of voters and interest groups will not matter much for developmental policies. He writes:

> When developmental policies are considered, attempts to ascertain the power of one or another individual or group are probably pointless, if not misleading. In this policy arena the city as a whole has an interest that needs to be protected and enhanced. Policies of benefit to the city contribute to the prosperity of all residents. Downtown business benefits, but so do laborers desiring higher wages, homeowners hoping house values will rise, the unemployed seeking new jobs, and politicians aiming for reelection. Those who seem to have 'power' over developmental policies are those who do the most to secure these benefits for all members of the city.[4]

Peterson's point is an important one, both as a statement about the politics of economic development and for its implications for a study of interest group influence. He argues that if business interests appear to get their way with developmental policies, it is not because they are successfully exerting political pressure, getting policy makers to do something they would not otherwise do. They are not having influence.[5] Rather, business *appears* to be getting its way because elected officials and policy makers want to make those business-friendly developmental policies anyway. Those policies are also in *their* interest. Because business interests are not distinct from the preferences of other important political actors, their activity should not result in policy that is different from what it otherwise would have been. Instead, he argues, environmental and contextual variables are the crucial ones for explaining local politics—much more than traditional political factors like voters, elections, and interest groups.[6]

Like the cities he is describing, however, Peterson's argument has its limits. It is mainly about the differences between city and national government; it is not as well suited to explaining the considerable variation across municipal governments. Oliver, Ha, and Callen clarify (and Peterson acknowledges) that not all municipalities are engaged in an endless pursuit of growth—especially smaller ones. But even if the goal is not growth, if incumbents' reelections hinge in part on whether they maintain an "equilibrium between taxes and services,"[7] as Oliver, Ha, and Callen propose, then city officials still have to be attentive to the local tax base, and they have to be thinking about local economic strength.

Also, if a successful local economy and a strong tax base (and thus strong service provision) are rewarded by voters, then presumably voters and political actors do make some difference. This, after all, is simply the idea of retrospective economic voting: voters reward local incumbents when economic performance is good and punish them when it is not. Setting aside debates about whether voters can do this well,[8] if this is a source of local elected officials' incentives to pursue economic prosperity, then by implication voters do have influence and local elections do serve a policy purpose.

Furthermore, putting all developmental politics into the same bucket and treating them as a win-win for all political actors overlooks key distinctions between policies that may be important for patterns of interest group influence. To see this, we need to clarify what is meant by developmental policies and what, exactly, city officials do to pursue economic prosperity. Peterson provides some illuminating examples.

> They can minimize their tax on capital and on profits from capital investment. They can reduce the costs of capital investment by providing low-cost public utilities, such as roads, sewers, lights, and police and fire protection. They can even offer public land free of charge or at greatly reduced prices to those investors they are particularly anxious to attract. They can provide a context for business operations free of undue harassment or regulation. For example, they can ignore various external costs of production, such as air pollution, water pollution, and the despoliation of trees, grass, and other features of the landscape. Finally, they can discourage labor from unionizing so as to keep industrial labor costs competitive.[9]

It is clear from these examples that many developmental policies do have costs and trade-offs—and thus political losers. Even if constituencies uniformly support a strong local economy and tax base, some might oppose particular policies because of those costs. It is even possible that some constituencies might perceive the costs of growth and development to be so great and so consistent that they become a regular force against cities' growth impulses. Once one considers these costs and trade-offs, there is reason to question whether the politics of economic growth and development is, in fact, consensual.

This is one of the main points made by Logan and Molotch in *Urban Fortunes*: growth policies have both winners and losers and are thus *not* in everyone's interest.[10] The clear winners, according to Logan and Molotch, are the businesses and developers that reap profits from the growth and the city officials who are complicit in that endeavor.[11] The losers are environmentalists, neighborhood associations, and local residents who want high quality of life. Not only might pro-development policies fail to actually create jobs and build the tax base, but growth can corrode the environment and detract from the interests of residents. An important implication is that there is indeed potential for political conflict over policies adopted in pursuit of a strong local economy.

Still, for a long time, urban politics scholars seemed to assume that business and growth interests would dominate any such conflict if it arose and that opposition groups would be weak and ineffectual. The picture painted was one of developers and growth-oriented businesses reigning supreme in American cities. More recently, there has been greater acknowledgment that urban politics is not (and perhaps never was) uniformly about the pursuit of growth,[12] that some cities also focus on sustainability,[13] and that neighborhood associations and environmental groups can actually be quite active in local politics.[14] But there is still very little work on whether these group dynamics are associated with city policies.[15]

The local political economy literature, meanwhile, suggests something very different: it is homeowners who reign supreme in local politics, and homeowners push back forcefully and effectively against growth, especially when the growth involves high-density housing. As William Fischel explains in *The Homevoter Hypothesis*, for many homeowners, their homes are their largest asset, and they cannot be moved.[16] Homeowners therefore engage in local politics to protect the value of their homes, which often means opposing new developments that might affect their view, local traffic and parking, the composition of local schools, the crowdedness of local parks, or the racial and ethnic composition of the neighborhood.[17] These kinds of NIMBY (Not in My Backyard) impulses cut across national ideological and partisan lines and can even be found among renters concerned about rising rent prices.[18] Moreover, public meeting requirements empower such residents in their efforts to delay and block new housing.[19] While this literature focuses much more on homeowners than on interest groups, it does offer a certain perspective on the local politics of growth and development, one in which a subset of city residents and voters has power, in which it is very difficult to pursue development, and in which growth interests are at a disadvantage.

This is a very different story from that of the urban politics literature, and there are different ways to interpret the gulf between the two accounts. It could be that growth interests dominated local politics in the past but that the anti-growth advocacy of residents is more powerful today. Another possibility is that both accounts dismiss elements of truth in the other: the political economy tradition does not place enough weight on the role of developers and other businesses, and the urban politics tradition—with its emphasis on business dominance—has not focused on the potential influence of residents and groups opposed to growth and development.

My own analysis in chapter 7 addresses this matter, but for now it is worth summarizing the most important points to be taken from these literatures. First, city officials have incentives to protect the tax base and maintain some balance between low taxes and service provision. The goal may not be growth—that impulse may be stronger for larger, less affluent cities—but economic development and property development everywhere are "central preoccupations of local politics."[20] Second, business may have clout when it comes to policies related to local economic development and growth, but it remains to be seen just how much clout and the conditions under which it exists. Business is an especially important constituency for elected officials, but business may also have less influence than it seems if policy makers would make the same decisions in the absence of its political activity. Moreover, there can be downsides of policies pursued in the name of economic development and growth, and organized groups and subsets of citizens might sometimes form effective opposition to business interests on those grounds. That some researchers point to the power of business and growth interests while others highlight the dominance of homeowners may even suggest that these are highly contentious issues in local politics—and that local policies depend on the balance of power between the opposing sides.

Local Public Service Provision

Compared to economic development and growth, there is far less research on the politics of local public service provision, including police and fire protection. The urban politics literature mostly ignores it, which is strange given that one of the reasons city officials feel pressure to maintain the tax base is that they need the revenue to pay for public services. It is also unclear why urban politics scholars emphasize the large, profit-oriented stakes of businesses and developers in local government, yet generally disregard vested interests in the case of public service provision: the public employees whose jobs, compensation, and working conditions depend on the policies cities make.[21] Regardless of what the explanation is, the urban politics literature's neglect of this core area of urban politics is a considerable oversight.

Then there is the quantitative local political economy literature: numerous studies have analyzed patterns of local government spending, but the focus is overwhelmingly on characteristics of residents and elected officials. Some emphasize the race and ethnicity of city residents, finding that more segregated cities with larger racial and ethnic minority populations have lower expenditures.[22] Others focus on the partisanship and ideology of city residents and elected officials,[23] as I discuss later. Throughout this work, interest groups like public-sector unions are conspicuously absent, and the researchers often seem more interested in the independent variable (namely, partisanship) than local spending per se. (Local spending data are typically used for the dependent variables because they are among the only city-level policy outcome data available.) If understanding the politics of public service provision was the main concern, not only would it be important to consider interest groups, but it would also be productive to go beyond aggregate spending variables to consider more detailed components of that spending as well as nonspending variables.[24]

This may point to one reason the politics of public service provision is less studied: many of the specific policies related to public service provision—such as employee compensation, staffing levels, work rules, and purchases of equipment—might at first seem like mere personnel matters that are not worthy of attention from political scientists.[25] But that would be a mistake. A very large share of what city governments spend money on is compensating employees for providing services, so policies governing compensation and employment have significant impacts on local government budgets. Also, rules that shape how government employees do their jobs are rules about how public services are provided, such as how police officers treat the accused and how teachers teach children. These are more than just personnel policies. They are highly public in their impacts and hugely important to how local governments operate.

Another possible reason these local policies are less studied is that in many cities, they are decided or shaped by collective bargaining—an avenue of potential influence that social scientists tend to overlook. Public-sector unions do engage in local politics in the more traditional ways, such as by contributing money to campaigns, as I have shown. But in many places they can also push their policy goals in collective bargaining. In most states, local government employers are required to negotiate and come to legally binding agreements with public-sector unions on matters of compensation and work rules. In some places, if the two sides do not reach agreement, public employees can threaten or carry out a strike—and thus halt or slow service provision. This, then, is a process through which a particular type of interest group—public-sector unions—pushes for public policies it favors. Because it is a channel of potential influence that other interest groups do not have and because it does not fit within traditional conceptualizations of interest group activity, it tends to get ignored or cordoned off as something different. But it is important to local public service provision, and that may be another reason researchers have paid less attention to public service provision than to economic development and growth.

While the existing literature on the politics of public service provision leaves much to be desired, there is a small political science literature on public-sector unions that is directly relevant. Research on teachers' unions, for example, sheds light on when public-sector unions will have more and less homogeneous interests and what types of local issues they are likely to focus on. Specifically, in an analysis of data from a national survey of teachers, Terry Moe finds that teachers are a heterogeneous group in terms of their views on national politics and policy: many, for example, are Republicans, and sizable shares do not agree with their national unions' Democratic positions. The issues that unite teachers are their occupational interests: better compensation, job protections, and favorable working conditions. On these issues, many of which are decided locally, teachers' interests are more homogeneous, and largely because of that, local teachers' unions tend to focus their efforts on them.[26]

As I showed in chapter 4, teachers' unions are not especially active in city politics—their local focus is on the school districts that employ teachers—but this insight should apply with equal if not greater force to other local government employees that *are* active in city politics, such as police officers and firefighters.[27] Compared to teachers, police officers and firefighters may exhibit even greater heterogeneity in their political views and greater tension between their support for their unions and their general political orientations. On the one hand, the law-and-order dimension of policing and the "culture of masculinity" in firefighting would seem to align with a more conservative worldview and alliance with the Republican Party.[28] On the other hand, the Democratic Party has long been more supportive of unions generally.[29] Yet even if police and firefighters vary considerably in ideology and party affiliation, they likely have homogeneous interests in more job security, better compensation, and better working conditions. Applying Moe's logic, this may well lead police and firefighters' unions to be ultra-focused on their members' locally determined occupational interests.

Research on public-sector unions also provides theoretical insight into the relationships between public-sector unions and elected officials—and how their goals often come into conflict. At the most basic level, they sit on opposite sides of the negotiating table in collective bargaining, with unions representing employees and elected officials serving as management. Elected officials presumably also want to retain discretion over how to manage the local government workforce if voters hold them accountable for government performance.[30] Public-sector unions, by contrast, often push for work rules that dictate how employees carry out their work.[31] Teachers' unions, for example, frequently advocate for rules that ensure that teachers are allocated to schools by seniority or that define the ways in which teachers can be evaluated, and those rules limit the discretion and authority of public managers.

One important example of the conflict between the interests of public-sector unions and those of local elected officials is the local government budget. Even if local elected officials feel pressure to be responsive to public-sector unions that are active in their own elections, many public-sector union demands cost money, and that money comes from government coffers. In considering employee requests for higher wages, better benefits, and staffing requirements that necessitate hiring more employees, the elected officials charged with governing have to weigh their desire to maintain service provision, the political difficulty of raising taxes, and the real limits of their budgets. The budget constraint creates a trade-off between hiring more employees and paying employees more. It also incentivizes elected officials to satisfy unions with concessions that seem "free," such as work rules they request, or with compensation increases whose costs can be hidden or pushed to the future, such as retirement benefit increases.[32] In these ways, then, local elected officials are pulled in different directions. They might feel pressure to be responsive to public-sector unions, but they also have to govern within the constraints of the local budget.

One final relevant insight that emerges from research on public-sector unions is that they often face weak or fragmented political opposition. For example, Moe finds that the groups that could potentially oppose teachers' unions in California school board elections, such as businesses, are less politically engaged in those elections than the unions themselves. Moreover, another potentially active constituency—parents of children in the district—either tend to be unorganized or are organized through parent-*teacher* associations and are thus not independent of teachers' interests.[33] This is not to say that organized opposition to public-sector unions never arises in local politics but rather that such opposition is usually the exception rather than the rule.[34]

This point is worth underscoring, because when there is an active political fight over an issue like local police reform or education policy, many people suddenly turn their attention to the issue, and it can be tempting to infer that those active political fights represent the normal politics of the issue. But one must be careful not to draw general inferences about the organization and clout of the opposition from a few salient, newsworthy events. For example, conservative networks have recently challenged public-sector unions in state politics, and the Black Lives Matter movement has recently challenged police unions in some cities, but that does not mean that groups like teachers' unions and police unions regularly face well-organized, ongoing opposition in local politics. That kind of inference would suffer from the same problem that befalls researchers trying to draw general conclusions about interest group influence from studies of roll-call votes: in some policy areas, the visible, high-profile, contentious cases are special. One also has to study power and influence when politics is quiet.

This is difficult to do, but a recent book by Moe shows how essential it is for understanding teachers' union influence.[35] By comparing the politics of education reform in New Orleans before and after Hurricane Katrina, he demonstrates how local teachers' unions had been successful in keeping reforms like charter schools off the agenda. After the hurricane, which caused many teachers to leave the city and the union to unravel, the very same policy makers who were active in the city and the state before the hurricane suddenly got busy proposing and adopting the union-opposed reforms that for years had gone nowhere. As he explains, it is only by "taking the lid off" that we really see the power dynamics that were in place when the lid was still on—when politics was quiet.

In addition, a few studies have evaluated the influence of public-sector unions using a quantitative approach. Most of them estimate the effect of unionization or collective bargaining on government employees' salaries, with mixed results: some find a positive effect of unionization or collective bargaining on salaries,[36] and others find no effect.[37] By contrast, scholars have found a clearer, positive relationship between union membership or collective bargaining and fringe benefits like health insurance and retirement benefits.[38] In addition, there are a small number of studies that go beyond indicators of union membership or collective bargaining to evaluate the effects of public-sector unions' more traditional political activities. Moe, for example, collected data on teachers' union endorsements in California school board elections and found a positive effect of those endorsements on candidates' win rates.[39] In a separate study, he found that when teachers' unions are more active in school board elections, the winners' views tend to be more favorable to collective bargaining for teachers.[40]

Viewed as a whole, then, research on public-sector unions establishes some important theoretical and empirical baselines. On the theoretical side, it speaks to public-sector unions' interests, how their interests often conflict with the interests of elected officials, and how direct organized opposition to their interests does not necessarily arise. And on the empirical side, there is research showing that unionization, collective bargaining, and unions' more traditional political activities make a difference to some local political and policy outcomes.

Expectations

The above discussion helps establish some more specific expectations for the empirical analyses in later chapters. The first condition of interest group influence I laid out earlier is that an interest group's political activity in a city should be more likely to affect policy when the group has relatively homogeneous preferences on that policy. Based on the discussion above, business groups will tend to have relatively homogeneous interests in the area of economic development and growth, and public-sector unions will generally have relatively homogeneous interests in local policies on compensation and work rules. For potential opposition groups, however, there is probably greater variation. In research on economic development and growth, scholars refer to environmental groups, neighborhood associations, and local homeowners as adversaries of business and developers. Research on public-sector unions suggests that they often do not face active opposition, but the opponents that are sometimes cited are businesses, taxpayer groups, and conservative groups. But do these potential opponents have homogeneous interests on all relevant outcomes? Probably not. It probably depends on the specific policy and the specific group in question.

The second condition is that we should be more likely to detect interest group influence when a group's interests on that policy are distinct from the preferences of other relevant political actors. As we have seen, the urban politics literature suggests that the interests of businesses and developers are aligned with those of local elected officials on policies that will expand or protect the local tax base. This suggests that for many policy outcomes related to economic development, the political activity of business and developers may not actually make much difference. It also suggests that their activity will be more likely to make a difference when what they want is not clearly aligned with elected officials' interests in maintaining the tax base. An example of this, as I explore in chapter 7, is business tax abatement, which is an economic development policy but one that also (at least in the short run) reduces tax revenue. Another example of conflict between the preferences of elected officials and interest groups comes from the literature on public-sector unions: unions' pushes for compensation increases and work rules (e.g., rules limiting how employees can be evaluated) clash with elected officials' interests in keeping public service costs down and retaining managerial discretion.

The third general condition that I identified earlier is that a group's influence depends on whether it is politically active and focused on the particular issue in question. Policy makers must know what the group wants on the issue and that it is willing to exercise its political clout to get what it wants. This is very likely true for most of the main group-issue pairs I am interested in: business groups tend to be politically focused on pro-growth and pro-economic development policies, and public safety unions are politically focused on higher employment, better compensation, and work rules that improve the daily lives of public safety workers. Even for these main group-policy pairs, however, the extent of the interest group's commitment to a particular city likely conditions whether that group's activity is focused on that local policy.

As I explained in chapters 2 and 4, some interest groups have no choice but to engage in local politics if they want to pursue their interests. A local chamber of commerce is one example. It represents the interests of businesses in a particular city. It cannot move across the state to a friendlier political environment; it has to focus on making the environment friendlier where it is. The same is true of police unions, firefighters' unions, and neighborhood associations: they are inextricably tied to a particular place. They cannot pursue their interests in some other city across the state. Developers, however, are different. My earlier findings show that they are very active in local politics, but if a developer finds that one city is inhospitable, it can attempt to take its business to another city. For many of these main groups, therefore, there is reason to expect that they will be politically focused on these issues. But because of their exit options, developers are probably less focused on city business-friendliness generally and more concentrated on the decisions that affect them very directly, such as city decisions about their own projects and proposals.

This third condition is also relevant for the opposition groups, and here, too, I can borrow the insight discussed earlier: the activity of interest groups hinges in part on whether the benefits and costs of a policy are concentrated or diffuse.[41] The main beneficiaries of the policies I explore here are the businesses, developers, and public safety unions in their respective areas. Those benefits, we can assume, are concentrated. The nature of the costs, however, varies by issue, and that variation stands to shape whether potential opposition will amount to focused, effective opposition.

While there are a number of features of policies' costs that could affect the organization and focus of potential opposition, a simple categorization is useful. We can think of the main trade-offs of a local policy as being in the form of land, budget, or constraints on the way government provides services. Of these three, the land-related costs of policies have received the most attention in urban and local politics research. And emphasizing land use makes sense, because most policies pursued in the name of economic development and growth probably do eventually have implications for land use. If a city successfully attracts a business, improves a downtown business district, or expands infrastructure or the housing supply to accommodate business investment, one consequence will be land use changes. Those land use changes probably have losers, whether it is homeowners worried about their property values; environmentalists angry over the loss of green space; residents worried about traffic, parking, and the quality of their local community; or something else. Especially in local government, policies' land use costs are an important type of trade-off.

But land use costs also have some unusual features: they are concentrated, highly visible, and easily attributable to policy makers' actions.[42] Typically, nearby residents are directly affected by new development—in large economic ways if it threatens their property values. New development also might directly threaten the goals of environmental groups (depending on the homogeneity of their interests). Furthermore, the results of land use decisions have a physical presence: residents and environmental groups can see or at least envision the building going up across the street, and if they experience decreased utility because of shade on their property, construction noise, or loss of parking, there is little ambiguity about the role of that new building in causing that decreased utility. The concentration and visibility of land use costs make them especially likely to generate active opposition—concentrated interest against concentrated interest—and thus open conflict. Because of this, when a policy's main costs come in the form of land use, potential opposition groups will likely be politically focused on the issue, and we should be more likely to see that those groups' political activity is associated with outcomes more in their favor. The costs in this case might even be sufficiently large, visible, and direct to mobilize individual, unorganized homeowners, consistent with what much of the housing politics literature has hypothesized and found.

But the main costs of a local policy need not be in the form of land use. Equally important are *budgetary* trade-offs. When government offi-

INFLUENCE: ISSUES, APPROACH, AND EXPECTATIONS

cials grant a salary increase to public employees or agree to pay the employees' share of their pension contributions, the effects appear in the government budget. There is no physically visible change, but the costs are real. If expenditures go up in one area of the budget, something else has to move: revenue has to go up, spending in another area has to go down, or debt has to increase. The key difference from land use, however, is that the costs are not visible and are often diffuse. And that should have consequences for the mobilization of opposition. Residents throughout the city experience the costs in the form of higher taxes, lower public-sector employment, or public parks maintained less well. But every resident is affected just a little, and most people would not attribute those costs to particular budgetary decisions made by elected officials.[43] Compared to land costs, then, budgetary costs may be less likely to generate active and targeted opposition. Exceptions might arise if incurring new expenses requires reallocating public funds from functions that have well-organized constituencies supporting them. But even if that is the case, the lower visibility of those costs (compared to land use change) may mean that the political activity of potentially opposed groups is less likely to affect outcomes.

This distinction implies potential differences both between and within the broad areas of economic development and public service provision. Economic development and growth more often lead to land use changes, whereas the costs of changes to public service provision policy are usually budgetary. One implication may be that opposition groups and even unorganized residents have greater influence on economic development and growth policies—and that there will be more open conflict as a result. But there could also be variation along these lines within these broad policy areas. For example, a proposal to build a new police station is in the realm of public safety and has budget consequences, but some of the major costs are land use costs, and directly affected groups and residents might view the station as a threat and mobilize to oppose it. Alternatively, consider tax abatement for businesses, an economic development policy I mentioned earlier. The most immediate trade-offs of tax abatement are budgetary: there is less revenue from taxes. It is true that attracting business to a city might eventually result in land use changes, and city officials hope that tax abatement will "pay for itself" by expanding the tax base down the road. But there is uncertainty in those projections. In the short run, the direct consequence of offering business tax incentives is lower tax revenue and thus less money for public service provision. This distinction between land and budget trade-offs might therefore be helpful for making predictions both across and within issue areas.

A third potential trade-off comes in the form of managerial discretion and the rules that govern how government employees do their work. Research on public-sector unions and education reform has emphasized how public managers (e.g., superintendents and school boards) want discretion in managing the public workforce (teachers, school nurses, bus drivers) so that they can pursue strong performance—for which they are held accountable.[44] Public-sector unions, on the other hand, advocate for policies that protect the interests of their members and usually their most active members, for example, rules that stipulate how employees will be evaluated, how they are assigned to certain tasks, and what constitutes grounds for termination.[45]

Because so little research has investigated the effects of institutions and policies that govern how public employees carry out their work, it is difficult to make broad, definitive statements about the costs and benefits of those institutions and policies. But in local politics, these provisions are often included in collective bargaining agreements. They are not included to serve the public but instead to protect employees, because public-sector unions push for them. Moreover, there are a few studies showing that such work rules and policies do affect public service provision, sometimes in a negative way.[46] In 2020, in particular, greater attention to long-standing issues of police brutality made salient questions about whether provisions in police collective bargaining contracts—such as provisions allowing officers to use chokeholds—have contributed to the problem. But this is a severely understudied topic and one that deserves much more attention going forward. What is clear is that the rules and processes that govern how employees do their work do have trade-offs. Very real ones, sometimes tragic ones. Like budgetary costs, these costs are often not visible, and they can be difficult to attribute to the actions of policy makers. Because they may be even more diffuse than budgetary costs, they are also probably less likely to engender regular, targeted, effective political opposition.

In sum, these are three forms of policy costs and trade-offs that might shape whether a group is politically focused on a particular issue and whether the political activity of that group affects particular policy outcomes. This discussion also provides general guidance for whether to expect effective opposition on a variety of specific policies related to economic development and growth and public service provision. Land use costs are usually direct, immediate, visible, and easily attributable to decisions made by local government. Budgetary costs do not have visible effects, are often felt indirectly or in the future, and can be difficult to attribute to any particular decisions of local government. Costs in the form of managerial discretion are similar to and possibly even less direct than budgetary costs. Because so much local politics research has developed in either a policy-neutral way or with an exclusive focus on land use, the relevance of managerial discretion costs for local politics has not yet been fully appreciated.

In addition, this line of thinking is helpful for making predictions about the politics of policies for which any trade-offs or costs are ambiguous. As I discuss in the next chapter, many common local economic development practices do not have clear costs associated with them: the costs are uncertain, ambiguous, and in the future. Such practices may well be in favor of business, but it is difficult to see how any active opposition would emerge. The same may be true of statements of broad policy principles, as one frequently hears from candidates during election campaigns. When local candidates say they are in favor of a business-friendly climate, a strong local economy, expansion of housing, or policies friendly to workers, it may or may not activate consideration of the costs and trade-offs of specific policies. It is possible that some groups know that expanding housing and creating a business-friendly environment will mean specific policies that impose costs on them. It is also possible that it is not until actual policies are adopted and actual costs are felt that opposition emerges. Both are theoretically plausible.

In general, though, this framework suggests that different policies have different costs and that those different costs are likely to be associated with different amounts of open conflict among groups and residents in a local government. With their direct, visible, immediate costs, land use changes are the most likely to result in open conflict, not just in a way that involves interest groups, but in a way that may involve residents or subsets of residents as well. Budgetary decisions may sometimes result in open conflict but often do not—probably less often than land use changes. And policies that affect managerial discretion and how employees do their jobs may be the least likely of all to result in open conflict. The nature of the policy and its costs, then, shapes the nature of the conflict.

Once one recognizes these differences across issues, it seems less likely that the focus on economic development and land use policies in the existing literature is a coincidence. In fact, this is probably another example of researchers channeling attention to where the visible conflict is. Local disputes about land use are common. Disputes about budgetary matters do happen in local politics, but they often involve a narrower set of actors when they occur. And under normal conditions, there appear to be far fewer open debates about work rules or policies that affect how public employees do their jobs. It seems that local politics scholars have tended to focus more on policy issues with more open conflict and more active competition.

That might not be problematic if the only goal were to draw conclusions about specific policy issues or specific groups. But often there is interest in understanding the nature of power and influence in society more generally. Political scientists studying responsiveness usually are not just trying to understand the relationship between public opinion and policy on a single issue; they are trying to understand whether policy is responsive to public opinion generally, because that tells us something about the quality of democracy. The reason interest group scholars favor studies of more than one issue and group over studies of a single issue or group is that they want to understand whether interest groups influence policy, not just on a single issue, but overall. If researchers are devoting more energy to issues with more active conflict, they may be drawing the wrong conclusions about power and influence in society. It would seem that even now, more than half a century later, we are still missing the primary lesson of the community power debates: to understand power and influence—*especially* the power and influence of the organized—you must also study what is happening where it looks like nothing is happening.

Endogeneity and Inference

Because the policy-focused approach is explicit about the endogeneity of public policy and interest group activity, moving from the theoretical to the empirical requires consideration of the challenges of inference. Earlier, when I was examining variation in interest group activity across cities, my empirical approach was to focus on relatively less malleable city characteristics—such as whether a city makes any policy at all in an issue area—to try to evaluate whether those city differences give rise to dif-

INFLUENCE: ISSUES, APPROACH, AND EXPECTATIONS

ferent patterns of interest group engagement. That is not a perfect solution, of course, because "relatively more fixed" does not mean those city characteristics aren't changeable, and in any case they only explain some of the variation in interest group activity across cities. But the task at hand is now even more challenging, because the particular policies a city makes could influence the activity of interest groups or local officials' perceptions of that activity, in addition to the other way around.

As a starting point, it needs to be acknowledged that these same issues apply with equal force to studies of political representation in which a cross-sectional relationship is shown between policy outcomes and public opinion. Some might call these descriptive studies, but they have been hugely influential, and there is usually some implicit or explicit claim that the public opinion is having a causal effect—that policy makers are *responding* to mass publics or some subset of the public (such as the affluent). Yet research by Gabriel Lenz shows evidence that the opinions of mass publics are also shaped by political elites.[47] Similarly, the policy feedback literature proposes that policies might affect political attitudes.[48] And as I will discuss shortly, there is a real theoretical question as to *how* public opinion would cause different policies, especially but not exclusively in local politics. This is not to dismiss the potential for reverse causality in my own analyses but rather to point out that there is a whole line of research that has this same structure and that many interpret as showing that public opinion has influence.

As for the potential for reverse causality in my evaluation of influence by interest groups, I have nothing close to a perfect solution. However, it helps to think through how it would work—and thus how it would affect inference. The first important clarification to make is that the likelihood of reverse causality probably depends on the group I am examining. The probability that the friendliness of city policy influences interest group activity seems fairly high for real estate developers because they do not have to devote their political energy to any one city: they might get more involved in cities where their projects are likely to be approved. This is less the case for groups like chambers of commerce, local public safety unions, and neighborhood associations, because they do not have the same ability to shop for friendly city environments. In addition, public-sector union activity is not only explained by local-level factors; their organization is heavily shaped by laws made at the state level.

Even in these latter cases, of course, the particulars of city policy could influence activity, but that could work in different ways. Most threatening to my efforts here would be a scenario in which city policies friendlier to an interest group either (1) cause city officials to perceive the group as more active or (2) cause that group to actually be more active in city politics. The first scenario seems unlikely even if I can't rule it out; I doubt, for example, that the absence of a requirement for police officers to wear body cameras would lead city officials to mistakenly assume that police unions are very active in city politics. The second scenario, however, is what is suggested by policy feedback theory: when government programs provide benefits to groups, those groups organize and strengthen to protect those benefits.[49] That said, while it seems likely that whether or not a city makes policy in an issue area would influence group activity in this way, I am examining issue areas in which almost all cities make policies. The key question then is, conditional on a city making policy in an area, would the cities with particular policies friendlier to a group cause greater political activity by that group? It isn't entirely obvious that the answer would be yes.

The opposite expectation seems just as likely if not more likely. Among similarly situated cities that have police departments, for example, it seems quite plausible that those with *lower* police compensation would inspire *more* political activity by police unions. More generally, policies that are unfriendly to a group could give rise to greater political activity by the group. In those cases, the group's grievances are greater, and there is more room to move policy in a friendly direction. And if the particulars of local policy affect interest group activity in *that* way, then it would make it less likely that I would find a positive relationship between the group's political activity and policy outcomes in its favor. It would bias the estimates downward.

I do not have a way of cleanly sorting this out empirically in this book. Most of the estimates of interest group influence in the following chapters are suggestive of causal relationships, but I recognize the limitations of the design and acknowledge that they need to be viewed and interpreted with a proper dose of caution and skepticism. That said, I would apply the same dose of caution and skepticism to studies using some seemingly more sophisticated causal inference methods to study interest group influence. One could imagine, for example, a study leveraging an exogenous shock that affects interest group activity to then examine how policy changes or does not change in the aftermath. Alternatively, one could imagine a difference-in-differences analysis of how within-unit changes in interest group activity are related to within-unit changes in policy. As I explained in chapter 2, these types of studies would be far less likely to detect interest group influence even if it exists. If interest group influence on policy is a slow-moving process, such that a group's policy gains accumulate slowly and gradually over time, anyone looking within a limited temporal window for a relationship between change in interest group activity and change in policy is unlikely to find it. Because of the empirical designs, many would view studies of this sort as more credible—and the null results more believable. But if the process of interest group influence works in the way I have proposed, those null results could be leading to the wrong inference. My cross-sectional analysis is a good empirical design for the causal process that I propose is at work, even with all its problems.

Mass Publics, Party, and Ideology

With the task now being the study of influence, it is important to discuss the political force that has received the lion's share of scholarly attention in research on political representation: mass publics. There are of course other factors that might be important in shaping local public policy, such as political institutions and city size (which I account for in my analyses), but the potential influence of mass publics deserves special attention up front. It has been central to the way political scientists have studied political representation and influence. Some have gone so far as to *define* responsiveness as the link between policies and public opinion. In some ways, it seems that the default expectation is that policies would be responsive to public opinion and that the onus is on the researcher to show otherwise.

I therefore take steps to account for the possibility that the policies I examine are explained by variation in the preferences of mass publics. Doing so in a satisfying way, however, is more difficult than it might seem. The major practical constraint is that there are no existing datasets of city residents' views on core local issues for any large number of cities—especially not for the kinds of local policies I examine. We simply do not know what people's positions are on economic development, growth, housing, police protection, fire protection, local public finance, or work rules for local employees in these hundreds of municipal governments. Until recently, researchers usually relied on proxies for local residents' opinions on local issues, such as variables describing the city's racial composition or the share of its residents who are homeowners. I include those variables in my analysis, and for some of the policies I explore, it is reasonable to assume something about the preferences of those subgroups of city residents. For example, the share of homeowners in a city may be a pretty good proxy for public opinion on multifamily housing development. In general, however, this is a very rough way of accounting for local residents' policy preferences.

An increasingly popular alternative is to use measures of city residents' partisanship or ideology to account for mass preferences in local governments,[50] and I incorporate those measures into my analysis as well: both the local-level two-party vote that went to Obama in 2012 and (alternatively) Tausanovitch and Warshaw's estimates of local citizen ideology.[51] In one way, these measures are preferable to using demographic variables as proxies: they are direct measures of city residents' preferences. However, I do not actually expect local Democratic presidential vote or the Tausanovitch and Warshaw ideology scores to be strong predictors of most of the local policies I examine. And given that there are now several studies concluding that party and ideology matter in local politics, that requires some explanation.

First, it is important to be clear that while Democratic presidential vote and the Tausanovitch and Warshaw ideology scores are undeniably measures of partisanship and ideology at the local *level*, that does not mean they are measures of preferences and positions on local government *issues*. Actually, these measures are more appropriately viewed as local-level preferences or positions on mostly *national* issues. And there is reason to doubt that city residents' nationally forged partisanship and ideology would be highly correlated with their positions on the main issues that animate municipal government.[52]

This is easiest to see for local-level measures of how people voted in US presidential elections: it is not obvious whether citizens' choices on the major parties' presidential candidates would be highly correlated with their views on local economic development, zoning, police and fire protection, and sewers and roads. Tausanovitch and Warshaw decouple the measurement of local-level preferences from the positions of presidential candidates, instead scaling policy question data from large national public opinion surveys, but most of the policy questions asked on those national surveys are about national policy issues, not core local government issues. Thus, the end result—their measure of mass ideology—is more a measure of local-level preferences on national issues than a measure of citizens' preferences on local government issues.[53] Because local issues are substantively different, it is far from clear that citizens' views on them would correlate strongly with their views on the national matters that divide the major political parties and define national-level ideology.

The reality is that the strength of any such link probably depends on the issue. If the substance of some local issue or decision is related to the substance of some national issue that divides the major parties, such as the environment, then it is perhaps reasonable to expect local residents' preferences on the local matter to be correlated with their national-level partisanship or ideology. But many local policy issues, such as policing, are cross-cutting and not a comfortable fit within the national party system. Other local issues, services, and priorities seem to have little partisan dimension, such as efforts to attract jobs to the city or having a well-functioning sewer system. It is not clear how national-level partisanship or ideology would be connected to residents' preferences on these local matters.

What is more, there is now a sizable empirical literature on the role of party and ideology in local politics, and the findings and conclusions are quite mixed. A handful of studies estimate whether the party affiliations of local elected officials predict local government spending, climate policies, and immigration enforcement, and while some find effects of partisanship,[54] others do not.[55] Then there are studies finding that the estimated ideologies of local residents (the Tausanovitch and Warshaw scores) and presidential vote predict local policy outcomes, including fiscal outcomes like total spending and policies related to sustainability.[56] Importantly, these empirical relationships are the basis of claims that local elected officials are responsive to the mass citizenry. And yet some newer public opinion studies find evidence that people's nationally forged party affiliations and views on national policy issues often do not map well onto their preferences on local government issues.[57]

On the basis of theory and the available empirical evidence, then, I do not expect that local residents' national-level partisanship and ideology will have strong relationships with most local government policies—especially core local government policies and especially the policies I examine in the following chapters. It is far from obvious how party and nationally oriented ideology of the mass public would relate to public opinion on local issues like economic development and growth, business tax expenditures, and firefighter salaries.

160   CHAPTER SIX

And that is assuming that mass publics even have well-developed views on these policies. On some local matters, they probably do. On others, it seems less likely. The crystallization of public attitudes on local issues is very likely correlated with the directness and visibility of the policies' costs. It seems quite plausible, for example, that local residents—especially homeowners—would have well-developed views on matters of local housing development. But how many residents would we expect to have strong views on their city's use of business tax expenditures? Before 2020, or even during 2020, how many city residents would we expect to have well-defined preferences on police spending? My point is that even if I could get access to public opinion data on these issues for hundreds of cities, I would not expect them to be strong predictors of many local policies. I would instead anticipate that most local residents do not have well-developed preferences on many of these issues and that they do not vote on the basis of them anyway—if they vote in local elections at all.

I cannot test for these things, of course. There is a wide-open research agenda for political behavior scholars interested in learning about people's views on and knowledge about core local government issues and how those issues do or do not factor into their vote choices and other political activities. For the time being, I incorporate mass preferences using the data currently available: city demographics, two-party presidential vote, and the Tausanovitch and Warshaw ideology scores. I do not expect them to matter much for the policies I examine, with the exception of homeownership rates and housing. And I would expect much the same even if I had better data on city-level public opinion on these issues. In the local government context, there are many reasons to doubt that city officials would design policies with an eye toward representing the interests of all adult city residents. Low voter turnout and scarce media coverage are just two of them. In contrast, when the conditions are right, interest groups are very focused, know what they want, and are active and engaged in politics, and there is good reason to expect that they are sometimes effective in pushing policy in their favor.

Conclusion

This chapter has laid important groundwork for the empirical analyses to come. The broad theoretical framework I developed in chapter 2 suggests that the extent of interest group influence is specific to both inter-

INFLUENCE: ISSUES, APPROACH, AND EXPECTATIONS

est groups and policies. It should depend on the homogeneity of a given group's interests in a policy, whether its interests conflict with those of other political actors on the policy, and whether it is politically focused on the issue. That means that moving from the broad theory to specific expectations requires selecting policies and interest groups to focus on—and some justification for that selection. Here I have explained my decision to focus on local economic development and growth and public safety provision. These are issue areas that are central to what municipal governments do. They feature theoretically relevant variation. And they are also issue areas with existing research literatures from which I could draw insights.

Using and building on these literatures, I formulated some more specific expectations for how interest groups will (or will not) influence outcomes in these two broad local policy areas—expectations that are specific to group-policy pairs. In general, I expect that businesses and developers have homogeneous preferences on the various economic development and growth outcomes and that public safety unions have homogeneous preferences on the various public safety outcomes. For these main groups, however, I expect the extent of their influence to depend on whether they are going against or with the grain. If the group is pushing for policies that are in line with what other actors would want to do otherwise, influence should be more limited. If the group is pushing for policies distinct from the interests of other political actors, the group's political activity should make a more pronounced difference to the outcome.

How active will the likely opposition be for these main groups and policies? The answer depends on the homogeneity of the group's interests in the policy and the form of the policy's trade-offs. For some group-policy pairs, the group may not even be homogeneously opposed to the policy, in which case the relationship between its political activity and that policy outcome is theoretically ambiguous. Even if the group's preferences are homogeneous, moreover, the likelihood that it will be politically active and focused on the issue depends on whether the policy's costs are direct, immediate, visible, and attributable to specific governmental decisions. Land use issues are more likely to generate effective opposition than issues with budgetary or managerial discretion trade-offs. These, then, are my expectations for how the political activity of interest groups will affect policy outcomes—and thus their influence.

In my analysis of interest group influence in the chapters that follow, I also take into account the potential for voters and residents to influence the policies I examine. However, because of both the shortcomings of the available measures of residents' preferences and my skepticism about how much these detailed policy decisions are made in response to residents' preferences, I do not expect to find clear relationships in most cases. When it comes to high-conflict areas in which subsets of residents have been shown to be highly engaged, such as homeowners on matters of housing development, there is reason to expect local governments to be responsive to them. But I do not expect that local residents' partisan or ideological leanings will matter for these local policies, nor would I expect most city residents to be knowledgeable about, attentive to, and focused on them.

Interest groups are different. They have their eye on the prize. I expect that under favorable conditions, their activity will make a difference. I turn to this question next.

CHAPTER SEVEN

Business and Growth

Economic development and growth is a natural place to begin an empirical analysis of interest group influence on local policy. Economic development is central to what municipal governments do and a major focus of city officials just about everywhere. It is also an area in which some of the most active interest groups in local politics—chambers of commerce and developers—likely have relatively homogeneous, concentrated interests, because when a city grows, builds, and becomes an economically strong, business-friendly place, businesses as a whole are better off. In this chapter, I evaluate whether cities with more politically active business communities have more pro-growth, business-friendly policies.

This is a difficult empirical endeavor. While I now have measures of interest group political activity for hundreds of cities, there are very few datasets of policies in US local governments. Most of the datasets that exist cover only some of the policies that are of greatest theoretical relevance, as I discuss below, and most of them also include only a sample of cities—often the largest ones and not necessarily the same cities that are covered by my data on local interest group activity. Moreover, while my focus here is on how business political activity influences policy, city policies may also influence the amount of business political activity. Making headway therefore calls for creativity and flexibility—as well as some tolerance for less than ideal design and measurement.

I proceed by casting a wide net and analyzing a variety of different policies related to economic development and growth. I rely on several different datasets, some of which align with my interest group activity data for only a few hundred municipal governments, others of which align for most of them. Importantly, these datasets span several aspects of economic development and growth—in ways related to the dimensions of my theoretical expectations. First, to provide the broadest overview of cities' economic development policies and practices, I use the 2014 Economic Development Survey dataset from the ICMA. Second, I turn my focus to the use of business tax incentives, relying on data on cities' tax abatement policies. Third, to investigate the politics of growth policies with clear land use implications, I analyze local housing development using both the 2016 US Census data on building permits and a 2006 dataset on land use procedures collected by Joseph Gyourko, Albert Saiz, and Anita Summers.[1] Together, these data provide a broad look at growth and development policies in municipal governments and allow me to evaluate whether, when, and the extent to which business groups influence them.

Overview of Local Economic Development and Growth Policies

To begin this discussion, it helps to get a sense of what, exactly, is meant by economic development and growth: what cities' goals are in this area and what kinds of policies they make in pursuit of those goals. For this purpose, I turn to data from the ICMA 2014 Economic Development Survey, which was mailed to 5,237 municipal and county governments in June 2014 and had a response rate of 23% (960 municipalities and 241 counties).[2] The ICMA survey includes questions about local governments' economic development goals, priorities, motivations, and obstacles, as well as some detail on what local governments do to pursue those goals.

The first important pattern that emerges in these data is that nearly all municipal governments are involved in developing local economic development strategies. Seventy percent of the cities indicate that their municipal government has *primary* responsibility for economic development, and an additional 7% say that their government shares primary responsibility with some other entity, such as a county or an economic development corporation. When I add in cities that indicate that their government *participates* in developing economic development strategies, the number reaches 97%. Therefore, nearly all municipal governments are active in making local economic development policies.

The survey also asks local governments to indicate whether five particular goals are priorities for them in developing their economic development plans: jobs, the tax base, quality of life, environmental sustainability, and social equity. The most common priorities for municipal governments are jobs (92%), the tax base (95%), and quality of life (92%). Only 52% report prioritizing environmental sustainability in their economic development strategies, and an even smaller share prioritize social equity (31%). The survey also asks local governments to explain why they adopt the economic development priorities they do, asking them to rate a list of possible motivations. The two motivations with the highest average ratings for municipal governments are "change in local economy" and "increased competition." "Concern about environmental sustainability" and "income inequality" are less commonly cited. This is broadly consistent with Peterson's account of cities:[3] in making developmental policies, city officials are mostly focused on strengthening the local economy and the tax base.

What, specifically, are cities doing to pursue those goals? What are the policies? On this point, the ICMA survey asks municipal governments to rate their use of 32 different economic development tools on a four-point scale from 0 (not at all) to 3 (high). I present the average rating for each of the activities in figure 7.1. In addition, the survey asks cities to indicate their level of use of 16 types of business incentives on the same four-point scale. In figure 7.2, I show the average rating for each type of incentive across all the cities in the ICMA dataset.

Two interesting patterns emerge in figure 7.1. The first is that some of the "tools" that local governments report being most important—such as "high-quality infrastructure" and "investments in high quality of life"— are not really tools or policies but rather aspirations or goals. And they are goals that presumably many cities would want, not just for economic development purposes, but also to be responsive to residents and other non-business constituencies. Moreover, the survey data do not tell us what cities are doing to invest in infrastructure and quality of life, only that they "use" them for economic development. Analytically, these variables are not as useful as some of the others, but it is nonetheless worth highlighting that city officials view high quality of life and infrastructure as some of the most important ways of developing the local economy.

Second, and relatedly, many of the economic development tools asked about in the ICMA survey seem difficult to object to: their costs are either ambiguous or small. Consider some of the most commonly used economic development tools: calling on prospective companies, surveying local businesses, and engaging in promotional and advertising activities. The costs and trade-offs of making calls to prospective

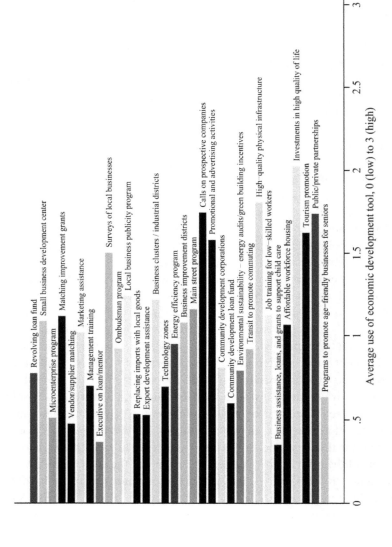

FIGURE 7.1 Municipal government use of economic development tools

BUSINESS AND GROWTH

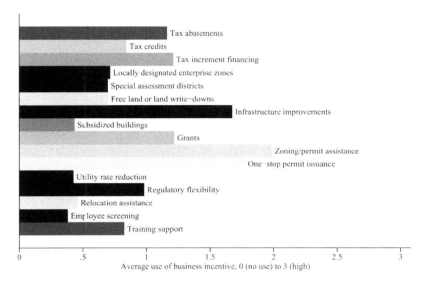

FIGURE 7.2 Municipal government use of business incentives

companies are ambiguous. Surveying local businesses and engaging in promotional and advertising activities may cost money, but those costs are probably small relative to the city budget. With such small and ambiguous costs, these pro-business, pro-growth policies may not engender much opposition. They instead seem like fairly straightforward things for a city to do if it is pursuing economic development.

What about municipal governments' use of business incentives, shown in figure 7.2? The picture there is somewhat different, because some of the more widely used incentives have clear associated costs. When cities offer businesses tax abatement, tax credits, grants, and tax increment financing, the result is either lower local tax revenue or the redirection of tax revenue to designated, business-friendly purposes (at least in the short run). But a number of the other widely used business incentives shown in figure 7.2 do not have obvious costs, such as providing assistance with zoning and permits. Infrastructure improvements, by contrast, certainly have costs, but they could be desired by a wide range of constituencies—not just business. And while offering businesses free land, subsidized buildings, or utility rate reduction all carry costs, these practices are far less common within the cities in the dataset.

Does this imply that the most common local economic development policies have small or ambiguous costs? Figures 7.1 and 7.2 might at first seem to suggest this—with the exception of business tax incentives and the like—but the answer is no. The reason is that (other than business tax incentives) the economic development and growth policies with the clearest costs cannot easily be assessed with a large survey: that is, economic development policies with land use costs. The ICMA data do not include measures of what cities do to develop land, not because of any shortcoming of the ICMA survey, but rather because decisions like building a business complex or expanding a road are specific to time and place and are thus less conducive to measurement through a survey. These kinds of policies are a crucial component of local economic development, and they do have costs. But they are the kinds of policies that are hard to ask about in a large survey.[4]

Exploring the politics of economic development therefore requires going beyond the ICMA survey data and analyzing policies with different kinds of costs. These cost considerations are directly relevant to my expectations for interest group influence. In general, local businesses and business groups probably have relatively homogeneous preferences on policies that make a city a business-friendly place, but whether their political activity influences those policies should depend on (1) whether their preferences are distinct from those of other political actors and (2) whether they focus their political energy on the issue. Moreover, the nature of the costs should affect the political focus of those opposed to the policies. When the costs of a policy are small or ambiguous, I do not expect the activity of any potential opposing groups to matter much. For policies like business tax incentives, the downsides are clearer, but they are primarily budgetary in nature, so it still isn't clear that focused, forceful opposition would emerge. Policies with land use costs are different: the costs are so visible and direct that it is more likely that those bearing the brunt of those costs will be activated and politically focused. In what follows, I test these expectations by analyzing three sets of economic development and growth policies that vary in key dimensions of the theoretical framework.

Policies with Small or Ambiguous Costs

I begin with the economic development policies for which I do not expect to see evidence of business or other group influence: those with small or ambiguous costs (see fig. 7.1). It's not that business groups do not have an interest in these policies. Surely they do. Chambers of commerce represent the interests of their business members, and these economic development tools may help make the city friendlier to business. While developers may not be politically focused on them (because most developers are not tied to a particular community), local chambers of commerce probably are. But I do not expect the activity of chambers of commerce to make much difference to these policies because city officials interested in maintaining a strong local economy would probably want to pursue them even without pressure from business. For these policies, the interests of chambers of commerce are not distinct from the interests of local officials.

I would not expect to see active, effective opposition to these policies either. Neighborhood associations and environmental groups are sometimes discussed as anti-growth forces, but it is unlikely that they would be monitoring cities' activities in surveying local businesses and connecting them to threats to their interests.[5] Likewise, local homeowners are probably not paying attention to whether a city is making pro-business moves such as calling on prospective businesses. And while some might expect more conservative cities to be more pro-business—and more likely to use these economic development tools—I do not expect nationally forged ideology and partisanship to matter here. Even if residents were paying attention to what cities are doing to try to attract and retain businesses, their views on what their city should and should not be doing need not be strongly correlated with their views on national issues.[6]

An interesting implication of all this is that economic development policies with small or ambiguous costs are actually a good fit for Peterson's model—a model in which traditional "political" considerations matter little, and policy variation across cities is mainly shaped by structural characteristics of cities.[7] I expect that city characteristics like size and affluence will probably affect the degree to which cities use these economic development tools. And if cities focus on economic development in large part because of competitive pressure, those that face greater competition from other jurisdictions should rely more heavily on these tools as well.

To test these expectations, I used the ICMA data on economic development tool usage summarized in figure 7.1. Because a thorough analysis of each of these variables would take a great deal of time, I created an index for each city, averaging the city's use of the tools in figure 7.1 except for the problematic ones I discussed earlier, such as high-quality infrastructure.[8] I then merged into the ICMA data my measures of city-level interest group activity. First, I merged the data from the City Interest Groups Survey, which contain the most general measures of interest group activity in each city. There are 155 cities in this dataset that are also in the ICMA survey data. I then merged the data from the City Elections Survey, which has measures of interest groups' activity in local elections (which, as I have shown, look very similar to the overall measures of interest group activity). This provides interest group activity information for an additional 76 cities in the ICMA survey data, bringing the total dataset to 231 cities.[9]

This number, though not large, is sufficient for getting a glimpse of what predicts the use of these economic development tools. I use OLS to regress the economic development tool index on the interest group activity variables that correspond to the groups I mentioned above: chambers of commerce, developers, neighborhood associations, and environmental groups. I also include the activity of building trade unions and taxpayer groups because they may be pro-growth, although like the other groups, I do not expect their activity to be positively associated with the use of these low-cost economic development tools. In addition to the interest group variables, I include most of the independent variables from earlier chapters: log population, log per capita income, percent homeowner, Democratic presidential vote, percent Black, percent Latino, percent rural, and the four indicators of city political institutions.[10] Finally, I add an indicator of the strength of local competition, which equals 1 for cities that reported on the ICMA survey that "competition is strong" for "economic development and tax base among local governments" in their region and 0 otherwise. Because of the relatively small sample size, I do not include fixed effects for each state but rather indicators for three of the four geographic regions in the United States. I cluster the standard errors by state.

The coefficient estimates and 95% confidence intervals for the main variables of interest are presented in figure 7.3. (In the interest of space, I do not present the coefficient estimates for some of the demographic variables and political institutions. Tests are two-tailed.) The results are broadly as expected: use of these economic development tools is best explained by demographic and competitive differences between the cities.

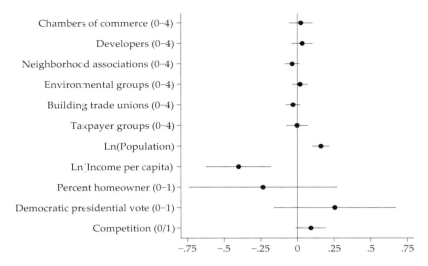

FIGURE 7.3 Use of economic development tools

Larger cities with lower per capita income report significantly higher use of these economic development tools. So do officials in cities that report strong competition with other jurisdictions in the region ($p = 0.08$). And none of the interest group activity variables—whether they are business groups or any other—are significant predictors of how much cities use these economic development tools. The share of city residents who are homeowners and the proportion who vote Democratic in presidential elections have statistically insignificant coefficients as well.[11]

Even as a merely suggestive set of results, this helps establish an important baseline. Many of the actions municipal governments take to strengthen or protect the local economy have small or ambiguous costs. For those policies, it is not always apparent who the political losers are—if there are any. Moreover, the interests of business on these policies are very likely aligned with the interests of city officials. Because of this, on these policies, we should expect little overt political conflict, little influence from political variables, and little sign that the political activity of the business community makes a difference to what cities do. And that is what I find. For these economic development policies, patterns seem to follow Peterson's model: it is mainly the structural characteristics of cities that explain the extent of their use.[12]

Tax Incentives for Businesses

Offering businesses tax breaks to entice them to move to or stay within the city is more likely to raise some objections. At a minimum, these tax breaks mean less tax revenue in city coffers in the short run and less money for local public service provision. The economic benefits of tax abatement are also disputed. With tax abatement, then, there is a clearer trade-off and greater potential for conflict, and I expect the political dynamics to vary accordingly.

To get oriented to the politics of business incentives, it is useful to consult Nathan Jensen and Edmund Malesky's book, *Incentives to Pander*.[13] Jensen and Malesky explain that governments around the world use a variety of tools to persuade business firms to locate, expand, or remain in a particular area rather than move to another jurisdiction. And economists tend to be skeptical that such policies deliver benefits: most research suggests that the incentives have little effect on firms' decisions about where to locate or that the effects are modest,[14] and the evidence is also mixed as to whether they generate job growth and expand tax revenue in the longer term.[15] Regardless, the use of such incentives is on the rise in the United States, and Jensen and Malesky argue that the reasons for that increase are mainly political. Most voters, they explain, care about the state of the economy and believe such incentives work. Politicians, on the other hand, know that there is little economic rationale for the incentives but offer them anyway—and advertise that fact—so that they can credibly claim that they did everything in their power to attract business to the city. At election time, voters reward that behavior. And in an empirical test, Jensen and Malesky show that cities with mayor-council governments—where city chief executives face electoral pressure—offer more generous tax incentives to businesses (although are not more likely to offer incentives in the first place).[16]

This is an important advance in the study of the politics of business incentives. As it stands, though, it is a model focused on the linkages between elected officials and voters, and the key source of variation exploited in the empirical analysis of US municipal governments is variation in political institutions (mayor-council as opposed to council-manager government). An important next step is to consider how businesses and other interest groups might shape the extent of local government tax abatement.

Theoretical Considerations and Expectations

As a general rule, it is probably safe to assume that the local business community—including both chambers of commerce and developers—have fairly homogeneous preferences in favor of the practice of offering incentives to businesses. The incentives make a city friendlier to business as a whole. But there is good reason to think that advocating for tax incentives is mainly a priority of chambers of commerce, not developers or any individual businesses other than the ones getting the tax breaks, because chambers are the organizations invested in enhancing the overall business-friendliness of their communities.

On this issue, moreover, the preferences of chambers of commerce are not necessarily aligned with the preferences of elected officials. To see this, it helps to reconsider the incentives of elected officials to offer business tax incentives. While Jensen and Malesky set out to explain why elected officials would offer such incentives given their unclear economic benefits, it does seem that elected officials' political incentives are mixed on the issue. If voters make decisions in local elections based on the state of the local economy, or on whether local incumbents have successfully maintained some balance of low taxes and quality service provision, local officials probably do not unequivocally favor business tax incentives. After all, the tax incentives may not actually help the local economy. They also reduce tax revenue, potentially leading to cuts to services. And if local voters are not paying attention to the actions local officials are taking to improve the local economy and instead focus only on economic and service provision outcomes, then local officials might opt to not offer business tax incentives. It is only when voters know officials are offering the incentives and think those incentives will work (and are unaware of the trade-offs) that elected officials' incentives should tip in favor of offering and advertising tax breaks to businesses.

Jensen and Malesky show that voters who are told about their governors' use of business tax incentives do tend to support those efforts. Moreover, they show that even at the state level, Democrats are not less supportive of their governors' use of tax incentives than Republicans, so this does not appear to be a partisan issue. Still, only 25% of their survey respondents report having knowledge of their state's investment incentives. Jensen and Malesky note that this is large enough for pandering on the issue of tax incentives to have electoral payoffs for state officials.[17] It does, however, raise the question of how much local voters know about their local governments' use of tax incentives. While there are no existing data that can answer the question definitively, voters probably know even less about their local governments' use of tax incentives than their state's.

This suggests that for local officials, incentives are not universally in favor of offering more and larger tax abatement to businesses; those politicians actually have to wrestle with a more complicated set of considerations. It is instead the business community, organized in local chambers of commerce, that has the clearest incentive to advocate for tax abatement. This is important, because it suggests that the interests of business and chambers of commerce may often not be aligned with the interests of elected officials on this issue. Unlike the policies analyzed earlier, business tax incentives are an issue on which businesses and local chambers of commerce are often swimming upstream, pushing elected officials to do something they might not otherwise want to do on their own. At a minimum, on the question of why cities continue to offer tax incentives when the economic benefits are so unclear, we should consider the possibility that they are doing it because businesses and local chambers of commerce are pressuring them to do it.

This provides some theoretical structure for how we should think about the interests of businesses, chambers of commerce, elected officials, and possibly voters on the issue of business tax incentives. But what about potentially opposing groups? It is not obvious what the preferences of neighborhood associations and environmental groups would be, nor is the position of taxpayer groups straightforward: they might oppose tax breaks if they reduce the tax base, but they might favor tax breaks because they lower taxes for businesses.

The nature of the trade-off also suggests that opposing groups might not be politically focused and active on the issue of business tax incentives. As I alluded to earlier, the broad societal benefits stemming from the use of business tax incentives are unclear, and if they exist, they are indirect and in the future. The costs of tax incentives, by contrast, are clear and immediate—but they are in budgetary form. They are not visible in the physical sense, as a building or a road would be. Tax incentives therefore do not directly threaten green space or the property value of local homeowners. The main way the negative impacts of business tax incentives might be experienced is through a decrease in services, but those decreases are probably slight and not perceived by most.[18] Thus, while local chambers of commerce are likely to be focused on and in

BUSINESS AND GROWTH

favor of business tax incentives, the budgetary nature of the costs makes it questionable whether there will be effective opposition to them.

Data

I evaluate these expectations by employing data on the use of tax incentives for businesses, by which I mean arrangements in which local governments offer businesses some reduction in taxes for relocating to or staying in the jurisdiction.[19] Business incentives can take a variety of forms, but the two most common are tax abatement and job creation tax credits, which together made up about 70% of all incentive costs in the United States as of 2015.[20] Tax abatement is especially analytically useful because it is an arrangement in which the local government gives a business a credit that reduces or eliminates its local tax payments, usually property tax payments. By contrast, with job creation tax credits, a firm receives tax benefits if it increases local jobs or payroll,[21] so the benefit to the business is contingent on its economic impact.

The ICMA survey data introduced earlier is a useful first stop in the empirical analysis, because the survey asks municipal government respondents to rate their use of two relevant tools: tax abatement and tax credits.[22] As I described earlier, cities rated their use of each tool on a four-point scale from 0 (no use) to 3 (high). Because it is unclear from the survey wording how tax abatement is different from tax credits, I treat them as substitutes and create a dependent variable equal to the maximum rating of the two variables within each city. Therefore, if a city reports high use of either tax abatement or tax credits, the city is coded as 3. A city is coded as 0 if it reports no use of either tax abatement or tax credits.

In their analysis of municipal tax incentives, Jensen and Malesky find that mayor-council government does not make use of tax incentives more likely but is associated with higher amounts of tax abatement.[23] Because of this and because the ICMA survey data only align with some of the cities in my interest group activity datasets, I also analyze a new dataset of the amount of local tax abatement in all the municipal governments included in the City Interest Groups Survey dataset.

As of 2016, the Government Accounting Standards Board (GASB) requires government entities to include in their comprehensive annual financial reports information about "limitations on revenue-raising capacity resulting from government programs that use tax abatements to induce behavior by individuals and entities that is beneficial to the government or its citizens."[24] Thanks to GASB Statement No. 77, therefore, governments are now technically required to disclose a description of any tax abatement agreements they have and the dollar amount of taxes abated during the reporting period.

However, as of fiscal year 2018, many local governments were still not in compliance with GASB 77. Good Jobs First, an organization that tracks the use of these incentives, finds that in the nation's 100 largest cities, only 71 of the cities' 2018 financial reports included the required GASB 77 note.[25] For the remaining 29 cities, one cannot tell from the reports whether they do not have tax abatement or simply did not report it. Even so, this is a major shift toward transparency about tax abatement, and we can potentially learn a great deal about the extent of tax abatement for the cities that are in compliance.

With all this in mind, I collected data on the total value of tax abatement in 2018 from all the cities in the City Interest Groups dataset. For the largest cities—most of those with 50,000 residents or more—I relied on data collected and generously shared by Nathan Jensen and Venus Shaghaghi.[26] I then acquired the 2018 comprehensive annual financial reports for the small to mid-size cities and collected information on tax abatement from the GASB 77 note in each one. At the time of this data collection (fall 2019), these reports were available for 87% of the cities, and 47% of those were compliant with GASB 77.[27] Thus, in addition to the 0–3 indicator of tax incentive use from the ICMA survey, I analyze the amount of tax abatement per capita in these cities.

Results

Starting with the ICMA indicator, of the cities included in the models that follow, 33% report no use of tax abatement or tax credits, 23% report low use, 26% report medium use, and the remaining 18% report high use. I model this dependent variable with all the independent variables from earlier: the interest group activity variables, city demographics, Democratic presidential vote, the ICMA survey measure of regional competitiveness, local political institutions, and regional fixed effects. The coefficient estimates and standard errors for most of the variables are summarized in table 7.1, column 1. I also present the coefficient estimates for the main interest group variables in the left-hand graph of figure 7.4.

BUSINESS AND GROWTH 177

TABLE 7.1 **Municipal government use of business tax incentives**

	(1)	(2)
Chambers of commerce	0.167**	0.121
	(0.076)	(0.082)
Developers	−0.038	−0.036
	(0.058)	(0.069)
Neighborhood associations	−0.109*	−0.097*
	(0.056)	(0.050)
Environmental groups	−0.05	−0.03
	(0.060)	(0.063)
Building trade unions	0.06	0.13
	(0.061)	(0.082)
Taxpayer groups	−0.003	0.003
	(0.066)	(0.087)
Ln(Population)	0.297**	0.216
	(0.142)	(0.167)
Ln(Income per capita)	−1.104***	−0.829
	(0.393)	(0.535)
Percent homeowner	1.011	0.768
	(0.800)	(1.081)
Strong competition	0.167	0.143
	(0.128)	(0.167)
Democratic presidential vote	−0.277	−0.831
	(0.355)	(0.660)
R−squared	0.4	0.5
Observations	212	212

Notes: Dependent variable is a 0–3 index of cities' use of business tax incentives. Model 1 includes regional fixed effects; model 2 includes state fixed effects. Both models include additional demographics and political institutions. Standard errors clustered by state.

*p < 0.1, **p < 0.05, ***p < 0.01 (two-tailed).

As with the economic development tool index, city size and income per capita are significantly associated with tax incentive use, but here I find that the political activity of chambers of commerce matters as well. The coefficient on chamber of commerce political activity is 0.167, significant at the 5% level. This indicates that, on average, a two-point increase in chamber of commerce political activity (e.g., from slightly active to very active) is associated with an increase in tax incentive use by about a third of a point on the 0–3 index. In column 2, I add state fixed effects to the model, keeping in mind that this places heavy demands on this relatively small dataset. The coefficient on the political activity of chambers of commerce is smaller and less precisely estimated than in column 1, but it is still positive (p = 0.149), suggesting that more political activity by local chambers of commerce is associated with slightly greater use of business tax incentives, as reported by local officials.

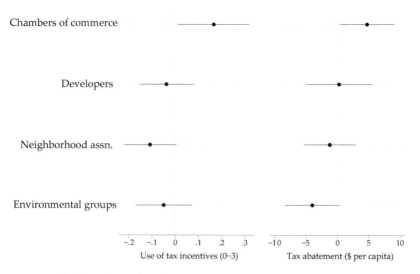

FIGURE 7.4 Tax incentives and tax abatement

By contrast, the political activity of most of the other interest groups seems to matter less—or at least less consistently. While developers are very active in local politics generally, the extent of their activity does not have a relationship to cities' reliance on business tax incentives. Neither is the political activity of environmental groups associated with tax incentive use, which is as expected given the ambiguity of their preferences and their low likelihood of being politically focused on the issue.[28] The one exception is the coefficient on the political activity of neighborhood associations: in both columns, it is negative and significant. Thus, it does look as though local governments report less reliance on business tax incentives in cities with more active neighborhood associations.[29]

Neither the share of city residents who are homeowners nor city residents' partisan leanings are significant predictors of cities' reliance on business tax incentives, as expected. Homeowners are often cited as active in opposition to housing development, but the costs of business tax incentives are budgetary and less visible. And Jensen and Malesky provide evidence that business tax incentives are not a partisan issue even at the state level, and even when voters are informed about them.[30] The theoretical case for partisanship on the issue is even weaker at the local

BUSINESS AND GROWTH

level, and table 7.1 shows that the share of city residents who vote for Democratic presidential candidates is not associated with cities' use of business tax incentives.

I turn next to the data on revenue lost to tax abatement.[31] For each city for which this information was available, I calculate the total value of revenue lost to tax abatement in 2018 per city resident. This value ranges widely across these cities, and there is a pronounced right skew to the distribution. A quarter of the cities lost less than $1.48 per city resident. The median is $6.02 per capita, and the 75th percentile is $18.81. But a small number of cities lost large amounts of revenue to tax abatement. Five percent lost more than $100 per capita, and five cities report having lost considerably larger amounts.

In modeling this dependent variable, I use two different approaches to deal with this right skew. In the first set of models, I model the dollar value of tax abatement per capita, excluding the five large outliers. In the second, I log the dependent variable, which drops cities with $0 in tax abatement. The distribution of logged tax abatement per capita has some outliers on the low end, so I exclude from the second set of models cities where the dependent variable is less than 1.5 times the interquartile range below the first quartile.[32]

Column 1 of table 7.2 starts with the model of tax revenue abated per capita, including the same set of predictors as before, except for the indicator of regional competition (which was only available in the ICMA survey dataset). I also present the main interest group coefficients graphically in the right-hand plot of figure 7.4. The estimates show that cities with more politically active chambers of commerce have significantly higher tax revenue abated. A two-unit change in the activity of chambers of commerce (e.g., from slightly active to very active) is associated with an additional $9.50 in tax revenue lost per city resident. Tellingly, the relationship is positive for chambers of commerce, not developers. For developers, there is no indication that more revenue is lost to tax abatement in cities where they are more politically active.[33]

The findings are broadly the same in column 2, where I add state fixed effects to this model, and in columns 3 and 4, where I estimate the same models but with logged tax abatement per capita as the dependent variable. In all three sets of results, more chamber of commerce political activity is associated with a larger amount of tax revenue lost to abatement. In columns 3 and 4 in particular, I find that, on average, a two-point increase in chamber of commerce activity is associated with

TABLE 7.2 **Local revenue lost to tax abatement, 2018**

	Revenue Lost per Capita		Ln(Revenue Lost per Capita	
	(1)	(2)	(3)	(4)
Chambers of commerce	4.754**	4.838*	0.299**	0.301*
	(2.132)	(2.738)	(0.124)	(0.160)
Developers	0.233	−0.49	−0.027	0.085
	(2.634)	(2.902)	(0.183)	(0.231)
Neighborhood associations	−1.226	−2.367	−0.107	−0.246*
	(2.049)	(2.338)	(0.124)	(0.140)
Environmental groups	−4.00*	−4.701*	−0.35*	−0.435*
	(2.151)	(2.737)	(0.177)	(0.253)
Building trade unions	1.483	0.586	0.041	0.025
	(1.899)	(2.185)	(0.133)	(0.179)
Taxpayer groups	−0.462	−0.925	0.01	0.002
	(2.411)	(2.884)	(0.151)	(0.188)
Ln(Population)	−0.312	1.108	0.021	0.062
	(2.125)	(2.674)	(0.148)	(0.185)
Ln(Income per capita)	10.922	2.885	0.955	0.759
	(6.718)	(10.131)	(0.578)	(0.953)
Percent homeowner	17.299	0.215	0.597	0.204
	(21.610)	(16.817)	(1.390)	(1.928)
Democratic presidential vote	−8.064	−4.141	−0.885	−0.574
	(20.574)	(31.855)	(1.327)	(2.048)
R-squared	0.12	0.34	0.14	0.31
Observations	185	185	170	170

Notes: Standard errors clustered by state in parentheses. Models 1 and 3 include regional fixed effects; models 2 and 4 include state fixed effects. All models include additional demographics and political institutions.

*p < 0.1, **p < 0.05, ***p < 0.01 (two-tailed).

an average 82% increase in tax revenue abated per capita. The activity of developers, by contrast, still has no discernible relationship with tax abatement.[34]

A look at potential opposition groups reveals interesting patterns as well. First, the coefficient on the political activity of neighborhood associations is negative, but it is only statistically significant in column 4. Thus, while greater activity by neighborhood associations was related to the extent of tax incentive use when the dependent variable was the ICMA 0–3 measure, it has a weaker relationship to the total amount of tax abated (in cities that report that information). But tax abatement amounts *do* tend to be lower in cities with more active environmental associations; the coefficients on environmental group activity are negative in all four models. In column 1 of table 7.2 and the right-hand graph in figure 7.4, the estimated coefficient is -4.00 (p = 0.071), indicating that a shift in environmental group activity from slightly active to very active is associated with an $8 decrease in revenue lost per capita.

Again, neither percent homeowner nor city residents' partisan leanings is a significant predictor of the tax abatement amounts. The same is true when I replace Democratic presidential vote with the Tausanovitch and Warshaw measures of city ideology:[35] in all four models, the coefficient is statistically insignificant (not shown). As I expected, these two characteristics of mass publics that are heavily emphasized in local politics research are unrelated to city reliance on business tax incentives.

The results in this section are illuminating both by themselves and in comparison to the earlier analysis of economic development tools with small and ambiguous costs. We see here that the amount of chamber of commerce political activity appears to make a difference to cities' use of business tax incentives. This is consistent with my argument that the difference a group makes to policy is contingent on whether the group's preferences are distinct from the preferences of other key political actors. For many of the economic development tools analyzed earlier, the costs were ambiguous or indirect, and thus there is little reason to expect anyone to object to them. For business tax incentives, the costs are clearer, and local elected officials are probably conflicted about whether to use them. In this case, then, business is swimming upstream, and we begin to see a relationship between their political activity and city policy.

That the relationship is positive for chambers of commerce and insignificant for developers is also notable. In urban politics accounts of cities as "growth machines,"[36] developers are depicted as powerful and influential on matters of growth and development. Yet here we have an important case where developers' political activity has no discernible relationship to local economic development policy. This cuts against accounts of developers as all-powerful, but it aligns well with my account in which developers focus their local political activity on matters that most directly affect them—and pay less attention to general efforts to make cities friendlier to business. Most developers are not locked into working within a particular city, so they do not need to invest heavily in such things. It makes sense, then, that their political activity would not be associated with greater use of tax incentives to attract business.

I also find some signs that cities with more active neighborhood associations and environmental groups tend to rely less on business tax incentives. The results are not as strong and consistent as those for chambers of commerce, but viewed together they suggest that effective organized opposition may emerge even when the costs of a policy are primarily budgetary. It could be that these opposition groups are actually attentive to local government budgets. It could also be that they anticipate the down-the-road land use costs that might come with any economic development and growth policy or that policy makers anticipate their likely objection when deciding whether to employ business tax incentives. A third possibility is that economic development and growth is a dimension of regular group conflict in many cities—one that consistently pits businesses and pro-growth interests against slow-growth groups like neighborhood associations and environmental groups across multiple issues.

My data analysis here cannot adjudicate between these different accounts. But if the third account is the right one—if economic development and growth is a defining issue of conflict in local politics, one that sorts players across multiple policies—the divide does not line up neatly with national partisan and ideological divisions. In every model I have estimated here, Democratic presidential vote does not have a significant relationship to cities' use of tax incentives. Business group political activity helps explain which cities are more reliant on business tax incentives, but variation in voters' political party commitments does not.

Land Use: Housing Development

Often the costs of economic development and growth policies are in the form of land use. For example, a new business complex might be an essential part of an effort to bring new jobs to a community, but it might also increase traffic and congestion or affect the views and values of nearby homes. And while many of the economic development policies I have discussed so far could eventually result in land use costs, the politics are likely to be different when those costs are direct and immediate, especially because land use costs are visible in a physical sense.

However, carrying out a quantitative analysis of economic development policies with land use costs requires a dependent variable that is comparable across cities: some kind of land use decision that almost all cities make on a regular basis, that can be measured, and that captures the degree to which local governments promote land development. And this is difficult to do. As I discussed earlier, it is not clear what kind of decision or policy one would ask cities about in a survey. Much of what cities do on land use is idiosyncratic—specific to particular cities and years.[37] One city might propose a new mixed-use development. A few years later it might propose a renovation of city hall. Another city might invest in the beautification of its business district. Cities are doing the same *kinds* of things—these are all about land use—but the particulars of what they are doing are different, and those differences affect the costs of the decisions. The costs, in turn, shape the politics.

Housing development is analytically useful in this regard. While there isn't complete overlap between housing development and economic development—cities sometimes work to attract more businesses and jobs without expanding the housing supply to match—building housing by definition involves land use. Moreover, almost all municipal governments have the authority to regulate how much housing is built, what kind of housing is built and where, and what processes must be followed in order to build it. Thus, as a way of evaluating cities' propensities to build and whether that is shaped by interest groups or other political forces, I examine what cities do to promote, delay, build, or block housing development.

Theoretical Considerations and Expectations

As I discussed in chapter 6, there is already a research literature on housing politics, but it has not carefully considered the role of interest groups. An underlying concern of this literature is the high cost of housing in the United States, so naturally much of it is focused on explaining why housing supply falls short of demand. Studies by economists and policy analysts focus on the effects of restrictive housing regulations such as bans on multifamily housing, minimum lot sizes, setback rules, and rules about parking.[38] Others emphasize the political influence of homeowners and other city residents who are opposed to building more housing, especially high-density housing.[39] And in a recent book, Katherine Einstein, David Glick, and Maxwell Palmer have highlighted the role of local institutions that empower residents to delay and block new housing developments. In many cities, development proposals that require a special permit or variance (as many do) trigger public meetings that invite anyone to comment on the proposal, and those meetings tend to be dominated by individuals strongly opposed to the proposed development. As Einstein, Glick, and Palmer explain, this selective participation in public meetings works to delay, reduce, or block the development of multifamily housing, contributing to housing shortages.[40]

What is mostly missing from these explanations is an account and analysis of the role of interest groups. Consider developers. They are sometimes mentioned in research on housing politics, but piecing together these snippets of arguments about the potential influence of developers produces a mixed, confused picture. The traditional urban politics literature depicts developers as having considerable clout in cities, pushing for more development and the bulldozing of minority neighborhoods.[41] Jessica Trounstine suggests that developers are influential but often on the side of white property owners who *resist* development, especially multifamily housing because it threatens the value of existing properties and therefore developers' profits.[42] Yet Einstein, Glick, and Palmer find that developers are often the only ones present at public meetings who *support* the project being discussed, and they conclude that developers are not very influential in pushing for more housing.[43]

What, then, should we expect the role of developers to be in housing politics, if they have any role at all? Do they support or oppose more housing? What are their preferences? And do they have influence? As a starting point, there is good reason to think that developers are generally supportive of proposals to build more housing. They have a concentrated interest in building.[44] As individual businesses, they make profits from building and developing. It is also not obvious that development firms would have different preferences on multifamily housing versus single-family housing. Both are opportunities for building and profits, and a developer might see considerable profit opportunity in building multifamily housing.

Moreover, the perspective that developers would work to oppose new developments hinges on conditions that seem somewhat unrealistic. Developers could potentially coordinate to limit development in order to keep existing property values high, but such an arrangement would be difficult to enforce given individual developers' profit interests in more development. Alternatively, a small number of incumbent developers could possibly persuade the city to ignore proposals from outside developers. But Einstein, Glick, and Palmer show that public meetings rarely, if ever, feature developers opposing the developers trying to expand housing.[45] Thus, it is probably safe to assume that developers are pro-development, not an active force pushing to limit development.

There is also reason to think that developers tend to engage in local politics as individual businesses and that to the extent they are coordinated, they are coordinated in the local chambers of commerce. As I have said, most developers are not committed to what goes on in any particular city.[46] They instead shop around for opportunities to develop. Because of this, we can expect developers to engage in city politics when the discussion at hand is about *their* project, which of course they will support. They probably would not get involved in one city's discussions about institutions, such as zoning or the procedures for considering housing development, because they have exit options. To the extent that they are involved, it is likely through the local chamber of commerce, which *is* committed to that particular city. And we can expect the relatively more invested chambers of commerce to advocate for local institutions and policies that encourage growth and development, not stifle it.

This much considers the role of business on land use policy, but what of the potential opposition? Land use should be especially contentious in local politics because the costs of the policies are direct and therefore readily apparent to those negatively affected by them. In fact, the costs in this case might be so large, direct, and visible to those affected that even unorganized, individual homeowners become politically engaged on the issue, as research on housing politics suggests. And that creates a dilemma for city officials. City officials, who are concerned with the economic strength of the city, might generally favor the construction of more housing, including multifamily housing. After all, a city's ability to attract and retain jobs can depend on the local cost and availability of housing. In the shorter run, however, homeowners who are angry about how a development decreased their property values will probably have intense preferences on the matter and vote on that issue in the next election; this may well hurt the politicians who allowed the development to move forward. Elected officials, then, are very likely pulled in different directions on the issue. For the city as a whole, they want to build housing, but doing so may make them electorally vulnerable.[47]

Opposed homeowners might also be bolstered by organized groups, particularly environmental groups and neighborhood associations. One study of neighborhood associations finds that most of them arise out of opposition to proposed developments and that they are mainly opposed to the efforts of real estate developers and business.[48] Neighborhood associations are therefore not only committed to their city or neighborhood but also may have as members the very residents who are negatively affected by proposed housing developments. We can thus expect

186   CHAPTER SEVEN

their activity to be focused on these land use debates—and that they will be opposed.

As I alluded to earlier, it is not clear where environmental groups would stand on housing development. They could be in favor of building high-density housing because of its potential to reduce commuting by car and thus greenhouse gas emissions. But they might just as likely oppose building and densification; note that many objections to new housing developments cite environmental concerns.[49] Many local environmental groups are also invested in their particular cities and advocate for institutions that empower them.[50] Whether and how environmental group activism influences housing development is therefore an empirical question.

More generally, though, this is an area in which I expect interest groups make a difference. Elected officials are conflicted. The costs are visible. Developers are active in advocating for their own projects, regardless of whether they are single-family or multifamily housing developments. Local chambers of commerce may even push cities toward more pro-development policies generally. And this is likely the type of local policy on which conflict is great and opposition effective. In the following analyses, I evaluate these expectations, first looking at the process of housing development, then analyzing how much new housing is permitted.

Process, Institutions, and Delay

Existing research highlights how opponents of new housing create and exploit local housing development institutions and processes to their advantage. For example, zoning ordinances often favor single-family housing.[51] Rules requiring public meetings allow opponents to stall, delay, and make efforts to build more housing more costly, which not only slows the process but also gives opponents key negotiating leverage.[52] A good place to begin this analysis is therefore with those kinds of institutions and processes.

Unfortunately, data on local housing development processes and institutions are sparse. Existing quantitative research on this topic tends to focus on a single state or city because that is where researchers have been able to locate data. In fact, the only existing dataset of housing regulations and processes that aligns with a large number of the cities I examine in this book is one collected by Gyourko, Saiz, and Summers. In

BUSINESS AND GROWTH

2006, they carried out a national survey of local governments to understand land use regulations and procedures in each city.[53] Over 400 municipal governments are in both my datasets and the Gyourko, Saiz, and Summers dataset.[54] These data were collected ten years before my measurements of interest group activity, but they are still a useful opening wedge for understanding variation in local processes for land use development.[55]

As a starting point, the Gyourko, Saiz, and Summers survey measures the presence of two types of rules that might work to limit multifamily housing development: whether there are outright limits on the number of building permits or units allowed for different types of housing and whether the city requires a certain minimum lot size. Very few cities place outright limits on the number of allowable building permits, but minimum lot sizes are common: 84% of the cities have them. And of the cities that have minimum lot sizes, those minimums vary by city: 46% are less than half an acre, 19% are between half an acre and one acre, 9% are between one and two acres, and 26% are more than two acres.

This second variable—the size of the minimum lot—is less than ideal both because it is not continuous and because many respondents who reported minimum lot sizes did not provide the information. With this in mind, I model two dependent variables: the first a binary indicator of whether the city has a minimum lot size requirement and the second an ordinal variable of the size of the minimum lot, which equals 0 if the city has no minimum lot size (least restrictive), 1 if the requirement is less than half an acre, 2 if it is half an acre to one acre, 3 if it is one to two acres, and 4 if it is two acres or more (most restrictive).[56] The independent variables I include are the same as those used earlier, and I estimate models first with regional indicators and then with state fixed effects.

The estimates in table 7.3 show several suggestive patterns. First, cities with more active chambers of commerce tend to have slightly less restrictive minimum lot sizes. In columns 1 and 2, which show the results of the models of the binary indicator, the coefficients on chamber of commerce activity are statistically insignificant, but in columns 3 and 4, the coefficients are negative, showing that minimum lot sizes tend to be less restrictive in cities with more active chambers of commerce. Interestingly, I also estimate negative coefficients on the political activity of building trade unions: minimum lot sizes are smaller where building trade unions have greater presence in local politics. Throughout, however, the coefficients on the political activity of developers are statisti-

188   CHAPTER SEVEN

TABLE 7.3 **Minimum lot size requirements**

	Requirement		Size of Minimum Lot	
	(1)	(2)	(3)	(4)
Chambers of commerce	−0.03	−0.036	−0.26***	−0.264***
	(0.021)	(0.023)	(0.082)	(0.095)
Developers	−0.01	−0.004	−0.03	−0.014
	(0.022)	(0.026)	(0.093)	(0.101)
Neighborhood associations	0.036**	0.038*	0.112	0.1
	(0.017)	(0.020)	(0.073)	(0.084)
Environmental groups	0.003	0.004	0.075	0.065
	(0.017)	(0.020)	(0.090)	(0.101)
Building trade unions	−0.04**	−0.038*	−0.176***	−0.167**
	(0.018)	(0.020)	(0.063)	(0.065)
Taxpayer groups	−0.01	−0.009	0.174**	0.14
	(0.020)	(0.024)	(0.084)	(0.097)
Ln(Population)	0.032*	0.033	0.142***	0.136**
	(0.018)	(0.021)	(0.052)	(0.054)
Ln(Income per capita)	−0.169***	−0.131*	−0.179	−0.178
	(0.054)	(0.071)	(0.367)	(0.461)
Percent homeowner	0.572**	0.601**	1.939**	1.813*
	(0.214)	(0.265)	(0.923)	(1.043)
Democratic presidential vote	−0.142	−0.194	−1.596*	−1.636
	(0.180)	(0.211)	(0.839)	(1.078)
R-squared	0.09	0.15	0.19	0.32
Observations	392	392	306	306

Notes: Standard errors clustered by state in parentheses. Models 1 and 3 include regional fixed effects; models 2
and 4 include state fixed effects. All models include additional demographics and political institutions.
*p < 0.1, **p < 0.05, ***p < 0.01 (two-tailed).

cally indistinguishable from zero. Thus, developers do not appear to be
investing in making local institutions more flexible to development—or
at least not effectively.

In a finding that aligns with expectations of the housing politics literature, cities with larger shares of homeowners tend to have more restrictive minimum lot size requirements. Moreover, the estimates in columns 1 and 2 of table 7.3 show that cities with more active neighborhood
associations are slightly more likely to have minimum lot sizes, even
though in columns 3 and 4, it does not appear that they have significantly
larger lot sizes. This, then, is some evidence that local homeowners and
neighborhood associations push for institutions that protect local property values. Notably, however, the coefficients on Democratic presidential vote share are statistically insignificant, except for column 3.

Next I turn to an analysis of why it takes longer to develop housing in some cities than in others. I use two variables from the Gyourko,

BUSINESS AND GROWTH

Saiz, and Summers survey dataset: the average duration, in months, of the review process for single-family housing units and the average duration of the review process for multifamily housing units.[57] In most of the cities I analyze here, city officials report the same average review duration for single-family and multifamily housing units, but unsurprisingly, when they differ, it is the multifamily housing that tends to take longer. For single-family housing, the median duration in these cities is 3 months, and for multifamily housing, it is 4 months. But there is some variation across cities: the standard deviation for single-family housing is 3.8 months and for multifamily housing, 4 months.[58]

In table 7.4, I model these variables with the same independent variables as before, with one addition. The Gyourko, Saiz, and Summers survey asked respondents to rate the importance of various factors in

TABLE 7.4 **Average duration of review for housing development (in months)**

	Single-Family Housing		Multifamily Housing	
	(1)	(2)	(3)	(4)
Chambers of commerce	−0.524***	−0.531***	−0.510***	−0.553***
	(0.170)	(0.195)	(0.159)	(0.200)
Developers	0.185	0.062	0.197	0.095
	(0.172)	(0.173)	(0.138)	(0.149)
Neighborhood associations	−0.09	−0.042	−0.072	−0.031
	(0.144)	(0.142)	(0.148)	(0.134)
Environmental groups	0.112	0.107	0.207	0.196
	(0.162)	(0.178)	(0.128)	(0.145)
Building trade unions	−0.116	−0.124	−0.228	−0.268
	(0.120)	(0.144)	(0.155)	(0.175)
Taxpayer groups	0.589**	0.523*	0.453**	0.363
	(0.225)	(0.264)	(0.202)	(0.241)
Ln(Population)	0.273**	0.289**	0.105	0.135
	(0.122)	(0.136)	(0.157)	(0.158)
Ln(Income per capita)	1.836***	1.031*	3.304***	2.140***
	(0.487)	(0.566)	(0.633)	(0.689)
Percent homeowner	1.142	1.984**	1.726	3.109**
	(0.991)	(0.933)	(1.190)	(1.165)
Democratic presidential vote	0.147	0.374	1.425	2.479*
	(1.056)	(1.096)	(1.238)	(1.461)
Citizen opposition	0.276**	0.216	0.251**	0.237**
	(0.117)	(0.131)	(0.094)	(0.110)
R-squared	0.20	0.29	0.28	0.38
Observations	396	396	396	396

Notes: Standard errors clustered by state in parentheses. Models 2 and 4 include state fixed effects; models 1 and 3 include regional fixed effects. All models include additional demographics and political institutions.

*p < 0.1, **p < 0.05, ***p < 0.01 (two-tailed).

shaping the rate of residential development in their cities, and one of the factors rated was the importance of "citizen opposition to growth," with separate ratings for single-family and multifamily housing. I include this 1–5 scale in the model to test whether greater citizen opposition is associated with longer review times for new housing. Higher values of this variable indicate greater citizen opposition to growth, so I expect it to be positively associated with housing review duration.

In columns 1 and 2 of table 7.4, I focus on the review duration for single-family housing developments, first with regional indicators (column 1) and then with state fixed effects (column 2).[59] The estimates show that cities with more active chambers of commerce tend to have shorter review periods for single-family housing development. On average, a two-point increase in the political activity of chambers of commerce is associated with a one-month reduction in the duration of the typical review. In columns 3 and 4, where I instead model the duration of the review process for multifamily housing, the results are substantively the same. The coefficient on the activity of chambers of commerce is strong and negative, suggesting that a more active local chamber of commerce is linked to an easier, shorter process for housing development—for multifamily housing as well as single-family housing.

As in table 7.3, the political activity of developers is unrelated to the review duration of a typical housing development project. This is consistent with an account in which developers get active in local politics to promote their own projects but not to make local government friendlier to development more generally. Whether it is single-family housing or multifamily housing in question, cities with more politically active developers do not have significantly shorter review times.[60]

These estimates do, however, support the argument that citizens and homeowners put up effective obstacles to developing housing. In three of the four models, greater citizen opposition to housing development is associated with longer review times, and per capita income is positive and significant in all of them. In addition, in the models with state fixed effects (columns 2 and 4), we see that cities with a higher share of homeowners report longer review times for both single-family and multifamily housing, especially for multifamily housing. Thus, in support of research that focuses on the role of voters and homeowners in housing politics, I find here that citizen opposition, higher income, and a higher concentration of homeowners are associated with longer review times for proposed housing developments.

BUSINESS AND GROWTH

Throughout this analysis, I find no evidence that more Democratic cities review housing development proposals more quickly than cities where residents lean Republican. The coefficient on Democratic presidential vote is insignificant in columns 1–3 and positive in column 4. Moreover, most of the other interest group activity variables are insignificant predictors of the length of the typical review: the coefficients on the activity of neighborhood associations, environmental groups, and building trade unions are not statistically distinguishable from zero.

The one exception is the positive coefficient on the activity of taxpayer groups, which suggests that cities with more active taxpayer groups tend to have longer review periods for housing development. This is an unexpected finding: based on preferences alone, I would expect taxpayer groups to favor more housing development and processes with fewer restrictions. The fact that I find the opposite relationship here probably reflects two things: first, the tendency for taxpayer groups to get involved in places where their interests are most threatened; and second, taxpayer group involvement adds to the conflict over housing development. As I showed in chapter 4, taxpayer groups are not highly active in most cities, and housing development is probably not one of their core concerns. I expect them to be much more engaged on matters of taxes and spending. Thus, it seems quite possible that if they get involved on housing development, they do so in a reactive way—in places where housing development is least likely to proceed as they would like. Moreover, taxpayer group involvement either adds to or reflects greater conflict over housing development; it is another group added to the mix. Viewed in this way, it may make sense that their political activity is associated with longer review times.

Stepping back, though, this suggests that institutions and processes related to housing development do vary with the activity of interest groups—at least the activity of chambers of commerce. But there are limitations to this analysis. Most notably, there is a ten-year gap between when Gyourko, Saiz, and Summers collected their data and when I measured local interest group activity. Also, their variables are only available for some of the cities in my interest group activity datasets, and they only contain information on some local institutions that could inhibit housing development. Still, the power to delay is an important weapon in battles over public policy, and housing politics experts have cited delay as a critical tactic and goal of opponents of new housing. My analysis here suggests that the process of housing development moves more slowly in places with more homeowners and more active citizen opposition and tends to be faster in cities with more politically engaged chambers of commerce.

Permitted Housing Units

For analyzing how much new housing is actually permitted, the best data source is the US Census Bureau's Building Permits Survey. The Census Bureau asks all permit-issuing governments for the number of building permits they issued each month for private residential buildings. The dataset includes information about the number of units and buildings permitted in four categories: residential buildings with one unit, two units, three to four units, and five or more units. I use the annual data from this survey in 2016, which has these permitting variables for most of the municipal governments covered in my interest group activity surveys.

I start with an analysis of the total number of housing units permitted in each city, including both single-family (one unit) and multifamily (two or more units) housing. Because a small number of cities have fewer than twelve months of permitting data tracked by the Building Permits Survey, I calculate the average number of units permitted per month.[61] As larger cities permit more housing units, I divide this monthly average by city population in thousands. Of the cities I analyze here, the median number of permits issued per month per thousand city residents is 0.2. The mean is 0.44, and the standard deviation is 0.9. Six percent of the cities permitted zero housing units in 2016, and a handful of mostly small cities permitted very large numbers of housing units relative to their populations.[62]

Because of these outliers and the right skew in the distribution of this variable, I model it in two ways. In all models, I include the same independent variables from earlier, including state fixed effects, but in the first model I exclude cities for which the amount of housing permitted is 1.5 times the interquartile range larger than the third quartile. In a second approach, I log the dependent variable, which drops the 6% of cities with no housing permitted but preserves the cities with large values. The estimates from those models are presented in table 7.5.

The first finding of note is that in cities where developers are more politically active, more units of housing are permitted. Based on the estimates in column 1, a two-unit increase in developer political activity is associated with an additional 0.076 units of housing permitted per

BUSINESS AND GROWTH

TABLE 7.5 **Total housing units permitted per month, 2016**

	Units per Thousand Residents (1)	Ln(Units per Thousand Residents) (2)
Chambers of commerce	−0.009	−0.006
	(0.015)	(0.071)
Developers	0.038***	0.219***
	(0.013)	(0.049)
Neighborhood associations	0.011	0.002
	(0.008)	(0.046)
Environmental groups	0.007	0.068
	(0.008)	(0.058)
Building trade unions	−0.018*	−0.035
	(0.011)	(0.047)
Taxpayer groups	−0.024*	−0.146**
	(0.013)	(0.061)
Ln(Population)	0.03**	0.049
	(0.012)	(0.036)
Ln(Income per capita)	0.021	0.555***
	(0.024)	(0.133)
Percent homeowner	0.14	0.003
	(0.095)	(0.472)
Democratic presidential vote	−0.112	−1.388***
	(0.089)	(0.424)
R−squared	0.25	0.32
Observations	785	798

Notes: Standard errors clustered by state in parentheses. Models include state fixed effects, additional demographic variables, and political institutions.

*p < 0.1, **p < 0.05, ***p < 0.01 (two-tailed).

month, per thousand city residents, on average.[63] In column 2, the results suggest that such a two-unit increase in developer activity comes with a 55% increase in housing units permitted. Thus, while all the analyses thus far have shown no connection between developers' political activity and local policy, here we see that it counts—where theory suggests it should.

More than for the other main interest group variables explored in this chapter, it is important to interpret this relationship with caution, because developers have greater ability to shop around. This positive coefficient could mean that developers' political activity influences local governments, pushing them to allow more housing development. It could also mean that business-minded developers are drawn to cities that are more inclined to build—that the pro-development environment attracts the developers' activity. With chambers of commerce and groups like neighborhood associations, this is less of a concern because they are locked into working within a single city. While local chambers of commerce and neighborhood associations could still vary their activity based on city policies, that relationship could go in either direction, as I discussed in chapter 6. With regard to developers, the findings in table 7.5 are notable because they are consistent with an account of influence, but they are less conclusive because of developers' stronger exit options.

Equally notable are the null results on most of the other interest group activity variables. The activity of chambers of commerce has no relationship to the amount of new housing permitted. The activity of neighborhood associations and environmental groups makes no difference either. There is some sign that greater activity of building trade unions is associated with fewer housing units, but that depends on the model specification. Again, the coefficient on the activity of taxpayer groups goes in the unexpected direction: more active taxpayer organizations are associated with fewer units of housing permitted.

Most of the other variables in the model are not significant predictors of the total number of units permitted. Of particular note, however, is the negative coefficient on Democratic presidential vote, which in column 2 is statistically significant. This suggests that in cities where residents lean Democratic, fewer housing units are permitted per month per capita. Just as important are the insignificant coefficients on percent homeowner: cities with more homeowners do not permit fewer housing units per capita in a typical month.

Importantly, however, much of the housing politics literature suggests that the political dynamics are different for multifamily housing and for single-family housing; in particular, the opposition of local homeowners and perhaps neighborhood associations is focused on multifamily housing. Thus, while I do not expect the type of housing to matter much for developers, it may matter for the opposition, so I next examine single-family units permitted and multifamily units permitted separately.

First it is important to note that most new housing permitted is single-family housing. In 2016, 92% of these cities permitted some new single-family housing, and of the cities that did not, nearly all permitted no new housing at all; it is extremely rare for a city to permit only multifamily housing. Moreover, of the cities that permitted at least some housing, the median share of units that were single-family units is 97%. Thus, for nearly all these cities, building more housing means building single-family, not high-density, housing. In interpreting the results in table 7.5,

BUSINESS AND GROWTH   195

TABLE 7.6 **Permits per month for single-family and multifamily housing, 2016**

	Single-Family Units per Thousand Residents	Ln(Single-Family Units per Thousand Residents)	Permitted Any Multifamily Units	Multifamily Units per Thousand Residents
	(1)	(2)	(3)	(4)
Chambers of commerce	0.001	0.001	−0.006	0.001
	(0.010)	(0.064)	(0.021)	(0.014)
Developers	0.018***	0.164***	0.051***	0.004
	(0.005)	(0.040)	(0.019)	(0.011)
Neighborhood associations	0.004	0.065*	−0.017	−0.009
	(0.007)	(0.036)	(0.014)	(0.012)
Environmental groups	0.0004	0.052	0.011	0.022**
	(0.006)	(0.062)	(0.014)	(0.010)
Building trade unions	−0.005	0.002	−0.026*	−0.012
	(0.006)	(0.056)	(0.014)	(0.011)
Taxpayer groups	−0.011	−0.102*	−0.022	−0.03*
	(0.010)	(0.060)	(0.014)	(0.015)
Ln(Population)	0.009	−0.125**	0.154***	0.016
	(0.010)	(0.058)	(0.011)	(0.010)
Ln(Income per capita)	−0.012	0.055	0.157*	0.125*
	(0.016)	(0.147)	(0.084)	(0.065)
Percent homeowner	0.23***	1.86***	−0.787***	−0.283**
	(0.070)	(0.317)	(0.158)	(0.134)
Democratic presidential vote	−0.114**	−1.713***	0.06	0.02
	(0.048)	(0.489)	(0.141)	(0.066)
R-squared	0.27	0.4	0.31	0.26
Observations	772	792	858	382

Notes: Standard errors clustered by state in parentheses. All models include state fixed effects, additional demographics, and political institutions.

*p < 0.1, **p < 0.05, ***p < 0.01 (two-tailed).

therefore, it is important to recognize that most of those new units are single-family units.

In columns 1 and 2 of table 7.6, I estimate the same models as in table 7.5 but examine only the number of single-family housing units permitted. As expected, I find that greater developer activity is associated with the permitting of more single-family homes. We can also see more clearly here that homeowners and neighborhood associations are not effective opposition to single-family housing: municipalities with more homeowners actually permit significantly more single-family housing, and in column 2, the coefficient on neighborhood association activity is positive as well. The results also show that cities with residents who lean Democratic permit significantly fewer units of single-family housing than cities with more Republican residents.

Does the pattern of local housing politics look different for multi-family housing? Because 53% of these cities permitted zero units of multifamily housing in 2016, I start by using OLS to model a simple indicator of whether a city permitted any multifamily housing at all. The estimates are shown in column 3 of table 7.6.

The coefficient on developers' political activity suggests that cities with very active developers are 10% more likely to permit multifamily housing than cities with only slightly active developers. The coefficients on the other interest group activity variables are insignificant, except for building trade unions, which is negative. Here, however, we see clearly that cities with more homeowners are far less likely to permit multi-family housing. Specifically, a city that is 75% homeowners is about 40% less likely to permit multifamily housing than a city with only 25% homeowners. More Democratic cities, however, appear no more inclined to permit multifamily housing than more Republican cities.

Of the cities that do permit multifamily housing, does interest group activity help explain the number of units permitted? I evaluate this in column 4 of table 7.6, modeling the number of multifamily housing units permitted in 2016 for those with nonzero values. Here, the only variable that predicts the number of multifamily units, as expected, is percent homeowner: of the cities that do permit multifamily housing, the cities with more homeowners permitted significantly fewer units. The political activity of chambers of commerce, developers, and neighborhood associations matters little. The coefficient on environmental group political activity is positive, and again, the coefficient on taxpayer groups is negative. As before, Democratic presidential vote has no relationship to the number of multifamily units permitted.

The Important and Unusual Case of Housing Development

One of the takeaways of this analysis of housing development is that when land use is at stake in a local government, there are clear signs that the political activity of business groups makes a difference. When it comes to the rules and processes governing housing development, more activity by chambers of commerce is associated with lesser restrictiveness and a more development-friendly environment. And in cities where developers are more politically active, more residential housing is permitted. Most new housing permitted is single-family housing, but greater developer activity is associated with more permitting of single-family

BUSINESS AND GROWTH

housing and a greater propensity to permit multifamily housing. These findings are an important contribution to our understanding of interest group influence and to our understanding of housing politics. Business interests and developers do play a role, and they are a force pushing cities in the direction of more and faster housing development.

Another major takeaway is that the strongest and most consistent pushback against these pro-growth business interests comes from city residents and homeowners—and not as clearly from interest groups. The relationships between housing development outcomes and the political activity of neighborhood associations and environmental groups are weaker than expected. What does emerge is a strong relationship between housing outcomes and the share of homeowners or the amount of citizen opposition in a city. Thus, there is open, regular conflict on land use issues, as I expected, but the opposition to business is not necessarily in the form I expected. Instead, the pattern is one of interest groups—chambers of commerce and developers—pushing for more housing and seemingly unorganized residents and homeowners working to slow and limit housing development, especially multifamily housing.

Why do the results not show stronger signs of influence of neighborhood associations and environmental groups? It may well be that these groups simply do not have influence on housing development in most cities. It could also be that these groups are not as consistent in their interests, goals, and political focus from city to city. Unlike chambers of commerce and developers, which probably act in similar, pro-development ways in cities across the country, neighborhood associations and environmental groups in different places may not be homogeneously in favor of slowing or blocking housing and may differ in their political focus on the issue. Local Sierra Club organizations, for example, might have very different agendas in different cities. Sorting out these potential explanations will take more focused research on these particular kinds of groups. What I can conclude, for the moment, is that the relationship between housing development outcomes and the political activity of neighborhood associations and environmental groups is weak and inconsistent.

Then there is the question of why the share of homeowners in a city has such a strong relationship with many of these housing development outcomes. Inasmuch as this variable can be interpreted as a proxy for city residents' preferences on housing, this may be read as a sign that the preferences of city residents do matter.[64] That is precisely what housing politics researchers have suggested, that is, that local voters and residents play a major role in slowing high-density housing development and that they are having influence mainly as individuals, not necessarily through organized groups.

The lesson is not that interest groups do not matter—business groups clearly do—but rather that in this case, the preferences of key subsets of residents matter as well. And this is very likely a special case, for reasons I have explained. In the scheme of city politics, the costs of land use policies are unusually direct and visible. For nearby homeowners, they are also large and economic.[65] City officials and developers can probably expect that if there are homeowners in close proximity to a proposed new development, there will be some backlash from residents.[66] Moreover, because of public meeting requirements, those residents have an established venue in which to voice their opposition;[67] they do not have to try to design an advocacy channel from scratch. All this combines to create a setup in which residents, acting mostly on their own, can be quite effective. But is this typical? Are unorganized city residents just as influential in other areas? Probably not. For many city policies, even in the area of economic development and growth, the costs are much less direct, much less visible, and much less likely to attract the attention of the average resident.

It is nonetheless striking what this implies for the politics of housing development. There is a force pushing for more land development, including more housing: chambers of commerce and developers. The clearest and most consistent opposition to more high-density housing is coming from a subset of city residents. Here, then, is an area where it appears that interest groups and residents are both engaged and active, and it is the residents who are pushing back against housing.

Conclusion

This attempt to understand the local politics of economic development and growth has taken me into many areas of municipal government decision making, from the seemingly mundane to the controversial, from policies with ambiguous costs to those whose costs are on full display. Do business interests influence what cities do on economic development and growth? The answer is that it depends: it depends on which specific policy is being considered and what type of business or business group is under examination.

My analysis in the first part of the chapter suggests that many of the actual decisions local governments make to pursue economic development and growth have small or ambiguous costs. There is little indication that the political activity of local chambers of commerce has any relationship to whether cities do or do not use these development tools. Local chambers of commerce can be assumed to want more pro-business city governments, but in this case, what they want is usually what city officials would want to do anyway. Nor is the use of economic development tools explained by other interest groups' activity, partisanship, or home-ownership rates. Instead, as Peterson argues,[68] the use of most of these economic development tools varies with city characteristics like size and per capita income. These types of activities receive less attention from researchers, probably because they are less conflictual and seemingly less interesting, but if the goal is to understand the politics of local economic development and business influence, this is an important part of the picture. Not all that is economic development is conflictual.

I then explored local growth policies that have clearer, more direct costs—but in two different forms: first, business tax abatement, whose costs come in the form of lower local tax revenue; and second, housing development, whose costs come in the form of land use. In both cases, what the business community prefers likely runs up against the interests of other city actors. Local chambers of commerce probably prefer a low-tax environment for businesses—and thus favor tax abatement— but city officials have to wrestle with the likelihood that offering such incentives will lower tax revenue. Developers and local chambers probably also favor an environment in which housing development is possible and not too cumbersome, but local residents often oppose new housing, especially multifamily housing, and that puts pressure on local officials as well. In my analysis, I found that cities with more active chambers of commerce are more likely to use business tax incentives and lose larger amounts of city revenue to tax abatement. They also tend to have less restrictive land use institutions and shorter review times for the permitting of new housing. Cities where developers are more active, moreover, issue permits for more single-family homes and are more likely to permit multifamily housing. Thus, on these issues, there is evidence that business groups make a difference to policy.

In some parts of my analysis of tax abatement and housing politics, I found signs that opposing interest groups sometimes succeed in pushing back on business interests. The activity of neighborhood associations and environmental groups appears to be weakly associated with lower use of business tax incentives and less revenue lost to tax abatement. But other than the finding that cities with more active neighborhood associations are slightly more likely to have minimum lot sizes, my analysis of housing politics does not show that these potentially opposing groups are a regular force slowing or blocking housing development. Instead, the variables that clearly and consistently predict slower permitting processes and fewer permits issued are the share of homeowners in the community, the amount of citizen opposition, and greater activity by taxpayer groups. Housing politics, then, often pits pro-growth business groups against anti-growth residents. Interest groups matter, but so do the voters.

A final pattern that deserves underscoring is the general failure of residents' partisan and ideological leanings to predict the local politics of economic development. Economic development and growth, including housing development, is a major function of municipal government almost everywhere. And while city policy making in this area does vary dramatically from city to city, that variation is not well explained by residents' national partisan and ideological commitments. A nationally focused perspective might lead one to think that Democratic cities would be less likely to grant businesses tax breaks or to grant them smaller tax breaks. They are not. Democratic presidential vote also is not a significant predictor of the length of the housing permitting process or the number of multifamily housing units permitted. Throughout these various analyses, the only place where partisanship appears to explain variation in what cities do is in the permitting of single-family homes: Democratic cities permit fewer of them. Otherwise, policies in this broad area are not well explained by residents' partisanship.

From this, then, we learn about the politics of local economic development and growth, the role of business in local politics, and how policy is different when certain groups are more or less active. In an area that has been such a heavy focus of the urban politics literature for the past few decades, I have presented a quantitative analysis that allows us to see the bigger picture and to assess more systematically what economic development and growth is about—and the conditions under which business does and does not have influence. The next step is to turn to the area of local politics that has gotten less attention: the role of interest groups in public service provision.

CHAPTER EIGHT

Unions, Public Safety, and Local Government Spending

During the summer of 2020, cities' public safety practices were in the spotlight. The killings of George Floyd and Breonna Taylor by police officers brought millions of Americans into the streets in protest. The Black Lives Matter movement surged. Calls for defunding, abolishing, or reimagining local police departments gained prominence. And while the roots of these injustices are deep, structural, and historical, the public also turned its gaze to local policies as a contributor. Suddenly, in 2020, advocates and policy makers across the nation started more active discussions about how much money is spent on public safety, what that money is spent on, and rules governing how police officers do their jobs.

If the widespread public attention to these policies is new, however, the policies themselves are not. Public safety policies are and have always been a central component of local government. Most municipal governments have police departments, a large majority have fire departments, and spending on public safety provision makes up a large share of municipal government budgets. Moreover, policies affecting public safety budgets and how government services are provided are made on a regular basis, whether or not the public is following the details. And it is fair to say that until recently, the public was not following the details. Perhaps today it is more apparent that local governments' "personnel policies" have large, important, and very public consequences. But most of the time matters of compensation and work rules seem technical and dull and do not attract much public scrutiny. The surge in public attention in 2020 likely changed the dynamics of local decision making on these matters in some cities, at least temporarily. But if we want to understand why local governments have the public safety policies and spending patterns they do, we have to look at what was happening before the scope of conflict expanded.[1]

Local politics scholars have generally not done this. These important matters of local public service provision have for the most part been ignored. Local politics research that does examine local policy is heavily focused on land use and housing. And while there are a number of quantitative studies examining local government spending and fiscal outcomes, they set out to explain those outcomes with variables measuring characteristics of local residents, voters, and elected officials. A central idea is that if some cities spend more than others, it is because city residents—or some subset of city residents—want them to.

That may well be true, but it is at best only part of the story. We have already seen that interest groups are also active in local politics and that unions of police officers and firefighters are among the most politically active of all. They have a tremendous stake in how much cities spend and what they spend it on. They also have a stake in other types of policies that recent protests against police brutality have brought into the spotlight: policies governing how public employees do their jobs and how they are managed—and thus how public services are provided. Surely an understanding of local politics and representation demands examination of whether and how these interest groups affect local public policies.

That is my goal in this chapter. As I discussed in chapter 6, some existing research on public-sector unions focuses squarely on their influence. Much of it analyzes state politics or the role of teachers' unions in public education and therefore does not speak directly to public safety unions and municipal government (although there are exceptions). But the general insights of this literature are helpful for structuring expectations for the particular cases of police and firefighters' unions in municipal government.

My analysis begins by revisiting the question of whether public-sector unions influence government employment and compensation. These are the main places researchers have looked for public-sector union influence in the past, but nearly all the existing studies rely on data from the 1980s or earlier, and their conclusions are mixed. To understand why, it helps to clarify some fundamental theoretical and empirical design issues inherent in this line of study. I lay out those clarifications as a first step, drawing on insights from an older economics literature on public-sector unions and more recent political science research. Given that employment and compensation have been studied by others, my own empirical contributions here are modest: I analyze more recent data on municipal government spending on police and fire protection salaries (from the 2017 Census of Governments), and I evaluate the effects of the political activity of interest groups, including public safety unions and their activity through collective bargaining. In addition, I examine which forms of extra pay police officers are eligible to receive, drawing on the 2013 Law Enforcement Management and Administrative Statistics (LEMAS) data.

I then connect the study of public safety union influence to local government spending more broadly. In recent years there have been empirical studies linking the ideology and partisanship of city residents and elected officials to patterns of city spending, with some studies concluding that city officials are responsive to city residents when making public policy. However, when I add public-sector unions and collective bargaining to models of local public spending, again relying on data from the 2017 Census of Governments, the picture changes—as does the conclusion about whom city government is responsive to.

To provide some detail on how all these factors fit together—local spending, taxes, fire protection, collective bargaining, and more traditional political activities—I describe a recent (and ongoing) political controversy in West Covina, California. The case illustrates how important public safety is to municipal government, how important public safety spending is to local government budgets, and how active firefighters' unions are in trying to protect fire department salaries, benefits, and employment levels. It also underscores the importance of collective bargaining to city fiscal outcomes, the absence of organized opposition to firefighters' unions' goals, and how the main opposition to their efforts comes from local officials who are forced to work within budget constraints.

In a final step, I present some preliminary thoughts and analysis on how police unions and police reform groups might influence rules governing how police officers do their jobs. Rules governing how public employees do their work are much more difficult to study than fiscal matters, both because the existing literature on the topic barely exists and because of the difficulty of collecting data on the rules and practices of interest. I attempt to make some headway by analyzing LEMAS data on community policing practices as of 2013 and the deployment of officer-worn body cameras as of 2016. The results, while only suggestive, help complete the picture of how public safety unions influence local policy.

Spending on Police and Fire Protection Compensation

Existing research on the influence of public-sector unions looks primarily for their effects on government compensation and employment levels, and that makes sense. Public-sector unions have clear interests in greater compensation and higher employment levels: it means more pay for employees, more dues-paying members for the union, and possibly more manageable workloads for each employee. If police and firefighters' unions have influence on local policy, we should expect to see it in compensation and employment.

As I mentioned in chapter 6, however, the conclusions of existing studies have been mixed. During the 1970s and 1980s, unionization and collective bargaining were still relatively new in the government sector, so estimating their effects on public-sector wages and employment was an active research enterprise, especially in economics. Most of the early studies found positive effects.[2] But the conclusions of more recent empirical research—most of which has focused on teachers—have varied. One study finds that the unionization of teachers in the late 1970s and 1980s caused increases in per-pupil spending, increases in teacher salaries, and decreases in student-teacher ratios.[3] Another compares three states' school districts before and after their first teacher union certification elections and finds no effect on teacher pay but a positive effect on teacher employment.[4] And an analysis of historical state-level data finds that the passage of state laws mandating collective bargaining for teachers did not cause changes in overall state spending on education, average teacher salary, or student-teacher ratios.[5] With such mixed findings, it would be easy to conclude that even on these matters most central to public-sector unions' interests, the unions do not seem to have much influence.

That conclusion would be premature, and a few simple considerations help clarify why. First, there is a trade-off for unions between increasing salaries and increasing employment levels,[6] and it is not clear which one any given union would prioritize.[7] What is clear is that if unions influence either one, that influence should be visible in *total* spending on their salaries (which reflects both employment and salary levels).

Second, a large portion of the compensation of public employees is above and beyond their base salaries. Many receive various forms of extra compensation, such as overtime pay and shift pay, that are not included in the most commonly available datasets on government salaries and wages—and therefore are not studied. Moreover, compared to the private sector, a disproportionately large share of public employee compensation is in the form of fringe benefits like health insurance, retiree health insurance, and pensions.[8] As Terry Moe and I have argued, unions are probably more successful influencing fringe benefits than salaries, because for elected officials the costs of granting more generous fringe benefits are ambiguous and in the future, whereas the costs of salary increases are clear and immediate.[9] Yet most studies look only at base salaries because those are the data available.

Third, nearly all studies examine data that are now quite old—from the 1980s or earlier. For the earliest research on this topic, of course, these data were contemporary. For more recent work, however, the decision to focus on old data is rooted in researchers' (and disciplines') prioritization of causal inference. Anyone wanting to estimate the effects of collective bargaining or unionization using difference in differences pretty much has to examine state and local governments during the 1960s, 1970s, or 1980s. Those were the years when the governments first adopted collective bargaining, and after the 1980s, there was very little within-government change.[10] Moreover, because collective bargaining and unionization were still new and salient during those years, government agencies (e.g., the US Census Bureau) and other organizations (e.g., the ICMA) collected data on them. They do not do so today. For these reasons, recent studies have continued to use data from this key historical period to study the impacts of collective bargaining and public-sector unionization.

There are two big problems with this. First, collective bargaining and public-sector unions did not end in the 1980s. Today, in the 2020s, they are defining features of many state and local governments and central to how they operate. Surely we want to know how they are affecting policy outcomes in the present day in addition to how they affected policy forty to fifty years ago. Anyone claiming to understand the modern influence of business on policy by studying policy variables from the 1970s would almost certainly be scrutinized and criticized, and we should apply the same critical eye in the case of public-sector unions. The second problem is linked to my argument in chapter 2: interest group influence on policy probably accumulates over time. Because of the focus on causal inference in political science and economics, the most highly regarded studies compare wages and employment before and after those governments first had collective bargaining or unions. But it is entirely possible that the biggest effects were not visible during the few years after onset but rather continued to accumulate in the years and decades that followed. If so, then even if examining more current data makes it difficult to use difference in differences, it is still worth examining those data because we want to understand how collective bargaining affects policy today as well as yesterday.

A fourth important consideration for estimating the influence of public-sector unions is that many of them may be able to influence public policies through collective bargaining, in addition to the channels available to other interest groups, such as lobbying and campaign finance.[11] These channels, moreover, can reinforce each other: by being active in elections, public-sector unions can help influence the selection of the officials they will be negotiating with, and if negotiations do not go well, the unions might be able to credibly threaten retaliation at the polls—in addition to the threat of a strike.[12] Political scientists tend not to consider collective bargaining as a form of political activity or channel of influence, but in fact it is a process in which elected officials are *required* to hear the positions of public-sector unions on policies central to their members' interests and are furthermore legally required to reach agreement with them on those policies. Meanwhile, studies of public-sector unions tend to focus on the effects of collective bargaining, not on any of their other political activities. Theoretically, it seems entirely appropriate for a study of public-sector union influence to include both measures, collective bargaining and unions' other more traditional political activities.[13]

To be sure, measuring and operationalizing these variables is complicated. First there is the issue that local employees' collective bargaining occurs at the local government level, yet today the presence of local public-sector bargaining is well predicted by state collective bargaining laws. For example, if a state has a mandatory bargaining law for firefighters, almost all local governments in the state that employ firefighters engage in collective bargaining with those firefighters.[14] Then there is the issue that the presence of collective bargaining is highly correlated with public-sector unions' other political activities. Government sanctioning of collective bargaining is largely what spurred the unionization of the public sector in the first place,[15] and where there is collective bargaining, there tend to be more politically active unions. To make matters even more complicated, in rating the political activity of police and firefighters' unions in their cities, some local officials who responded to my surveys might have considered the unions' collective bargaining activity in providing their ratings, since that is a way in which public-sector unions engage in politics in many places.

But this measurement and data issue aside, the theoretical and empirical design basics are pretty clear. To study public-sector union influence, we should be examining current data in addition to data from the 1980s and earlier, even if it means we cannot use difference in differences. In addition, we should be cognizant of the possibility that unions might influence employment or salaries but sometimes not both. We should recognize that government employees' pay often includes salary above and beyond base salary and that public officials have greater flexibility to respond to unions' requests on matters of fringe benefits than on salaries. And ideally we want to consider both collective bargaining and public-sector unions' more traditional political activities in evaluating their influence.

Data and Empirical Design

A few years ago, Moe and I tackled many of these issues in a study of police and firefighters' unions in US municipal governments.[16] We first carried out a study of the 1970s and 1980s, examining employment and salary outcomes within the same cities before and after their police and firefighters unionized. The results show positive effects on both salaries and employment. But we also carried out an analysis of more recent data, up through 2010, including data on fringe benefit spending as well as salaries. From the ICMA Police and Fire Personnel and Expenditure Surveys, we acquired measures of cities' expenditures on police and firefighters' salaries that include their extra pay in addition to base salaries, and we found clear evidence that cities where police and firefighters have collective bargaining spend more per capita on their salaries. We also found that the effect of collective bargaining is larger for cities' expenditures on police and firefighters' health benefits. And finally, while we noted that our indicators of collective bargaining likely pick up some of the effects of unions' other political activities, we also did a preliminary analysis that includes an indicator—albeit a crude one—of whether the unions endorse candidates in local elections. The results suggest that both collective bargaining and the indicator of other political activity increase spending on salaries and health benefits.

These results are a strong indication that police and firefighters' unions influence policy in municipal government. What I do here is update that analysis with more recent data and my interest group activity variables. Unfortunately, the ICMA stopped running its Police and Fire Personnel and Expenditures Survey in 2013, which rules out looking at city spending on salaries including extra pay and fringe benefits. Even so, a lot has happened since 2010, especially for public-sector unions—most notably the Great Recession and Republican efforts to weaken collective bargaining in many states. It is therefore worthwhile to examine more recent data, even if they are more limited in the variables they include.

To do this, I use the 2017 Census of Governments Employment data, which contain employment numbers and payroll expenditures for every government in the United States broken down by employee function. When I merge my interest group activity variables with these data, the result is a dataset of over nine hundred municipal governments to analyze, most of which report positive payroll expenditures for police and fire protection.

I first model the amounts cities spent on monthly payroll for police protection employees and fire protection employees, per city resident. In the models of police protection payroll expenditures, I include the political activity of police unions in the city, and in the model of fire protection payroll expenditures, I include the activity of firefighters' unions. As I discussed above, however, it is also important to test for the unions' influence through collective bargaining as another form of political activity available to them.

There are no comprehensive datasets on which local governments across the United States have collective bargaining, especially for particular types of employees, so I use a multipronged approach to code the collective bargaining status of the cities in this dataset. First, for all cities that are also in the Anzia and Moe dataset, I use our collective bargaining indicators from that study, which we constructed using the 1972–87 Census of Governments surveys on collective bargaining and unionization status, the 1989 and 1999 ICMA labor-management relations surveys, and, for police, data from LEMAS.[17] Second, I rely on data from my own surveys described in chapter 3, in which I asked local officials whether police officers and firefighters in their cities have collective bargaining. Third and finally, cities that do not have collective bargaining information from these sources are coded as having collective bargaining for police officers if the state has a duty-to-bargain law for police officers, and the same for firefighters.

As I explained above, including both the collective bargaining indicator and the measure of unions' political activity in these models has advantages and disadvantages. The advantage is that this approach allows me to test for union influence through both channels. The disadvantage is that the two are correlated, both because of how political activity is measured and because (measurement aside) unions are more politically active in other ways when they also have collective bargaining. In addition, as I discussed above, most states have little within-state variation in collective bargaining by municipality, which raises issues of how to interpret the coefficients on collective bargaining in models with state fixed effects. Taking all this into consideration, I estimate two different models for each dependent variable: the first with only regional fixed effects and both the collective bargaining indicator and the measure of political activity and the second with state fixed effects and only the political activity variable (no collective bargaining indicator).

My expectation throughout is that either through their traditional political activities or through collective bargaining—or both—police and firefighters' unions will influence city spending on their salaries. As I discussed in chapter 6, research is clear that this is an area in which public-sector unions have homogeneous preferences. It is also an area in which public-sector unions are swimming upstream, that is, pushing for policies that are likely not the same as those elected officials would otherwise adopt. Elected officials have to wrestle with the budget constraint; they are balancing the need to keep taxes low and service provision steady. These realities of governing often put them at odds with public-sector union pushes for higher compensation and staffing.

With regard to the potential for interest group competition, as I discussed earlier, there may not be much under normal political circumstances. Thinking purely in terms of interests, it is not clear which groups would be homogeneously opposed to higher public-sector salaries and employment levels. Taxpayer groups are one possibility. In the case of police, racial and ethnic minority organizations such as Black Lives Matter are another. But it is far from clear that any other groups would be homogeneously opposed to efforts to hire more public safety employees and pay them more. More important, there is the question of whether any groups other than the grassroots police reform groups will be politically focused on these matters. Salaries and employment have long been primarily budgetary matters (even if the size and budgets of police departments are now viewed by some as part of the problem of police misconduct). Moreover, according to my data, as of 2015 and 2016, taxpayer groups and racial and ethnic minority groups were not very active in most cities. And when it comes to collective bargaining, no group other than the union is able to take part.[18]

In the models that follow, to cover the most likely opponents of higher salaries and greater employment, I include the activity of taxpayer groups, and in models of police salary expenditures in particular, I also include the activity of racial and ethnic minority groups. Because it is possible that some neighborhood associations are politically active on matters other than land use issues, I include their political activity as well but without an expectation that it will make a difference. In addition, I include the other predictors from the models in chapter 7, including city demographics, political institutions, and Democratic presidential vote.

Two final considerations are important to discuss. The first is the general difference in public support for police officers and firefighters. The nature of police officers' and firefighters' jobs is quite different, and that—even before 2020 or the rise of Black Lives Matter—affects public perceptions of them. Those differences in reputation, in turn, may shape their influence; previous research provides evidence that firefighters' unions are more influential than police unions.[19] While it is difficult to measure these differences in public perceptions across a large number of cities, it does lead to a general expectation that firefighters' union influence will be greater than that of police unions.

The second consideration is the theoretical ambiguity about how residents' party affiliations will be related to spending on firefighters' and police officers' salaries. There is evidence that even in local politics, more Democratic and liberal cities tend to tax and spend more,[20] and a large proportion of municipal government spending is *for* police and fire protection—the vast majority of which goes to compensating employees. This suggests that perhaps public safety salary spending will be higher in more Democratic cities. Others have noted that the law-and-order, anticrime dimension of public safety provision aligns more with the Republican Party and a conservative agenda.[21] Still others suggest that public

UNIONS, PUBLIC SAFETY, AND LOCAL GOVERNMENT SPENDING

safety is bipartisan or nonpartisan.[22] It simply is not clear, as a theoretical matter, what role if any partisanship will play.

Results

I begin by analyzing city police protection payroll expenditures per capita in 2017. The median city in this dataset spent \$13.33 per month per city resident on police payroll, with a standard deviation of \$8.30. I first model this variable, including both the main police union activity measure, the collective bargaining indicator, and regional fixed effects.[23] The estimates are shown in table 8.1, column 1. The coefficients on both the collective bargaining indicator and the political activity measure are positive and statistically significant. On average, cities where police have collective bargaining spend an additional \$1.95 per city resident per month on police protection payroll. Moving from a city with slightly active police unions to very active police unions—a two-point increase in

TABLE 8.1 **Police and fire protection payroll per capita**

	Police Protection		Fire Protection	
	(1)	(2)	(3)	(4)
Police union political activity	0.227*	0.336		
	(0.131)	(0.213)		
Police collective bargaining	1.948*			
	(1.157)			
Firefighters' union political activity			0.603***	0.617***
			(0.198)	(0.165)
Firefighter collective bargaining			2.767***	
			(0.894)	
Taxpayer groups	0.0002	0.048	−0.262	−0.129
	(0.158)	(0.162)	(0.157)	(0.152)
Racial and ethnic minority groups	0.073	−0.011		
	(0.200)	(0.234)		
Neighborhood associations	0.001	0.011	−0.239	−0.168
	(0.145)	(0.155)	(0.228)	(0.236)
Democratic presidential vote	0.496	2.401**	−1.171	−0.014
	(1.226)	(1.085)	(1.574)	(1.933)
R-squared	0.22	0.29	0.32	0.41
Observations	779	779	608	608

Notes: Standard errors clustered by state in parentheses. Models 1 and 3 include regional fixed effects; models 2 and 4 include state fixed effects. All models include city demographic variables and political institution variables from earlier analyses.

*p < 0.1, **p < 0.05, ***p < 0.01 (two-tailed).

the political activity variable—is associated with an increase of $0.45 per capita. In column 2, where I drop the collective bargaining indicator and include state fixed effects, that relationship is larger, although not statistically significant at the 10% level (p = 0.12, two-tailed).

In columns 3 and 4, I estimate the same models for monthly fire protection payroll per capita. More cities have police departments than fire departments (some contract with a county or have a special district or volunteer fire department), and in cities that have them, they tend to be smaller than the police departments: median fire protection payroll expenditures per month in this dataset are $8.93, with a standard deviation of $7.81. But the results in columns 3 and 4 clearly indicate that expenditures are greater in places where firefighters have collective bargaining and are politically active. On average, cities with collective bargaining spend $2.77 more on fire protection payroll per capita. And a two-point increase in firefighters' union political activity is associated with an increase in payroll expenditures of about $1.20 per month per capita, in the models with and without state fixed effects.[24]

This, then, is additional evidence that more politically active public safety unions, including collective bargaining activity, influence payroll expenditures in a positive direction—and more for firefighters' unions than police unions.[25] As for other interest groups, I see little sign that they make a difference to public safety salary spending. Democratic presidential vote, moreover, is only significant in one of the models, and it is positive there: in column 2, higher Democratic presidential vote is associated with higher police payroll expenditures; this is not the case in column 1 or in the models of firefighter payroll.[26]

Viewed together, these findings paint a picture of firefighters' unions and police unions positively influencing the amounts cities spend on their salaries, both through collective bargaining and through their other political activities. And they suggest that the unions do not face much interest group opposition in the typical city, at least as of 2017. But all the caveats I mentioned above should be kept in mind. These data only contain information about salaries, not fringe benefits, even though the effects on fringe benefits are probably larger. Moreover, these salary variables only include base pay, even though public safety workers in many places receive forms of extra pay that could be substantial.

While there are no data on the amounts of extra pay police officers and firefighters earn in the cities in my dataset, the 2013 LEMAS dataset provides a glimpse at what is available to police officers in some of them.

Every few years, LEMAS collects information from all large state and local law enforcement agencies (those with at least one hundred sworn officers) and a sample of smaller agencies, and the most recent basic survey asked questions about whether officers are eligible for certain pay incentives. The questions cover several forms of extra pay, most of which are likely desired by officers and their unions and a few of which may be more controversial, such as residence incentives and merit or performance incentives. In table 8.2, I first show the share of municipal government law enforcement agencies that make each form of incentive available to its officers, including all cities in the LEMAS dataset. Then, for the 304 cities that have these data in this LEMAS dataset and for which I have the relevant interest group activity data, I use OLS to regress each of these binary indicators on the independent variables from table 8.1, column 1. In the lower rows of table 8.2, I present the coefficient estimates on police collective bargaining and the main police union political activity variable.

The top rows of table 8.2 show that the most common types of incentives are for educational achievement, such as a college degree (47%); special duty assignments, such as K-9 or horse patrol (43%); and shift differential (34%), which means extra pay for working a less desirable shift, such as overnight. The next two most common incentives, for special skills or vocational training and merit or performance, are available in 23% of the cities. Other incentives, such as for bilingual or multilingual ability, hazardous duty assignments, and residence (living within a certain geographic area), are less common. In addition to the incentives shown here, sworn officers are compensated for overtime work in 97% of the cities.

The coefficient estimates in table 8.2 also show some suggestive patterns. First, cities with collective bargaining and otherwise more politically active police unions are significantly more likely to offer incentives for both educational achievement (column 1) and shift differential pay (column 6). In addition, where police officers have collective bargaining, they are more likely to receive extra pay for special duty assignments and hazardous duty assignments (although the latter estimate is imprecise). There is no indication that either collective bargaining or generally more active unions are associated with incentives for vocational training or language ability. But also interesting are the negative coefficients in columns 7 and 8, the models of residence and merit incentives, respectively.

While in general it would seem that opportunities to earn extra pay

TABLE 8.2 **Pay incentives for police officers**

	Educational Achievement (1)	Vocational Training (2)	Bilingual or Multilingual Ability (3)	Special Duty (4)	Hazardous Duty (5)	Shift Differential (6)	Residence (7)	Merit or Performance (8)
Share of cities	0.471	0.234	0.171	0.432	0.114	0.339	0.038	0.231
Police union activity	0.049*	−0.005	0.005	−0.0004	0.026	0.05**	0.002	−0.037*
	(0.028)	(0.019)	(0.027)	(0.038)	(0.022)	(0.023)	(0.016)	(0.019)
Collective bargaining	0.225***	0.091	−0.09	0.361***	0.118	0.286***	−0.069**	−0.102
	(0.055)	(0.099)	(0.094)	(0.084)	(0.075)	(0.076)	(0.034)	(0.066)
R-squared	0.24	0.15	0.48	0.25	0.17	0.22	0.08	0.14
Observations	304	304	304	304	304	304	304	304

Notes: Models include the covariates from table 8.1, column 1, as well as regional fixed effects. Standard errors clustered by state in parentheses.

*p < 0.1, **p < 0.05, ***p < 0.01 (two-tailed).

would be broadly desired by police unions, there is some evidence that police officers and their unions oppose requirements that they live in or near the cities where they work.[27] It is perhaps notable, then, that less than 4% of cities offer incentives based on residence and that they tend to be cities without police collective bargaining. Moreover, in public education, teachers' unions usually oppose merit pay or pay for performance, preferring instead the uniform salary schedule in which pay increases are tied to education and professional training.[28] The negative coefficients on both collective bargaining and police union activity in column 8 suggest that police unions may take a similar position and successfully oppose merit pay in cities where they are more politically active.

These findings on police pay incentives are therefore preliminary but suggestive. The results in table 8.1 show that overall city spending on police and especially firefighter salaries is higher in cities where those public safety workers have collective bargaining and where their unions are more broadly politically active. But that is only a part of the picture. The weight of the evidence in table 8.2 suggests that police unions in such cities are also more likely to be eligible for certain forms of extra pay—although only those viewed as not threatening to officers' interests and their unions. This, combined with the evidence in my work with Moe, suggests that both collective bargaining and other union political activity influence spending on police and firefighter compensation.

Total Spending and the Share for Police and Fire Protection

While research on public-sector unions has focused on particular forms of government spending that are most clearly linked to the interests of employees and their unions—salaries, benefits, and employment—the local politics literature on representation has examined broader local fiscal patterns, such as total spending and total tax revenue.[29] Other local politics scholars have also investigated the amounts or shares of spending dedicated to certain functions like police protection, fire protection, streets and sanitation, and parks and recreation.[30] These studies do not measure or estimate the effects of interest group activity, but given public-sector unions' interests in higher employment and higher compensation, it is well worth asking whether we should expect these unions to influence taxing and spending more generally.

Theoretically, the answer to this question could go either way, even if public-sector unions do successfully influence local spending on their own compensation. It is spending's components rather than spending totals that most directly affect their interests. Their main focus should be on spending that affects them—and not necessarily on the broad goal of increasing the size of government. While this means that unions will usually favor efforts to increase local revenue, it is not because they care about the total amount of revenue per se but rather because some of that revenue can be used to increase spending on budget items they care about. As Daniel DiSalvo explains:

> To understand public employee unions' lobbying agenda, it is helpful to think of a set of concentric circles. At the core are the bread-and-butter occupational interests of the unions' membership. This includes the things that affect workers' lives on a day-to-day basis: salary, benefits, job protections, and working conditions. At the second level are broader issues affecting workers more generally, including issues such as labor law, healthcare policy, and the minimum wage. At the outer edge are broad liberal causes that unions support—sometimes half-heartedly—in order to forge alliances and good will with other progressive groups.[31]

Total local government spending fits within the "core" DiSalvo describes only inasmuch as it is used to pay for the items within that core. For police officers and firefighters in city governments, there is good reason to think that link is quite strong. Spending on police protection and fire protection compensation makes up a large share of overall city spending in a typical city. Because of this, it could be that more public safety union political activity and collective bargaining does increase overall spending levels of municipal governments. But it is also possible that local governments respond to public safety unions by reallocating spending from other areas to public safety compensation, and that might be just as satisfactory to public safety unions. If so, then active public safety unions may not actually lead to higher municipal government spending overall.

Now that the discussion is focused on total local government spending, moreover, what about the influences of partisanship and ideology? Tausanovitch and Warshaw find a strong relationship between the partisanship and ideology of city residents and total city spending and tax revenue.[32] One interpretation of this is that the broad size-of-government issue that defines ideological and partisan divisions in national politics carries over into the local context. How this works is still an open question,[33] but the general idea seems plausible. Liberals and Democrats may be more tolerant of higher taxes and bigger government regardless of whether the government or issue in question is local, state, or federal. If so, then on broad questions about the size of the pie in government, it seems reasonable that outcomes would vary with national-level partisanship and ideology.

But work along these lines does not consider interest groups; it is focused on public opinion. Yet both the presence of collective bargaining and the measure of the political activity of public safety unions are positively correlated with Democratic presidential vote, because the Democratic Party has long been more favorable to unions. It is worth asking, then, whether some of the relationship between total spending and ideology or partisanship is explained by collective bargaining and other union activity. While Tausanovitch and Warshaw conclude from their analysis that city policy is responsive to residents,[34] it could also be that those same city policies are responsive to unions.

Then there are questions not about the overall size of the government pie but rather how the pie is divided. These questions have gotten less attention from scholars focused on the effects of partisanship and ideology, and the little research that has been done has generated some debate. Elisabeth Gerber and Daniel Hopkins, for example, use a regression discontinuity design and find that local governments that barely elect a Republican mayor devote a larger share of spending to police protection and fire protection but no other clear relationships to the allocation of spending.[35] Justin de Benedictis-Kessner and Christopher Warshaw, however, conclude that this is because the denominator (of total spending) is smaller under Republican mayors—not because Republicans actually spend more on public safety.[36]

Debates of this kind are a productive starting point, but I suspect one reason this issue has gotten less attention and generated inconclusive findings is that it is not theoretically clear how national-level partisanship and ideology should map onto how local governments allocate spending. Once again, the functions of local government—what they actually *do*—do not line up nicely with the issues that divide the national political parties. More Democratic residents may well be more open to paying higher taxes than Republicans, but are Democrats' preferences on parks versus roads systematically different from those of Republi-

218   CHAPTER EIGHT

cans? We don't know, but I suspect not. It isn't even obvious that residents have well-defined preferences on these issues.[37]

Here, however, is exactly where interest groups come in. Police unions *do* prefer more spending on police protection. Firefighters' unions *do* prefer more spending on fire protection. And the same goes for any group with a similarly vested interest in what city governments do. Once we shift from a focus on the whole to a focus on the parts, theoretical expectations about the role of citizens and public opinion become murky, but the expectations about the role of interest groups are strong.

To explore these questions, I use data from the 2017 Census of Governments Finance file, which provide detailed breakdowns of every government's spending by function and type. Combined with my interest group variables, the result is a dataset of over nine hundred cities to examine. For comparison purposes, I start with a model that is very similar to the one presented by Tausanovitch and Warshaw: focusing on cities with more than 20,000 in population, it uses OLS to regress the city's total current operating expenditures per capita on Democratic presidential vote, income per capita, city population, and percent Black. The estimates of this model are shown in table 8.3, column 1.[38] The results are similar to those of Tausanovitch and Warshaw: cities with more Democratic residents have higher overall spending per capita. The same is true when I instead use their MRP measure of residents' ideology and when I include cities with fewer than 20,000 residents.

In column 2, I instead model this total spending variable with most of the covariates from my earlier models—city demographics and political institutions—with cities of all sizes, including those with fewer than 20,000 residents. For the moment, I leave out the regional fixed effects, the interest group activity variables, and the collective bargaining indicator. The coefficient on Democratic presidential vote is still positive and statistically significant, indicating that local partisanship is positively associated with total city spending per capita.

In column 3, I add one variable: an indicator for whether firefighters have collective bargaining in the city. The results show that the presence of collective bargaining is associated with a significant $194 increase in total spending per capita—about 13% of a standard deviation. The coefficient on Democratic presidential vote is reduced by half. And in column 4, where I add the regional indicators and measures of the political activity of firefighters' unions, taxpayer groups, and neighborhood associations, the results are the same. The interest group activity variables,

UNIONS, PUBLIC SAFETY, AND LOCAL GOVERNMENT SPENDING

TABLE 8.3 **Total current operating expenditures per capita**

	(1)	(2)	(3)	(4)
Democratic presidential vote	598.69***	366.37*	183.68	162.82
	(157.78)	(183.43)	(192.72)	(180.51)
Collective bargaining			194.12***	271.76***
			(72.00)	(75.54)
Firefighters' union activity				−10.13
				(19.07)
Taxpayer groups				16.33
				(25.92)
Neighborhood associations				6.81
				(30.48)
Ln(Income per capita)	420.88***	564.21***	578.80***	558.39***
	(141.34)	(69.28)	(65.50)	(62.70)
Ln(Population)	154.02***	57.67	50.85	42.90
	(29.61)	(34.54)	(30.94)	(30.99)
Percent Black	317.61	−138.44	65.50	−187.80
	(324.25)	(209.50)	(236.78)	(233.64)
Percent homeowner		−1,814.94***	−1,756.11***	−1,923.27***
		(285.74)	(275.55)	(250.41)
Percent Latino		−538.69***	−541.53***	−455.41***
		(142.63)	(144.91)	(121.35)
Percent rural		395.13**	380.40**	277.99**
		(153.31)	(156.53)	(119.31)
Off-cycle		58.99	51.97	86.39
		(73.03)	(74.63)	(54.37)
Nonpartisan		−44.88	−81.71	24.75
		(143.32)	(137.51)	(90.98)
District elections		81.24	89.91	97.31*
		(59.92)	(56.44)	(48.39)
Mayor-council government		−17.41	−35.59	−29.26
		(41.08)	(39.95)	(38.13)
R-squared	0.12	0.17	0.18	0.22
Observations	478	895	895	884

Notes: Standard errors clustered by state in parentheses. Model 1 includes only cities with more than 20,000 in population. Model 2 includes regional fixed effects.

*p < 0.1, **p < 0.05, ***p < 0.01 (two-tailed).

including firefighters' union political activity, are not associated with higher overall spending, nor is Democratic presidential vote. But the indicator for collective bargaining is.[39]

These results put an asterisk on claims that patterns of city spending are responsive to the preferences of city residents. Some of the correlation between Democratic presidential vote (or ideology) and overall city spending has to do with the fact that liberal and Democratic cities are more likely to have collective bargaining for their public employees. And it makes sense that collective bargaining would have this relationship with spending. Collective bargaining is a process in which government employee unions negotiate directly with city officials for higher compensation and more employees—among the biggest expenses of city government. Comparatively, the mechanisms by which city residents affect spending are theoretically less clear. And my results here show that a sizable proportion of the relationship between Democratic presidential vote and total spending is explained by collective bargaining.

Does this mean citizens' preferences don't matter? As I have discussed, the analysis does not allow me to answer this question. The results show that national-level partisanship and ideology appear to matter less for local spending than some researchers previously thought. But Democratic presidential vote (and ideology) may or may not capture local residents' preferences on the amount of local spending. We will not know for sure until we have public opinion questions that ask directly about local government spending preferences. At a minimum, though, these findings demand that scholars of local political representation consider interest groups—public-sector unions in particular—when thinking about local government policy and responsiveness.

Having considered total spending, I now turn to the amount of spending dedicated to police protection and fire protection. Here is where my expectations about public safety union influence are the clearest: if these unions have influence, we should see larger amounts per capita spent on public safety functions. In table 8.4, I model total police protection expenditures per capita, first with regional indicators (column 1) and then with state fixed effects.[40] The results are unambiguous. Having collective bargaining is associated with an increase in police protection spending of $35 per capita, which is about one-fifth of a standard deviation. (The median city in this dataset spent $270 per resident on police protection.) More politically active police unions are associated with more spending as well: a two-point increase in police union political activity is associated with a $13 increase in police protection spending per city resident. I find the same relationship in column 2, where I add state fixed effects. Thus, through both collective bargaining and other political activity, police unions seem to have influence on local police protection spending.

The other estimates show some interesting patterns as well. Wealthier cities and cities with larger racial and ethnic minority populations spend more per capita on police protection. Cities with a higher share of homeowners spend significantly less. And the coefficients on Democratic presidential vote are positive and significant. I had no reason to expect this—one could tell a story about why it should be positive, negative, or

UNIONS, PUBLIC SAFETY, AND LOCAL GOVERNMENT SPENDING

TABLE 8.4 **Per capita expenditures on police protection, fire protection, and parks and recreation**

	Police Protection		Fire Protection		Parks and Recreation
	(1)	(2)	(3)	(4)	(5)
Collective bargaining	34.90***		49.57***		−5.99
	(9.98)		(13.55)		(7.60)
Police union activity	6.57**	8.06***			
	(2.67)	(2.63)			
Firefighters' union activity			10.47***	9.62***	−1.62
			(2.58)	(2.32)	(1.75)
Taxpayer groups	4.44	3.11	−3.48	−5.49**	1.20
	(3.53)	(3.61)	(3.23)	(2.46)	(2.29)
Neighborhood associations	−5.22*	−5.32	−3.77	−1.07	1.60
	(2.86)	(3.19)	(3.26)	(3.02)	(2.44)
Minority groups	−5.65	−6.22*			
	(3.47)	(3.19)			
Ln(Population)	4.39	2.87	9.22*	10.10*	11.45***
	(3.47)	(3.49)	(4.76)	(5.58)	(2.66)
Ln(Income per capita)	148.36***	136.43***	80.08***	83.38***	87.41***
	(14.44)	(20.41)	(16.31)	(17.07)	(5.79)
Percent homeowner	−277.03***	−288.59***	−163.91***	−154.51***	−157.90***
	(35.01)	(39.62)	(23.49)	(21.34)	(20.28)
Democratic presidential vote	58.52**	81.55**	19.95	35.33	−1.20
	(27.04)	(30.62)	(32.44)	(40.96)	(21.26)
Percent Black	147.12***	99.40***	12.97	4.60	−72.66***
	(38.53)	(32.41)	(28.89)	(31.43)	(23.93)
Percent Latino	81.14*	45.79	−74.03***	−70.11***	−11.87
	(44.20)	(53.33)	(22.25)	(20.52)	(16.67)
R-squared	0.32	0.38	0.30	0.37	0.27
Observations	890	890	726	726	864

Notes: Standard errors clustered by state in parentheses. Models 1, 3, and 5 include regional fixed effects; models 2 and 4 include state fixed effects. All models include additional demographic variables and political institutions.

*p < 0.1, **p < 0.05, ***p < 0.01 (two-tailed).

null—but these results show that more Democratic cities spend more per capita on the police.

Just as striking are the negative coefficients on the political activity of neighborhood associations and racial and ethnic minority groups. While existing research suggests that neighborhood associations are primarily focused on land use and development issues, these results indicate that cities with more active neighborhood associations spend less per capita on police protection. It also appears that more active racial and ethnic minority organizations can be an effective counterforce against the interests of police unions: moving from a city where such groups are slightly active to one where they are very active is associated with a \$12 decrease in police protection spending per capita. For police, then, there are signs that there is resistance to their influence on spending on police protection.

In columns 3 and 4 of table 8.4, I model total spending on fire protection per capita. For context, the median city in this dataset spent \$164 per city resident on fire protection. The coefficients on collective bargaining and other union political activity are even larger here than for the police. Collective bargaining is associated with a \$50 increase in spending on fire protection per capita, which is about one-third of a standard deviation. In addition, a two-point increase in firefighters' union political activity is associated with about \$20 more in fire protection spending per capita, regardless of whether the model includes regional fixed effects or state fixed effects.

The estimates for the other variables in these models are somewhat different from those in the models of police protection spending. Here we continue to see that wealthier cities with fewer homeowners spend more on fire protection. But cities with larger Latino populations spend less, and Democratic presidential vote has no significant relationship to fire protection spending. As for group competition, column 4 suggests that more active taxpayer groups are associated with less spending on fire protection per capita, but there is no such relationship for neighborhood associations.

Finally, in column 5, I run a placebo test, modeling total spending per capita on parks and recreation in each city. This, like police and fire protection, is a relatively large municipal government spending item, but I would not expect collective bargaining or the political activity of public safety workers to influence it. In column 5, that is what I find. Neither collective bargaining nor firefighters' union political activity has a significant relationship with parks and recreation spending. Therefore, I find relationships for budget items where I expect it and do not find relationships where I do not expect it, suggesting that this is influence and not some unmeasured feature of cities that makes them more pro-spending.

I carry out one final analysis of these spending data to complete the connection to existing research: whether public safety union political activity is associated with larger shares of city spending devoted to public safety. As I explained above, even if the unions are having influence, it may or may not result in a large *share* of spending devoted to public safety. The unions care more about the numerator than the denomina-

UNIONS, PUBLIC SAFETY, AND LOCAL GOVERNMENT SPENDING 223

TABLE 8.5 **Share of total current operating expenditures, police protection and fire protection**

	Police Protection		Fire Protection	
	(1)	(2)	(3)	(4)
Collective bargaining	0.005		0.021**	
	(0.007)		(0.009)	
Police union activity	0.01***	0.01***		
	(0.002)	(0.002)		
Firefighters' union activity			0.008**	0.009***
			(0.003)	(0.003)
Taxpayer groups	0.001	−0.001	0.0002	−0.002
	(0.004)	(0.005)	(0.002)	(0.002)
Minority groups	−0.009***	−0.011***		
	(0.002)	(0.002)		
Neighborhood associations	−0.012***	−0.012***	−0.004*	−0.002
	(0.003)	(0.003)	(0.002)	(0.002)
Ln(Population)	−0.005*	−0.003	−0.0003	0.002
	(0.003)	(0.003)	(0.002)	(0.003)
Ln(Income per capita)	0.047***	0.033**	0.019**	0.021**
	(0.010)	(0.015)	(0.008)	(0.008)
Percent homeowner	0.018	0.028	0.012	0.015
	(0.032)	(0.030)	(0.017)	(0.015)
Democratic presidential vote	0.01	0.024	−0.011	−0.001
	(0.021)	(0.025)	(0.021)	(0.022)
Percent Black	0.159***	0.107***	0.01	−0.009
	(0.041)	(0.033)	(0.022)	(0.019)
Percent Latino	0.161***	0.127***	−0.005	−0.008
	(0.022)	(0.029)	(0.018)	(0.022)
R-squared	0.22	0.32	0.17	0.30
Observations	914	914	733	733

Notes: Standard errors clustered by state in parentheses. Models 1 and 3 include regional fixed effects; models 2 and 4 include state fixed effects. All models include additional demographic variables and political institutions.
*p < 0.1, **p < 0.05, ***p < 0.01 (two-tailed).

tor. Still, when I model the share of total city operating expenditures devoted to police protection and fire protection, respectively, the results indicate that larger shares of city spending go to public safety when public safety unions are more active.

Column 1 of table 8.5 shows that police collective bargaining is not associated with a larger share of the budget devoted to police protection, but in columns 1 and 2, more activity by police unions in general is. On average, a two-point increase in police union activity is associated with a two-percentage-point increase in the share of the budget spent on police protection. In columns 3 and 4, both firefighter collective bargaining and more politically active firefighters' unions in general are associated with a larger proportion of the budget being spent on fire protection. For collective bargaining, the coefficient shows a two-percentage-point increase. A two-point increase in firefighters' union activity is also associated with about a two-point increase in the share of the budget devoted to fire protection. Thus, cities with more active public safety unions spend more overall and a larger share of their budgets on public safety. Moreover, Democratic presidential vote is not associated with either a larger or smaller share of spending devoted to police protection or fire protection.

Fiscal Pressure and Fire Protection in West Covina, California

An in-depth look at events in West Covina, California, illustrates how these dynamics can play out and how local political matters of spending, taxes, salaries, benefits, collective bargaining, and union activity all fit together. West Covina is a city of just over 100,000 residents east of downtown Los Angeles. Registered Democrats outnumber Republicans. A slight majority of city residents are Latino. Median household income was about $83,000 in 2019, similar to that of California as a whole.

As was the case for many cities, the budget situation in West Covina in 2011 was grim. In the aftermath of the Great Recession, the city had massive annual budget shortfalls, caused by both declining revenues and increasing costs—with pensions and retiree health care being especially large drivers of the latter. The city workforce was already shrinking. Between 2008 and 2010, the total size of the city staff declined from 445 to 385, with the fire department going from 78 to 66 employees. And that year even more fire department jobs were on the chopping block: facing an overall city shortfall of $7.3 million, the city eliminated one of the fire department's five engines—Engine 4—along with the nine personnel associated with it.[41]

Engine 4 and those firefighter jobs were temporarily restored thanks to a $3 million FEMA Staffing for Adequate Fire and Emergency Response (SAFER) grant the city received in 2011. As part of the grant deal that restored the funding, moreover, the city adopted two pension reforms. First, the city council and the West Covina Firefighters' Association (FFA) agreed to increase the pension eligibility retirement age for new hires from 50 to 55.[42] Then, the following year, they also approved a contract that required firefighters to pay their share (the employees' share) of the city's pension contributions—which previously the city had

UNIONS, PUBLIC SAFETY, AND LOCAL GOVERNMENT SPENDING   225

paid on firefighters' behalf out of the general fund.[43] For the moment, open conflict was minimal.

That started to change when the SAFER grant expired in 2013. The city then laid off six firefighters, demoted another three, and once again put Engine 4 out of commission.[44] The next year the city received a second SAFER grant of $1.5 million, which covered thirteen fire department positions and Engine 4, but this time the city itself had to find the funds needed for any associated overtime, equipment, and hiring costs.[45] Those extra costs turned out to be a lot for the cash-strapped city to bear. When the second SAFER grant funding ran out in May 2017, city officials opted not to apply for another grant—and thus not to seek the federal funding to help pay for the extra firefighter positions.

Meanwhile, collective bargaining negotiations between the city and the FFA were growing tense. Negotiations over a new contract in 2014 stalled when the two sides disagreed about bonuses and staffing. Ultimately, a mediator from the state Public Employment Relations Board was brought in to try to help resolve the dispute.[46] When that new contract lapsed at the end of 2016,[47] just before the second SAFER grant ran out, negotiations once again stalled. The city was proposing to eliminate Engine 4 and six vacant positions and to demote six other fire department employees. It wanted to replace Engine 4 with something called a quint, which is like a mix between a truck and an engine and can be operated by fewer firefighters. The FFA, opposed to the staffing cuts and requesting benefit increases, picketed outside city hall.[48] As FFA president Matt Jackson explained, "The significance here is that the area of West Covina which is served by that station, when an engine is cut, does not have a piece of equipment to deliver water to a fire. . . . The citizens in that district, should they have a fire, are waiting for an engine to respond from a further away station. This puts life and property needlessly at risk."[49] Replacing Engine 4 with a quint was thus framed by the FFA as a threat to public safety.

In the midst of all this, the FFA accused Fire Chief Larry Whithorn of retaliating against union members for drawing out negotiations and for picketing. It filed a tort claim against the city and Whithorn and issued a vote of no confidence in Whithorn.[50] (When Whithorn was eventually fired in April 2019, the *San Gabriel Valley Tribune* cited no reasons other than the 2017 vote of no confidence and tense relations between the chief and the union.)[51]

With the labor dispute ongoing in 2018, the city and the union entered into arbitration, the outcome of which was the arbitrator recommending that the city put a tax measure on the ballot to generate funding for the contested fire department positions. Chris Freeland, the city manager, called the arbitrator's decision "very overreaching" and stated, "You have a state agency recommend to solve a labor dispute with a tax on the community, which is shocking and surprising."[52]

Shortly afterward, the city council voted 3 to 2 to reject the city's *own* best and final offer to the FFA—a vote that had the effect of keeping Engine 4 in service for the time being. At that city council meeting, a number of firefighters spoke during the public comment period. Their overwhelming message was that Engine 4 needed to remain in service and that risks to public safety would ensue should it be replaced with a quint. Some speakers gestured to their colleagues in the audience as they spoke, indicating that there was a sizable firefighter presence at the meeting. The culmination of this was that one city council member, Lloyd Johnson, switched his vote from supporting the best and final offer to opposing it—thereby moving the council from 3 to 2 in support to 3 to 2 in opposition. After the council vote, the audience erupted in applause.[53]

Reactions to that city council decision illustrate the various considerations that were involved. Jackson was pleased, saying, "We're excited about the fact the council is starting to believe us and have faith in us. . . . They trusted our opinion on this matter even though it was a complex issue to sort through." James Toma, one of the two councilmembers who voted to eliminate Engine 4, worried about the prospect of West Covina going the way of Vallejo and Stockton (which declared bankruptcy): "I understand where the firefighters are coming from, and it is frustrating. . . . I feel for them because they're doing their jobs. But ours is to look out for the bigger picture."[54] Councilmember Tony Wu, on the other hand, voted to keep Engine 4 in operation. Wu had been elected in 2015 as a pro-business candidate ("I'm going to run the city like a business") with the endorsements of the FFA and the West Covina Police Association.[55] In explaining his vote on this issue, he said that West Covina was much stronger on economic growth than Stockton and highlighted the importance of robust public safety provision to attracting investment: "We can't cut to make money, we have to spend money to attract people to come in. . . . We want to create an environment comfortable to invest in, with good public safety and proud firefighters."[56]

Regardless, the city council vote to keep Engine 4 in operation was only temporary. When it came time to do the budget for 2018–19, the outlook was bleak: an $8.7 million deficit. To close the gap, the city voted 3 to 2 to make 10% cuts in almost all city departments, including the police department and the number of maintenance workers in the Public Works Department.[57] The only departments that saw less than a 10% cut were Planning, which was already short staffed,[58] and the fire department. Cuts to the fire department amounted to less than 10% because any more would have necessitated salary reductions—which would require negotiations with the union.[59] Still, Engine 4 was decommissioned and fire department employment levels were reduced. In November 2018, James Toma lost his reelection to Planning Commissioner Dario Castellanos, who had been endorsed by the FFA. A second councilmember who had voted to decommission Engine 4 (and had also done so earlier in 2018) decided not to seek reelection.[60] Lloyd Johnson, the councilmember who had switched his vote earlier that year, voted in support of the 2018–19 budget and thus to decommission Engine 4 and then lost his reelection bid in November 2020, garnering the smallest vote share of the three candidates running.

Even with the 2018–19 city budget balanced by a thread, some city council members set out to find ways to restore previous police and fire department staffing levels. The problem was that no one knew where that money would come from.[61] While a majority on the city council was now supportive of the efforts of the FFA, the council could not muster a majority to put a tax measure on the ballot to increase revenue. The FFA and the West Covina Police Officers Association therefore joined with residents to gather signatures to place a sales tax increase initiative on the March 2020 ballot—one that would increase the local sales tax to the state maximum of 10.25%.[62]

Meanwhile, in late 2019, the California State Auditor released an online dashboard ranking the fiscal health of the state's cities, and West Covina was rated as having the seventeenth highest fiscal risk.[63] Yet, a month later, the city and the FFA together approved a 12% raise for firefighters, even though it wasn't clear how it would be paid for.[64] Moreover, with the pay increases locked in, the dispute over Engine 4 seemed to die down: Engine 4 was not put back in service, and the quint remained in place despite the FFA's warning. Then, in March 2020, the sales tax measure failed at the polls, with 80% of city residents voting against it. In July 2020, the state auditor declared that West Covina was at risk of bankruptcy. Scrambling to cover costs, the city issued pension obligation bonds and proposed selling city land, but those onetime measures would of course be limited in their effectiveness in addressing the city's structural deficit problem. Meanwhile, roughly 80% of West Covina's general fund goes to public safety expenses.[65] What lies ahead remains to be seen.

While the controversy in West Covina should not be taken as representative of city and fire department politics everywhere, it gives some substance to the quantitative findings shown above. The FFA works to increase firefighters' salaries and benefits and keep employment levels high. It is active through both collective bargaining and more traditional political activities, such as trying to elect sympathetic candidates to the city council. It faces little opposition from organized groups and can actually end up on the same side as business in local policy debates. But that does not mean it can get the city council to enact whatever it wants. First, there is a trade-off between staffing and salaries. Second, its influence is limited by cost commitments made in the past—most notably, on pensions. Third, even in this city that now leans Democratic, there is public resistance to tax increases. The opposition, therefore, comes from city officials who are forced to cope with what Toma called "the big picture" and tasked with governing under a budget constraint.

Two final points are worth highlighting. Even with the public controversy in West Covina, no one is openly *against* the FFA. There is no direct opposition to it. Further, these costs and these services really matter to city government. They are the essence of city government. Seemingly technical disputes about whether a less expensive quint would work almost as well as an engine are ultimately disputes about jobs, which in turn are disputes about city expenditures, taxes, and the size of government. And clearly public safety unions play an important role in shaping decisions on those matters.

Work Rules and the Police

My analysis so far has considered outcomes that have been the main focus of research on public-sector unions: fiscal variables. As local policies, their direct costs are primarily budgetary. That researchers have focused on these makes sense given both public-sector unions' interests in them and the importance of local budget constraints to public service provision. But public-sector unions also have an interest in policies whose costs are not primarily budgetary: rules that govern how employees do their work and rules for what their managers can and cannot do to manage them.

As I discussed in chapter 6, research on the causes and effects of work rules is much more limited than research on fiscal outcomes. Yet as a very small body of work on teachers' unions has shown, school districts' collective bargaining contracts typically have many provisions that structure what the managers in public education—superintendents, principals, and state education officials—can and cannot do. A typical contract goes far beyond civil service protections that prohibit termination for political reasons. Contracts often include, for example, rules for how employees can be hired and evaluated, who gets priority in transfer requests, how many faculty meetings are allowed, how often teachers can be required to communicate with parents, and how employees can be evaluated and disciplined.[66] As a theoretical matter, most of these rules could have either positive or negative social welfare effects, but research on these questions is in very short supply,[67] and much more is needed. At the very least, it is important to recognize that contracts contain these provisions because teachers' unions advocate for them. The rules are there to protect teachers, and they are negotiated in private, out of public view.

Regardless, one need not definitively establish the social welfare implications of each rule before making some headway on understanding the politics involved, particularly the role of interest groups. We can assume that government employees and their unions tend to favor provisions that give them greater protections, that do not impose cumbersome or stressful requirements, and that create favorable conditions on the job. Their managers—both appointees and elected officials—probably prefer to have flexibility and managerial discretion given that they are held accountable for agency or government performance.[68] And there is already some evidence from public education that where teachers' unions are stronger, their collective bargaining agreements tend to include more restrictive work rules.[69]

We currently have far less understanding of how police and firefighters' unions influence work rules—or for that matter whether and how work rules structure public safety provision. Work rules in public education have received some attention in part because for years they have been central to high-profile controversies, such as that in New York City, when teachers accused of misconduct were put in "Rubber Rooms": they were removed from the classroom but paid full salaries and benefits for doing nothing, because contract provisions made it nearly impossible to fire them. Until recently, the work rules and accountability of public safety workers received less attention. But that began to change in 2014 when a police officer fatally shot Michael Brown in Ferguson, Missouri, and as the Black Lives Matter movement gained momentum and visibility. Even before 2020, a number of reform groups were actively working to increase accountability in local police agencies, many of them with a focus on the rules governing how police do their jobs. In 2020, these rules were front and center in active debates about police reform.

Campaign Zero, for example, is an organization focused on ending police-based violence. Through its ten-point plan, it proposes a number of changes to how police officers do their work and how they are managed. It advocates for citizen oversight of investigations of police misconduct, standards for how police officers can use force, and enhanced reliance on community input for determining police agency policies. It wants to put body cameras on police officers and require training on de-escalation techniques and implicit bias. Furthermore, it seeks the removal of provisions in police collective bargaining contracts that reduce accountability, such as provisions that "allow officers to wait 48 hours or more before being interrogated after an incident," to "expunge or destroy records of past misconduct (both sustained and unsustained) from their disciplinary file," and "prevent an officer from being investigated for an incident that happened 100 or more days prior."[70] Many of these goals are shared by other organizations, such as PolicyLink and the Police Reform Organizing Project.

Unfortunately, research on the prevalence and effects of these types of provisions still lags reform group interest. Currently, there are no readily available datasets on these policies for large numbers of municipal police departments. Campaign Zero itself has compiled a dataset of controversial collective bargaining contract provisions in 81 US cities, but so far it only covers the largest cities—and naturally only those that have collective bargaining. Even so, it finds that 72 of the 81 contracts have at least one provision that makes it difficult to hold police officers accountable,[71] and most have multiple such provisions. Stephen Rushin has also carried out a study of police collective bargaining contract provisions in 178 of the largest US cities and found that 156 contained provisions "that could thwart legitimate disciplinary actions against officers engaged in misconduct."[72] Thus, while there is still little to no research on the effects of these provisions, it seems very likely that they are important to how policing is conducted. As with teachers, moreover, the provisions are in the contracts because police unions push for them. They are designed to protect workers, not to serve the public interest, and they are hashed out behind closed doors in mostly private negotiations.

Case studies of particular cities also suggest that police unions are vocal and active on such issues and that even before 2020—at least in some large cities—reform groups were active as well. Historically, the media has covered work rules only when there has been active controversy about them, but the controversial cases provide insight into the positions and activities of the key actors—and therefore their interests— even if they are less useful for drawing conclusions about power.

In Dallas, for example, Chief of Police David Brown implemented a series of reforms after a number of officer-involved shootings in the city in 2012 and 2013. Those reforms included requiring more detail in officers' "resisting arrest reports," changes in Taser training, and a new foot patrol policy to reduce the likelihood of dangerous chases. Furthermore, he released to the public details on all officer-involved shootings in the city from 2002 to 2012.[73] In 2013, he implemented a new requirement for officers to receive use-of-force training every two months instead of every two years.[74] But perhaps the biggest break from the past was the shift from a "command and control" approach to "de-escalation," which *Governing* called "nothing less than an attempt to change a century of police practice."[75]

Pushing for these reforms were a number of organizations, including Mothers Against Police Brutality, Next Generation Action Network, Dallas Communities Organizing for Change, and the Texas Chapter of the American Civil Liberties Union (ACLU).[76] The Texas ACLU praised the shift to de-escalation,[77] but other activists felt that Brown's reforms didn't go far enough. Many called for deeper reforms, including having a special independent prosecutor appointed by the local US attorney to investigate fatal police shootings, regular drug testing and psychological evaluations for officers, body cameras for all officers, compensation for victims, federal investigations of civil rights violations by officers, and a federal database of problem officers.[78] As Stephen Benavides, organizer with the Dallas Communities Organizing for Change, said in 2016, "Training and body cameras run parallel to, but are not solutions to, the core issue of systemic racism."[79]

At the same time, many of the reforms Brown implemented were criticized by the local police unions. Of the department's changes in its use-of-force policy, president of the Dallas Federation of Police, Richard Todd, said, "They're [the officers are] going to be so worried about whether they're going to get in trouble that they're not going to react. They need to know about what levels of force they can use and when they should act."[80] The Dallas police unions supported the deployment of body cameras but expressed concerns about officer privacy and how the video would be used.[81] They warned that releasing officers' names to the public after they were involved in shootings put them in danger.[82] And many viewed the training and use-of-force reforms as making the police force less effective, less cohesive, and less safe.[83] According to *Governing*, "Many people believed that Brown's reforms, along with low salaries and extended hours for cops on the beat, had decimated morale on the force. Scores of officers had quit over the past year [2015–16]. The exodus was so great—more than 40 officers resigned in the month of May—that the department reportedly couldn't process the paperwork quickly enough, and cops were being told they had to wait to quit."[84]

Based on what we know, then, contract provisions, work rules, and employee protections are important features of how local public services are provided. While this topic deserves a much more thorough treatment than I can provide here, I can contribute a starting point. I do not have detailed data on the work rules and employee protections in place in the hundreds of cities in my dataset, but using data from recent LEMAS datasets, I carry out a preliminary analysis of whether and how police collective bargaining and other union political activity is associated with two common goals of police reform groups: community policing and officer-worn cameras.

Community policing has long been sought by reformers, although it is more a philosophy than a set of well-defined policies or practices. The goal of community policing is to improve relationships between police officers and the communities they serve. It is an approach in which police officers directly involve the community—businesses and residents—in developing priorities and addressing crime.[85] The specific practices can include "talking to local business owners to help identify their problems and concerns, visiting residents in their homes to offer advice on security, and helping to organize and support neighborhood watch groups and regular community meetings."[86] We might expect that where racial and ethnic minority groups are more active, community policing will be more prevalent.

Should we expect police officers and their unions to be actively opposed to community policing, however? It is not obvious that they would be. Community policing can be implemented in many different ways, some of which officers might have no objection to. Many community policing practices might even be favored by the police, especially if they involve little cost to them and improve their relationships with and reputation among their communities. In this case, then, police union interests are not clearly homogeneous, so we may not see a relationship between their political activity and the prevalence of community policing.

To explore this, I turned to data in the 2013 LEMAS survey. Those data show that even as of 2012, community policing—at least in the abstract—was widespread among municipal police departments. All but 11% of the municipal police agencies surveyed reported having a written mission statement, and 88% of those said that their mission statements contained a "community policing component." Of the cities with a mission statement, moreover, cities with police collective bargaining were slightly *more* likely to have a community policing component. In table 8.6, column 1, I model this binary indicator of community policing on the same set of independent variables from earlier, and the coefficient

TABLE 8.6 **Community policing**

	Community Policing Statement (1)	8 Hours of Training for Recruits (2)	SARA Model Encouraged (3)	Proportion of Officers Using SARA (4)
Collective bargaining	0.158**	−0.334*	−0.053	−0.041
	(0.068)	(0.178)	(0.079)	(0.069)
Police union activity	−0.029	0.016	−0.024	−0.018
	(0.029)	(0.044)	(0.049)	(0.024)
Taxpayer groups	0.027	−0.001	0.028	−0.009
	(0.026)	(0.062)	(0.029)	(0.012)
Neighborhood associations	−0.027	−0.072	−0.005	0.003
	(0.027)	(0.052)	(0.021)	(0.016)
Minority groups	0.026	−0.002	0.042*	0.038*
	(0.018)	(0.081)	(0.023)	(0.019)
Democratic presidential vote	−0.063	0.037	−0.354	0.112
	(0.164)	(0.272)	(0.249)	(0.125)
R-squared	0.08	0.15	0.1	0.08
Observations	305	259	302	291

Notes: Standard errors clustered by state in parentheses. Models include fixed effects for region as well city demographic variables and political institution variables from earlier analyses.

*p < 0.1, **p < 0.05, ***p < 0.01 (two-tailed).

on police collective bargaining is positive and statistically significant. Moreover, neither the coefficient on police union activity nor that of racial and ethnic minority organizations is significant, whether in a model with regional fixed effects (column 1) or in a model with state fixed effects (not shown).

The estimates in column 2 suggest that the issue may be complicated, however, and that more detailed measures are needed. The LEMAS survey asked local agencies whether officers are required to do at least eight hours of community policing training. The dependent variable in column 2 equals 0 if no recruits are required to do such training, 1 if some recruits are, and 2 if all recruits are. On average, cities with police collective bargaining are less likely to require all police recruits to do a minimum of eight hours of community policing training. Again, minority organization activity does not seem to make a difference, whether in this model with regional fixed effects or in a model with state fixed effects (not shown). But in a model with state fixed effects, the coefficient on police union political activity is actually positive.

This ambiguity in the results may well reflect varied definitions of what community policing actually is and what any such training involves. In columns 3 and 4, therefore, I turn to another set of variables in the LEMAS data: measures of whether the agency actively encourages SARA-type problem-solving projects. SARA, which stands for Scanning, Analysis, Response, and Assessment, is a particular model of problem-solving that is commonly used in community policing. The dependent variable in column 3 equals 1 if the agency encouraged its use, 0 if it did not. In column 4, the dependent variable is the proportion of police officers in the agency who are engaged in such projects.

In neither set of results is there indication that police collective bargaining or other police union political activity is associated with encouragement to use the SARA model. Here, however, the coefficient on the activity of racial and ethnic minority organizations is positive. A two-point increase in the political activity of such groups is associated with an 8-percentage-point increase in the likelihood that SARA-type projects are encouraged. Such an increase is also associated with a 7.6-percentage-point increase in the share of officers using such projects. However, when I add state fixed effects to these last two models and drop the collective bargaining indicator, the coefficients on minority group political activity are no longer statistically significant. Thus, there are weak signs that the activity of racial and ethnic minority groups might matter for these community policing practices, but they are sensitive to the model specification. More central to my focus here, it is not clear that police unions are actively or successfully opposed to them.

Body cameras may be another matter. This, too, is a reform commonly sought by police reform groups and one that is asked about in the 2016 LEMAS Body-Worn Camera Supplement. I know of no data on police officers' or unions' positions on body cameras. But while the views of individual officers probably vary, there is strong reason to think that many police unions tend to be opposed to them. Some officers might welcome the increased transparency or at least not feel threatened by it. But the union's job is to protect *all* officers. The underlying logic is the same for police unions as it is for other unions. The education reform community has long pointed to teachers' unions' defense of practices that keep teachers in the classroom even when they have been accused of serious misconduct. As one New York City principal once put it (describing the then-president of the United Federation of Teachers), "Randi Weingarten would protect a dead body in the classroom. That's her job."[87]

The relative clarity of police unions' positions on the body camera issue makes it useful to explore here, but it also has one significant analytical downside: deploying body cameras involves significant financial costs. I have argued that it is important to study policies that govern how public safety employees do their work because often the trade-offs are not primarily budgetary. With body cameras, however, police unions have reasons to oppose them because of the potential to weaken the unions' ability to protect officers but also because they are expensive. On the one hand, adopting body cameras might mean increases to police department budgets, which all else equal might be viewed as a positive by police themselves. On the other hand, money spent on body cameras is money that could go to hiring and compensating officers. This is therefore far from perfect as a test of police union influence on policies with primarily nonbudgetary costs. But it is still an interesting opening into the study of how public safety unions might influence policies beyond compensation and employment.

What, then, can we learn from the LEMAS data about the use of officer-worn cameras? As of the 2013 survey data collection, only 28% of responding municipal government police agencies had deployed them, and by 2016, 50% had. According to the 2016 supplement, of the city agencies that had deployed body cameras, most reported doing so

236   CHAPTER EIGHT

to improve officer safety (81%), improve officer/agency accountability (75%), improve evidence quality (77%), reduce agency liability (77%), and more quickly resolve citizen complaints (81%). Of those agencies that had not deployed body cameras, the main reported reasons were related to costs: costs of the hardware, costs of ongoing maintenance and support, and costs of video storage and disposal.

In table 8.7, I evaluate whether cities with police collective bargaining and more politically active police unions are less likely to deploy body cameras. The dependent variable equals 1 if the city had deployed officer-worn cameras as of 2016 and 0 if it had not. Column 1 includes the collective bargaining indicator and regional fixed effects, and column 2 drops the collective bargaining indicator and includes state fixed effects. In column 1, the collective bargaining indicator is not significant, showing that police agencies with collective bargaining are not less

TABLE 8.7 **Deployment of body cameras for police officers**

	(1)	(2)
Collective bargaining	0.029	
	(0.088)	
Police union activity	−0.033	−0.068**
	(0.023)	(0.029)
Taxpayer groups	0.008	0.011
	(0.028)	(0.030)
Neighborhood associations	0.008	0.02
	(0.031)	(0.036)
Minority groups	0.044	0.059
	(0.036)	(0.037)
Ln(Population)	0.02	0.029
	(0.027)	(0.028)
Ln(Income per capita)	0.055	−0.033
	(0.100)	(0.110)
Percent homeowner	−0.329	−0.268
	(0.248)	(0.293)
Democratic presidential vote	−0.322	−0.031
	(0.228)	(0.218)
Percent Black	0.464*	−0.096
	(0.257)	(0.307)
Percent Latino	0.209	−0.271
	(0.205)	(0.227)
R-squared	0.14	0.3
Observations	325	325

Notes: Standard errors clustered by state in parentheses. Model 1 includes regional fixed effects; model 2 includes state fixed effects. Both models include additional demographics and political institutions.

*p < 0.1, **p < 0.05, ***p < 0.01 (two-tailed).

likely to deploy body cameras. Suggestively, however, the coefficient on police union activity is negative, and for minority group organizations it is positive—although neither is statistically significant in column 1. Still, cities with higher percentages of Black residents are more likely to have deployed body cameras as of 2016.

In column 2, however, the negative coefficient on police union political activity is statistically significant. This suggests that cities with more politically active police unions were less likely to have adopted body cameras as of 2016. A two-point increase in police union activity is associated with about a 14-percentage-point drop in the probability that a city had deployed body cameras. There is also stronger indication that minority group activity makes a difference here. The two-sided p-value of the coefficient estimate is 0.123, but the result suggests that a two-point increase in the political activity of racial and ethnic minority groups is associated with a 12-point increase in the likelihood of body camera deployment. Notably, the partisanship of city residents has no relationship to whether a city's police force is using body cameras.

The results of this analysis are therefore suggestive but also highlight that more research is needed. It is not theoretically clear that police unions would be homogeneously opposed to reforms falling under the umbrella of community policing; in table 8.6, my results show that greater police union activity has weak and inconsistent relationships with these practices. Table 8.7 shows a bit more clearly that cities with very politically active police unions were less likely to have deployed body cameras as of 2016. But what is needed is much more research attention to the many specific policies and practices that govern how police officers perform their work and how police chiefs and city elected officials manage the day-to-day operations of police protection. More detailed data on these practices, as well as more current and detailed data on the activities of police reform organizations, would help clarify the questions of how interest groups influence work rules and how politics shapes policing and law enforcement.

Conclusion

In this chapter, I evaluated whether and how police unions and firefighters' unions influence local policies related to compensation, employment levels, total spending, spending by function, and some of the rules that govern how police and firefighters do their work. Questions about public-sector union influence on compensation and employment have been explored in numerous studies, but here I analyzed newer data and focused on both collective bargaining and measures of public safety unions' overall political activity. The results show clearly that collective bargaining *and* unions' other political activities are associated with greater spending on police and firefighter salaries—and more for firefighters than police. These quantitative results also show few signs that organized groups work successfully to counter the salary and employment interests of public safety unions.

I then bridged research on public-sector unions and research on local political representation—the latter of which has studied patterns in local public spending but not the role of public-sector unions. My findings show that while there is indeed a positive correlation between Democratic presidential vote and total municipal government spending per capita, much of that is due to the positive correlation between Democratic presidential vote and collective bargaining. When I add collective bargaining to the model, the relationship between residents' partisanship and city spending is reduced by half and is no longer statistically significant. As I argue, there is a clear theoretical argument for why public safety collective bargaining is associated with greater city spending—clearer even than the argument for why residents' nationally based partisanship would matter.

I also showed that collective bargaining and public safety union political activity is associated with greater spending on police protection and fire protection and that generally cities with more active police and firefighters' unions spend a larger share of their budgets on police and fire protection. This is an area in which accounts based on partisanship and ideology do not yield clear predictions. But an account based on local interest groups does make clear predictions, and I find support for those predictions here.

To provide detail on how all this fits together, I described events in West Covina, California, where a conflict involving firefighters' unions erupted over matters of taxing, spending, employment levels, and compensation. The case demonstrates the importance of collective bargaining as well as more traditional political activity, and it shows that the main opposition firefighters face comes not from opposing groups or anti-firefighter residents but rather from city officials trying to deal with limited budgets and the political difficulty of raising taxes.

Finally, I turned to rules governing how local government employees do their work—and thus how public services are provided. Analysis of how unions might influence work rules is much more difficult because so little progress has been made in existing research, but given its importance, I attempted to make some headway. First, examining variables related to community policing, the evidence that police unions stifle these practices is quite mixed—perhaps because even police unions are not homogeneously opposed to them. Second, my analysis of a 2016 LEMAS survey on the deployment of officer-worn cameras suggests that cities with more politically active police unions are less likely to have adopted them.

Together, these analyses show how interest group influence extends beyond the economic development and land use issues prominent in the urban politics literature and how interest groups play an important role in shaping outcomes that have been a focus of research on local political representation—most notably, government spending. Police and firefighters' unions are highly active in local politics, and it shows in local policy.

CHAPTER NINE

Interest Group Influence in Local Elections

As a final step of the empirical analysis, I examine one potentially important stage of influence: local elections. When an interest group is more active in local elections, are the winning candidates more favorable to the group's policy goals?

By focusing on elections, I do not mean to suggest that all or even most group influence occurs through the electoral process. Interest groups can engage in a variety of other ways, such as lobbying, testifying at hearings and public meetings, participating on commissions and boards, and, for public-sector unions, engaging in collective bargaining. But elections are one possible stage of influence, and they also receive considerable emphasis in American politics research. An interest group's influence at later policy-making stages might also depend on its activity in elections. One of the main reasons elected officials may feel compelled to listen and respond to a group when it lobbies or testifies is that it has some clout in elections: perhaps the official was recruited by the group, received electoral support from the group, or is concerned that the group will campaign against them in the next election. Thus, while there are a number of stages or channels through which interest groups might exert influence, this is a good one to investigate.

I begin the chapter by explaining how local politics research has been strangely bifurcated in its treatment of elections and interest groups. Some local politics experts make local elections a major focus of their work but mostly ignore interest groups. Others seek to explain local policies—and sometimes consider certain types of interest groups—but use an approach that downplays the role of local elections. My analysis in this chapter bridges these two approaches by examining local elections with a policy orientation and with an emphasis on whether and how interest groups might influence outcomes.

Using data from the City Elections Survey, I first describe city candidates' positions on issues relevant to economic development, housing, and public safety. This is an important step; it gets at candidates' positions on core municipal government issues that are also presumably the focus of the main interest groups I am examining. I then evaluate whether greater electoral activity by a particular interest group is associated with the winning candidates having policy positions more favorable to the group. Those results provide some indication of whether interest group activity influences elections and serve as an opening to important questions that other researchers should continue to explore.

Local Elections and Interest Groups

In studying local elections in the United States, political scientists have mainly focused on questions related to voters, candidates, and elected officials. For example, researchers have answered questions about the kinds of people who run for local office and how voters make choices in local elections.[1] They have made progress in explaining how voter turnout in local elections affects the demographic composition of the electorate and how electoral institutions affect the demographic makeup of city councils.[2] Numerous studies have examined the incumbency advantage and retrospective voting in local politics.[3] And yet as productive and informative as this research has been, it has not paid much attention to what interest groups do in local elections, nor does it usually explore the public policy implications of election outcomes.

Other research has focused on local policies and policy processes but has tended not to examine the role of elections specifically. Consider local political economy studies that seek to explain variation in public spending: they are more explicitly focused on local policy, but they typically do not examine the role local elections might play in affecting those outcomes.[4] Similarly, the urban politics tradition focuses on economic development and land use but downplays the ways in which local elections could shape the policy-making process.[5] Perhaps this is somewhat justified by this tradition's major theoretical arguments: if policy is made by a stable governing coalition of businesses and city officials, then local elections might not be all that important. But the fact is that local elections *do* take place, some voters *do* participate, and interest groups *are* involved. If most local policy decisions are made in informal, smoke-filled-room negotiations between businesses and city officials, that raises the question of why interest groups bother to get active in local elections—as we have seen they do.

Rarely discussed in local politics research is the major challenge involved in carrying out a study of interest group influence in elections, even beyond the difficulty of measuring interest group activity: How does one determine whether election outcomes are or are not favorable to a particular interest group? Until very recently,[6] there have not been any datasets of the policy positions of local elected officials, let alone local candidates. And as I have argued, local candidates' party affiliations will at best be a rough proxy and at worst could be uncorrelated with local candidates' positions on local government issues.[7]

Some existing research simplifies matters by studying ballot measures or by emphasizing the effects of electoral institutions. With ballot measures, voters are making policy directly and on a single issue, so with some reasonable assumptions about groups' preferences on ballot measure outcomes, one can test whether election outcomes are more or less favorable to particular groups under certain electoral conditions.[8] Another approach is to test whether local policies or election outcomes are more or less favorable to certain interest groups under particular electoral institutions.[9] What is missing from work of this kind, however, are direct measures of interest group activity in elections, as well as direct measures of whether interest groups are electing the candidates they favor. As a result, the conclusions from these studies have more to do with how electoral institutions shape policy than with how the amount or type of interest group activity shapes local election outcomes.

Studies that both measure interest group activity in local elections and analyze dependent variables related to local public policy are few and far between. But Moe's studies of teachers' union activity and influence in school board elections are examples of how this can be done. In one study, he estimates the effect of teachers' unions' endorsements on candidates' likelihood of winning a school board election and finds that the effect is positive and as large as the effect of incumbency.[10] In a second study, he surveyed California school board candidates to learn what teachers' unions do in school board elections and to measure the relevant policy positions of the candidates, finding that in districts where teachers' unions are more active in school board elections, the winning candidates' policy positions are friendlier to teachers' unions.[11]

Thus, while there are obstacles, research on local interest groups' electoral influence can and should be done. The local elections literature that neglects interest groups might be missing an important contributor to who wins and who loses. And the local politics literature that neglects elections could be overlooking an avenue by which interest groups influence policy

Local Candidates' Positions on Local Issues

As a way to learn about city candidates' positions on core local issues relevant to interest groups, I included in the City Elections Survey questions about their opinions on local policy matters related to economic development and growth and public safety provision.

First, what are local candidates' positions on economic development? Is there meaningful variation across cities or candidates? To explore this, I asked city candidates three questions about their perceptions of how economic growth would affect their community: "If your city were to attract more investment and economic development in the coming years, what do you consider the most likely effects on . . . ?" Candidates were asked how it would affect city government revenue, city government costs, and the quality of the community, and for each question, the response options were "increase," "decrease," and "no effect."

I summarize the responses at the top of table 9.1. There is near-unanimous agreement that economic development would increase city revenue (94%), but there is more variation in the responses to the other two questions. Sixty-seven percent reported that economic growth would increase local government costs, indicating that most see a potential downside to growth and expansion. As for how it would affect the quality of the city community, most but not all were positive: 78% said growth would increase the quality of the community, 9% said it would have no effect, and 13% said it would decrease the quality of the community. Thus, nearly all these city candidates agree that more economic development would be good for the tax base, but there is some disagreement about whether it would be desirable overall.

I also asked two questions that more explicitly mention possible trade-offs to pursuing more economic growth. First, I asked respondents

TABLE 9.1 Candidates' responses to local policy questions

Effects of economic development on ...	Increase	Decrease	No effect		
City revenue	0.94	0.02	0.04		
City costs	0.67	0.09	0.24		
Quality of city community	0.78	0.13	0.09		

Focus more on economic growth or environmental sustainability?	Much more growth	Somewhat more growth	Equal	Some-what more sustain.	Much more sustain.
	0.31	0.11	0.43	0.07	0.08

Focus on protecting existing conditions or attracting development?	Much more protect	Somewhat more protect	Somewhat more attract	Much more attract	
	0.17	0.19	0.37	0.28	

Effects of increasing housing supply on ...	Increase	Decrease	No effect		
City revenue	0.11	0.10	0.78		
City costs	0.77	0.08	0.15		
Quality of city community	0.60	0.24	0.17		

What do you think about spending on the fire department in your city?	More spending	Enough spending	Lower spending		
	0.33	0.55	0.12		

Do you think the money spent on your city's fire department is ...	All well spent	Other priorities			
	0.73	0.27			

Effects of collective bargaining with firefighters on ...	Increase	Decrease	No effect		
City costs	0.79	0.04	0.17		
Quality of fire protection service	0.48	0.06	0.46		
Efficiency of city fire protection service	0.44	0.10	0.46		

Attitude toward collective bargaining for firefighters?	Very positive	Somewhat positive	Neutral	Somewhat negative	Very negative
	0.19	0.21	0.37	0.15	0.08

Effects of collective bargaining with police on . . .	Increase	Decrease	No effect		
City costs	0.85	0.05	0.10		
Quality of policing and law enforcement	0.50	0.09	0.41		
Crime	0.05	0.38	0.57		
Accountability of police	0.39	0.13	0.48		
Police recruitment and retention	0.70	0.04	0.26		

Attitude toward collective bargaining for the police?	Very positive	Somewhat positive	Neutral	Somewhat negative	Very negative
	0.19	0.23	0.34	0.14	0.09

if they think their city should focus more on economic growth or more on environmental sustainability, with response options on a five-point scale. Second, I asked them whether their city should focus more on protecting existing conditions or more on attracting development, with four possible response options.

As I show in table 9.1, 42% of city candidates said their city should focus more on economic growth, with 31% saying much more and 11% saying somewhat more. Forty-three percent of respondents chose the neutral response. But 15% said their city's focus should be more on environmental sustainability than growth. Moving to the next row, 17% said the city should focus much more on protecting existing conditions than on growth, and 19% said the city should focus somewhat more on protecting existing conditions. Thus, while pro-economic development positions are overall more common in this sample, a non-negligible share of the candidates lean more toward environmental sustainability and protecting existing conditions.

I also asked the candidates a three-step question about the desirability of increasing the local housing supply: If their city were to increase the supply of housing, what do they consider the most likely effects on city revenue, city costs, and the quality of the local community? As I show in table 9.1, 77% of respondents indicated that increasing the supply of housing would increase city costs, and 78% said it would have no effect on city revenue. On the question of how it would affect the quality of the local community, however, responses were more divided. The majority—60%—said increasing the housing supply would increase the quality of their community. But 24% said it would decrease the quality, and 17% said it would have no effect. When it comes to expanding the city's housing supply, then, candidates' views do vary—especially their views on how it would affect the quality of the local community.

Compared to economic development and housing, eliciting candidates' views on public safety was more complicated. Economic development and housing are issues on which it is reasonable to expect that some candidates might want more and others might want less, and the questions to the candidates could be designed in that way. Most of public service provision is different. Presumably few candidates—at least the ones hoping to succeed—would take the position that there should be lower levels of fire protection or less refuse collection.[12] Instead, concerns about public service provision are often budgetary, about the allocation of scarce resources, about whether the effectiveness of or need for a service justifies the spending, and perhaps, for some, about the desirability of smaller government generally. There may also be debates about how public employees provide services; for the police, for example, there are questions about racial profiling, use of force, whether and how officers are held accountable to the public, and whether officers should wear body cameras. The bottom line is that the basic characteristics of public service provision as a policy area are different from those of land use and development, so designing questions to gauge candidates' positions on service provision issues was less straightforward.

I therefore took a two-pronged approach to measuring candidates' positions on public safety. In a first set of questions, I asked candidates for their views about spending on the fire department in their city. One question allowed respondents to indicate that "increasing spending would make the fire department more effective," that "the fire department is effective enough at current spending levels," or that "the fire department would be just as effective at lower spending levels." (They could also indicate that their city does not have a fire department.) In a second question, I asked whether they think all the money spent on their city's fire department is well spent or whether some of the money would be better spent on other city priorities.

Returning to table 9.1, I find that 33% supported greater spending on the fire department, saying that it could be more effective with more spending. Fifty-five percent took the status quo position, saying that the fire department is effective enough at current spending levels. But 12% said that the fire department could be just as effective if spending levels were decreased. (Here I exclude respondents who indicated that their city does not have a fire department.) On the second question, 73% said that all the money spent on fire protection is well spent, and 27% reported that some of the money going to fire protection would be better spent on other city priorities. Overall, then, most of the city candidates are supportive of spending on fire protection, but there is variation in their views.

My second approach was to consider the policy preferences and priorities of key public safety interest groups—police and firefighters' unions—and then ask candidates' for their views on those issues. This could be done in a variety of ways as local government employees and their unions have a large number of important interests at stake in local government, including their compensation, employment levels, the quality of the working environment, and rules governing how they do their jobs. One way of getting at all these issues at the same time—and assessing how friendly local candidates are to public safety unions' interests overall—is to ask for their opinions on collective bargaining. Electing local officials who are supportive of collective bargaining is a priority of public-sector unions. But local candidates' views on collective bargaining need not be uniformly supportive: they may have concerns that it increases government costs, reduces their discretion to manage the public workforce, and results in work rules that detract from effective service provision. This, then, is another way of assessing whether candidates are friendly to the policy priorities of key interest groups on public safety.

To implement this approach, I first asked respondents for their views of the long-term effects of collective bargaining for firefighters on city costs, the quality of fire protection service, and the efficiency of fire protection service. For police, I asked about the likely effects of collective bargaining on city costs, the quality of policing and law enforcement, crime levels, the accountability of the police, and police recruitment and retention. For all these questions, the response options were "increase," "decrease," or "no effect." For both police and firefighters, I also asked respondents about their general attitude toward collective bargaining, allowing them five response options ranging from very positive to very negative.

The responses to these questions are summarized in table 9.1. Seventy-nine percent reported that collective bargaining for firefighters increases city costs, with most of the remaining respondents saying that it has no effect on costs. (This by itself is notable because while there is some debate in the literature about whether collective bargaining increases the costs of government, over three-fourths of these city candidates reported that it does.) Respondents were roughly evenly divided between whether firefighter collective bargaining increases the quality of fire protection service (48%) or has no effect on it (46%). There was a similar divide between whether respondents think collective bargaining improves the efficiency of fire protection, with 44% saying it does and 46% saying it would have no effect. Ten percent said that firefighter collective bargaining decreases the efficiency of fire protection. And respondents' general attitudes about firefighter collective bargaining were mixed: 23% were either somewhat or very negative, 37% were neutral, and the remaining 40% were positive.

For the analogous questions about police, 85% of respondents reported that collective bargaining increases city costs. Most respondents were split between whether police collective bargaining increases the quality of police and law enforcement (50%) or has no effect (41%); the remaining 9% said that it decreases the quality. The majority of respondents—57%—said police collective bargaining has no effect on crime levels, whereas 38% said that it decreased crime. Likewise, there was relative agreement on the effects on recruitment and retention of police officers: 70% of candidates said collective bargaining helps with recruitment and retention; most of the remaining respondents said that it has no effect. Respondents were somewhat more divided on the effects of police collective bargaining on the accountability of the police. Thirty-nine percent were very positive, saying it improves accountability, 48% said it has no effect, and 13% said that it decreases the accountability of the police. In terms of their overall views on collective bargaining, 23% were either somewhat or strongly negative, 34% were neutral, and the remaining 42% were either somewhat or strongly positive.

Another useful question to ask is whether the candidates' views on different issues "go together" in the same way that the positions of national political elites do. Are local candidates' positions on fire protection spending and police collective bargaining correlated with their views on housing or economic development, similar to national politicians' positions on issues like taxing and spending, gun control, and abortion? Does it look like local candidates' preferences could be usefully arrayed on a single dimension, as many have argued is the case for the preferences of national politicians?

A simple factor analysis provides a preliminary answer to this question. For all the policy questions in table 9.1, I reordered the responses so that low values mean that the candidate is most negative (on economic development, housing, and public safety) and high values mean that the candidate is most positive. Then, for all the questions about the various effects of a policy, I created additive indexes. For the questions about the effects of economic development, for example, I summed the candidates' responses to the questions about city costs and the quality of the city community to create an index that ranges from 0 to 4. (I did not include the responses to the question about revenue because virtually all respondents agreed that economic development would increase city revenue.) For the effects of housing, the index ranges from 0 to 6, with 0 being most negative about increasing the supply of housing and 6 being most positive. For firefighter collective bargaining, I combined the responses about cost, quality, and efficiency in a 0–6 index, with 0 being most negative and 6 being most positive. And for police officers, I did the same, with the index ranging from 0 to 10.

Table 9.2 presents the results of a factor analysis of these variables. Because there are two eigenvalues greater than one, I show the factor loadings for each variable on the first two factors. The variables that load

TABLE 9.2 **Factor loadings, principal components analysis**

	Factor 1	Factor 2
Effects of economic development	0.08	0.51
Environmental sustainability or development	−0.05	0.61
Protect existing conditions or development	0.07	0.62
Effects of expanding housing supply	0.17	0.43
Effectiveness of fire department spending	0.55	0.06
Is all spending on fire department well spent	0.45	0.01
Effects of firefighter collective bargaining	0.7	−0.004
General attitude toward firefighter collective bargaining	0.82	−0.15
Effects of police collective bargaining	0.74	0.04
General attitude toward police collective bargaining	0.81	−0.09

250   CHAPTER NINE

heavily onto the first factor are all the variables related to public safety—both those about collective bargaining for public safety workers and those about firefighter spending. The variables that load onto the second factor are the questions about economic development and, more weakly, housing. This pattern suggests that a single dimension would not explain most of the variance on these key local issues.[13] Just by asking about a limited number of areas in which most municipal governments make decisions, I find that there are two clusters of policy positions among candidates running for city office.

One final descriptive matter is whether the positions of the winning candidates are systematically different from those of the candidates who lost. To make these comparisons, I limited the analysis to states where at least a quarter of the respondents in the sample lost their elections: California, South Carolina, and Washington. (Recall that for some states included in this sample, I was only or mainly able to contact candidates who won.) Table 9.3 shows the results of t-tests for each policy variable, comparing the average responses of losing candidates and winning candidates. The winning candidates tend to be significantly more pro-economic growth than the losing candidates, and they are also significantly more pro-housing. In addition, the winners are more supportive of spending on the fire department than the losing candidates. However, there is no clear relationship for candidates' views on collective bargain-

TABLE 9.3 **Comparing the policy positions of winning and losing candidates**

	Effects of Economic Development	Sustainability or Growth	Protect Existing Conditions or Growth	Effect of Increasing Housing
Winning candidates	2.09	2.47	1.86	2.73
Losing candidates	1.78	2.25	1.42	2.36
Difference	0.307	0.226	0.439	0.379
p-value	0.002	0.047	0.000	0.003

	Effectiveness of Fire Dept. Spending	Fire Dept. Funding Well Spent	Fire Collective Bargaining Effects	Fire Collective Bargaining Attitude	Police Collective Bargaining Effects	Police Collective Bargaining Attitude
Winning candidates	1.28	0.76	2.92	2.25	5.72	2.3
Losing candidates	1.12	0.64	3.07	2.43	5.71	2.37
Difference	0.155	0.119	−0.148	−0.184	0.01	−0.071
p-value	0.027	0.013	0.267	0.098	0.963	0.540

ing for police and firefighters. Winning candidates are not more likely to view police or firefighter collective bargaining more positively than losing candidates; if anything, it looks as though the losing candidates may be slightly more supportive of firefighter collective bargaining, on average. Therefore, while there is some early indication that being pro–economic growth, pro-housing, and pro–public safety spending are winning positions, there is not a strong bivariate relationship between winning and favorability to public safety collective bargaining.

Interest Group Activity and the Positions of Winning Candidates

I now turn to tests of whether interest group activity is associated with election outcomes, asking, When a group is more active in an election, is the election outcome more favorable to it? My general approach is to model the policy positions of the individual winning candidates using OLS, clustering the standard errors by municipality.[14] The main independent variables, again, are the interest group activity variables: each candidate provided a 0–4 rating of the activity of several kinds of groups in their most recent city election, where 0 means the group was "not at all active" and 4 means the group was "extremely active." For cities in which more than one candidate responded to the survey, I average their group activity ratings for each individual group and city.

Local Economic Development and Housing

To explain winning candidates' positions on local economic development, I again begin with business interests, specifically, chambers of commerce and developers. If the electoral activity of business groups is positively associated with winning candidates having pro-growth views, that would suggest that they have influence in local elections. As I discussed earlier, however, the interests of chambers of commerce and developers might be very closely aligned with the interests of city officials in maintaining and growing the tax base. If so—and if the default is for city candidates to take a pro-development stance—then the amount of business group activity might actually make little difference to election outcomes.

In addition to chambers of commerce and developers, I include the measures of the activity of building trade unions and taxpayer groups, both of which might help elect more pro-growth candidates, and the activity of environmental groups and neighborhood associations. While my focus here is on the electoral activity of interest groups, I include the other city-level variables from the earlier chapters as well as whether the candidate was running for mayor or the city council and whether the candidate ran unopposed. Because they are often active in local elections, variables measuring the activity of the two major political parties are included but without any expectations that they will have strong relationships with the policy positions of the winning candidates. In the model results shown, I include state fixed effects, but the substantive conclusions do not change when I exclude them.

See columns 1–3 of table 9.4 for a summary of the model estimates. The first finding of note is that the coefficient estimates on chamber of commerce and developer activity are weak and inconsistent across models. When the question to the candidate is phrased in terms of a trade-off between environmental sustainability and economic growth (column 2), I do find a positive association between chamber of commerce electoral activity and more pro-growth views of the winning candidates, but the coefficient on developers' activity is insignificant. For the other two dependent variables—the perceived effects of economic growth (column 1) and whether the priority should be protecting existing conditions or encouraging growth (column 3)—the coefficients on both business electoral activity variables are statistically insignificant.

The coefficients on the electoral activity of other potential pro-growth groups are also mixed. In column 1, for example, I estimate a positive coefficient on the activity of taxpayer groups, indicating that with more taxpayer group activity, the winning candidates tend to have more positive views on the effects of economic development. But in columns 2 and 3, those effects are not significant. Moreover, in none of the models is the activity of building trade unions statistically significant. Thus, overall, while there are some signs that the activity of pro-development groups influences winning candidates' positions on economic growth, those signs are weak and not consistent across different measures of candidates' views.

What about the groups potentially opposed to economic development? Here I find one very clear pattern. For every question asked, the activity of environmental groups has a negative relationship with the growth attitudes of winning candidates. In column 1, increasing the

INTEREST GROUP INFLUENCE IN LOCAL ELECTIONS

TABLE 9.4 **Winning candidates' positions on economic development and housing**

	Effects of Economic Development (1)	Environmental Sustainability or Growth (2)	Protect Existing Conditions or Growth (3)	Expand Housing Supply (4)
Chambers of commerce	0.036	0.105*	0.027	0.036
	(0.052)	(0.055)	(0.043)	(0.055)
Developers	−0.029	−0.02	−0.047	−0.069
	(0.046)	(0.062)	(0.057)	(0.063)
Taxpayer groups	0.129**	0.096	0.065	0.108
	(0.054)	(0.062)	(0.054)	(0.067)
Building trade unions	−0.009	−0.032	−0.015	0.061
	(0.052)	(0.056)	(0.050)	(0.058)
Environmental groups	−0.158***	−0.302***	−0.189***	−0.105
	(0.052)	(0.061)	(0.046)	(0.067)
Neighborhood associations	−0.019	−0.013	0.035	0.012
	(0.047)	(0.051)	(0.044)	(0.057)
Democratic Party	0.023	0.005	0.123***	0.045
	(0.044)	(0.054)	(0.043)	(0.052)
Republican Party	0.002	0.032	−0.048	0.043
	(0.041)	(0.052)	(0.040)	(0.047)
Ln(Population)	0.025	0.126**	0.11**	−0.075*
	(0.040)	(0.050)	(0.043)	(0.045)
Ln(Income per capita)	−0.752***	−0.98***	−0.976***	−0.392*
	(0.186)	(0.193)	(0.145)	(0.200)
Percent homeowner	−0.144	0.849*	0.332	−1.993***
	(0.426)	(0.470)	(0.366)	(0.489)
Democratic presidential vote	0.625	−0.805*	−0.864**	0.388
	(0.422)	(0.465)	(0.401)	(0.433)
R-squared	0.17	0.24	0.30	0.20
Observations	551	550	540	543

Notes: Standard errors clustered by city in parentheses. All models include state fixed effects, additional demographic variables, and political institutions.

*p < 0.1, **p < 0.05, ***p < 0.01 (two-tailed).

electoral activity of these groups from "slightly active" to "very active" (a two-point change) is associated with a decrease in winning candidates' perceptions of the benefits of economic growth by about one-third of a point on a scale of 0 to 4. The estimates in column 2 show that the same two-point shift is associated with a downward shift of 0.6 (also on a scale of 0 to 4) on the question about whether to prioritize sustainability or growth. And in column 3, the same pattern holds. A two-point increase in environmental group electoral activity makes the winning candidates more likely to say the city should focus on protecting existing conditions.

However, in none of the three models does the activity of neighborhood associations have a clear relationship with winning candidates' attitudes about economic growth. Nor do the party variables have clear, consistent effects. In column 3, when the question is about protecting existing conditions or attracting development, Democratic Party activity is actually associated with more pro-growth attitudes among the winners. In contrast, more Democratic constituencies tend to have winning candidates who are more in favor of environmental sustainability and protecting existing conditions.[15] And there is no evidence in these three models that communities with larger shares of homeowners are less in favor of economic development: in two of the three, percent homeowner is statistically insignificant, and in column 2, it is actually positive.

Viewed together, these patterns of group activity and the positions of the winners suggest that the electoral activity of business groups matters less for election outcomes than the activity of environmental groups. One plausible interpretation of this is the one I discussed earlier, in chapter 6: business groups could get more active in local elections when their policy interests are more threatened. A second possibility is that the extent of business activity in local elections matters little for the growth views of the winners because the winners are inclined to be pro-growth regardless of business activity levels. Environmental groups, by contrast, are fighting an uphill battle against the pro-growth impulses of city officials, so the extent to which they are able to have an impact depends on the extent to which they pose an electoral threat.

In column 4 of table 9.4, I turn to a model of the winning candidates' views on building more housing. The patterns of results among the group activity variables are similar to those for the economic development models. There is no clear relationship between the activity of chambers of commerce or developers on winning candidates' views of the likely effects of expanding the housing supply. Again, this may seem surprising given that developers have such large economic interests at stake, but it is consistent with the idea that developers mainly get active in local politics when their own projects are being discussed—and less so to influence local elections generally.

Two other patterns are important to note in the housing model results. The first is the very strong negative coefficient on the share of homeowners in the city. This finding is consistent with my findings in chapter 7 and with what the literature on housing politics and local politics suggests. In the case of housing, more than for economic development, there is evidence that homeowners resist development and growth and that the share of homeowners matters for winning candidates' positions on expanding the housing supply. The second pattern is that the activity of the political parties is not significantly related to winning candidates' views on expanding the housing supply, nor is the city's Democratic presidential vote share.

One takeaway from this analysis of candidates' views on economic development and housing is that opposition to growth in elections does seem to make a difference. When environmental groups are more active, the winning candidates have more anti-growth views. And in cities with more homeowners, the winning candidates are less favorable to expanding housing. This further suggests, then, that when it comes to economic growth, there often are two sides competing with each other. And the nature of that competition appears to shape election outcomes: how favorable the winners are to one side or the other.

Public Safety

In the models of winning candidates' positions on fire protection spending and public safety collective bargaining, the main independent variables of interest are the electoral activity of firefighters' unions and the electoral activity of police unions. As for groups that are opposed to the goals of firefighters' unions, it is not clear that there will be any—or at least not consistently across cities. Just as cutting Social Security benefits doesn't make for a winning campaign platform in national elections, neither should cutting firefighter budgets or reducing the frequency of garbage collection make for a winning campaign in municipal elections. Instead, any opposition to public services usually takes the form of arguments about how scarce local government funds should be allocated differently or about seemingly technical matters such as what makes for good or better fire protection. As I showed in chapter 4, these usually aren't active issues in most municipal elections—even though they are important issues for municipal governance. So while taxpayer groups, for example, might push candidates to lower spending and oppose collective bargaining, this is likely to be an area in which there is a politically active group on one side without any consistent opposition.

Policing is a different matter. Policing and crime are more often active issues in municipal elections. Taxpayer groups may be even more likely to pay attention to police spending because it represents a larger share of the typical city budget than fire protection. And in some cities, groups committed to racial justice may be active opponents of the police.

In the models of winning candidates' views on police collective bargaining, therefore, I also include the activity of racial and ethnic minority groups. As above, I include the electoral activity of neighborhood associations and the two major political parties, without clear expectations for how they would be related to winning candidates' views on public safety.

The estimates for the public safety models are shown in table 9.5, and the coefficients on firefighters' union and police union electoral activity are presented graphically in figure 9.1. I start with the two questions about spending on the fire department. When the dependent variable is a binary indicator for whether all the money spent on the fire department is well spent or whether some of the money spent on the fire department would be better spent on other priorities, the coefficient on the firefighters' union activity variable is statistically insignificant. But when the question is about the relationship between fire department spending and its effectiveness (see column 1 of table 9.5 and the top plot of fig. 9.1), the coefficient on the electoral activity of firefighters' unions is positive. It shows that, on average, a two-point increase in firefighters' union electoral activity is associated with a 0.17-point increase (on a

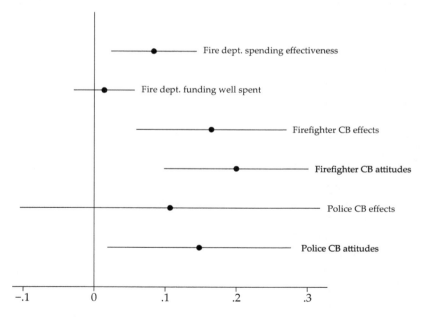

FIGURE 9.1 Public safety union activity and winning candidates' positions

INTEREST GROUP INFLUENCE IN LOCAL ELECTIONS

TABLE 9.5 **Public safety positions of winning candidates**

	Effectiveness of Fire Dept. Spending (1)	Fire Dept. Funding Well Spent (2)	Fire Collective Bargaining Effects (3)	Fire Collective Bargaining Attitude (4)	Police Collective Bargaining Effects (5)	Police Collective Bargaining Attitude (6)
Firefighters' unions	0.084***	0.014	0.165***	0.2***		
	(0.031)	(0.022)	(0.054)	(0.052)		
Police unions					0.107	0.148**
					(0.107)	(0.066)
Taxpayer groups	−0.101**	−0.031	−0.091	−0.098	0.025	−0.107
	(0.046)	(0.029)	(0.086)	(0.071)	(0.121)	(0.076)
Neighborhood assn.	0.046	−0.008	−0.005	0.085	0.096	0.105*
	(0.034)	(0.024)	(0.061)	(0.055)	(0.100)	(0.058)
Minority groups					0.065	0.082
					(0.134)	(0.071)
Democratic Party	−0.058*	−0.029	0.043	0.1	0.243***	0.088
	(0.035)	(0.024)	(0.064)	(0.061)	(0.088)	(0.055)
Republican Party	0.069**	0.031	0.098*	−0.029	−0.06	−0.073
	(0.035)	(0.023)	(0.059)	(0.054)	(0.089)	(0.056)
Ln(Population)	−0.049*	−0.032	−0.134**	−0.057	−0.08	−0.043
	(0.029)	(0.022)	(0.061)	(0.049)	(0.092)	(0.052)
Ln(Income)	−0.259**	−0.071	−0.579**	−0.469**	−1.271***	−0.522**
	(0.116)	(0.082)	(0.236)	(0.203)	(0.359)	(0.207)
Percent homeowner	0.488*	0.208	0.367	0.251	1.405	0.752
	(0.274)	(0.225)	(0.636)	(0.513)	(0.937)	(0.557)
Dem. pres. vote	0.544*	0.339*	0.551	0.745	−0.634	0.015
	(0.315)	(0.199)	(0.646)	(0.534)	(0.822)	(0.514)
R-squared	0.10	0.06	0.07	0.14	0.11	0.13
Observations	461	446	495	526	487	516

Notes: Standard errors clustered by city in parentheses. All models include state fixed effects, additional demographics, and political institutions.

*p < 0.1, **p < 0.05, ***p < 0.01 (two-tailed).

scale of 0 to 2) in the winning candidates' favorability toward spending on the fire department.

Moreover, the electoral activity of firefighters' unions is positively associated with the winning candidates' favorability to collective bargaining for firefighters. A two-point increase in their activity (such as from slightly active to very active) is associated with a 0.33-point increase in the winning candidates' views about the effects of firefighter collective bargaining on a 0–6 scale. And it is also associated with a 0.4-point increase in candidates' overall attitudes toward collective bargaining for firefighters on a 0–4 scale. Thus, there is evidence that the extent of firefighter activity is positively associated with winning candidates' positions being friendlier to firefighters.

The same is true of police officers' activity, although only one of the coefficients on police union activity is statistically significant, as shown in columns 5 and 6 of table 9.5 and the bottom two plots of figure 9.1. When the dependent variable is an index of the perceived effects of police collective bargaining, the overall amount of police union activity does not have a significant relationship. On general attitudes toward collective bargaining for police, however, it does: a two-point increase in the activity of police unions in elections is associated with a 0.3-point increase in winning candidates' favorability to collective bargaining for police.

What of any opposition to firefighters' and police unions? The other group activity estimates in table 9.5 suggest that there was little such electoral opposition to speak of in these 2015 and 2016 elections. In most of the models, the activity of taxpayer groups has a negative association with the public safety views of winning candidates, but that negative association is only significant in column 1, which is the question about favorability to firefighter spending. Neighborhood associations are not a force of opposition to public safety; the coefficient in column 6 (for police collective bargaining favorability) is actually positive. In the models related to the police, the activity of racial and ethnic minority groups has no association with winning candidates' positions on police collective bargaining. And the coefficients on political party activity are not consistent across models.[16] Thus, while the relationships for police and firefighters' union activity are generally consistent, that is not the case for any of the other group activity variables.

Winning and Losing Candidates in the Same City

As a final way of examining whether more electoral activity by an interest group is associated with election outcomes more in its favor, I analyze the magnitude and direction of any differences between the views of winning and losing candidates within the same city. I only have the reported policy positions of both winning and losing candidates in seventy-six cities, so the dataset for this analysis is small, but it may still be informative even if merely suggestive. As an interest group's activity increases, does it become more likely that the candidates with policy views more favorable to the group are elected?

I first calculate the average position of the winning candidates and the average position of the losing candidates for each policy question and each city. Then, for each city and policy question, I calculate the difference between the average position of the winners and the average position of the losers. Both the magnitude and the direction of the differences vary across cities. In some cities, where these variables equal zero, there is no difference in the winning and losing candidates' positions on these issues. In many others—the ones with positive values on these variables—the candidates with views more favorable to economic development, housing, and public safety won. In other cities, the values are negative, indicating that candidates less favorable to economic development, housing, and public safety won.

Starting with the three economic development and growth variables, I test whether the activity of the relevant interest groups in a city's elections can explain some of this variation. Because I am dealing with such a small number of cases here, I only include the group activity variables and state fixed effects as predictors, but when I add the remaining predictors, the results are substantively the same.

I present the estimates of these models in columns 1–3 of table 9.6. The weight of the evidence suggests that greater activity by environmental groups is associated with the winners being the less pro-development candidates. In column 3, the coefficient is not significant, but in columns 1 and 2, I find that as the electoral activity of environmental groups increases, the winners are increasingly more skeptical of economic development than the losers. I also find the opposite for taxpayer groups: the more active taxpayer groups are in the elections, the more the winners are the ones more favorable to economic development. Once again, the relationships for business are inconsistent. In column 2, more developer activity is associated with the winners being more pro-development than the losers, but the same is not true for the other two economic development variables in columns 1 and 3. And if anything, greater activity by neighborhood associations in elections is associated with the winners being more pro-economic development.

In modeling the difference between winners' and losers' positions on expanding the housing supply, I add percent homeowner as a predictor because of its importance for explaining housing development outcomes in chapter 7. The estimates, presented in column 4 of table 9.6,

260   CHAPTER NINE

TABLE 9.6 **Within-city differences in winning and losing candidates' positions, growth**

	Effects of Economic Development (1)	Environmental Sustainability or Growth (2)	Protect Existing Conditions or Growth (3)	Expand Housing Supply (4)
Chambers of commerce	0.234	0.141	0.278	0.357*
	(0.230)	(0.283)	(0.310)	(0.207)
Developers	−0.193	0.448*	−0.166	−0.445**
	(0.194)	(0.242)	(0.260)	(0.183)
Taxpayer groups	0.274	0.36**	0.364*	0.231
	(0.186)	(0.175)	(0.194)	(0.222)
Building trade unions	−0.137	0.164	0.003	0.263**
	(0.196)	(0.129)	(0.164)	(0.129)
Environmental groups	−0.451**	−0.478**	−0.119	0.046
	(0.174)	(0.195)	(0.156)	(0.192)
Neighborhood associations	0.37*	0.474**	0.408*	0.277
	(0.211)	(0.220)	(0.224)	(0.176)
Percent homeowner				2.885**
				(1.316)
R-squared	0.23	0.43	0.25	0.24
Observations	75	76	75	75

Notes: Robust standard errors in parentheses. Dependent variables are the average of the winning candidates' positions minus the average of the losing candidates' positions for each question in each city.

*p < 0.1, **p < 0.05, ***p < 0.01 (two-tailed).

are a bit murkier than those of the economic development variables. Interestingly, there is evidence that as building trade unions become more active in elections, the winners are also more pro-housing compared to the losers. The same is true for more chamber of commerce activity. But the coefficient on developers' activity in column 4 is negative. Environmental group activity, moreover, is not a significant predictor of the preference gap between winners and losers in this case. And one of the variables that one might expect to lead to the election of anti-housing candidates—percent homeowner—is actually associated with the winners being relatively more *pro*-housing than the losing candidates. While this seems counterintuitive, it is important to remember that the dependent variable here is the difference between winners' and losers' positions on housing within the same city (and for a small number of cities). It is still the case that cities with larger shares of homeowners elect candidates less favorable to expanding the housing supply (see table 9.4), and the data suggest that the losing candidates in those cities tend to be less favorable to housing as well.

The findings of this winner-loser comparative analysis are a bit clearer for the public safety variables, as shown in table 9.7. In columns 1 and 2, even though there are only 57 and 53 cities in the analysis, respectively, greater electoral activity by firefighters' unions is associated with the winning candidates being more favorable to fire department spending than the losing candidates. There is also some evidence that greater electoral activity by firefighters' unions is associated with the winners having overall more favorable perceptions of the effects of collective bargaining for firefighters (column 3), even if it is not the case that the winners are generally more prone to liking firefighter collective bargaining overall (column 4). And in column 5, I find that greater electoral activity of police unions is associated with the winning candidates having more favorable views of the effects of police collective bargaining than the losing candidates. In column 6, the effect of police union activity is not significant, but to find a fairly consistent pattern with such a small number of cases is telling. When there are two candidates with different views on public safety policy, the likelihood of the winners being the more pro-safety candidates increases with the electoral activity of public safety unions.

TABLE 9.7 **Within-city differences in winning and losing candidates' positions, public safety**

	Effectiveness of Fire Dept. Spending (1)	Fire Dept. Funding Well Spent (2)	Fire Collective Bargaining Effects (3)	Fire Collective Bargaining Attitude (4)	Police Collective Bargaining Effects (5)	Police Collective Bargaining Attitude (6)
Fire unions	0.27***	0.105*	0.322*	0.03		
	(0.085)	(0.057)	(0.180)	(0.183)		
Police unions					0.708*	0.174
					(0.404)	(0.255)
Taxpayer groups	−0.249**	0.018	−0.238	−0.097	−0.267	−0.516*
	(0.123)	(0.106)	(0.284)	(0.263)	(0.587)	(0.288)
Neighborhood assn.	0.107	−0.137	−0.303	0.05	0.145	−0.004
	(0.141)	(0.085)	(0.362)	(0.262)	(0.650)	(0.329)
Minority groups					−0.29	0.405
					(0.429)	(0.317)
R-squared	0.30	0.25	0.11	0.03	0.08	0.14
Observations	57	53	67	71	55	62

Notes: Robust standard errors in parentheses. Dependent variables are the average of the winning candidates' positions minus the average of the losing candidates' positions in each city.

*p < 0.1, **p < 0.05 ***p < 0.01 (two-tailed).

Conclusion

As I explained in chapter 2, the policy-focused approach does not put special emphasis on elections compared to other stages and venues of political activity; elections are only one avenue through which interest groups might have political influence. Yet elections are a focus of a great deal of American politics research, including the local politics literature. As a way of connecting this work on interest group influence to studies of elections and as an exploration of one of the stages at which interest groups might be able to push policy in their favor, I have carried out a preliminary analysis of how interest group activity shapes election outcomes by examining some of the local policy preferences of city candidates.

Because this is only one stage of the policy-making process, and because here I am looking only at interest groups' activity in elections, it would not be surprising to find more muted relationships than those in chapters 7 and 8, where I looked at policies as dependent variables. Some interest groups might have greater influence through nonelectoral channels. A group might "lose" a particular election, but that does not necessarily mean it is ineffective in the longer run. And, perhaps especially for elections, an interest group might get more active in elections when its policy goals are most threatened—and when candidates opposed to their views are poised to win. I cannot adjudicate between these possible accounts with my analysis, but there are many reasons influence might not show up in an analysis of local elections, even if the bigger picture is one of interest group influence.

Nevertheless, this chapter provides some evidence that the winning candidates in these local elections are friendlier to certain interest groups' goals when those groups are more active. On matters of economic development and growth, the activity of chambers of commerce and developers has little relationship to how pro-growth the winning candidates are, but in cities where environmental groups are more electorally active, the winning candidates are significantly less favorable to growth. In cities where firefighters' unions are more engaged in local elections, moreover, the winning candidates express more favorable views on spending on fire departments and stronger support for collective bargaining for firefighters. The latter is also the case for police: cities with more electorally active police unions feature winning candidates who are more supportive of police collective bargaining.

On housing, by contrast, none of the interest group activity variables is strongly predictive of winning candidates' views. The variable that does significantly predict those positions is the share of homeowners in the city: in cities with larger shares of homeowners, winning candidates report more negative views on expanding housing development, on average. Again, this is not to say that the political activity of developers and chambers of commerce doesn't make a difference generally—just that it doesn't appear to in these local elections. And these findings are once again broadly consistent with housing politics research that emphasizes the importance of local homeowners on matters relating to housing development.

The data analysis in this chapter also sheds light on local candidates' positions on some core local issues and the dimensionality of local politics. Notably, although I am focused here on elections, I measured the dependent variables in a policy-relevant way. And while much more can and should be done, the patterns I find suggest that local political decision making may often not be structured by a single dimension. I asked candidates about just a few local issues, yet there appear to be two distinct clusters of candidate positions on these issues. Moreover, local political party activity is not a strong predictor of winning candidates' local policy positions, and the partisan leanings of city residents only sometimes are: winning candidates in more Democratic cities express greater preference for environmental sustainability, protecting existing conditions, and spending on the fire department but not for police or firefighter collective bargaining or housing.

This only begins to scratch the surface; one could do an entire study of candidates' views on economic development, housing, policing, spending, or public service provision. And these are just a few of the topics that are relevant in local government. My hope is that scholars continue along this trajectory and collectively produce a more complete picture of the policy dynamics of local elections—and the role of interest groups, political parties, and voters in shaping local election outcomes. For my purposes here, these results suggest that local elections are one potential avenue for interest group influence. They are not the only avenue, and by focusing on them I do not mean to suggest that they are. What is clear, however, is that any account of power and influence in local elections cannot ignore the role of interest groups.

CHAPTER TEN

Local Interests and Power

It can be easy to take local governments for granted in the United States because of the kinds of policies they make. When local governments are running smoothly—when the garbage is picked up, the snow is removed, the schools are open to educate children, and clean water comes out of the faucet—it can be easy to ignore what goes on behind the scenes.

But when there is a crisis in local governance, people take note. In Jackson, Mississippi, when a winter storm caused pipes to freeze and put 70% of city residents under a boil-water notice for more than a month, public attention turned to the city's infrastructure.[1] During the COVID-19 pandemic, when public schools in large, urban school districts remained fully in remote (online) instruction several months after private schools and public schools in smaller districts opened for in-person instruction, outraged parents turned their sights to school board meetings.[2] When a city like Detroit goes through bankruptcy, people write about what happened and what brought the city to that point.[3]

In recent years, it has seemed as though these kinds of crises have been adding up and that researchers, advocates, and concerned citizens have been paying more attention to local politics as a result. That increase in attention is a positive development. But it has also put a spotlight on the extent to which local politics is not well understood and the extent to which existing political science accounts of local government do not seem to fully capture what has been happening around the country. What I have offered in this book is a perspective on local politics that tries to better account for some of these dynamics. It is a perspective centered on local policies and interest groups.

It can be tempting to view conflict in local politics as idiosyncratic, or to say that the real problems in the examples above were the winter storm, the pandemic, or the Great Recession. And there is of course some truth to that: every city is a bit different from the next, and disasters and recessions do create enormous challenges. But crises like these also expose broader underlying problems with local government—problems that had been building for a long time. The crisis may light the match, but the city had been piling up tinder for years. And regardless of whether there is a fire in a particular place or at a particular time, some of the underlying political dynamics in American cities are strikingly similar from place to place. There is a rhythm and regularity in local politics and some pattern to the outcomes. Those patterns come into focus when we consider local interests.

Not only are there interest groups active in municipal governments, but the overall amount of their activity varies with the size and scope of government. The types of interest groups that are most active in local politics tend to be those with a large, direct, and regular economic stake in local policy making and those that have few alternatives to local politics for achieving their goals. Because issues like economic development and growth, housing, and public safety provision are important charges of municipal governments almost everywhere, some of the most consistently active interest groups in cities are chambers of commerce, developers, police unions, firefighters' unions, and neighborhood associations. But the activity of these and other interest groups varies depending on what a specific local government does and the nature of a group's interests in those policies. And under some conditions, the political activity of these groups appears to make a difference to local public policies. Crises and open conflict may be relatively rare in local politics, but there are still regular issues, regular interests, and predictable politics. And interest groups are at the heart of that.

Concerned citizens learn this the hard way when they start to engage in local politics in the midst of a crisis. Like Jefferson Smith in *Mr. Smith Goes to Washington*,[4] typically they are newcomers wading into an entrenched, existing power structure. They may manage to organize, even if on a temporary basis, but they find that interest groups are already there—groups with an enormous stake in local policy making that have been actively engaged on an ongoing basis for years. Sometimes those groups are woven into the very fabric of local policy making, aided by institutions that amplify their voices and power, in ways concerned citizens could only dream of. The interest groups and their stake in local policy making are regular and predictable. It is the attention of citizens that is the irregular part.

This is why conceiving of local politics mainly in terms of interactions between citizens, voters, and elected officials has led political scientists off-course in their efforts to understand local democracy and representation. Most citizens do not follow local politics closely, and their main political act is voting—if they even do that. By contrast, interest groups like public-sector unions and local chambers of commerce have a large and ongoing stake in the policies local governments make, and they cannot leave the city in search of better conditions. They focus intensely on the local policies they care most about. And my findings in this book show that local policy is often responsive to them.

My approach also underscores the importance of examining issue areas without open political conflict. The urban politics tradition has focused heavily on land use and growth, and those are of course central to local governance, but they are also unusual in the amount of active political conflict they engender. Developers and chambers of commerce have a stake in furthering growth and development. But the costs of land use policies are highly visible, and those who are negatively impacted by them are profoundly aware of those impacts. As housing politics experts have long said, moreover, those impacts can be very large and economic for nearby homeowners, and that spurs them into political action.[5] The result, very often, is active political conflict. But there are other local issues with major public impacts for which active conflict is far less common. When it comes to public service provision, some of the most important policies are either budgetary or related to rules governing how public employees carry out their work. These policies garner less attention from the public and from researchers, but they still have costs, and they still get attention from interest groups. From my findings in this book, it appears that those interest groups can be quite influential on these matters.

Finally, regardless of whether conflict on a local issue is active or quiet, there is little to suggest that that local political conflict cleanly follows national partisan or ideological lines. City residents' nationally based ideological and partisan leanings are not significantly associated with most of the local policies I examine in this book. Moreover, the most active interest groups in local politics do not coalesce and clash in the ways we would expect if local politics were structured similarly to national politics. And while political parties are sometimes active in

LOCAL INTERESTS AND POWER   267

local elections, they are not active everywhere, and it does not look as though they are coordinating the activity of interest groups. This is not to say that there is *no* ideology in local politics—there could be distinctively local, and possibly multidimensional, ideology at play—but rather that most of local politics does not appear to be heavily structured by nationally based ideology or partisanship. Local politics is distinctive.

Political Representation

There is a bigger lesson about political representation here that transcends the local government context. Up to this point, much of the mainstream study of political representation has conceived of good representation as a link between policy (or elites' positions on policy) and citizens' preferences, where citizens' preferences are measured using public opinion data. This approach makes sense given that public opinion data tell us something about what the public wants. But there are some disadvantages to using public opinion data as the only gauge of the quality of political representation—or the quality of democracy—and advantages to considering a wide range of policies as well as interest groups as major political actors.

As is well known, public opinion does not always form organically from the ground up. It can be influenced by political elites, public policies, and probably even interest groups.[6] In addition, standard public opinion polls tell us little about salience or intensity—whether a citizen feels strongly about an issue and would vote on the basis of that issue—even though politicians surely consider salience in making public policy. Moreover, there are important issues that are not asked about in public opinion polls on a regular basis, and those issues get boxed out of mainstream assessments of representation. There are seemingly technical policies that are important to how cities operate—and how the public is served—that rarely (if ever) get asked about in public opinion polls, if the public even has well-formed opinions about them.

Interest groups, however, often have very well-formed positions on policy matters—and strong ones. In addition, they have many ways of making these preferences known to policy makers: they can lobby, encourage members to attend and speak at public meetings (and give those members talking points), specify certain policy positions as conditions for receiving their endorsements, and more. Sometimes interest groups are in positions of direct policy-making authority, as regime theory scholars have suggested about business in city politics[7] and as scholars of public-sector unions have noted about their role in collective bargaining and decision making on pension funding.[8] And if interest groups have strong preferences, effectively communicate those preferences, and demonstrate willingness to act politically on the basis of those preferences, it raises questions about why policy would be responsive to mass public opinion or the conditions under which that would occur.[9]

My approach in this book has been to instead examine a broad range of core local public policies and prioritize interest groups as political actors while still attempting to consider the role of mass publics. There are some disadvantages to approaching political representation in this way—including the inability to test whether the policies align with local public opinion—but the advantages are considerable. We gain insights into the politics of important policies like cities' use of business tax expenditures. We begin to understand the conditions under which interest group activity shapes those local policies. And we have to wonder whether most city residents have well-developed preferences on these matters anyway.

Finally, it is worth noting that even if city residents have well-developed preferences on a local policy (uninfluenced by elites) and if there is a match between policy and public opinion, that does not necessarily mean the outcome is good policy or good for local governance. For example, if a large majority of a city's residents are opposed to a proposed high-density housing development, a city decision to block the development would be in line with what the public wants. But only the public in that city. Blocking the development could actually be quite bad for those who would like to live in the city but cannot afford to. But because they are outside the city—kept out of the city by that very policy— their opinions would not be included in a measure of public opinion in that jurisdiction. There would be a policy-opinion match, and it would look like good representation by that standard. But it may not be an example of local democracy working well.

None of this is to say that we cannot or should not use public opinion as a benchmark; my point is that it is not a perfect benchmark or the only one and that assessments of political representation should not be defined or constrained by it. Research on political representation should examine a wide range of policies. It should seriously consider and evaluate policy responsiveness to interest groups as well as mass publics. I have tried to do that here. And the results suggest that local policy is

LOCAL INTERESTS AND POWER

often responsive to interest groups—perhaps even more responsive than it is to mass publics.

Interest Groups

Inserting interest groups into the study of local politics has not been a simple matter of borrowing insights and approaches from the existing literature on interest groups and applying them to the local context. Reconceptualizing local democracy in this way has required a broader reconceptualization of interest groups.

Over the past few decades, there have been many attempts to empirically evaluate whether interest groups have influence in American politics, but the findings have been mixed and inconclusive. One interpretation could be that interest groups may not actually have much influence—at least not in the context studied, which is almost always national politics.[10] Another is that perhaps interest groups do have influence, but quantitative studies just have not been able to show it.[11] In part because of these challenges, interest group scholars have devoted more attention to answering questions about interest group activity than about influence. And even the literature on interest group activity has developed in a fragmented way: it is disconnected from the study of interest group influence, examines certain forms of activity in isolation, and puts the theoretical focus on resources. All this has meant that in studying interest groups in local politics, I have had to revisit, unpack, and address some of the broader challenges of the interest group literature in order to make headway.

I have argued that there is a lot to be gained from thinking about interest group activity in a way that is connected to the study of their influence and from conceiving of interest group activity as in large part growing out of their interests in shaping public policies. Solving collective action problems, maintaining organization, and acquiring resources are of course important. But theories of interest groups have focused so heavily on these group dilemmas that they have neglected groups' policy interests as major motivators of their activity. I bring the interests back in. And one would be hard-pressed to explain the patterns of local interest group activity that I found in chapter 4 without consideration of groups' interests. I also adopt an expansive view of interest group activity, recognizing that these groups use and combine a variety of different tools to try to influence policy, including not just campaign contributions and lobbying but also less studied activities like speaking at public meetings and collective bargaining.

This reorientation of the study of interest group activity is an important component of my reoriented approach to evaluating interest group influence. Another is the recognition that interest group influence on policy likely accumulates gradually, over a long period of time, through both decisions and nondecisions. Determining whether they have influence therefore calls for looking at the accumulation of their successes and failures, and that means looking at the content of public policy. That is hard to do quantitatively when the case being studied is the federal government; in searching for units to compare within a single government, researchers have turned to data on roll-call votes and indicators of policy change that have the policy content stripped away. But in subnational governments, where different governments make policies in many of the same areas and have many of the same types of groups involved to varying degrees, the dependent variables can be actual policies. And when I approach the assessment of interest group influence in this way, I find strong signs that interest groups do make a difference.

This, then, is the first twist on the usual way of doing things, because it shows how subnational government—and especially local government—can put the analyst in a better position to evaluate interest groups than the federal government. Usually, when there is interest in a general topic of American politics, such as legislatures, political parties, or voting in elections, the impulse is to start with the federal government and national politics. For instance, much of the way American politics scholars understand legislatures is from theories of Congress, and theories of political parties are built from observations of parties in national elections and national institutions. Eventually those theories are applied to state politics and maybe even local politics. And while it is certainly not always assumed that everything works exactly the same way in state and local governments as in Washington, DC, the theoretical structure builds from the top down, with the federal government understood as the natural starting point and state and local governments the extensions and later applications.

Interest group scholarship has developed in much the same way, with a heavy focus on national politics and the federal government, eventually trickling down to the states and barely reaching local politics at all. But this developmental pathway has hindered its progress. For this particular set of questions—about interest group activity and influence—there is a tremendous advantage to starting with the subnational context and then testing whether the implications extend upward. And local governments in particular provide an especially good vantage point for observing interest group behavior and effectiveness, because there are fewer groups overall, the pull of partisanship is weaker, and they are more limited in their policy scope. None of this is to say that we should stop studying interest groups in national politics or to claim that the specific findings of interest group influence here would carry over into the very different national context. But through local politics we can learn some general lessons about interest groups—about how policy issues help generate certain patterns of interest group activity and about the conditions of interest group influence—that may well be transferable to national politics. Perhaps those insights might someday help to clear the logjam in the study of interest group influence in the federal government.

Of course, the empirical approach I developed and used in this book cannot be directly applied to national politics, so the most direct extensions of this work are to other local and state governments. States, for example, make many of the same types of policies, and there is a great deal more to be done in assessing whether greater activity by certain types of interest groups leads to state policies more in their favor. There is already some research that uses this kind of comparative, cross-state approach, such as Alexander Hertel-Fernandez's research on the influence of conservative networks[12] and empirical studies of states' public-sector retirement costs and the role of public-sector unions.[13] But more of this needs to be done. Working toward an understanding of interest group influence in state politics calls for more research on different kinds of groups and different kinds of policies.

With regard to extending this work to other local governments, studies of politics in local school districts, for example, have already shown how interest groups—especially teachers' unions and other district employees' unions—get involved in a variety of ways. In many districts, they engage through the more traditional channels, such as by giving money in elections and endorsing candidates, but they also engage in collective bargaining, campaign during elections, and more. And there is evidence that their activities affect political and policy outcomes. A new book by Michael Hartney shows this clearly, bringing together an impressive array of data to evaluate just how and how extensively teachers' unions influence school board politics and local education policy in the United States.[14]

All of this seemed to come into sharp relief during the COVID-19 pandemic; it would have been difficult to explain patterns of school district decision making during that period without considering union influence. The onset of the pandemic rapidly shut down businesses and social gatherings across the country, and as part of that, schools of all types shifted to remote instruction. Yet as the pandemic wore on, as knowledge of virus transmission expanded, and as mitigation measures were put in place, many private schools and certain public school districts began to open to in-person instruction on a part-time basis, then many of them on a full-time basis. But certain public school districts remained fully in remote learning. A number of studies show that those decisions had more to do with politics than science. Democratic partisanship is one predictor of whether districts stayed in remote learning. Another is the strength of local teachers' unions.[15]

A closer look at one large, urban school district in California—West Contra Costa Unified School District (WCCUSD)—allows for a more detailed, inside view of how all this worked and how teachers' and other school employees' unions slowed and weakened the district's return to in-person instruction. First, there were hints of agenda setting and blocking: well into fall 2020 and winter 2020–21, even as private and some public Bay Area schools had opened in hybrid mode (part in-person, part remote), the prospect of reopening schools had not appeared on the WCCUSD school board meeting agendas.[16] Collective bargaining played a role too: parents of children in the district, puzzled by the lack of movement toward reopening, eventually learned that early in the pandemic the district had signed a memorandum of understanding (MOU) with its unions that made it nearly impossible to reopen: the MOU stipulated that reopening required the district to meet criteria that county health officials said were unmeasurable, unmeasured, or wildly unrealistic.[17] When parents began to prod the school board to consider reopening, only one of the five board members was clearly supportive, and it happened to be the one board member who had run unopposed in the most recent board election and who had not received several thousand dollars in campaign contributions from the local teachers' union.[18] By appearances, at least, elections and money mattered. And in the earliest meetings at which reopening was discussed, most of the public comments were from educators opposed to reopening to in-person instruction. Scholars often talk about status quo bias in policy, and in WCCUSD, this is how the status quo of remote instruction was allowed to persist for so long.

Eventually, a group of WCCUSD parents got organized, advocated more forcefully for reopening, and threatened to sue the district. Even then, with education employees having been eligible and prioritized for vaccines for many weeks, the district opened for in-person instruction in late April 2021 for only some children for a few hours per week—and made teachers' return voluntary. It seems fairly clear that outcomes in this case—outcomes affecting nearly 29,000 kids and their families—would have been different absent public-sector union political activity. And so the perspective on local politics and interest groups I have offered does seem relevant beyond the municipal governments analyzed in this book.

In addition to proposing this flipped perspective on how we learn about interest groups—that instead of starting from national politics and working downward, we would do well to start with local politics and work upward—my approach departs from the usual way of doing things in its emphasis on the importance of cross-sectional variation. The study of interest group influence is an awkward one in that it is focused on a causal question—the effect of interest group activity on policy—but one for which widely used methods for estimating causal effects are probably not well suited to detecting effects that might exist. Any approach to studying interest group influence therefore carries big downsides. Perhaps the conventional path would be to opt for the widely used causal inference methods—or to not study such questions at all. I have taken the other route, analyzing cross-sectional variation in policies. The downside is that I cannot be sure that the relationships I have estimated are causal; there remain concerns about whether it is in fact the activity of interest groups that is causing the differences in policies. But even with this drawback, there is value in this empirical research, just as scholars have long recognized the value of research on whether policies are associated with public opinion.

Much the same is true of the data and measures I have used throughout this book: they have many flaws, but they also move the study of interest groups forward. Now that we have seen that the policy-focused approach has merit, we should work to collect better data on local interest group activity and local public policies. Datasets like those of the US

Census of Governments are invaluable, but they do not capture all that we might want to know about local public finance, such as tax rates, business tax breaks, spending on pension contributions, or how much local governments spend on lobbying other governments.[19] Moreover, there are important local policies and outcomes that would not be reflected in local finance data even in the best of scenarios, such as rules governing how employees provide public services, emergency response times, and indicators of water or infrastructure quality. Local politics scholars have begun to investigate some such policies and outcomes,[20] but more should be done. Our understanding of local government and local politics depends on it.

Furthermore, now that we better understand the general lay of the land of interest group activity in municipal governments, researchers should pursue answers to some of the unanswered questions I have raised. In addition to more detailed and more comprehensive measures of what interest groups do in local politics, there is much to be learned from in-depth studies of particular types of interest groups, such as local chambers of commerce. As I discussed in chapter 4, there are a number of factors that shape how well organized certain groups are across the country. I have placed the focus on interests because interests have been downplayed in existing theories, and they are clearly important to motivating group political activity. But just as research has shown the importance of state laws to the organization of public-sector unions,[21] it is important for researchers to try to explain variation in the organization of other groups like local chambers of commerce and to consider the historical, institutional, and political factors that may have contributed to patterns of their organization and activity today.

In-depth studies would also be productive for local environmental groups and neighborhood associations. Some of my empirical findings pertaining to these groups were not as I expected, and making more sense of them and their influence will require better understanding of how they are organized and what their preferences and priorities are — and how heterogeneous they are within and across cities. For environmental groups in particular, it will be important to consider the extent to which they are organized from the bottom up or the top down. Just as Michael Hartney and Leslie Finger have shown for teachers' unions,[22] some environmental groups like the Sierra Club have a federated structure, and that may well influence how they behave and what they priori-

LOCAL INTERESTS AND POWER

tize in local politics. Furthering our understanding of local politics and interest group influence will depend on a much more thorough, comprehensive understanding of what these groups do, how they do it, and to what effect.

In the end, the data collection and empirical analyses I have done in this book are just a start—but an important one. They show that there is merit to the policy-focused approach. We have seen that it helps us understand local interest group activity and interest group influence. And that suggests that it should be pursued further with better data and more in-depth attention to particular kinds of interest groups.

Power, Influence, and Public Policy

More than sixty years ago, in one of the most famous studies of city politics and American politics more generally, Robert Dahl posed the question, who governs? The answer, he ultimately concluded, was that it depended on the issue. Different individuals and groups were more active and influential on matters of urban redevelopment than on matters of education, and influence in both of these areas looked different from the dynamics of party nominations. There was inequality of influence on any given issue but not one set of political actors with power over all of city decision making.[23] And so while Dahl's question may seem to imply that we are searching for a single, comprehensive answer—a concise statement about who or what has power in American society—the answer he landed on was that there wasn't one.

I have examined hundreds of cities and multiple city policies in the modern era, and I have also found that influence depends on the policy and the group in question. In cities across the country, one can generally expect to find one set of active groups on matters of policing, a different set of active groups on many questions of economic development, and still a different set of active groups and residents in debates about housing. This aligns in some fundamental ways with Dahl's perspective. But by insisting that the policy details are important for understanding the politics, and that influence is often policy-specific, it departs from modern mainstream approaches to studying American politics.

In a great deal of American politics research today, the emphasis is on particular political actors or institutions, such as voters, legislators, or political parties. Most of the time, there isn't much attention to how their behavior or their effects vary by policy area. And perhaps that makes sense for the questions being asked; perhaps the policy particulars are incidental when the main questions are about, for example, how voters or legislators behave. Most voters are not fixated on the fine details of policy. So much of legislative behavior in national politics today is explained by party affiliation and ideology. For many questions, then, the policy specifics may not be all that important.

For interest groups, however, the policy specifics are crucial. Thinking about policies is a key to understanding interest group activity. It is the key to understanding interest group influence as well, and the ways in which influence is likely to be conditional. And once we engage in questions of interest group influence, we also have to consider the possibility that other actors—such as mass publics—are influential as well, and that forces us to consider whether the influence of those other actors is also conditional on policy. Perhaps the policy specifics are important for understanding those other political actors after all.

There is great value, then, in some of the core elements of the pluralist approach, and we would gain a great deal by reinserting them into the mainstream study of American politics. Importantly, though, the bigger takeaway here is not what the pluralists suggested. Dahl's work in *Who Governs?* is often summarized as implying that power in American society is (or was) dispersed. That statement has appeal in that it sounds like a single answer. But it is misleading. In trying to boil down a complex reality into a single statement, the suggestion is that perhaps we don't really have to worry about concentrated power in American democracy. But unequal power in one issue area does not neutralize or counteract unequal power in another area. It simply means that power in both areas is unequal.

To return to the cases in this book one last time, the finding that police unions are barely active on matters of land use does not change the significance of the finding that police unions are often highly active on matters of police budgets. This does not even the normative score. Rather, it is crucial to understand that police unions are active and have influence in that single issue area. We want to know those specifics. They affect local policies on policing. There is nothing about relative police union inactivity on other issues that averages away the importance of their influence on matters of policing.

In the end, there probably is no single satisfying statement to be made about who or what has power in American society. It depends. And so we would do well to move on and try to understand why we get the public policies we do and whether and when the policies we get are in the public interest. What we have learned is that in local politics in the United States, interest groups are an important part of the picture. But we have to be willing to look at the policy details to see it.

Acknowledgments

It took several years for this book to take shape, and I spent much of that time trying to figure out why the way I was thinking about local interest groups didn't seem to fit within the standard literatures on very closely related topics (interest groups, local politics, political representation, political parties). During some of my early presentations of draft chapters, I got the impression that I left many audience members feeling bewildered, because I wasn't yet able to clearly articulate my contribution or situate it within a debate that was recognizable. But a few people were intrigued and seemed to understand what I was trying to do. They saw value in it and helped me put words to my thoughts. For their encouragement and guidance, I am deeply grateful.

First and foremost, I want to thank my mentor, frequent coauthor, and good friend, Terry Moe. My conversations with Terry over the years have shaped my thinking about public-sector unions, state and local politics, and public policy in ways that are impossible to separate out. His research on education politics and the second face of power has been a major influence on my own work. And I'm sure it's clear to everyone who has read our coauthored articles on public-sector unions and public pensions that many of the seeds of this book were planted in those earlier collaborations. On top of all this, Terry has been an incredibly strong supporter of this project—always encouraging, always constructive.

Two of my colleagues at UC Berkeley, Paul Pierson and Eric Schickler, have also had an especially large impact on this book. Eric helped me talk through the broad themes of the book, provided detailed comments on early drafts of multiple chapters, and provided outstanding mentorship more generally. Paul also gave me feedback on early drafts and pushed me to schedule a book conference when I needed the nudge.

As is surely clear, moreover, Paul's research—including his coauthored work with Jacob Hacker—is foundational to the ideas and approaches I put forward in this book.

I am very grateful to a number of others who helped me make this book what it is. Kathy Bawn and John Zaller saw value in what I was doing early on, encouraged me to keep working on it, and offered helpful suggestions. Jessica Trounstine, Eric Oliver, Matt Grossmann, Liz Gerber, and David Broockman read the first draft of the book (along with the others mentioned above) and provided extensive feedback. Nathan Jensen and Venus Shaghaghi generously shared data on city tax abatement. Parts of chapter 5 started as a collaboration with Olivia Meeks; she and I wrote a paper for a June 2016 conference on political parties run by the Hewlett Foundation and the University of Maryland, College Park, in which we offered some theoretical and empirical preliminaries on the relationship between interest groups and parties. I am indebted to Olivia for her help with that working paper and chapter 5. And I am grateful to Chuck Myers, Chad Zimmerman, and Sara Doskow at the University of Chicago Press for their support of the book.

I also presented chapters of this book at other conferences and workshops over the past few years and benefited from the helpful comments of numerous discussants and audience members, including those at UC Berkeley, Stanford, Vanderbilt, Princeton, Columbia, and USC, as well as the annual meetings of the APSA and MPSA. It was for the USC conference on subnational politics and policy making, convened by Jeff Jenkins, that I originally wrote the article, "Looking for Influence in All the Wrong Places: How Studying Subnational Policy Can Revive Research on Interest Groups," *Journal of Politics* 81, no. 1 (2019): 343–51 © 2019 Southern Political Science Association. It was in that article that I began to lay out some of the core elements of the theoretical framework and approach I develop in chapter 2 of this book. Many thanks to Jeff Jenkins for inviting me to write that piece and attend the conference.

Outside of these workshops and conferences, I had helpful conversations with a number of people, including (but not limited to) Henry Brady, Steve Teles, Michael Hankinson, Hye Young You, Chuck Cameron, Dan Butler, Michael Hartney, Julia Payson, Justin de Benedictis-Kessner, Sarah Reckhow, Alexander Sahn, Sam Trachtman, Brad Barber, John Ellwood, and others. I was also fortunate to have excellent research assistants on the project, including Natalie Ahn, Amir Amerian, Annie Benn, Khulan Erdenebaatar, Charlotte Hill, Julia Hubbell, Khalid Kaldi,

ACKNOWLEDGMENTS 281

Caroline Lefever, Sita McGuire, Olivia Meeks, Anna Mikkelborg, Sophie Morris, Davina Srioudom, and Alex Thibodo. Natalie Ahn deserves special thanks for her incredible work on the surveys.

Most important, I am grateful for the love and support of my family, friends, and community. A lot happened in life during the years I worked on this book, and I was only able to persevere—on this book and in general—because I was lucky enough to have the support of Dan, Joan, Jill, David, Carolyn, Maura, Chris, Lauren, Lijie, Rob, Eliza, Eliana, and Alethea and Daniel. And I wouldn't have been able to do any of this if my children weren't so great. They have been patient, understanding, and lighthearted as I've worked to bring this project to a close during a very difficult year. And after the year we've just had, they might even be starting to get interested in local politics.

Notes

Chapter One

1. Raj Chetty, Nathaniel Hendren, Patrick Kline, and Emmanuel Saez, "Where Is the Land of Opportunity? The Geography of Intergenerational Mobility in the United States," *Quarterly Journal of Economics* 129, no. 4 (2014): 1553–1623; Chang-Tai Hsieh and Enrico Moretti, "Housing Constraints and Spatial Misallocation," *American Economic Journal: Macroeconomics* 11, no. 2 (2019): 1–39; Jessica Trounstine, *Segregation by Design: Local Politics and Inequality in American Cities* (New York: Cambridge University Press, 2018).

2. See, e g., Joanna Stern, "They Used Smartphone Cameras to Record Police Brutality—and Change History," *Wall Street Journal*, June 13, 2020, www.wsj.com/articles/they-used-smartphone-cameras-to-record-police-brutalityand-change-history-11592020827; Heather Kelly and Rachel Lerman, "America Is Awash in Cameras, a Double-Edged Sword for Protesters and Police," *Washington Post*, June 3, 2020, www.washingtonpost.com/technology/2020/06/03/cameras-surveillance-police-protesters/; James Pilcher, "New Investigation Reveals Widespread Police Misconduct Never Publicly Revealed," interview by Amna Nawaz, *PBS News Hour*, PBS, April 25, 2019, audio 6:29, www.pbs.org/newshour/show/new-investigation-reveals-widespread-police-misconduct-never-publicly-revealed.

3. See, e.g., Tracy Gordon, "State and Local Budgets and the Great Recession," Brookings, December 31, 2012, www.brookings.edu/articles/state-and-local-budgets-and-the-great-recession/; Carl Smith, "Government Falls into a Recession and Job Cuts Soar," *Governing*, June 3, 2020, www.governing.com/work/Government-Falls-into-a-Recession-and-Job-Cuts-Soar.html; Sarah F. Anzia, "Pensions in the Trenches: How Pension Spending Is Affecting U.S. Local Government," *Urban Affairs Review* (forthcoming).

4. See Alana Semuels, "From 'Not in My Backyard' to 'Yes in My Back-

yard,'" *The Atlantic*, July 5, 2017, www.theatlantic.com/business/archive/2017/07/yimby-groups-pro-development/532437/.

5. Rashawn Ray, "What Does 'Defund the Police' Mean and Does It Have Merit?" Brookings, June 19, 2020, www.brookings.edu/blog/fixgov/2020/06/19/what-does-defund-the-police-mean-and-does-it-have-merit/.

6. See, e.g., Ali Budner, "A Case Study on Pension Reform: San Jose's Grand Compromise," KQED, January 1, 2017, www.kqed.org/news/11243683/a-case-study-on-pension-reform-san-joses-grand-compromise; Mary Williams Walsh, "Rhode Island Averts Pension Disaster without Raising Taxes," *New York Times*, September 25, 2015, www.nytimes.com/2015/09/26/business/dealbook/rhode-island-averts-pension-disaster-without-raising-taxes.html.

7. Conor Dougherty, "California, Mired in a Housing Crisis, Rejects an Effort to Ease It," *New York Times*, January 30, 2020, www.nytimes.com/2020/01/30/business/economy/sb50-california-housing.html.

8. See Steve Eder, Michael H. Keller, and Blacki Migliozzi, "As New Police Reform Laws Sweep across the U.S., Some Ask: Are They Enough?" *New York Times*, April 18, 2021, www.nytimes.com/2021/04/18/us/police-reform-bills.html; Astead W. Herndon, "How a Pledge to Dismantle the Minneapolis Police Collapsed," *New York Times*, September 26, 2020, updated January 2, 2021, www.nytimes.com/2020/09/26/us/politics/minneapolis-defund-police.html; Rachel Swan, "Collision in Oakland: Move to Defund Police Meets Homicide Spike," *San Francisco Chronicle*, November 1, 2020, www.sfchronicle.com/crime/article/Oakland-pledged-to-cut-its-police-budget-in-half-15689857.php.

9. See, e.g., Pivot Learning, "The Big Squeeze: How Unfunded Pension Costs Threaten Educational Equity," Pivot Learning Research Report, April 19, 2019, www.pivotlearning.org/resources/the-big-squeeze-how-pension-costs-threaten-educational-equity/.

10. Jessica Dyer, "City Council to Consider Housing Project Near Wetlands," *Albuquerque Journal*, June 19, 2019, www.abqjournal.com/1330591/city-council-to-consider-housing-project-near-wetlands.html.

11. Jessica Dyer, "City Council Sends Oxbow Plan Back to Board," *Albuquerque Journal*, August 5, 2019, www.abqjournal.com/1350095/city-council-sends-oxbow-plan-back-to-board-ex-proposed-west-side-housing-development-remains-in-limbo.html.

12. Nick Harrison, "Oxbow Preservation and Poole Purchase Outlined," *Albuquerque West Side*, November 24, 2020, www.abqwestside.com/oxbow-preservation-and-poole-purchase-outlined/; "City Close to Purchasing Property Near Bosque," KRQE, February 7, 2021, updated March 10, 2021, www.krqe.com/news/albuquerque-metro/city-close-to-purchasing-property-near-bosque/.

13. Steve Miletich, "Seattle City Council Passes Historic Police-Accountability Legislation," *Seattle Times*, May 22, 2017, www.seattletimes.com/

NOTES TO CHAPTER ONE

seattle-news/crime/seattle-city-council-passes-historic-police-accountability-legislation/; Steve Miletich, "Seattle's Community Police Commission Urges City Council to Reject Proposed Police Contract," *Seattle Times*, October 17, 2018, www.seattletimes.com/seattle-news/politics/seattles-community-police-commission-unanimously-urges-city-council-to-reject-proposed-police-contract/.

14. Melissa Hellmann, "Oversight Group Rebukes Seattle's Proposed Police Contract," *Seattle Weekly*, October 18, 2018, www.seattleweekly.com/news/oversight-group-rebukes-seattles-proposed-police-contract/.

15. Steve Miletich, "'Our Chance to Fix What Went Wrong': Pressure Mounts on Seattle's Leaders to Enact More Police Reforms," *Seattle Times*, December 6, 2019, www.seattletimes.com/seattle-news/politics/pressure-mounts-on-seattles-leaders-to-enact-more-police-reforms/.

16. Ibid.

17. See "Community Update from Mayor Jeff Ira—Structural Change Needed in Budget," Redwood Shores Community Association, April 2, 2011, www.rsca.org/community-update-from-mayor-jeff-ira-structural-change-needed-in-budget/; Sierra Lopez, "With Strong Budget, Redwood City May Offer Community Help," *Daily Journal*, February 22, 2021, www.smdailyjournal.com/news/local/with-strong-budget-redwood-city-may-offer-community-help/article_6c46fe60-7324-11eb-b174-5f9ff66dae5e.html.

18. Sierra Lopez, "Redwood City Explores Cuts," *Daily Journal*, October 24, 2020, www.smdailyjournal.com/news/local/redwood-city-explores-cuts/article_c8a62982-15ab-11eb-9f98-2f1fc77d5827.html; Aldo Toledo, "Redwood City's Downtown Fire Station Spared from Closure, but Police May Lose Nine Vacant Positions," *Mercury News*, October 30, 2020, www.mercurynews.com/2020/10/29/redwood-citys-downtown-fire-station-spared-from-closure-but-police-may-lose-nine-vacant-positions/.

19. See City of Redwood City, "Revised Budget Fiscal Year 2020–2021," https://webapps.redwoodcity.org/files/finance/main/Revised-Budget-FY-20-21-w-covers-links.pdf.

20. For research on local elections, local voters, and the types of people who run for office, see J. Eric Oliver, Shang E. Ha, and Zachary Callen, *Local Elections and the Politics of Small-Scale Democracy* (Princeton, NJ: Princeton University Press, 2012). The local political economy literature emphasizes the importance of homeowners, variables related to race and ethnicity, and local political institutions. See, e.g., Alberto Alesina, Reza Baqir, and William Easterly, "Public Goods and Ethnic Divisions," *Quarterly Journal of Economics* 1144, no. 4 (1999): 1243–84; Katherine Levine Einstein, David M. Glick, and Maxwell Palmer, *Neighborhood Defenders* (New York: Cambridge University Press, 2019); William A. Fischel, *The Homevoter Hypothesis* (Cambridge, MA: Harvard University Press, 2001); David Schleicher, "City Unplanning," *Yale*

Law Journal 122 (2013): 1670–1737; Trounstine, *Segregation by Design*. When the local politics literature does consider the role of interest groups, it focuses more on electoral institutions than on the groups themselves. See, e.g., Sarah F. Anzia, *Timing and Turnout: How Off-Cycle Elections Favor Organized Groups* (Chicago: University of Chicago Press, 2014); Christopher R. Berry and Jacob E. Gersen, "The Timing of Elections," *University of Chicago Law Review* 77, no. 1 (2010): 37–64; Elisabeth R. Gerber, *The Populist Paradox: Interest Group Influence and the Promise of Direct Legislation* (Princeton, NJ: Princeton University Press, 1999).

21. E.g., Brian F. Schaffner, Jesse H. Rhodes, and Raymond J. La Raja, *Hometown Inequality: Race, Class, and Representation in American Local Politics* (New York: Cambridge University Press, 2020); Chris Tausanovitch and Christopher Warshaw, "Representation in Municipal Government," *American Political Science Review* 108, no. 3 (2014): 605–41.

22. Marie Hojnacki, David C. Kimball, Frank R. Baumgartner, Jeffrey M. Berry, and Beth L. Leech, "Studying Organizational Advocacy and Influence: Reexamining Interest Group Research," *Annual Review of Political Science* 15 (2012): 379–99.

23. For an eloquent articulation of the merits of "policy-focused political science," as compared to a Downsian approach centered on voters, elected officials, and elections, see Jacob S. Hacker and Paul Pierson, "After the 'Master Theory': Downs, Schattschneider, and the Rebirth of Policy-Focused Analysis," *Perspectives on Politics* 12, no. 3 (2014): 643–62.

24. See Christopher Warshaw, "Local Elections and Representation in the United States," *Annual Review of Political Science* 22 (2019): 461–79.

25. Paul E. Peterson, *City Limits* (Chicago: University of Chicago Press, 1981).

26. Oliver, Ha, and Callen, *Local Elections and the Politics of Small-Scale Democracy*.

27. E.g., Katherine Levine Einstein and Vladimir Kogan, "Pushing the City Limits: Policy Responsiveness in Municipal Government," *Urban Affairs Review* 52, no. 1 (2016): 3–32; Tausanovitch and Warshaw, "Representation in Municipal Government."

28. Justin de Benedictis-Kessner and Christopher Warshaw, "Mayoral Partisanship and Municipal Fiscal Policy," *Journal of Politics* 78, no. 4 (2016): 1124–38; Justin de Benedictis-Kessner and Christopher Warshaw, "Politics in Forgotten Governments: The Partisan Composition of County Legislatures and County Fiscal Policies," *Journal of Politics* 82, no. 2 (2020): 460–75. However, see also Fernando Ferreira and Joseph Gyourko, "Do Political Parties Matter? Evidence from U.S. Cities," *Quarterly Journal of Economics* 124, no. 1 (2009): 399–422; Daniel M. Thompson, "How Partisan Is Local Law Enforcement? Evi-

NOTES TO CHAPTER ONE

dence from Sheriff Cooperation with Immigration Authorities," *American Political Science Review* 114, no. 1 (2020): 222–36.

29. Anzia, *Timing and Turnout*; Mark Lubell, Richard C. Feiock, and Edgar E. Ramirez De La Cruz, "Local Institutions and the Politics of Urban Growth," *American Journal of Political Science* 53, no. 3 (2009): 649–65; Jessica Trounstine, *Political Monopolies in American Cities: The Rise and Fall of Bosses and Reformers* (Chicago: University of Chicago Press, 2008).

30. Elisabeth R. Gerber and Daniel J. Hopkins, "When Mayors Matter: Estimating the Impact of Mayoral Partisanship on City Policy," *American Journal of Political Science* 55, no. 2 (2011): 326–39; Oliver, Ha, and Callen, *Local Elections and the Politics of Small-Scale Democracy*; Peterson, *City Limits*.

31. See Christopher R. Berry, *Imperfect Union: Representation and Taxation in Multilevel Governments* (New York: Cambridge University Press, 2009).

32. See Oliver, Ha, and Callen, *Local Elections and the Politics of Small-Scale Democracy*.

33. Some cities and counties are responsible for public education, and when they are, education makes up a large share of their spending. However, in most parts of the United States, public education is provided by independent school districts.

34. On vested interests, see Terry M. Moe, "Vested Interests and Political Institutions," *Political Science Quarterly* 130, no. 2 (2015): 277–318.

35. Some prominent examples are Larry M. Bartels, *Unequal Democracy: The Political Economy of the New Gilded Age* (Princeton, NJ: Princeton University Press, 2008); Robert S. Erikson, Gerald C. Wright, and John P. McIver, *Statehouse Democracy: Public Opinion and Policy in the American States* (New York: Cambridge University Press, 1993); Martin Gilens, *Affluence and Influence: Economic Inequality and Political Power in America* (Princeton, NJ: Princeton University Press, 2012); Jeffrey R. Lax and Justin H. Phillips. "The Democratic Deficit in the States," *American Journal of Political Science* 56, no. 1 (2012): 148–66.

36. A simple search for "police and policing" on Roper's iPoll data base yields a total of 47 public opinion poll questions in 2011, 37 in 2019, and 311 in 2020. There was also an earlier uptick in 2014 after the killing of Michael Brown and subsequent protests in Ferguson, Missouri, but even that year, there were only 146 questions.

37. See Jacob S. Hacker and Paul Pierson, *Winner-Take-All Politics: How Washington Made the Rich Richer—and Turned Its Back on the Middle Class* (New York: Simon & Schuster, 2010).

38. Hacker and Pierson, "After the 'Master Theory.'"

39. Some studies of representation ignore interest groups altogether. Others cite interest groups as one possible reason public opinion does not align with

policy as well as expected, yet do not study interest group influence empirically. Rare are studies of representation that attempt to incorporate interest groups. For examples, see Gilens, *Affluence and Influence*; Lax and Phillips, "The Democratic Deficit in the States." Even these latter studies put heavy emphasis on the explanatory power of public opinion—not on interest groups.

40. Frank Baumgartner and Beth L. Leech, *Basic Interests: The Importance of Groups in Politics and in Political Science* (Princeton, NJ: Princeton University Press, 1998).

41. Robert Alan Dahl and Charles Edward Lindblom, *Politics, Economics and Welfare: Planning and Politico-Economic Systems, Resolved into Basic Processes* (New York: Harper & Brothers, 1953); Nelson W. Polsby, "How to Study Community Power: The Pluralist Alternative," *Journal of Politics* 22, no. 3 (1960): 474–84; E. E. Schattschneider, *The Semi-Sovereign People* (New York: Holt, Rhinehart and Winston, 1961); David Truman, *The Process of Government* (New York: Knopf, 1951).

42. Robert Alan Dahl, *Who Governs? Democracy and Power in an American City* (New Haven, CT: Yale University Press, 1961).

43. Peter Bachrach and Morton S. Baratz, "Two Faces of Power," *American Political Science Review* 56, no. 4 (1962): 947–52.

44. Paul Pierson, "Goodbye to Pluralism? Studying Power in Contemporary American Politics," paper presented at the Wildavsky Forum for Public Policy, April 2015, 10; Nelson W. Polsby, *Community Power and Political Theory: A Further Look at Problems of Evidence and Inference* (New Haven, CT: Yale University Press, 1980); Raymond E. Wolfinger, "Nondecisions and the Study of Local Politics," *American Political Science Review* 65, no. 4 (1971): 1063–80.

45. Hacker and Pierson, "After the 'Master Theory.'"

46. Mancur Olson's rational choice theory of collective action was both a boon and a blow to the study of groups: it provided insight into the collective action problem many organizations face, but it also raised the puzzle of why interest groups would form at all. Mancur Olson, *The Logic of Collective Action: Public Goods and the Theory of Groups* (Cambridge, MA: Harvard University Press, 1965).

47. Ironically, around the same time, there was an explosion of interest groups on the national political scene. See Jeffrey M. Berry, *The New Liberalism: The Rising Power of Citizen Groups* (Washington, DC: Brookings Institution, 1999). But instead of inspiring new work on interest group influence, it inspired new theories of how groups are organized into loose issue networks—a move that further separated the substance and methods of interest groups research from those used in the mainstream study of political representation. See Hugh Heclo, "Issue Networks and the Executive Establishment," in *The New American Political System*, ed. Samuel Hutchison Beer and Anthony Stephen King (Wash-

NOTES TO CHAPTER TWO

ington, DC: American Enterprise Institute for Public Policy Research, 1978), 87–124.

48. See, e.g., Baumgartner and Leech, *Basic Interests*; Frank R. Baumgartner, Jeffrey M. Berry, Marie Hojnacki, Beth L. Leech, and David C. Kimball, *Lobbying and Policy Change: Who Wins, Who Loses, and Why* (Chicago: University of Chicago Press, 2009); Hojnacki et al., "Studying Organizational Advocacy and Influence"; Richard A. Smith, "Interest Group Influence in the U.S. Congress," *Legislative Studies Quarterly* 20, no. 1 (1995): 89–139.

49. Beth L. Leech, "Lobbying and Influence," in *The Oxford Handbook of American Political Parties and Interest Groups*, ed. Jeffrey M. Berry, L. Sandy Maisel and George C. Edwards III (Oxford: Oxford University Press, 2010), 534.

50. There are a few large cities that track lobbying activity, and in principle it is possible to collect local campaign finance data (as I discuss later).

51. John R. Logan and Harvey Luskin Molotch, *Urban Fortunes: The Political Economy of Place* (Berkeley: University of California Press, 1987).

52. Einstein, Glick, and Palmer, *Neighborhood Defenders*; Fischel, *The Homevoter Hypothesis*; Schleicher, "City Unplanning."

53. Sarah F. Anzia and Terry M. Moe, "Public Sector Unions and the Costs of Government," *Journal of Politics* 77, no. 1 (2015): 114–27.

54. Tausanovitch and Warshaw, "Representation in Municipal Government."

55. Peter Bucchianeri, "Party Competition and Coalitional Stability: Evidence from American Local Government," *American Political Science Review* 114, no. 4 (2020): 1055–70.

Chapter Two

1. See Bartels, *Unequal Democracy*; Lax and Phillips, "The Democratic Deficit in the States."

2. Jacob M. Grumbach, "From Backwaters to Major Policymakers: Policy Polarization in the States, 1970–2014," *Perspectives on Politics* 16, no. 2 (2018): 416–35; Hacker and Pierson, *Winner-Take-All Politics*.

3. For more discussion of this point, see my related article, Sarah F. Anzia, "When Does a Group of Citizens Influence Policy? Evidence from Senior Citizen Participation in City Politics," *Journal of Politics* 81, no. 1 (2019): 1–14. See also, e.g., R. Douglas Arnold, *The Logic of Congressional Action* (New Haven, CT: Yale University Press, 1990); Betsy Sinclair, *The Social Citizen: Peer Networks and Political Behavior* (Chicago: University of Chicago Press, 2012).

4. See, e.g., John R. Zaller, *The Nature and Origins of Mass Opinion* (New York: Cambridge University Press, 1992).

5. Arnold, *The Logic of Congressional Action*.

6. Kathleen Bawn, Martin Cohen, David Karol, Seth Masket, Hans Noel, and John Zaller, "A Theory of Political Parties: Groups, Policy Demands and Nominations in American Politics," *Perspectives on Politics* 10, no. 3 (2012): 571–97. See also Benjamin I. Page and Robert Y. Shapiro, "Effects of Public Opinion on Policy," *American Political Science Review* 77, no. 1 (1983): 175–90.

7. This is an assumption but a reasonable one, and I am not alone in making it. Scholars studying interest group influence have long assumed that interest groups are pushing for policies they favor. See, e.g., Baumgartner et al., *Lobbying and Policy Change*; Berry, *The New Liberalism*; Hacker and Pierson, "After the 'Master Theory.'"

8. Hacker and Pierson, "After the 'Master Theory,'" 648.

9. See also Andrea Louise Campbell, *How Policies Make Citizens: Senior Political Activism and the American Welfare State* (Princeton, NJ: Princeton University Press, 2003); Moe, "Vested Interests and Political Institutions."

10. This was the pluralists' approach, after all. See, e.g., Theodore J. Lowi, *The End of Liberalism* (New York: Norton, 1969); Grant McConnell, *Private Power and American Democracy* (New York: Knopf, 1966); Schattschneider, *The Semi-Sovereign People*. It is also the central idea put forward by Moe in his argument about how "vested interests" are crucially important to stability and change in political institutions; see Moe, "Vested Interests and Political Institutions." And it is a core idea of work on the politics of public policy; see, e.g., Sarah F. Anzia and Terry M. Moe, "Polarization and Policy: The Politics of Public-Sector Pensions," *Legislative Studies Quarterly* 42, no. 1 (2017): 33–62; Campbell, *How Policies Make Citizens*; Eric M. Patashnik, *Reforms at Risk: What Happens after Major Policy Changes Are Enacted* (Princeton, NJ: Princeton University Press, 2008).

11. For statements on the dearth of interest groups in local government, see Oliver, Ha, and Callen, *Local Elections and the Politics of Small-Scale Democracy*; Peterson, *City Limits*.

12. Olson, *The Logic of Collective Action*.

13. One line of this research puzzles over which groups lobby independently as opposed to through trade associations. See, e.g., John M. de Figueiredo and Emerson H. Tiller, "The Structure and Conduct of Corporate Lobbying: How Firms Lobby the Federal Communications Commission," *Journal of Economics & Management Strategy* 10, no. 1 (2001): 91–122. Another asks whether lobbyists are valuable because of their expertise or their connections; see Marianne Bertrand, Matilde Bombardini, and Francesco Trebbi, "Is It Whom You Know or What You Know? An Empirical Assessment of the Lobbying Process," *American Economic Review* 104, no. 12 (2014): 3885–3920. Still another explains which legislators lobbyists choose to target; see David Austen-Smith and John R. Wright, "Counteractive Lobbying," *American Journal of Political Science* 38, no. 1 (1994): 25–44; Marie Hojnacki and David C. Kimball, "The Who and

How of Organizations' Lobbying Strategies in Committee," *Journal of Politics* 61, no. 4 (1999): 999–1024.

14. See, e.g., Alexander Fouirnaies and Andrew B. Hall, "The Financial Incumbency Advantage: Causes and Consequences," *Journal of Politics* 76, no. 3 (2014): 711–24; Richard L. Hall and Frank W. Wayman, "Buying Time: Moneyed Interests and the Mobilization of Bias in Congressional Committees," *American Political Science Review* 84, no. 3 (1990): 797–820; Eleanor Neff Powell and Justin Grimmer, "Money in Exile: Campaign Contributions and Committee Access," *Journal of Politics* 78, no. 4 (2016): 974–88. Much of the research on campaign contributions isn't exclusively about interest groups, however; it instead examines contributions by groups and individuals, hoping to understand what motivates different actors to give money to candidates. See, e.g., Stephen Ansolabehere, John M. de Figueiredo, and James M. Snyder Jr., "Why Is There So Little Money in U.S. Politics?," *Journal of Economic Perspectives* 17, no. 1 (2003): 105–30.

15. E.g., Kay Lehman Schlozman and John T. Tierney, *Organized Interests and American Democracy* (New York: HarperCollins, 1986); Kay Lehman Schlozman, Sidney Verba, and Henry E. Brady, *The Unheavenly Chorus: Unequal Political Voice and the Broken Promise of American Democracy* (Princeton, NJ: Princeton University Press, 2013); Jack L. Walker, *Mobilizing Interest Groups in America: Patrons, Professions, and Social Movements* (Ann Arbor: University of Michigan Press, 1991).

16. E.g., Walker, *Mobilizing Interest Groups in America*; Schlozman, Verba, and Brady, *The Unheavenly Chorus*.

17. See Kay L. Schlozman, "Who Sings in the Heavenly Chorus? The Shape of the Organized Interest System," in Berry, Maisel, and Edwards, *The Oxford Handbook of American Political Parties and Interest Groups*, 425–50.

18. Virginia Gray and David Lowery, *The Population Ecology of Interest Representation* (Ann Arbor: University of Michigan Press, 1996).

19. Ibid., 38, 61–63. The embedded quote here is from Paul R. Ehrlich and Jonathan Roughgarden, *The Science of Ecology* (New York: Macmillan, 1987), 322.

20. Instead, it generates hypotheses about the number of organizations *within a guild*, for example, how many gay and lesbian rights groups there will be in a polity. See, e.g., Anthony J. Nownes, "The Population Ecology of Interest Group Formation: Mobilizing for Gay and Lesbian Rights in the United States, 1950–98," *British Journal of Political Science* 34, no. 1 (2004): 49–67.

21. Their second dependent variable—interest group population "diversity"—sounds like it's related to questions about the types of interest groups that will be active, but their theory doesn't identify independent variables that will explain it. See Gray and Lowery, *The Population Ecology of Interest Representation*, 74, 162, 174–75.

22. For a helpful discussion, see Terry M. Moe, "Toward a Broader View of Interest Groups," *Journal of Politics* 43, no. 2 (1981): 531–43.

23. Olson, *The Logic of Collective Action*.

24. Walker, *Mobilizing Interest Groups in America*, 75, 77.

25. Also, many interest groups are not made up of individuals making a decision about whether to join; many are businesses, institutions, groups of organizations, or individuals who join because doing so is related to their occupations.

26. This is also true of James Q. Wilson, *Political Organizations* (Princeton, NJ: Princeton University Press, 1995).

27. Gray and Lowery, *The Population Ecology of Interest Representation*, 65.

28. As Moe explains, we should not just be focused on the *resources* groups have to influence politics but also their *incentives* to influence politics. Terry M. Moe, *Special Interest: Teachers Unions and America's Public Schools* (Washington, DC: Brookings Institution Press, 2011); Moe, "Vested Interests and Political Institutions."

29. E.g., Schlozman, Verba, and Brady, *The Unheavenly Chorus*.

30. See Smith, "Interest Group Influence in the U.S. Congress."

31. See Sarah F. Anzia and Terry M. Moe, "Interest Groups on the Inside: The Governance of Public Pension Funds," *Perspectives on Politics* 17, no. 4 (2019): 1059–78; Lowi, *The End of Liberalism*; McConnell, *Private Power and American Democracy*.

32. Sarah F. Anzia and Terry M. Moe, "Public Sector Unions and the Costs of Government," *Journal of Politics* 77, no. 1 (2015): 114–27; Daniel DiSalvo, *Government Against Itself: Public Union Power and Its Consequences* (New York: Oxford University Press, 2015).

33. Alexander Hertel-Fernandez, *Politics at Work: How Companies Turn Their Workers into Lobbyists* (New York: Oxford University Press, 2018).

34. Peterson, *City Limits*.

35. Specifically, they argue that electoral politics in any government will depend on its size (the number of constituents), its scope (its power or capacity for action), and its bias (how unevenly it distributes resources among its constituents). See Oliver, Ha, and Callen, *Local Elections and the Politics of Small-Scale Democracy*.

36. See, e.g., Arnold, *The Logic of Congressional Action*; Andrea Louise Campbell, "Policy Makes Mass Politics," *Annual Review of Political Science* 15 (2012): 333–51.

37. This is not to say that they never do, of course, but rather that regulating abortion is not a core function of most city governments. See Elaine B. Sharp, *Morality Politics in American Cities* (Lawrence: University Press of Kansas, 2005).

38. See Oliver, Ha, and Callen, *Local Elections and the Politics of Small-Scale Democracy*, 106.

NOTES TO CHAPTER TWO

39. Ibid., 25.

40. To be clear, I am not arguing that a lack of activity means a lack of interest (I discuss this further in subsequent chapters). I am also not arguing that interests are the only factor that matters for explaining interest group activity. I am simply saying that groups' interests in policies are important to consider for explaining patterns of interest group activity and that research on interest group activity has tended to downplay or ignore the role of interests.

41. See Campbell, "Policy Makes Mass Politics."

42. Arnold, *The Logic of Congressional Action*; Campbell, *How Policies Make Citizens*; Moe, "Vested Interests and Political Institutions."

43. Campbell, "Policy Makes Mass Politics," 339; see also Eric M. Patashnik and Julian E. Zelizer, "The Struggle to Remake Politics: Liberal Reform and the Limits of Policy Feedback in the Contemporary American State," *Perspectives on Politics* 11, no. 4 (2013): 1071–87.

44. E. E. Schattschneider, *Politics, Pressures and the Tariff* (New York: Prentice-Hall, 1935), 127–28.

45. Olson, *The Logic of Collective Action*; see also Terry M. Moe, *The Organization of Interests: Incentives and the Internal Dynamics of Political Interest Groups* (Chicago: University of Chicago Press, 1980).

46. Moe, "Vested Interests and Political Institutions."

47. People of course join groups for social, purposive, and ideological benefits as well. See Wilson, *Political Organizations*. In fact, Berry argues that the proliferation of citizen groups in Washington, DC, during the 1970s and 1980s reflected a rise in "post-materialism." See Berry, *The New Liberalism*. But there are reasons to question whether the same rise in post-materialism happened in local politics.

48. Arnold, *The Logic of Congressional Action*; Moe, "Vested Interests and Political Institutions"; Walker, *Mobilizing Interest Groups in America*.

49. Arnold, *The Logic of Congressional Action*.

50. Ibid., 137.

51. E.g., Peterson, *City Limits*.

52. Charles M. Tiebout, "A Pure Theory of Local Expenditures," *Journal of Political Economy* 64, no. 5 (1956): 416–24.

53. Fischel, *The Homevoter Hypothesis*; Albert O. Hirschman, *Exit, Voice, and Loyalty: Responses to Decline in Firms, Organizations, and States* (Cambridge, MA: Harvard University Press, 1970).

54. See, e.g., Baumgartner and Leech, *Basic Interests*; Paul Burstein and April Linton, "The Impact of Political Parties, Interest Groups, and Social Movement Organizations on Public Policy: Some Recent Evidence and Theoretical Concerns," *Social Forces* 81, no. 2 (2002): 380–408; Allan J. Cigler, "Interest Groups: A Subfield in Search of an Identity," in *Political Science: Looking to the Future*, ed. William J. Crotty (Evanston, IL: Northwestern University

Press, 1991), 99–135; Hojnacki et al., "Studying Organizational Advocacy and Influence."

55. Baumgartner et al., *Lobbying and Policy Change.*

56. See, e.g., Baumgartner and Leech, *Basic Interests*; Leech, "Lobbying and Influence."

57. See Hojnacki et al., "Studying Organizational Advocacy and Influence."

58. Baumgartner and Leech also refer to a dependent variable problem in their discussion of the interest group influence literature, but it is not the same problem that I lay out here. They argue that because scholars working in this literature have used different dependent variables in their studies, it is hard to review the literature as a whole and draw general conclusions about interest group influence. I am instead pointing to specific problems with some of the commonly used dependent variables in this literature. See Baumgartner and Leech, *Basic Interests.*

59. Hacker and Pierson, "After the 'Master Theory,'" 648.

60. This is not to say that interest groups aren't sometimes myopic in weighing the trade-offs of policies. See Anzia and Moe, "Interest Groups on the Inside."

61. E.g., Douglass Cater, *Power in Washington* (New York: Random House, 1964); A. Lee Fritschler, *Smoking and Politics: Policymaking and the Federal Bureaucracy* (New York: Appleton-Century-Crofts, 1975); Arthur Maass, *Muddy Waters: The Army Engineers and the Nation's Rivers* (Cambridge, MA: Harvard University Press, 1951).

62. E.g., Raymond A. Bauer, Ithiel de Sola Pool, and Lewis Anthony Dexter, *American Business and Public Policy: The Politics of Foreign Trade*, 2nd ed. (Chicago: Aldine-Atherton, 1972); Schattschneider, *Politics, Pressures and the Tariff.*

63. Lowi, *The End of Liberalism*; McConnell, *Private Power and American Democracy.*

64. Baumgartner and Leech, *Basic Interests*, 139.

65. For reviews of this work, see Ansolabehere, de Figueiredo, and Snyder, "Why Is There So Little Money in U.S. Politics?"; Baumgartner and Leech, *Basic Interests.*

66. See David R. Mayhew, *Congress: The Electoral Connection* (New Haven, CT: Yale University Press, 1974).

67. See Gilens, *Affluence and Influence*; Pierson, "Goodbye to Pluralism?"

68. Bachrach and Baratz, "Two Faces of Power"; Hacker and Pierson, "After the 'Master Theory'"; Moe, "Vested Interests and Political Institutions."

69. Moe, *Special Interest*; Terry M. Moe, *The Politics of Institutional Reform: Katrina, Education, and the Second Face of Power* (New York: Cambridge University Press, 2019).

70. Baumgartner and Leech, *Basic Interests*, 137.

71. Pierson, "Goodbye to Pluralism?"

NOTES TO CHAPTER TWO

72. E.g., Gary W. Cox and Mathew D. McCubbins, *Setting the Agenda: Responsible Party Government in the U.S. House of Representatives* (New York: Cambridge University Press, 2005).

73. Baumgartner et al., *Lobbying and Policy Change*.

74. See Sarah F. Anzia, "Looking for Influence in All the Wrong Places: How Studying Subnational Policy Can Revive Research on Interest Groups," *Journal of Politics* 81, no. 1 (2019): 343–51.

75. For important new research on the second face of power, see Moe, *The Politics of Institutional Reform*.

76. For research using a similar approach, see Gilens, *Affluence and Influence*; Martin Gilens and Benjamin I. Page, "Testing Theories of American Politics: Elites, Interest Groups, and Average Citizens," *Perspectives on Politics* 12, no. 3 (2014): 564–81.

77. Paul Pierson, "Big, Slow-Moving, and . . . Invisible," in *Comparative Historical Analysis in the Social Sciences*, ed. James Mahoney and Dietrich Rueschemeyer (Cambridge: Cambridge University Press, 2003), 117–207; Paul Pierson, *Politics in Time: History, Institutions, and Social Analysis* (Princeton, NJ: Princeton University Press, 2004).

78. "Bringing policy back in" is from Hacker and Pierson, "After the 'Master Theory,'" 655; see Pierson, *Politics in Time*.

79. Pierson, *Politics in Time*.

80. Ibid.

81. See, e.g., Alexander Hertel-Fernandez, *State Capture: How Conservative Activists, Big Businesses, and Wealthy Donors Reshaped the American States—and the Nation* (New York: Oxford University Press, 2019).

82. E.g., Gilens, *Affluence and Influence*.

83. See Campbell, *How Policies Make Citizens*; Moe, "Vested Interests and Political Institutions"; Leah Cardamore Stokes, *Short Circuiting Policy: Interest Groups and the Battle over Clean Energy and Climate Policy in the American States* (New York: Oxford University Press, 2020).

84. Moe, *Special Interest*; George Tsebelis, *Veto Players: How Political Institutions Work* (Princeton, NJ: Princeton University Press, 2002).

85. Leech, "Lobbying and Influence," 549.

86. See, e.g., Gilens, *Affluence and Influence*; Lax and Phillips, "The Democratic Deficit in the States"; Tausanovitch and Warshaw, "Representation in Municipal Government."

87. For examples, see Richard C. Feiock, Kent E. Portney, Jungah Bae, and Jeffrey M. Berry, "Governing Local Sustainability: Agency Venues and Business Group Access," *Urban Affairs Review* 50, no. 2 (2014): 157–79; Zoltan L. Hajnal and Terry Nichols Clark, "The Local Interest-Group System: Who Governs and Why?," *Social Science Quarterly* 79, no. 1 (1998): 227–41.

88. Research by Lax and Phillips and Gilens are excellent examples of how

this can be done at the state level and national level. Still, the emphasis in their work is on the link between public opinion and policy, with a simple measure of interest group balance. Gilens, *Affluence and Influence*; Lax and Phillips, "The Democratic Deficit in the States."

89. E.g., Katherine Levine Einstein and Vladimir Kogan, "Pushing the City Limits: Policy Responsiveness in Municipal Government," *Urban Affairs Review* 52, no. 1 (2016): 3–32; Tausanovitch and Warshaw, "Representation in Municipal Government."

90. Einstein, Glick, and Palmer, *Neighborhood Defenders*; Fischel, *The Homevoter Hypothesis*; Trounstine, *Segregation by Design*.

91. Baumgartner and Leech, *Basic Interests*; Baumgartner et al., *Lobbying and Policy Change*.

92. In later chapters, I provide a more detailed description of how I contend with these various forces in my empirical analyses.

93. Richard L. Hall and Alan V. Deardorff, "Lobbying as Legislative Subsidy," *American Political Science Review* 100, no. 1 (2006): 69–84.

94. Dahl, *Who Governs?*

95. Moe's recent analysis of New Orleans public schools post–Hurricane Katrina highlights just how difficult it can be to see the full second face of power. Moe, *The Politics of Institutional Reform*.

96. In this way, the approach incorporates agenda-setting as a channel through which policy is shaped: within an issue area, interest groups can block certain policies from being considered and push others forward. Because cities vary in the issue areas they make policy on, however, there is another form of agenda-setting that is important to consider as well: "what cities do" might be shaped by interest groups. For example, an active interest group in one city might persuade city officials to make policy on a new issue, whereas a less active interest group somewhere else might not. I discuss this latter form of agenda-setting in chapter 3.

97. Anzia and Moe, "Interest Groups on the Inside"; Hertel-Fernandez, *Politics at Work*; Hertel-Fernandez, *State Capture*.

98. Dahl, *Who Governs?*, 271, 273 (emphasis in original).

99. As a side note, actual union membership in Mississippi is probably a pretty good measure of potential activity if it is reasonable to assume that a large share of those members could be mobilized for political action. This gets closer to capturing potential activity than, say, a corporation's net worth.

100. If we had data on the opinions of group members, it would be possible to empirically explore this variation in preference homogeneity and test its relationship to policy outcomes. Measuring interest group preferences has not been a major focus of the interest group literature, however, and this is a promising area for future study. Research by Moe on the political and policy views of pub-

NOTES TO CHAPTER THREE

lic school teachers is an excellent example of how this could be done. I discuss this work later. See Moe, *Special Interest*.

101. Just as it would be possible to measure the within-group homogeneity and across-group distinctiveness of policy preferences, it could also be possible to measure the activity of groups on specific issues or sets of issues, as Moe does in his studies of teachers' unions and education policy. See Terry M. Moe, "Teacher Unions and School Board Elections," in *Besieged: School Boards and the Future of Education Politics*, ed. William G. Howell (Washington, DC: Brookings Institution Press, 2005), 254–87. Those issue-specific measures of activity would then rule out the need to theoretically consider how a group will channel its political attention and resources. In this book, however, I use city-level measures of interest group activity, so my empirical tests require consideration of whether a group would focus its efforts on a particular policy.

102. Leech, "Lobbying and Influence."

103. Dahl, *Who Governs?*

104. Wilson, *Political Organizations*.

105. Arnold, *The Logic of Congressional Action*.

106. Timothy Barnekov and Daniel Rich, "Privatism and the Limits of Local Economic Development Policy," *Urban Affairs Quarterly* 25, no. 2 (1989): 212–38; Karen Mossberger and Gerry Stoker, "The Evolution of Urban Regime Theory: The Challenge of Conceptualization," *Urban Affairs Review* 36, no. 6 (2001): 810–35; Clarence N. Stone, *Regime Politics: Governing Atlanta, 1946–1988* (Lawrence: University Press of Kansas, 1989).

107. Peterson, *City Limits*, 25.

108. Logan and Molotch, *Urban Fortunes*, 13.

Chapter Three

1. Dahl, *Who Governs?*, 137.

2. John Hilliard, "Referendum Could Decide Future of Newton's Biggest Mixed-Use Development," *Boston Globe*, January 3, 2020, www.bostonglobe .com/metro/globelocal/2020/01/03/referendum-could-decide-future-newton -biggest-mixed-use-development/0pkkT3fdaSUaElNGZ7T2WL/story.html.

3. Nick Marnell, "MOFD Elections: Firefighters Union Achieves 100 Percent ROI," *Lamorinda Weekly*, December 12, 2018, www.lamorindaweekly .com/archive/issue1221/MOFD-elections-Firefighters-union-achieves-100 -percent-ROI.html; Nick Marnell, "Plenty of Money and Plenty of Nastiness Define MOFD Board Races," *Lamorinda Weekly*, October 31, 2018, www.lamorindaweekly.com/archive/issue1218/Plenty-of-money-and-plenty-of -nastiness-define-MOFD-board-races.html.

NOTES TO CHAPTER THREE

4. One can try to piece together relevant bits of intuition and empirical analysis that are scattered across disparate strands of research, but it does not add up to a satisfying account of interest group activity in local politics. For example, Peterson argues that there should be fewer interest groups in city politics than in national politics but is not more specific than that. See Peterson, *City Limits*. Oliver, Ha, and Callen argue that interest groups are important players in some local governments and not others, but their empirical analysis is focused on voters and candidates, not interest groups. See Oliver, Ha, and Callen, *Local Elections and the Politics of Small-Scale Democracy*. Urban politics scholarship on "regimes" offers a window onto the interest group environment in American cities, but its focus is overwhelmingly on the politics of economic development and growth and the role of business interests (and more recently environmental groups), and it has mostly explored this through case studies of large cities. See, e.g., Stone, *Regime Politics*; Mossberger and Stoker, "The Evolution of Urban Regime Theory"; Jeffrey M. Berry, "Urban Interest Groups," in Berry, Maisel, and Edwards, *The Oxford Handbook of American Political Parties and Interest Groups*, 502–18; Kent E. Portney and Jeffrey M. Berry, "The Impact of Local Environmental Advocacy Groups on City Sustainability Policies and Programs," *Policy Studies Journal* 44, no. 2 (2016): 196–214.

5. For details on these data bases, see, e.g., Baumgartner et al., *Lobbying and Policy Change*; Gray and Lowery, *The Population Ecology of Interest Representation*.

6. Other researchers have also used surveys to gather information about local politics, recognizing that there is often no other way to collect the needed information about local governance. There are even some studies that use surveys to gather information about local interest groups. For example, Hajnal and Clark use a survey to measure the activity and influence of privileged and nonprivileged groups in local politics. See Hajnal and Clark, "The Local Interest-Group System." Moe uses a survey to study teachers' union and other group involvement in school board elections. See Moe, "Teacher Unions and School Board Elections." And Cooper, Nownes, and Roberts also use a survey to measure local interest group activity and influence in a set of 68 large cities. Christopher A. Cooper, Anthony J. Nownes, and Steven Roberts, "Perceptions of Power: Interest Groups in Local Politics," *State and Local Government Review* 37, no. 3 (2005): 206–16.

7. Note that the target unit of analysis is a municipal government, although the way to obtain information about municipal governments is through the individuals holding elective office.

8. Specifically, I used web forms to request individual email addresses in 77 cities and received at least some emails from 26 of them. I also obtained email addresses in 30 cities by requesting them from a staff person.

9. Four percent of the cities did not provide any way to communicate elec-

NOTES TO CHAPTER THREE

tronically with city officials. The remaining cities that were dropped did not respond to my web form requests for individual email addresses.

10. I used Qualtrics to administer the survey. The project was approved as exempt by the Office for the Protection of Human Subjects at the University of California, Berkeley (February 24, 2015).

11. E.g., Samuel H. Fisher III and Rebekah Herrick, "Old versus New: The Comparative Efficiency of Mail and Internet Surveys of State Legislators," *State Politics & Policy Quarterly* 13, no. 2 (2013): 147–63.

12. E.g., Gray and Lowery, *The Population Ecology of Interest Representation*, 12; Schlozman, Verba, and Brady, *The Unheavenly Chorus*, 319.

13. Dahl, *Who Governs?*, 137–39.

14. The response options ranged from 1, "All are informal and temporary," to 10, "All are formal and permanent." This variable is rescaled to a 0–9 measure for the analysis.

15. It could be that officials who have been in city office longer have more accurate (and systematically different) perceptions of the amount of interest group activity in their cities than officials who are newer to city office. However, when I use OLS to regress interest group activity on an ordinal measure of how long the respondent has held elected office in the city, ranging from 0 (less than one year) to 4 (more than ten years), including city fixed effects, the coefficient on seniority is not statistically significant.

16. E.g., Schlozman, "Who Sings in the Heavenly Chorus?"

17. Peterson, *City Limits*.

18. See Gerber and Hopkins, "When Mayors Matter."

19. There are also other reasons why larger cities might have more interest groups. For example, Oliver, Ha, and Callen argue that electoral politics tends to be more formal in larger places—and groups more involved—because relationships between citizens and elected officials are more remote. In smaller places, candidates can more easily go door-to-door to campaign, whereas in larger places, groups are needed for mobilization and information provision. Larger cities also tend to be more heterogeneous, and their governments do more, which means they will tend to "sprout more organized groups." Oliver, Ha, and Callen, *Local Elections and the Politics of Small-Scale Democracy*, 18.

20. E.g., Campbell, "Policy Makes Mass Politics."

21. As I'll discuss, the "policy stakes" can also vary within cities.

22. The spending categories are air transportation, corrections, elementary and secondary education, higher education, fire protection, police protection, health, hospitals, highways, housing and community development, libraries, natural resources, parking facilities, parks and recreation, protective inspection and regulation, public welfare, sewers, solid waste, sea and inland port facilities, liquor stores, water supply utilities, electric supply utilities, gas supply utilities, and transit system utilities. Because not all city functions necessarily involve

expenditures—most important, the regulation of land use—I also construct an alternative measure of scope using data from the survey: I asked respondents to indicate whether their city makes policy on 18 issues, including land use planning, zoning, and economic development (see Cooper, Nownes, and Roberts, "Perceptions of Power"), and I constructed an index of the number of functions, averaged by city. The results with this alternative measure are substantively the same (not shown).

23. The negative slope for the smallest cities is heavily influenced by two very small cities whose officials reported that they have many active interest groups.

24. For example, it may be that regardless of whether there are 100 residents or 2,000 residents in a city, interest groups are rare.

25. The results don't change in any substantive way when I include the square of population to account for the relationship between population and interest group activity in the smallest cities.

26. E.g., Einstein and Kogan, "Pushing the City Limits"; Tausanovitch and Warshaw, "Representation in Municipal Government."

27. Tausanovitch and Warshaw, "Representation in Municipal Government."

28. E.g., Einstein, Glick, and Palmer, *Neighborhood Defenders*; Fischel, *The Homevoter Hypothesis*; Schleicher, "City Unplanning."

29. E.g., Zoltan L. Hajnal, *America's Uneven Democracy: Race, Turnout, and Representation in City Politics* (New York: Cambridge University Press, 2009); Zoltan Hajnal and Jessica Trounstine, "What Underlies Urban Politics? Race, Class, Ideology, Partisanship, and the Urban Vote," *Urban Affairs Review* 50, no. 1 (2014): 63–99; Trounstine, *Segregation by Design*.

30. E.g., Jessica Trounstine and Melody E. Valdini, "The Context Matters: The Effects of Single-Member versus At-Large Districts on City Council Diversity," *American Journal of Political Science* 52, no. 3 (2008): 554–69.

31. For any cities missing values of the political institutions variables, I collected the data from cities' websites. I am missing data on partisan or nonpartisan election status for three cities.

32. According to the 2011 ICMA Municipal FOG Survey, 80% of US cities hold nonpartisan elections. While the literature on nonpartisan elections is small and dated, the work that exists suggests that political parties are much less involved in nonpartisan local elections than in state and national politics, even though there is variation across localities. See Charles R. Adrian, "Some General Characteristics of Nonpartisan Elections," *American Political Science Review* 46, no. 3 (1952): 766–76; Eugene C. Lee, *The Politics of Nonpartisanship: A Study of California City Elections* (Berkeley: University of California Press, 1960); Gerald C. Wright, "Charles Adrian and the Study of Nonpartisan Elections," *Political Research Quarterly* 61, no. 1 (2008): 13–16.

33. See, e.g., Bawn et al., "A Theory of Political Parties."

34. Amy Bridges, *Morning Glories: Municipal Reform in the Southwest*

NOTES TO CHAPTER THREE

(Princeton, NJ: Princeton University Press, 1997); Trounstine, *Political Monopolies in American Cities*.

35. The number of observations is smaller in this model because I am missing some responses to the two additional interest group activity questions.

36. This most likely reflects an underlying difference in municipalities. Cities with mostly homeowners tend to be smaller, narrower, and politically quieter—and also have less interest group activity overall. It is the inclusion of this independent variable in particular that makes a difference to the estimated coefficient on per capita income: it is only when the homeownership rate is accounted for that the positive relationship emerges between per capita income and city interest group activity.

37. The measure of district elections is a binary indicator equal to one if the city elects any city council members by district. The indicator of off-cycle elections equals one if the city holds elections at a time other than state and national general elections.

38. This could suggest that interest groups get more involved when political parties are less involved. It could also suggest that in cities with partisan elections, interest groups engage in politics through political parties—and therefore city officials have fewer direct interactions with interest groups. I explore this question later in the book; for now it is worth noting that having nonpartisan elections is positively associated with overall interest group activity in a city.

39. See, e.g., Hertel-Fernandez, *State Capture*.

40. E.g., Tausanovitch and Warshaw, "Representation in Municipal Government."

41. Many respondents did not answer these questions, which is why the number of observations in table 3.3 is smaller than 902.

42. All candidates in Washington have to file an F-1 for Personal Financial Affairs in any jurisdiction that has at least 1,000 registered voters and does not span a whole county. In addition, if a candidate is running in a jurisdiction with at least 5,000 registered voters and expects to raise more than $5,000 for the campaign or single contributions of $500 or more, they have to also file a C-1, which requires itemized contribution reporting. The dataset is therefore constructed from candidates' C-1 forms.

43. In 19 city races, there were positive contributions but $0 from interest groups. To preserve them for this model, I add one to the interest group contribution amounts before taking the log.

44. When I drop the one extremely large city and the one extremely small city in this dataset—Seattle and a South Carolina city of 89 people—these three relationships do not change in any substantive way (not shown).

45. See Oliver, Ha, and Callen, *Local Elections and the Politics of Small-Scale Democracy*.

Chapter Four

1. There are arguments and suggestions of this flavor in existing research. See, e.g., Hajnal and Clark, "The Local Interest-Group System."

2. See Peterson, *City Limits*. Even for cities that are not pursuing growth, there is pressure to be attentive to the local tax base, because it is the source of city government revenue.

3. A reading of the urban politics literature could give the impression that economic development, growth, and land use are most or all of what city governments do. Even as urban politics scholars have acknowledged that the growth impulse is not uniform across cities and that some cities also prioritize sustainability, their substantive focus has remained on economic development and land use. See, e.g., Martin Horak, Juliet Musso, Ellen Shiau, Robert P. Stoker, and Clarence N. Stone, "Change Afoot," in *Urban Neighborhoods in a New Era*, ed. Clarence N. Stone and Robert P. Stoker (Chicago: University of Chicago Press, 2015), 1–32; Kent E. Portney and Jeffrey M. Berry, "Participation and the Pursuit of Sustainability in U.S. Cities," *Urban Affairs Review* 46, no. 1 (2010): 119–39.

4. Logan and Molotch, *Urban Fortunes*, 13.

5. E.g., Mossberger and Stoker, "The Evolution of Urban Regime Theory."

6. There are, of course, exceptions to this. For example, Chevron, which has a large refinery in Richmond, CA, cannot easily leave Richmond. Also, large corporations and trade associations might get involved in city politics out of fear that one city's decision will affect the decisions of other cities.

7. Olson, *The Logic of Collective Action*.

8. These union membership rates are from Barry T. Hirsch and David A. Macpherson, "Union Membership and Coverage Database from the Current Population Survey: Note," *Industrial and Labor Relations Review* 56, no. 2 (2003): 349–54. Their data are updated annually and are available on unionstats .com.

9. State and national union organizations could still get active in city politics, however. Also, individual carpenters, electricians, and plumbers can be active in politics even if they are not unionized; they can still have these interests as individuals. But as I discussed early in chapter 2, groups serve an important role in informing individuals of their interests, shaping their preferences, and identifying particular policies and policy proposals of relevance to them. Groups are more than just the sum of autonomous individual members. And many of the political activities groups engage in (such as lobbying) are more effective in conveying policy preferences than the most common individual political activity (voting).

10. For an account of why private-sector union membership rates vary across the country, see Ryan Nunn, Jimmy O'Donnell, and Jay Shambaugh, "The Shift in Private Sector Union Participation: Explanation and Effects," The Hamilton

NOTES TO CHAPTER FOUR

Project, August 2019, www.hamiltonproject.org/assets/files/UnionsEA_Web_8 .19.pdf.

11. See, e.g., Campbell, "Policy Makes Mass Politics"; Michael T. Hartney, *How Policies Make Interest Groups: Governments, Unions, and American Education* (Chicago: University of Chicago Press, forthcoming); Moe, *Special Interest*; Paul Pierson, "When Effect Becomes Cause: Policy Feedback and Political Change," *World Politics* 45, no. 4 (1993): 595–628.

12. Leslie K. Finger and Michael T. Hartney, "Financial Solidarity: The Future of Unions in the Post-*Janus* Era," *Perspectives on Politics* 19, no. 1 (2021): 19–35.

13. See Olson, *The Logic of Collective Action*.

14. Berry, "Urban Interest Groups."

15. Walker, *Mobilizing Interest Groups in America*, 61.

16. John R. Logan and Gordana Rabrenovic, "Neighborhood Associations: Their Issues, Their Allies, and Their Opponents," *Urban Affairs Quarterly* 26, no. 1 (1990): 68–94.

17. Toledo, "Redwood City's Downtown Fire Station Spared from Closure."

18. See Berry, "Urban Interest Groups"; Hajnal and Clark, "The Local Interest-Group System."

19. Hirsch and Macpherson, "Union Membership and Coverage Database from the Current Population Survey: Note."

20. See Hartney, *How Policies Make Interest Groups*.

21. See Moe, *Special Interest*; Gregory M. Saltzman, "Bargaining Laws as a Cause and Consequence of the Growth of Teacher Unionism," *Industrial and Labor Relations Review* 38, no. 3 (1985): 335–51.

22. DiSalvo, *Government Against Itself*.

23. Hartney, *How Policies Make Interest Groups*; Moe, *Special Interest*.

24. Terry Moe and I calculated these figures using data from the CPS from 2003 to 2010. Current data on union membership rates at the city level do not exist. To calculate the unionization rates of different types of government employees by state, we pooled several years of CPS data (the same source that Hirsch and Macpherson use) because there are a limited number of police, firefighters, and teachers in the CPS sample for each year. This is a reasonable approach as public-sector unionization rates do not vary much year to year (with exceptions of states like Wisconsin after 2011). For those three local government occupations, we pooled data from 2003 to 2010 to estimate the unionization rates, including only full-time employees. For local employee unions, I am using the three-year average of local government employee unionization from 2008 to 2010.

25. See Amy E. Lerman and Vesla M. Weaver, *Arresting Citizenship: The Democratic Consequences of American Crime Control* (Chicago: University of Chicago Press, 2014). But see also Hannah L. Walker, *Mobilized by Injustice:*

Criminal Justice Contact, Political Participation and Race (Oxford: Oxford University Press, 2020).

26. Other interest groups are sometimes mentioned as active in local politics whose policy interests are difficult to characterize in any generalizable way. For example, large nonprofits like universities, civic associations, and faith-based organizations can be quite active in their home cities, but theory doesn't point to any single policy or set of policies on which they would be focused and have homogeneous interests. Similarly, senior citizens are highly active in local politics in many places and can be organized, but characterizing their interests in city politics is not always straightforward. See Anzia, "When Does a Group of Citizens Influence Policy?" These types of groups do not fit as cleanly into my theoretical setup. It may be that they are sometimes or even often active in city politics, but their activity and influence would be better studied through case studies of particular cities and issues.

27. I asked, "Below is a list of different kinds of interest groups. For each one, please rate how active it is in politics in your city." The response options were Not at all active, Slightly active, Somewhat active, Very active, and Extremely active.

28. Respondents within the same cities also tend to give similar ratings to these groups. For example, for cities with more than one respondent, the maximum and minimum within-city ratings of chambers of commerce were within one point in 67% of the cities and within two points in 89% of the cities. For developers, the maximum and minimum within-city ratings were within two points for 84% of the cities; and for neighborhood associations, they were within two points in 89% of the cities.

29. For cities with multiple respondents, the maximum and minimum ratings for firefighters' unions were within two points in 91% of the cities. For police unions, they were within two points in 90% of the cities, and for miscellaneous employee unions, 93% of the cities.

30. City officials in the larger cities (those with more than 50,000 residents) also said there would be less conflict between interest groups over the police budget issue than the land use issue.

31. This ranking does not vary much with city size. Matters of economic development and land use are as common in large and small city elections. Issues of police, crime, and the public safety budget are more commonly election issues in larger places but still not as common as economic development and land use.

32. I drew these questions from Moe's survey of school board candidates. See Moe, "Teacher Unions and School Board Elections."

33. Three of the Washington city council races analyzed in chapter 3 are not included here because the candidates' contributions were not itemized.

34. Some of the largest remaining non-individual contributions in Washington came from Native American tribes, affordable housing groups, liberal and

NOTES TO CHAPTER FIVE

progressive groups and PACs, and the Democratic Party (which I discuss in the next chapter).

35. To be clear, in showing these relationships, I am *not* arguing that local partisanship drives union political activity. I am pointing out that local partisanship is correlated with union political activity—and that this is mainly because of state laws.

36. The state-level unionization rates here are again the estimates Moe and I created using CPS data.

37. As a placebo test, I also ran the same models for police union activity. Neither development potential nor business exit potential is a significant predictor.

38. Both waves of the survey were administered using Qualtrics. The project was approved as exempt by the Office for the Protection of Human Subjects at the University of California, Berkeley (January 8, 2016, and April 10, 2017).

Chapter Five

1. The analysis in this chapter began as a coauthored working paper with Olivia Meeks, which we wrote for a June 2016 conference, "Parties, Polarization, and Policy Demanders," at the University of Maryland, College Park, and co-sponsored by the Hewlett Foundation. That working paper was titled, "Political Parties and Policy Demanders in Local Elections."

2. Einstein and Kogan, "Pushing the City Limits"; Michael W. Sances, "When Voters Matter: The Limits of Local Government Responsiveness," *Urban Affairs Review* 57, no. 2 (2021): 402–27; Tausanovitch and Warshaw, "Representation in Municipal Government." A separate but related question is whether political behavior in the United States has nationalized. See Daniel J. Hopkins, *The Increasingly United States: How and Why American Political Behavior Nationalized* (Chicago: University of Chicago Press, 2018). See also my discussion of these topics in Sarah F. Anzia, "Party and Ideology in American Local Government: An Appraisal," *Annual Review of Political Science* 24 (2021): 133–50.

3. De Benedictis-Kessner and Warshaw, "Mayoral Partisanship and Municipal Fiscal Policy"; de Benedictis-Kessner and Warshaw, "Politics in Forgotten Governments"; Elisabeth R. Gerber, "Partisanship and Local Climate Policy," *Cityscape* 15, no. 1 (2013): 107–24.

4. See, e.g., Gary W. Cox, *Making Votes Count: Strategic Coordination in the World's Electoral Systems* (New York: Cambridge University Press, 1997); Nolan McCarty and Eric Schickler, "On the Theory of Parties," *Annual Review of Political Science* 21 (2018): 175–93.

5. E.g., Edward G. Carmines and James A. Stimson, *Issue Evolution: Race and the Transformation of American Politics* (Princeton, NJ: Princeton University Press, 1989); Neil A. O'Brian, "Before Reagan: The Development of Abor-

tion's Partisan Divide," *Perspectives on Politics* 18, no. 4 (2020): 1031–47; Eric Schickler, *Racial Realignment: The Transformation of American Liberalism, 1932–1965* (Princeton, NJ: Princeton University Press, 2016).

6. Anzia, *Timing and Turnout*; Bridges, *Morning Glories*; Lee, *The Politics of Nonpartisanship*; Trounstine, *Political Monopolies in American Cities.*

7. Bawn et al., "A Theory of Political Parties"; Marty Cohen, David Karol, Hans Noel, and John Zaller, *The Party Decides: Presidential Nominations Before and After Reform* (Chicago: University of Chicago Press, 2008).

8. See, e.g., John H. Aldrich, *Why Parties? The Origin and Transformation of Political Parties in America* (Chicago: University of Chicago Press, 1995).

9. When other parties were rated as active in city elections, the most common ones were the Libertarian Party and the Green Party, although respondents also sometimes listed groups that are not parties, such as neighborhood groups or police officers.

10. I asked respondents to rate the activity of 14 interest groups in the City Elections Survey: chambers of commerce, real estate developers, retail businesses, building trade unions, police unions, firefighters' unions, miscellaneous municipal employee unions, neighborhood associations, environmental organizations, anti-growth or preservationist organizations, ethnic or racial minority organizations, taxpayer organizations, Tea Party or conservative organizations, and senior citizens' organizations.

11. E.g., Bawn et al., "A Theory of Political Parties"; Carmines and Stimson, *Issue Evolution.*

12. It is possible that local interest groups could form their own, locally based political parties based on local issues, but table 5.1 shows that this does not seem to be happening on any large scale.

13. Of the 75 contests for mayor and city council in the Washington State campaign finance dataset, some of the city council contests had multiple races for different seats, and some of the races were uncontested.

14. To put this in relief, the contributions of businesses *not* clearly associated with growth and development are somewhat more spread out: non-growth businesses were active in 77 of the 103 races, and that money went to back more than one candidate in 31 of them.

15. See also Verlan Lewis, *Ideas of Power: The Politics of American Party Ideology Development* (New York: Cambridge University Press, 2019).

16. Robert Alan Dahl, *Pluralist Democracy in the United States: Conflict and Consent* (Chicago: Rand McNally & Company, 1967), 429.

17. Cohen et al., *The Party Decides*, 31.

18. See Berry, "Urban Interest Groups."

19. Bawn et al., "A Theory of Political Parties."

20. Charles R. Adrian, "A Typology for Nonpartisan Elections," *Western Political Quarterly* 12, no. 2 (1959): 449–58.

NOTES TO CHAPTER SIX

21. This is not a useful exercise for South Carolina, where only two candidates got money from the Republican Party and only one from the Democratic Party.

22. See Peter Bucchianeri, "Party Competition and Coalitional Stability: Evidence from American Local Government," *American Political Science Review* 114, no. 4 (2020), 1055–70.

23. E.g., Oliver, Ha, and Callen, *Local Elections and the Politics of Small-Scale Democracy.*

24. David R. Mayhew, *Placing Parties in American Politics: Organization, Electoral Settings, and Government Activity in the Twentieth Century* (Princeton, NJ: Princeton University Press, 1986).

25. Bucchianeri, "Party Competition and Coalitional Stability."

26. Fran Spielman, "Lightfoot Says CPS Would 'Never Have Opened without Mayoral Control,' Fuels Speculation of Backing Away from Elected School Board," *Chicago Sun-Times*, February 15, 2021, https://chicago.suntimes.com/city-hall/2021/2/15/22284118/lightfoot-chicago-public-schools-elected-board-teaches-union-ctu-strike-new-york-times-interview.

Chapter Six

1. In principle, one could measure the within-group homogeneity and across-group distinctiveness of policy preferences as well as the activity of groups on specific issues or sets of issues (as I attempted to do in chapter 4 with the land use and police budget vignettes). Those issue-specific measures of activity would then rule out the need to theoretically consider how a group will channel its political attention and resources. In my analyses in the following chapters, however, I use city-level measures of interest group activity, so my empirical tests require consideration of whether a group would focus its efforts on a particular policy.

2. Peterson, *City Limits.*

3. Ibid, 22.

4. Ibid, 147.

5. This is similar to the concept of coincidental representation described by Schaffner, Rhodes, and La Raja in *Hometown Inequality.* See also Gilens, *Affluence and Influence*; Hall and Deardorff, "Lobbying as Legislative Subsidy."

6. It is also important to note that Peterson's book was a corrective to the literature as it had developed up to that point: major literatures had conceived of local governments as mini-federal governments—places in which voters, parties, and interest groups operated in much the same way as they did in national politics.

7. Oliver, Ha, and Callen, *Local Elections and the Politics of Small-Scale Democracy*, 7.

8. See, e.g., Christopher H. Achen and Larry M. Bartels, *Democracy for Realists: Why Elections Do Not Produce Responsive Government* (Princeton, NJ: Princeton University Press, 2016).

9. Peterson, *City Limits*, 28.

10. Logan and Molotch, *Urban Fortunes*.

11. Regime theory also emphasizes the importance of business in city governing regimes and how business influences city politics through its informal, collaborative, and symbiotic relationships with city officials. See Mossberger and Stoker, "The Evolution of Urban Regime Theory"; Stone, *Regime Politics*.

12. Horak et al., "Change Afoot."

13. E.g., Portney and Berry, "Participation and the Pursuit of Sustainability in U.S. Cities."

14. Berry, "Urban Interest Groups."

15. There are studies related to these questions, but very few feature dependent variables that capture cross-city variation in local policies related to economic development and land use. For an exception, see Lubell, Feiock, and Ramirez De La Cruz, "Local Institutions and the Politics of Urban Growth." Some other studies ask policy makers which interest groups are influential and then analyze those perceptions of influence as the dependent variable, as I discussed in chapter 2. Also, nearly all these studies use proxies for interest group activity or "civic capacity," typically city demographic variables like income, education, and race. See, e.g., Elaine B. Sharp, Dorothy M. Daley, and Michael S. Lynch, "Understanding Local Adoption and Implementation of Climate Change Mitigation Policy," *Urban Affairs Review* 47, no. 3 (2011): 433–57.

16. Fischel, *The Homevoter Hypothesis*; see also Schleicher, "City Unplanning."

17. See Trounstine, *Segregation by Design*.

18. Michael Hankinson, "When Do Renters Behave Like Homeowners? High Rent, Price Anxiety, and NIMBYism," *American Political Science Review* 112, no. 3 (2018): 473–93; William Marble and Clayton Nall, "Where Interests Trump Ideology: Liberal Homeowners and Local Opposition to Housing Development," *Journal of Politics* 83, no. 4 (2021).

19. Einstein, Glick, and Palmer, *Neighborhood Defenders*.

20. Oliver, Ha, and Callen, *Local Elections and the Politics of Small-Scale Democracy*, 10.

21. See DiSalvo, *Government Against Itself*; Moe, "Vested Interests and Political Institutions."

22. Alesina, Baqir, and Easterly, "Public Goods and Ethnic Divisions"; Daniel Hopkins, "The Diversity Discount: When Increasing Ethnic and Racial

NOTES TO CHAPTER SIX 309

Diversity Prevents Tax Increases," *Journal of Politics* 71, no. 1 (2009): 160–77; Trounstine, *Segregation by Design*.

23. Einstein and Kogan, "Pushing the City Limits"; Tausanovitch and Warshaw, "Representation in Municipal Government."

24. Jessica Trounstine's analysis of city sewer extensions and overflows is an excellent example of how this can be done; Trounstine, *Segregation by Design*.

25. See Anzia and Moe, "Public Sector Unions and the Costs of Government."

26. Moe's research also shows that occupational self-interest is an especially strong political motivator for teachers: teachers who live and work in the same school district and can thus vote for their own employers vote in school board elections at significantly higher rates than teachers who live and work in different districts and thus cannot vote for their own employers. See Terry M. Moe, "Political Control and the Power of the Agent," *Journal of Law, Economics, and Organization* 22, no. 1 (2006): 1–29; see also Hartney, *How Policies Make Interest Groups*.

27. See DiSalvo, *Government Against Itself*.

28. Joshua Page, *The Toughest Beat: Politics, Punishment, and the Prison Officers Union in California* (Oxford: Oxford University Press, 2011); Mark Tebeau, *Eating Smoke: Fire in Urban America, 1800–1950* (Baltimore, MD: Johns Hopkins University Press, 2003).

29. Taylor E. Dark, *The Unions and the Democrats: An Enduring Alliance* (Ithaca, NY: Cornell University Press, 1999).

30. John E. Chubb and Terry M. Moe, *Politics, Markets, and America's Schools* (Washington, DC: Brookings Institution, 1990).

31. Terry M. Moe, "Collective Bargaining and the Performance of the Public Schools," *American Journal of Political Science* 53, no. 1 (2009): 156–74; Katharine O. Strunk and Jason A. Grissom, "Do Strong Unions Shape District Policies? Collective Bargaining, Teacher Contract Restrictiveness, and the Political Power of Teachers' Unions," *Educational Evaluation and Policy Analysis* 32, no. 3 (2010): 389–406.

32. Anzia and Moe, "Public Sector Unions and the Costs of Government."

33. See Moe, "Teacher Unions and School Board Elections."

34. New research by Michael Hartney also shows that school board members are more responsive to teachers than to parents. See Hartney, *How Policies Make Interest Groups*.

35. Moe, *The Politics of Institutional Reform*.

36. Anzia and Moe, "Public Sector Unions and the Costs of Government"; Caroline Minter Hoxby, "How Teachers' Unions Affect Education Production," *Quarterly Journal of Economics* 111, no. 3 (1996): 671–718.

37. Michael F. Lovenheim, "The Effect of Teachers' Unions on Education Production: Evidence from Union Election Certifications in Three Midwest-

ern States," *Journal of Labor Economics* 27, no. 4 (2009): 525–87; Agustina S. Paglayan, "Public-Sector Unions and the Size of Government," *American Journal of Political Science* 63, no. 1 (2019): 21–36.

38. Anzia and Moe, "Public Sector Unions and the Costs of Government"; Daniel DiSalvo and Jeffrey Kucik, "Unions, Parties, and the Politics of State Government Legacy Cost," *Policy Studies Journal* 46, no. 3 (2018): 573–97.

39. Moe, "Political Control and the Power of the Agent."

40. Moe, "Teacher Unions and School Board Elections."

41. See, again, Wilson, *Political Organizations.*

42. See Arnold, *The Logic of Congressional Action.*

43. Ibid.

44. Chubb and Moe, *Politics, Markets, and America's Schools.*

45. Strunk and Grissom, "Do Strong Unions Shape District Policies?"

46. Sarah F. Anzia and Terry M. Moe, "Collective Bargaining, Transfer Rights, and Disadvantaged Schools," *Educational Evaluation and Policy Analysis* 36, no. 1 (2014): 83–111; Michael F. Lovenheim and Alexander Willén, "The Long-Run Effects of Teacher Collective Bargaining," *American Economic Journal: Economic Policy* 11, no. 3 (2019): 292–324; Moe, "Collective Bargaining and the Performance of the Public Schools"; Jonathan Mummolo, "Militarization Fails to Enhance Police Safety or Reduce Crime but May Harm Police Reputation," *Proceedings of the National Academy of Sciences* 115, no. 37 (2018): 9181–86.

47. Gabriel S. Lenz, *Follow the Leader? How Voters Respond to Politicians' Policies and Performance* (Chicago: University of Chicago Press, 2013).

48. See Campbell, "Policy Makes Mass Politics."

49. E.g., Pierson, "When Effect Becomes Cause."

50. E.g., Einstein and Kogan, "Pushing the City Limits"; Schaffner, Rhodes, and La Raja, *Hometown Inequality.*

51. Tausanovitch and Warshaw, "Representation in Municipal Government."

52. For a more thorough discussion of this and the points to follow, see Anzia, "Party and Ideology in American Local Government: An Appraisal."

53. Attempts to estimate mass ideology based on local issues have been limited to a few cities. See Cheryl Boudreau, Christopher S. Elmendorf, and Scott A. MacKenzie, "Lost in Space? Information Shortcuts, Spatial Voting, and Local Government Representation," *Political Research Quarterly* 68, no. 4 (2015): 843–55; Michael W. Sances, "Ideology and Vote Choice in U.S. Mayoral Elections: Evidence from Facebook Surveys," *Political Behavior* 40, no. 3 (2018): 737–62. Schaffner, Rhodes, and La Raja also use a measure of citizen ideology in municipal governments, but because it is a proprietary measure developed by Catalist, it is unclear whether it is constructed using mainly national or local issues. See Schaffner, Rhodes, and La Raja, *Hometown Inequality.*

54. De Benedictis-Kessner and Warshaw, "Mayoral Partisanship and Munic-

NOTES TO CHAPTER SEVEN

ipal Fiscal Policy"; de Benedictis-Kessner and Warshaw, "Politics in Forgotten Governments"; Gerber, "Partisanship and Local Climate Policy."

55. Ferreira and Gyourko, "Do Political Parties Matter?"; Thompson, "How Partisan is Local Law Enforcement?"

56. Einstein and Kogan, "Pushing the City Limits"; Tausanovitch and Warshaw, "Representation in Municipal Government."

57. Marble and Nall, "Where Interests Trump Ideology"; Amalie Jensen, William Marble, Kenneth Scheve, and Matthew J. Slaughter, "City Limits to Partisan Polarization in the American Public," *Political Science Research and Methods* 9, no. 2 (2021): 223–41.

Chapter Seven

1. Joseph Gyourko, Albert Saiz, and Anita Summers, "A New Measure of the Local Regulatory Environment for Housing Markets: The Wharton Residential Land Use Regulatory Index," *Urban Studies* 45, no. 3 (2008): 693–729.

2. The ICMA partnered with HR&A Advisors on the survey; HR&A is a consulting firm specializing in real estate, economic development, and public policy.

3. Peterson, *City Limits*.

4. One could also view the policies listed in figure 7.1 as *potentially* or *eventually* leading to decisions about land use, but any potential land use costs of those policies are uncertain, in the future, and in any case won't be easily attributable to the policy itself.

5. Exceptions may come about when a particular tool is directly linked to environmental groups' goals, such as the use of energy efficiency programs or green building incentives. For these, environmental groups might be focused on the issue and have homogeneous preferences.

6. Again, exceptions might arise when a local economic development policy is linked to an issue that defines national-level ideology and partisanship, such as corporate taxation or environmental sustainability.

7. Peterson, *City Limits*.

8. The items I exclude are transit to promote commuting, high-quality physical infrastructure, affordable workforce housing, and investments in high quality of life. For cities that are missing only one of the 28 included indicators, I average over the 27 that have data.

9. The number of cities in the analysis is slightly lower than this because of missing data on the economic development tool index as well as some of the independent variables.

10. Except for city size and income, I do not have any expectations about how these variables would be correlated with the use of these economic development

tools. I add them to the models because they feature prominently in the local politics literature.

11. When I model each of the 28 economic development tools separately (not shown), moreover, chamber of commerce political activity is significantly associated with only one of them (promotional and advertising activities). In addition, there are only five tools for which Democratic presidential vote in the city is a significant predictor, and in all five cases, the results show that more Democratic cities are *more* likely to use the economic development tools, not less. The pattern of findings also suggests that the degree to which national-level partisanship or ideology predicts local policy depends on whether that policy shares something in common with national political and ideological alignments: two of the tools that more Democratic cities are more likely to use are energy efficiency programs and programs to promote environmental sustainability, both of which line up with the Democratic Party's relatively greater support for green energy and environmental activism.

12. Peterson, *City Limits*.

13. Nathan M. Jensen and Edmund J. Malesky, *Incentives to Pander: How Politicians use Corporate Welfare for Political Gain* (New York: Cambridge University Press, 2018).

14. See, e.g., Raffaello Bronzini and Guido De Blasio, "Evaluating the Impact of Investment Incentives: The Case of Italy's Law 488/1992," *Journal of Urban Economics* 60, no. 2 (2006): 327–49; Alexander Klemm and Stefan Van Parys, "Empirical Evidence on the Effects of Tax Incentives," *International Tax and Public Finance* 19, no. 3 (2012): 393–423.

15. See Terry F. Buss, "The Effect of State Tax Incentives on Economic Growth and Firm Location Decisions: An Overview of the Literature," *Economic Development Quarterly* 15 (2001): 90–105; Carlianne Patrick, "Does Increasing Available Non-Tax Economic Development Incentives Result in More Jobs?," *National Tax Journal* 67, no. 2 (2014): 351–86.

16. Jensen and Malesky, *Incentives to Pander*.

17. Ibid.

18. See Gordon Tullock, "The Economics of Politics," in *The Selected Works of Gordon Tullock*, ed. Charles K. Rowley (Carmel, IN: Liberty Fund, 2005), vol. 4.

19. Timothy J. Bartik, "A New Panel Database on Business Incentives for Economic Development Offered by State and Local Governments in the United States," Technical Report, Pew Charitable Trusts, W. E. Upjohn Institute for Employment Research, 2017, https://research.upjohn.org/cgi/viewcontent.cgi ?referer=&httpsredir=1&article=1228&context=reports.

20. Ibid.

21. Ibid.

NOTES TO CHAPTER SEVEN

22. The ICMA survey also asks about cities' use of tax increment financing (TIF) districts, enterprise zones, and special assessment districts, but as Bartik ("A New Panel Database on Business Incentives for Economic Development Offered by State and Local Governments in the United States") explains, these tools are typically used to finance redevelopment projects, housing, and public projects—not to lower the tax payments of businesses to entice them to move to or stay in the city. In some places, enterprise zones are general incentives for development rather than a tool offered to help lure a particular business. Enterprise zones can also incorporate benefits beyond tax benefits. TIF incentives are also different because typically the firm pays its normal tax rates; it is just that the funds are used to develop the area around the firm. Special assessment districts are typically areas where a special tax is levied on properties in the area in order to fund redevelopment, so it is not a reduction in taxes paid.

23. Jensen and Malesky, *Incentives to Pander.*

24. Government Accounting Standards Board, "Tax Abatement Disclosures," *Financial Accounting Foundation, Governmental Accounting Standards Series* no. 353, August 2015, www.gasb.org/jsp/GASB/Document_C/DocumentPage?cid=1176166283745&acceptedDisclaimer=true.

25. Good Jobs First, "Tax Abatement Disclosures in 2018: 100 Largest US Cities," Good Jobs First, www.goodjobsfirst.org/tax-abatement-disclosures-2018 -100-largest-us-cities; accessed April 22, 2020.

26. The value of tax abated for New York, NY, comes from Good Jobs First.

27. One other city—Rockford, IL—reports that it committed a portion of its sales tax revenue to a local retailer for the years 2002 to 2022, but the amount of tax abated in 2018 is not clear, so it is not included.

28. The same is true of taxpayer groups. In the model with state fixed effects, moreover, the coefficient estimate on the political activity of building trade unions is positive, hinting that they may push cities in a more pro-business direction, but I find no such relationship in column 1.

29. While not shown, the coefficients on the institutional variables show that cities with off-cycle elections and partisan elections report greater use of business tax incentives. Those coefficients are not significant in the model with state fixed effects, but there isn't much within-state variation in those variables in this dataset. I find that mayor-council government is not a significant predictor of local government use of tax incentives.

30. Jensen and Malesky, *Incentives to Pander.*

31. Of the cities in the City Interest Groups Survey dataset for which this information was available, 92% reported losing some revenue due to tax abatement in 2018. This could mean that most cities use tax abatement, or it could mean that many of the cities did not report tax abatement amounts because they did not have any. It will be impossible to know which is more accurate until more

cities are compliant with GASB 77, but for now, I can evaluate whether city characteristics and interest group activity explain variation in the amounts of tax abatement for cities that are compliant.

32. The results do not change in any substantive way when I add one before taking the log.

33. When I use different approaches to handling outliers, including dropping the top 5% of the distribution and dropping cities where abatement per capita is more than 1.5 times the interquartile range larger than the 3rd quartile, the coefficient on chambers of commerce is still positive and significant. However, it is not significant when I include all of the outliers. For a small number of cities, these amounts include tax abatement from TIF districts, and TIF districts are usually created through agreements between cities and developers. However, for most cities, these tax abatement amounts are from tax incentives given to companies to develop or expand a business in the city.

34. The estimates from the models with state fixed effects are more sensitive to the approach to handling outliers. For the model in column 2, when I drop the top 5% of the distribution, the coefficient on chambers of commerce is positive and significant, but it is not when I include all outliers or drop cities with abatement per capita greater than 1.5 times the interquartile range larger than the 3rd quartile. In column 4, when I include the small outliers, the coefficient on chambers of commerce is no longer significant.

35. Tausanovitch and Warshaw, "Representation in Municipal Government."

36. Logan and Molotch, *Urban Fortunes*; Harvey Molotch, "The City as a Growth Machine: Toward a Political Economy of Place," *American Journal of Sociology* 82, no. 2 (1976): 309–32.

37. See Oliver, Ha, and Callen, *Local Elections and the Politics of Small-Scale Democracy.*

38. See, e.g., Edward L. Glaeser and Bryce A. Ward, "The Causes and Consequences of Land Use Regulation: Evidence from Greater Boston," *Journal of Urban Economics* 65, no. 3 (2009): 265–78; John M. Quigley and Larry A. Rosenthal, "The Effects of Land Use Regulation on the Price of Housing: What Do We Know? What Can We Learn?" *Cityscape* 8, no. 1 (2005): 69–137.

39. E.g., Fischel, *The Homevoter Hypothesis*; Schleicher, "City Unplanning"; Trounstine, *Segregation by Design.*

40. Einstein, Glick, and Palmer, *Neighborhood Defenders.*

41. E.g., Logan and Molotch, *Urban Fortunes.*

42. Trounstine, *Segregation by Design.*

43. Einstein, Glick, and Palmer, *Neighborhood Defenders.*

44. Einstein, Glick, and Palmer argue that it is mainly the costs that are concentrated in the case of housing development. Ibid., 36. However, there are also concentrated benefits for the developer.

45. Einstein, Glick, and Palmer, *Neighborhood Defenders.*

NOTES TO CHAPTER SEVEN

46. See also Lubell, Feiock, and De La Cruz, "Local Institutions and the Politics of Urban Growth."

47. See Michael Hankinson and Asya Magazinnik, "The Supply-Equity Tradeoff: The Effect of Spatial Representation on the Local Housing Supply," Working Paper, George Washington University and MIT (2021).

48. Logan and Rabrenovic, "Neighborhood Associations."

49. See Einstein, Glick, and Palmer, *Neighborhood Defenders*.

50. See, e.g., Elisabeth R. Gerber and Justin H. Phillips, "Direct Democracy and Land Use Policy: Exchanging Public Goods for Development Rights," *Urban Studies* 41, no. 2 (2004): 463–79.

51. See Alexander Sahn, "Racial Diversity and Exclusionary Zoning: Evidence from the Great Migration," Working Paper, University of California, Berkeley (2021).

52. See Einstein, Glick, and Palmer, *Neighborhood Defenders*, 15, 28. On the power of delay more generally, see Christian Fong and Keith Krehbiel, "Limited Obstruction," *American Political Science Review* 112, no. 1 (2018): 1–14.

53. Gyourko, Saiz, and Summers, "A New Measure of the Local Regulatory Environment for Housing Markets." The mail survey was sent to the planning director or chief administrative officer of 6,896 municipal governments, and the response rate was 38%.

54. Again, however, the numbers for the analysis are slightly lower because of missing data on some variables.

55. Most researchers use the Gyourko, Saiz, and Summers data's indexes: one or more of the eleven subindexes in the dataset or the combined index of regulatory restrictiveness. I instead look at the set of variables that are included in those indexes, which include information on rules about land use and the review time for typical projects.

56. For the results presented here, I use OLS, but the results are not substantively different when I use logit (for modeling whether there is a minimum lot size requirement) or ordered logit (for the size of the minimum lot).

57. The question is phrased as follows: "What is the current length of time required to complete the review of residential projects in your community?" The respondent entered the number of months for single-family units and multi-family units.

58. In the analysis that follows, I drop one city that reports a negative number of months for single-family housing.

59. In all of these models, I exclude one large outlier in which the city reported a 42-month review process. These results for chambers of commerce are robust to various approaches to handling the right skew in the data: logging the dependent variables, dropping cities with processes longer than 20 months, and dropping cities with values 1.5 times the interquartile range larger than the 3rd quartile.

60. In some of the models that use different approaches to handling the right skew in the data, the coefficient on developers' political activity is positive.

61. Some cities are reported as having zero months represented in the data but have a positive number of housing units permitted. I include them in the analysis and assume that they have twelve months of data represented. Results do not change in any substantive way when I exclude these cities. I exclude the few cities coded as having zero months represented and zero total units permitted.

62. I exclude New York City because it is an outlier and because its permits are reported by borough rather than for the city as a whole.

63. When I include the outliers, the coefficient on developers' political activity more than doubles in magnitude.

64. It should be noted that this is an issue area in which this widely available, city-level demographic variable probably captures local preferences on the issue pretty well, which is not necessarily the case for other issues.

65. See Fischel, *The Homevoter Hypothesis*.

66. If it is generally the homeowners nearest to a proposed development who object forcefully, that may actually make it difficult for anti-development interests to come together as a consistent organized group, because the affected constituency is constantly shifting, depending on the location of the development. It is not the same people who are being affected time after time.

67. Einstein, Glick, and Palmer, *Neighborhood Defenders*.

68. Peterson, *City Limits*.

Chapter Eight

1. On the scope of conflict, see Schattschneider, *The Semi-Sovereign People*.

2. E.g., Peter Feuille and John Thomas Delaney, "Collective Bargaining, Interest Arbitration, and Police Salaries," *Industrial and Labor Relations Review* 39, no. 2 (1986): 228–40; Clayton W. Hall and Bruce Vanderporten, "Unionization, Monopsony Power, and Police Salaries," *Industrial Relations* 16, no. 1 (1977): 94–100.

3. Hoxby, "How Teachers' Unions Affect Education Production."

4. Lovenheim, "The Effect of Teachers' Unions on Education Production," 525–87.

5. Paglayan, "Public-Sector Unions and the Size of Government."

6. Richard B. Freeman and James L. Medoff, *What Do Unions Do?* (New York: Basic Books, 1984).

7. Anzia and Moe, "Public Sector Unions and the Costs of Government."

8. See Alicia H. Munnell, Jean-Pierre Aubry, Josh Hurwitz, and Laura Quinby, *Comparing Compensation: State-Local versus Private Sector Workers* (Boston: Center for Retirement Research at Boston College, 2011); Jason

NOTES TO CHAPTER EIGHT

Richwine and Andrew G. Biggs, *Assessing the Compensation of Public-School Teachers* (Washington, DC: Heritage Center for Data Analysis, 2011).

9. Anzia and Moe, "Public Sector Unions and the Costs of Government."

10. More recently, some states have limited public-sector collective bargaining rights, but the effects of limiting collective bargaining during the modern era may not be exactly the inverse of the effects of introducing collective bargaining for the first time.

11. See Jeffrey Zax and Casey Ichniowski, "The Effects of Public Sector Unionism on Pay, Employment, Department Budgets, and Municipal Expenditures," in *When Public Sector Workers Unionize*, ed. Richard B. Freeman and Casey Ichniowski (Chicago: University of Chicago Press, 1988), 323–64.

12. See, e.g., DiSalvo, *Government Against Itself*; Thomas A. Kochan, "A Theory of Multilateral Collective Bargaining in City Governments," *Industrial and Labor Relations Review* 27, no. 4 (1974): 525–42.

13. On this point, see Timothy D. Chandler and Rafael Gely, "Toward Identifying the Determinants of Public-Employee Unions' Involvement in Political Activities," *American Review of Public Administration* 26, no. 4 (1996): 417–38; Kevin M. O'Brien, "Compensation, Employment, and the Political Activity of Public Employee Unions," *Journal of Labor Research* 13, no. 2 (1992): 189–203.

14. Even so, it could be problematic to look at the timing of the passage of state mandatory bargaining laws to see whether there was a subsequent effect on policies that were decided at the local level, such as salaries. Some local governments might have had collective bargaining before the passage of the state laws; others might not have gotten to their first contract until several years later. It is probably safer to use state-level labor laws as indicators of whether the state's local governments have collective bargaining in the present day, because most local governments that were going to adopt collective bargaining had done so by the late 1980s.

15. Hartney, *How Policies Make Interest Groups*; Saltzman, "Bargaining Laws as a Cause and Consequence of the Growth of Teacher Unionism."

16. Anzia and Moe, "Public Sector Unions and the Costs of Government."

17. Ibid.

18. For discussions of the democratic implications of public-sector collective bargaining, see DiSalvo, *Government Against Itself*. See also Myron Lieberman, *Public-Sector Bargaining: A Policy Reappraisal* (Lexington, MA: Lexington Books, 1980).

19. See Anzia, *Timing and Turnout*; Anzia and Moe, "Public Sector Unions and the Costs of Government."

20. E.g., Tausanovitch and Warshaw, "Representation in Municipal Government."

21. E.g., Gerber and Hopkins, "When Mayors Matter."

22. E.g., Page, *The Toughest Beat*.

23. Municipal governments with no expenditures on police payroll are excluded, as are those with police payroll expenditures per capita that are more than 1.5 times the interquartile range above the third quartile.

24. When I include the outliers, the coefficients on union political activity are much larger in all four models. In column 1, the coefficient on police collective bargaining is no longer significant at the 10% level, but in column 3, the coefficient on firefighter collective bargaining is larger and statistically significant.

25. When I analyze police and firefighter average wages and employment levels (not shown), the results are consistent with the findings of my coauthored work with Terry Moe. For firefighters, having collective bargaining and more politically active unions is associated with *both* higher fire protection employment per capita and higher average firefighter wages. For police officers, the findings are more mixed. In the models that include both collective bargaining and police union political activity, both are associated with higher average wages for police officers but not higher employment levels. See Anzia and Moe, "Public Sector Unions and the Costs of Government."

26. When I include the outliers, the coefficient on Democratic presidential vote is negative and significant in the models of fire protection payroll per capita.

27. Batya Ungar-Sargon and Andrew Flowers, "Reexamining Residency Requirements for Police Officers," *FiveThirtyEight*, October 1, 2014, https:// fivethirtyeight.com/features/reexamining-residency-requirements-for-police -officers/.

28. See Moe, *Special Interest.*

29. E.g., Tausanovitch and Warshaw, "Representation in Municipal Government."

30. E.g., Gerber and Hopkins, "When Mayors Matter."

31. DiSalvo, *Government Against Itself*, 119.

32. Tausanovitch and Warshaw, "Representation in Municipal Government." See also Einstein and Kogan, "Pushing the City Limits."

33. For more discussion of this, see Anzia, "Party and Ideology in American Local Government: An Appraisal."

34. Tausanovitch and Warshaw, "Representation in Municipal Government."

35. Gerber and Hopkins, "When Mayors Matter."

36. De Benedictis-Kessner and Warshaw, "Mayoral Partisanship and Municipal Fiscal Policy."

37. Moreover, as Matt Grossmann demonstrates in his study of state spending, the main things state governments spend money on—such as K–12 education— are popular among Republican and Democratic citizens alike. See Matt Grossmann, *Red State Blues: How the Conservative Revolution Stalled in the States* (New York: Cambridge University Press, 2019).

38. See Tausanovitch and Warshaw, "Representation in Municipal Government." I use Democratic presidential vote instead of the Tausanovitch and War-

shaw measure of ideology because I was able to collect Democratic presidential vote at the city level for more cities. There are several high-end outliers, which I exclude from this analysis. Specifically, for the results shown, I exclude cities for which total current operating expenditures per capita is 1.5 times the interquartile range greater than the third quartile. When I include the outliers (not shown), the coefficient on Democratic presidential vote is larger.

39. The same patterns hold when I use police collective bargaining and police union political activity (although the coefficient on police union activity is negative in this case). They also persist when I replace Democratic presidential vote with the Tausanovitch and Warshaw measures of city ideology and when I include the outliers. When I limit the estimation to cities of more than 20,000 residents, the coefficient on Democratic presidential vote is 291.18 (p = 0.151), and the coefficient on collective bargaining is 338.43, significant at the 1% level. When I replace Democratic presidential vote with city ideology in the model of cities with more than 20,000 residents, both the coefficients on collective bargaining (329.21) and city ideology (-286.81) are statistically significant.

40. In all of these models, and in the models shown in table 8.5, I exclude cities where the spending variable is 1.5 times the interquartile range larger than the third quartile. The results are robust to including these outliers as well.

41. "More Downsizing on the Way for West Covina," *San Gabriel Valley Tribune*, April 20, 2011, www.sgvtribune.com/2011/04/20/more-downsizing-on-the-way-for-west-covina/; "Federal Grant Funds 12 New Firefighter Positions in West Covina," *San Gabriel Valley Tribune*, August 24, 2011, www.sgvtribune.com/2011/08/24/federal-grant-funds-12-new-firefighter-positions-in-west-covina/.

42. "Federal Grant Funds 12 New Firefighter Positions in West Covina"; "West Covina Approves Ordinance Affecting Pension Plans for New Firefighter Hires," *San Gabriel Valley Tribune*, July 20, 2011, www.sgvtribune.com/2011/07/20/west-covina-approves-ordinance-affecting-pension-plans-for-new-firefighter-hires/.

43. "West Covina Public Safety Units Agree to Begin Paying Retirement Costs," *San Gabriel Valley Tribune*, July 19, 2012, www.sgvtribune.com/2012/07/19/west-covina-public-safety-units-agree-to-begin-paying-retirement-costs/.

44. Jason Henry, "Six West Covina Firefighters Laid Off after Loss of Grant," *San Gabriel Valley Tribune,* December 18, 2013, www.sgvtribune.com/2013/12/18/six-west-covina-firefighters-laid-off-after-loss-of-grant/.

45. Christopher Yee, "Fate of Long-Disputed West Covina Fire Engine Company to Be Decided Tuesday," *San Gabriel Valley Tribune*, March 3, 2018, www.sgvtribune.com/2018/03/03/fate-of-long-disputed-west-covina-fire-engine-company-to-be-decided-tuesday/.

46. Stephanie K. Baer, "State to Mediate Labor Negotiations for West Covina Firefighters," *San Gabriel Valley Tribune,* October 6, 2015, www.sgvtribune.com/2015/10/06/state-to-mediate-labor-negotiations-for-west-covina-firefighters/;

Sandra T. Molina, "Can West Covina and Its Firefighters Agree on a New Contract?," *San Gabriel Valley Tribune,* June 9, 2016, www.sgvtribune.com/2016/06/09/can-west-covina-and-its-firefighters-agree-on-a-new-contract/.

47. Christopher Yee, "Cash-Strapped West Covina Approves a Raise for Its Firefighters," *San Gabriel Valley Tribune,* November 7, 2019, www.sgvtribune.com/2019/11/07/cash-strapped-west-covina-approves-raise-for-its-firefighters/.

48. Stephanie K. Baer, "Why West Covina Firefighters Are Protesting at City Hall," *San Gabriel Valley Tribune,* November 30, 2016, www.sgvtribune.com/2016/11/30/why-west-covina-firefighters-are-protesting-at-city-hall/.

49. Ibid.

50. Stephanie K. Baer, "West Covina Firefighters Accuse Fire Chief of Retaliation amid Labor Dispute," *San Gabriel Valley Tribune,* August 2, 2017, www.sgvtribune.com/2017/08/02/west-covina-firefighters-accuse-fire-chief-of-retaliation-amid-labor-dispute/.

51. Christopher Yee, "West Covina Fires Its Police, Fire Chiefs," *San Gabriel Valley Tribune*, April 24, 2019, www.sgvtribune.com/2019/04/24/west-covina-fires-its-police-fire-chiefs/; Christopher Yee, "West Covina Residents to City Council: Do You Support Proposed Sales Tax Increase?," *San Gabriel Valley Tribune,* August 21, 2019, www.sgvtribune.com/2019/08/21/west-covina-residents-to-city-council-do-you-support-proposed-sales-tax-increase/.

52. Yee, "Fate of Long-Disputed West Covina Fire Engine Company to Be Decided Tuesday."

53. City of West Covina City Council Meeting, City Hall in the City of West Covina, March 6, 2018, www.youtube.com/watch?v=XTG3UeREspE&t=13242s.

54. Christopher Yee, "West Covina to Keep Disputed Fire Engine Company—for Now," *San Gabriel Valley Tribune,* March 7, 2018, www.sgvtribune.com/2018/03/07/west-covina-to-keep-disputed-fire-engine-company-for-now/.

55. Stephanie K. Baer, "Election 2015: Johnson, Wu Win Seats on West Covina City Council," *San Gabriel Valley Tribune,* November 3, 2015, www.sgvtribune.com/2015/11/03/election-2015-johnson-wu-win-seats-on-west-covina-city-council/.

56. Yee, "West Covina to Keep Disputed Fire Engine Company."

57. Kayiu Wong, "Financially Pinched West Covina Cuts Half of Its Maintenance Division," *San Gabriel Valley Tribune,* July 19, 2018, www.sgvtribune.com/2018/07/19/financially-pinched-west-covina-cuts-half-of-its-maintenance-division/.

58. Christopher Yee, "West Covina Finally Adopts a Budget for 2018–19—a Month into New Year," *San Gabriel Valley Tribune,* August 3, 2018, www.sgvtribune.com/2018/08/03/west-covina-finally-adopts-a-budget-for-2018-19-a-month-into-new-year/.

59. Ibid.

60. "West Covina Councilmember Loses Re-Election Bid," *Rafu Shimpo,*

NOTES TO CHAPTER EIGHT 321

November 12, 2018, www.rafu.com/2018/11/west-covina-councilmember-loses
-re-election-bid/.

61. Christopher Yee, "West Covina Leaders Propose Restoring Cut Police,
Fire Resources, but with What Money?" *San Gabriel Valley Tribune,* December 24, 2018, www.sgvtribune.com/2018/12/24/west-covina-leaders-propose
-restoring-cut-police-fire-resources-but-with-what-money/.

62. Christopher Yee, "With Signature Gathering Underway, West Covina
Mayor Wants Council to Opine on Sales Tax Hike," *San Gabriel Valley Tribune,* September 16, 2019, www.sgvtribune.com/2019/09/16/with-signature
-gathering-underway-west-covina-mayor-wants-council-to-opine-on-sales-tax
-hike/; Christopher Yee, "State Auditor Finds West Covina to Be 17th Most Financially Challenged City in California," *San Gabriel Valley Tribune,* October
24, 2019, www.sgvtribune.com/2019/10/24/state-auditor-finds-west-covina-to-be
-17th-most-financially-challenged-city-in-california/.

63. Yee, "State Auditor Finds West Covina to Be 17th Most Financially Challenged City in California."

64. Yee, "Cash-Strapped West Covina Approves a Raise for Its Firefighters."

65. Romy Varghese, "California City That Sold Pension Debt Now at Fiscal
Brink," Bloomberg, December 1, 2020, www.bloomberg.com/news/articles/2020
-12-01/california-city-that-sold-pension-debt-in-july-at-fiscal-brink.

66. See DiSalvo, *Government Against Itself*; Moe, *Special Interest.*

67. See Moe, "Collective Bargaining and the Performance of the Public
Schools."

68. See Chubb and Moe, *Politics, Markets, and America's Schools.*

69. Strunk and Grissom, "Do Strong Unions Shape District Policies?"

70. Campaign Zero, "Fair Police Contracts," www.joincampaignzero.org/
contracts: accessed April 22, 2020.

71. See DeRay McKesson, Samuel Sinyangwe, Johnetta Elzie, and Brittany
Packnett, "Police Union Contracts and Police Bill of Rights Analysis," Campaign Zero, June 29, 2016, checkthepolice.org.

72. Stephen Rushin, "Police Union Contracts," *Duke Law Journal* 66, no. 6
(2017): 1224.

73. John Buntin, "David Brown: Caught between Reform and a Hard Place,"
Governing, November 2016, www.governing.com/topics/public-justice-safety/
gov-dallas-police-chief-david-brown.html.

74. Radley Balko, "What the Dallas Police Department Does Right—and Why
Doing Those Things Could Now Be More Difficult," *Washington Post,* July 8,
2016, www.washingtonpost.com/news/the-watch/wp/2016/07/08/what-dallas-pd
-does-right-and-why-doing-those-things-could-now-be-more-difficult/.

75. Buntin, "David Brown."

76. Ibid.; Jeremy Gorner, "A Racially Charged Police Shooting. A City
on Edge. Chicago's Likely Next Police Leader Has Been There Before," *Chi-*

cago Tribune, April 14, 2020, www.chicagotribune.com/news/criminal-justice/ct-chicago-police-david-brown-profile-20200415-xep7kg74g5fovj64yrtfrpznjm-story.html.

77. Gorner, "A Racially Charged Police Shooting."

78. Buntin, "David Brown."

79. George Joseph, "Is the Dallas Police Department a Model for Reform? Depends on Which Part of Dallas You're From," CityLab, July 14, 2016, www.citylab.com/equity/2016/07/is-the-dallas-police-department-a-model-for-reform/490610/.

80. Ken Kalthoff, "Dallas Police Leaders Oppose Use of Force Training Plan," NBC Dallas-Fort Worth, January 13, 2014, www.nbcdfw.com/news/local/dallas-police-leaders-oppose-use-of-force-training-plan/1972168/.

81. Ibid.

82. Tristan Hallman, "Dallas Police Association Wants Department to Stop Releasing Officers' Names after Shootings," *Dallas Morning News,* September 8, 2015, www.dallasnews.com/news/crime/2015/09/08/dallas-police-association-wants-department-to-stop-releasing-officers-names-after-shootings/.

83. "Editorial: Dallas Police Chief Risks Looking Reactive on Overhaul," *Dallas Morning News,* January 8, 2014, www.dallasnews.com/opinion/editorials/2014/01/09/editorial-dallas-police-chief-risks-looking-reactive-on-overhaul/.

84. Balko, "What the Dallas Police Department Does Right"; Buntin, "David Brown."

85. Charlotte Gill, David Weisburd, Cody W. Telep, Zoe Vitter, and Trevor Bennett, "Community-Oriented Policing to Reduce Crime, Disorder and Fear and Increase Satisfaction and Legitimacy among Citizens: A Systematic Review," *Journal of Experimental Criminology* 10, no. 4 (2014): 399–428.

86. Bureau of Justice Assistance, "Understanding Community Policing: A Framework for Action" (Washington, DC, 1994), www.ojp.gov/pdffiles/commp.pdf.

87. Steven Brill, "The Rubber Room: The Battle over New York City's Worst Teachers," *New Yorker,* August 24, 2009, www.newyorker.com/magazine/2009/08/31/the-rubber-room.

Chapter Nine

1. See Patricia A. Kirkland, "Mayoral Candidates, Social Class, and Representation in American Cities," *Journal of Political Institutions and Political Economy* 1, no. 1 (2020): 105–36; Oliver, Ha, and Callen, *Local Elections and the Politics of Small-Scale Democracy.*

2. Melody Crowder-Meyer, Shana Kushner Gadarian, and Jessica Trounstine, "Electoral Institutions, Gender Stereotypes, and Women's Local Representa-

NOTES TO CHAPTER NINE

tion," *Politics, Groups, and Identities* 3, no. 2 (2015): 318–34; Hajnal, *America's Uneven Democracy*.

3. E.g., Christopher R. Berry and William G. Howell, "Accountability and Local Elections: Rethinking Retrospective Voting," *Journal of Politics* 69, no. 3 (2007): 844–58; Craig M. Burnett and Vladimir Kogan, "The Politics of Potholes: Service Quality and Retrospective Voting in Local Elections," *Journal of Politics* 79 no. 1 (2017): 302–14; Julia Payson, "When Are Local Incumbents Held Accountable for Government Performance? Evidence from US School Districts," *Legislative Studies Quarterly* 42, no. 3 (2017): 421–48.

4. E.g., Einstein and Kogan, "Pushing the City Limits."

5. See, e.g., Mossberger and Stoker, "The Evolution of Urban Regime Theory."

6. In a recent study, Bucchianeri assembles a dataset of city council roll-call votes. See Bucchianeri, "Party Competition and Coalitional Stability."

7. Even beyond questions about whether national party divisions map onto local preferences, it is rare for the top two contenders in a city to be a Democrat and a Republican. See, e.g., de Benedictis-Kessner and Warshaw, "Mayoral Partisanship and Municipal Fiscal Policy." This raises questions about whether national political party affiliation is a key distinguishing feature between candidates in most local contexts.

8. See, e.g., Vladimir Kogan, Stephane Lavertu, and Zachary Peskowitz, "Election Timing, Electorate Composition, and Policy Outcomes: Evidence from School Districts," *American Journal of Political Science* 62, no. 3 (2018): 637–51; Marc Meredith, "The Strategic Timing of Direct Democracy," *Economics & Politics* 21, no. 1 (2009): 159–77; Jacob S. Rugh and Jessica Trounstine, "The Provision of Local Public Goods in Diverse Communities: Analyzing Municipal Bond Elections," *Journal of Politics* 73, no. 4 (2011): 1038–50.

9. See, e.g., Anzia, *Timing and Turnout*; Berry and Gersen, "The Timing of Elections"; Adam M. Dynes, Michael T. Hartney, and Sam Hayes, "Off-Cycle and Off-Center: Election Timing and Representation in Municipal Government," *American Political Science Review* 115, no. 3 (2021): 1097–1103; Michael T. Hartney and Sam Hayes, "Off-Cycle and Out of Sync: How Election Timing Influences Political Representation," *State Politics and Policy Quarterly* (2021).

10. Moe, "Political Control and the Power of the Agent"; see also Michael T. Hartney, "Teachers Unions and School Board Elections: A Reassessment," Working Paper, Boston College (2021).

11. Moe, "Teacher Unions and School Board Elections."

12. For a helpful discussion of these differences across local policy areas, see the discussion of sewer overflows in Trounstine, *Segregation by Design*.

13. This is consistent with the patterns of interest group coalitions I found in chapter 5 and with Bucchianeri's recent study of city council roll-call votes. See Bucchianeri, "Party Competition and Coalitional Stability."

14. None of the results discussed below change in a substantive way when I use ordered logit rather than OLS.

15. When I exclude the smallest municipalities from the estimation, moreover, the negative coefficients on Democratic presidential vote in columns 2 and 3 are no longer significant, and the positive coefficient on Democratic presidential vote in column 1 is statistically significant. It is therefore not clearly the case that municipalities with more Democratic constituents elect candidates who are less favorable to economic development and growth. Separately, I also analyzed whether (both winning and losing) candidates' self-reported party identification and ideology are related to their stated positions on economic growth. On average, Democratic and liberal candidates express positions less favorable to economic development and growth. Democratic candidates also express more pro-housing positions than do Republican candidates, but the relationship between candidate ideology and housing positions is not significant.

16. When I exclude the state fixed effects, Democratic presidential vote is a positive and significant predictor of winning candidates' views on firefighter collective bargaining. While these models do not include candidates' party identification and ideology (because my focus is on the local policy positions of winning candidates and whether they are favorable to the key interest groups), my separate analysis shows that Democratic and liberal candidates are more in favor of fire department spending than are Republican and conservative candidates. They are also more favorable to collective bargaining for police officers and firefighters.

Chapter Ten

1. Ellen Ann Fentress and Richard Fausset, "'You Can't Bathe. You Can't Wash': Water Crisis Hobbles Jackson, Miss., for Weeks," *New York Times*, March 12, 2021, www.nytimes.com/2021/03/12/us/jackson-mississippi-water -winter-storm.html.

2. Kris Maher and Jennifer Calfas, "School Reopening Pits Parents against Teachers: 'Is There a Word beyond 'Frustrating'?," *Wall Street Journal*, February 16, 2021, www.wsj.com/articles/school-reopening-covid-classroom-cdc -parents-teachers-union-students-11613512932.

3. Nathan Bomey, *Detroit Resurrected: To Bankruptcy and Back* (New York: Norton, 2016).

4. Frank Capra, dir., *Mr. Smith Goes to Washington* (Columbia Pictures Industries, Los Angeles, 1939).

5. E.g., Fischel, *The Homevoter Hypothesis*.

6. E.g., Campbell, "Policy Makes Mass Politics"; Lenz, *Follow the Leader*.

7. E.g., Mossberger and Stoker, "The Evolution of Urban Regime Theory."

NOTES TO CHAPTER TEN

8. Anzia and Moe, "Interest Groups on the Inside"; DiSalvo *Government Against Itself*; Hartney, *How Policies Make Interest Groups.*

9. See Dynes, Hartney, and Hayes, "Off-Cycle and Off-Center."

10. See Ansolabehere, de Figueiredo, and Snyder, "Why Is There So Little Money in U.S. Politics?"; Hojnacki et al., "Studying Organizational Advocacy and Influence."

11. Baumgartner et al., *Lobbying and Policy Change*; Leech, "Lobbying and Influence."

12. Hertel-Fernandez, *State Capture.*

13. E.g., DiSalvo and Kucik, "Unions, Parties, and the Politics of State Government Legacy Cost."

14. Hartney, *How Policies Make Interest Groups.*

15. Corey DeAngelis and Christos Makridis, "Are School Reopening Decisions Related to Union Influence?," *Social Science Quarterly* (2021); Matt Grossmann, Sarah Reckhow, Katharine Strunk, and Meg Turner, "All States Close but Red Districts Reopen: The Politics of In-Person Schooling during the COVID-19 Pandemic," *Educational Researcher* (2021); Michael Hartney and Leslie Finger, "Politics, Markets, and Pandemics: Public Education's Response to Covid-19," *Perspectives on Politics* (2021); Bradley D. Marianno, Annie Hamphill, Ana Paula Loures-Elias, Libna Garcia, and Cooper Deanna, "Power in a Pandemic: Teachers' Unions and Their Responses to School Reopening," Working Paper, University of Nevada, Las Vegas.

16. WCCUSD board meeting agendas and minutes are available at https:// simbli.eboardsolutions.com/SB_Meetings/SB_MeetingListing.aspx?S= 36030499. Other than one agenda item on November 4, 2020, which was about the criteria for school reopening, a dedicated discussion of reopening was not on the agenda until January 20, 2021.

17. WCCUSD Board of Trustees Study Session, January 20, 2021, www .youtube.com/watch?v=vE3K0OEpTZI; Mike Aldax, "Coalition Urges WCCUSD to Resume In-Person Learning," *Richmond Standard*, February 10, 2021, https://richmondstandard.com/community/education/2021/02/10/parent -coalition-urges-wccusd-to-resume-in-person-learning-quickly-and-safely/.

18. Isabella Bloom and Cameron Nielsen, "WCCUSD Candidates Backed by the UTR Headed for Victory; One Race Remains Too Close to Call," *Richmond Confidential*, November 6, 2020, https://richmondconfidential.org/2020/11/06/ wccusd-candidates-backed-by-the-utr-headed-for-victory-one-race-remains-too -close-to-call/. See the Contra Costa County Public Portal for Campaign Finance Disclosure for candidates' campaign finance reports: https://public.netfile .com/pub2/?aid=CCC.

19. On governments lobbying other governments, see Julia Payson, *When Cities Lobby: How Local Governments Compete for Power in State Politics* (Oxford: Oxford University Press, 2021). See also Rebecca Goldstein and Hye

Young You, "Cities as Lobbyists," *American Journal of Political Science* 61, no. 4 (2017): 864–76.

20. E.g., Burnett and Kogan, "The Politics of Potholes"; Trounstine, *Segregation by Design*.

21. See Hartney, *How Policies Make Interest Groups*.

22. Finger and Hartney, "Financial Solidarity."

23. Dahl, *Who Governs?*

Index

Page numbers in *italics* indicate a figure or table.

abortion groups, 95
abortion rights, 30
Adrian, Charles, 124
Albuquerque, New Mexico, proposed housing development in, 2
American Community Survey (ACS), 66
Anderson, Steve, 55
Arkansas, 98
Arnold, Douglas, 32, 53

Baumgartner, Frank, 33–34, 35, 36, 37, 39, 294n58
Benavides, Stephen, 231
Benedictis-Kessner, Justin de, 217
Black Lives Matter movement, 77, 91, 146, 209, 230
Brown, David, 231, 232
Brown, Michael, 230, 287n36
businesses, 142–43; business incentives, 167; business resources, 83–85; different types of, 83–84; electoral activity of business groups, 254; and the importance of business interest groups, 83; mobilization of employees to engage in politics 28; political activity of, 106–7; political activity of in cities, 89–90, 108; potential for businesses to have a large, direct, and economic stake in city politics, 83; pushback against pro-growth business interests, 197; relationship between business and labor in local politics, 119–22, 121. *See also* businesses, tax incentives for

businesses, tax incentives for, 151–52, 172, 313n29; cost of tax incentives, 174; data concerning, 175–76; municipal government use of business tax incentives, 177; results of the study concerning, 176–82; tax abatements, 174, 175 178, 180, 199; tax credits, 175; theoretical considerations concerning, 173–75

California, 98, 113, 147
Callen, Zachery, 29–30, 140, 299n19
campaign contributions/financing, 23, 28, 75, 291n14; city campaign finance data in South Carolina and Washington State, 103–5, 104; in Democratic cities, 75; per capita income as a positive predictor of total campaign contributions by individuals, 76
Campaign Zero, 230–31
Census of Governments, 63, 66, 110, 203; employment data of, 208; Finance file of, 218
chambers of commerce, 84–85, 94, 100, 106–7, 137, 169, 181, 187, 199, 251, 266, 304n28, 315n59; activity in local politics, 85, 95–96, 107–8, 193–94, 254, 312n11
cities, 301n36; common policy concerns of, 31, 138–39; cross-city variation in local policies, 79, 308n15; direct expenditures of, 66, 299–300n22; distinction between whether a city makes policy on an issue, or more fixed

cities (*continued*)
characteristics of cities, 65; limitations in the ability to pursue a wide range of policies, 64; number of cities by interest group and political party activity, *125*; particular details of city policies, 65; policy making of, 29; political activity of businesses in cities, 89–90, *108*; and the possibility of population growth due to interest group policies, 64–65; and the range of issues on which a city makes policy decisions, 64–65. *See also* city interest group activity, explaining variation in

City Elections Survey, 57, 98–99, 100, 111–13, *112*, 118–19, 170, 241, 305n38, 306n10

city interest group activity, explaining variation in, 66, *67, 68*, 68–73, *73*; and insights from local campaign finance data, 73–76, *75*; and "normal" interest group politics, 76–79, *78*; and partisanship, 68–69; using city demographics, 69; using local politics literature examining the effects of political institutions, 69–70; using multilevel regression and post-stratification (MRP) measures of citizen ideology, 69; using the two-party vote in the 2012 presidential election, 69, 71–72

City Interest Groups Survey, 56, 92, 107, 120, 170, 175

City Limits (Peterson), 138

coalitions, 70, 119; of interest groups, 115, 129, 323n13; national coalitions, 127; party coalitions, 122, 123, 124–25, 126, 129; strength of, 32–33

collective bargaining, 2, 18, 144, 147, 208–9, 210, 218–19, 238, 317n14, 318nn24–26; estimating the effects of using difference in differences analysis, 205; of firefighters, 223–24, 247–48, 318n25, 324n16; laws mandating collective bargaining for teachers, 204; likely effects of collective bargaining on city costs, 247–48; limiting of, 317n10; local public-sector bargaining, 206–7; mandatory, 89, 204; police collective bargaining, 152, 213, 215, 223, 230–34, 236, 248–49, 256, 258, 261, 262, 318n24,

319n39; process of, 219–20; and public-sector unionization, 205; state laws concerning, 91; weakening of through state legislation, 41–42

compensation, for police and fire protection, 204–7, 318n25; compensation beyond base salaries, 205; data and empirical design of the study of, 207–11; pay incentives for police officers, *214*, 215; police and fire protection payroll/ expenditures per capita, *211, 221*; results of the study concerning, 211–213, 215; role of city residents' party affiliations in, 210–11; total spending and the share for police and fire protection, 215–24, *219*; and the trade-off for unions between increasing salaries and increasing employment levels, 204

COVID-19 pandemic, 264, 272

"culture of masculinity," in firefighters, 145

Current Population Survey (CPS), 89, 90, 303n24

Dahl, Robert, 9, 47, 48, 51, 59–60, 275, 276; on the options for political movements to influence policy, 122

Dallas Communities Organizing for Change, 231

Dana Point, California, 77, 78, *78*

Danziger, Steve, 55

data, 18, 26, 28, 63, 69, 72, 74, 175–76, 273–74; campaign contribution, 14–15, 75, 76; on city institutions, 58; cross-sectional, 41; the data hurdle, 56–57; datasets, 76, 79, 157, 163–64, 187, 191, 205, 208, 230, 232, 242; historical, 40; public-opinion, 8–9, 10, 19, 52, 160, 267; quantitative, 28, 57. *See also* Law Enforcement Management and Administrative Statistics (LEMAS) data

Democratic Party, 116–18, 119, 128, 129, 130, 132, 145, 217; active presence of in Washington State and South Carolina, 126; coalitions of, 127

Democratic presidential vote, 71–76, 106–7, 158, 176, 181–82, 188, 191, 194, 196, 200, 210, 212, 217–24, 238, 312n11, 318–19nn38–39, 324nn15–16; coefficients on Democratic presidential vote, *105*, 170–71

INDEX   329

Democrats, 72, 77, 79, 105–6, 144, 195, 210, 217, 224; Democratic partisanship, 111

dependent variable, solutions to the problem of, 40–43; comparing policies across subnational governments, 40–41; historical analysis, 40

dependent variables: "policy as prize" and the dependent variable, 34–38; policy change as, 35; problems concerning, 34; public policy as, 38–39; removing policy content from, 39–40; roll-call votes as, 35. *See also* dependent variable, solutions to the problem of

Detroit, bankruptcy of, 264

developers, 100, 102, 110, 137, 149, 181, 186, 251, 265; competition with other groups in the selection of political candidates, 123–34; political activity of, 107–8, 187–88, 190, 254. *See also* land use

development firms, 96

difference in differences analysis, 41, 43, 156–57, 205, 206–7

directness 31, 32, 160

DiSalvo, Daniel, 216

Dodd-Frank Act (2010), 21

Durkan, Jenny, 2

economic development and growth, 16, 53, 82, 88, 99, 138–43, 148, 163–64, 200, 239, 241, 249, 265, 311n6; economic development tools, 165, *166*, 167, 311n9, 312n11; economic development policies with small or ambiguous costs, 168–71; and the importance of business interest groups, 83; local candidate positions concerning, 251–55. *See also* housing development; land use; economic development and growth policies, overview of

economic development and growth policies, overview of, 164–65; politics of, 198–99; and the use of business incentives, 167–68, *167*; use of economic development tools, 170–71, *171*

education. *See* public education

Einstein, Katherine, 183–84

El Cerrito Chamber of Commerce, 85

elected officials: Democratic, 5; Republican, 5

elections, 30–31; city elections, 98–99, 126–29, 304n31; correlates of political party activity in municipal elections, *131*; district elections, 301n37; influence of political parties and interest groups on, 123–24; national party incentives to be involved in city elections, 126–29; nonpartisan municipal elections, 124, 300n32, 301n38; off-cycle elections, 69, 71, 111, 118, 130, 301n37, 313n29; partisan elections, 301n38; patterns of interest group activity in city elections, 99–100; political parties in city elections, 116–18, *117*, 129–33. *See also* elections, local

elections, local, 18, 114; comparison of the policy positions of winning and losing candidates in, 250–51, *250*; interest group influence on, 240–41, 262–63; and interest groups, 241–43; local candidates' positions on local issues, 243, *244–45*, 245–51, *249*. *See also* interest group activity, and the positions of winning candidates in local elections

environmental groups, 26, 28, 49–50, 94–95, 98, 106, 127, 141, 148, 150, 170, 174, 181–82, 185–86, 194, 197, 200, 274, 298n4, 311n5; as active in city policies, 87, 95; as an anti-growth force, 169; political activity of, 178, 181, 252, 254, 255, 259, 262

environmental sustainability, 165, 311n6

Farm Hill Neighborhood Association, 3

FEMA Staffing for Adequate Fire and Emergency Response (SAFER) grant, 224–25

Finger, Leslie, 274

firefighters. *See* compensation, for police and fire protection; firefighters' unions

firefighters' unions, 17–18, 90–91, 94–95, 100, 102, 103, 111, 137, 149, 202, 203, 204, 207, 218, 223–24, 239, 247, 25, 261, 262, 265, 304n29; activity of in city politics, 109–10; electoral activity of, 257–58; influence of, 208, 209–10, 212, 229, 237–38

Fischel, William, 141

Floyd, George, 201

Freeland, Chris, 226

330 INDEX

Gamma Development, 2

Gerber, Elisabeth, 217

Glick, David, 183–84

Good Jobs First, 176

Governing, 231, 232

Government Accounting Standards Board (GASB), 175–76

government(s): competition among for mobile, taxpaying citizens, 33; research literature focus on the federal government, 38–39. *See also* government(s), local/municipal

government(s), local/municipal, 1, 2, 4, 6–7, 12, 14, 17, 18, 23, 29, 40, 43, 56–57, 58, 74, 95, 118, 119, 164–65, 176, 178, 193, 199, 217, 264, 298n7, 307n6, 317n14; group activities in, 14, 15; influence of municipal government policies, 137–38; as mini-federal governments, 307n6; research on the policies of, 53–54; state limitations on, 70–71

Gray, Virginia, 24–25

Great Recession, 77, 224, 265

Green Party, 306n9

"growth machine," the, 53, 83

guilds, 291n20; definition of, 24–25

Gyourko, Joseph, 164, 186–87, 188–90, 191, 315n55

Hacker, Jacob, 22, 34

Hartney, Michael, 271–72, 273

Hertel-Fernandez, Alexander, 271

Hirsch, Barry, 89

Homevoter Hypothesis (Fischel), 141

Hopkins, Daniel, 217

housing, 153, 265; housing prices, 1; housing supply, 245–46. *See also* housing development

housing development, 1, 182–83, 198–200, 251–55; average duration of reviews for housing development, 189–91, *189*; and city residents' preferences concerning, 197–98; longer development times in some cities as opposed to others, 188–89; and minimum lot size requirements, 188, *188*; multifamily housing development, 158, 196, 197; opposition to, 185–86, 190, 200, 316n66; permitted housing units, 192–96, *193*, *195*, 316n61; process, institutions, and delay in, 186–92; rules

limiting multifamily housing, 187–88; single-family housing units, 194–95, 196; theoretical considerations and expectations concerning, 183–86; the unusual case of housing development, 196–98

ideology, 5, 6, 143, 266–67; citizen ideology, 310n53; city ideology, 72, 181, 318–19nn38–39; estimating ideology's effect on policy, 45; mass publics, party, and ideology, 157–60; measuring of at the local level, 45, 158–59, 181; national ideology, 19, 159, 220; relationship of to city residents and total city spending, 216–17

Incentives to Pander (Jensen and Malesky), 172

income inequality, 165

independent variables, 16, 41, 44, 46, 47, 48; activity as, 49; resources as, 48

Indiana, 98, 112, 130

influence: centrality of, 21; of conservative networks, 271; "influencers," 20. *See also* influence, of interest groups

influence, of interest groups, 27–29, 33–34, 39, 43, 48–49, 135–37, 160–62, 205–6, 294n58, 307n1; comparing and controlling the influence of other political actors, 45; conditions of influence, 49–51; cross-sectional analysis as a means of testing for, 41–42; as the effect of group activity, 14, 15, 47; and the estimates of "influence," 44, 156–57; gradual accumulation of, 270; and influence as the dependent variable in the evaluation of, 44–45; on local elections, 240–43; of municipal government group activities, 14, 15; policy-focused approach to the evaluation of, 44–49; and "policy as prize" and the dependent variable, 34–38; and the potential for reverse causality, 155; of public-sector unions, 205–6; representation and influence in local politics, 51–54. *See also* influence, of interest groups, and municipal government policies

influence, of interest groups, and municipal government policies, 137–38; and budgetary trade-offs, 150–53; city policy

INDEX

will influence political activity, 155–56;
conditions of interest group influence,
148–49; endogeneity of public policy
and interest group activity, 154–57; expectations concerning, 148–54; influence of public-sector unions, 145–47;
on local economic development and
growth, 138–43; on local public service
provision, 143–47; three forms of policy
costs and trade-off that shape political
focus, 152–53. *See also* mass publics
interest group activity, 23–25, 47–48, 135,
202, 293n40; and city expenditures, *63*;
in Democratic and liberal cities, 72–
73; and the disconnect between the
amount of literature on interest groups
and the lack of theoretical guidance on
basic interest group activity, 25–29; endogeneity of public policy and interest
group activity, 154–57; group activity
flows from what governments actually
do, 27; influence-oriented conception
of, 29; interest group activity focusing primarily on resources, 27; interest
group activity in large versus small cities, 30–31; interest group systems, 27–
28; in municipal governments, 265, 274;
patterns of interest group activity in
city elections, 99–100; potential activity, 48; and the problems of collective
action and group maintenance, 26–27;
and putting policy interests first, 29–33;
puzzle of cities with more Democratic
residents having greater interest group
activity than cities whose residents lean
Republican, 105–6, 110–11; when and
how interest groups are active, 95–102,
96, 97, 99, 100, 101. *See also* city interest group activity, explaining variation in; interest group activity, and the
positions of winning candidates in local elections; interest group activity, by
type of group; interest group activity,
in local politics; interest group activity,
measuring of
interest group activity, and the positions of
winning candidates in local elections,
251–55, 256, 257; and housing model
results. 254–55; lack of relationship between the activity of chambers of com-

merce or developers on winning candidates' views, 254; on local economic
development and housing, 251–55, 253;
on public safety, 255–58; winning and
losing candidates in the same city, 258–
61, 260, 261
interest group activity, by type of group,
92–95, 92, 95; building trade unions,
94; chambers of commerce, 94; developers, 93; environmental groups, 95;
firefighters' unions, 94, 95; local labor
councils, 94; miscellaneous employee
unions, 94; neighborhood associations,
94, 95, 97; nonprofit service providers,
94; police unions, 94, 95; racial and ethnic minority organizations, 94, 95; retail businesses, 93; taxpayer organizations, 94, 95; teachers' unions, 94
interest group activity, in local politics,
55–56, 59, 60, 62, 82, 149, 242, 298n4,
299n15, 304n26; different interest
groups as active on different policy issues, 97–98; within-group variation in
activity across cities, 102–10, 103, 104,
105
interest group activity, measuring of, 56–
57, 296–97n100, 297n101; design of the
survey concerning, 57–62; and policy
stakes, 62–66; scarcity of data concerning, 56–57
interest groups, 267–68, 269–75, 288–
89n47, 291n21, 292n25; citizen groups,
24; in the context of the federal government, 30; data concerning, 14–15; defining an interest group, 59–60; growth-
oriented interest groups, 16; and the
importance of business interest groups,
83; influencing policy as the main goal
of, 27; interest groups with a federated structure, 86; interests of, 22–23;
in local government, 3–4; in local policy making, 265–66; long-term game
of, 34–35; non-occupational groups,
86–87; occupationally based groups,
24; patterns of local group activity, 11–
12; political parties as coalitions of interest groups, 115; public policy as the
main concern of, 4, 21–22, 34–35; research on interest group influence,
11–12; research on interest groups as

interest groups (*continued*)
descriptive, 23; scholarship concerning, 270–71; strategy of, 25; survival as a goal of, 26; and the theoretical puzzle of how interest groups form, 25–26; as unimportant according to political scientists, 9. *See also* interest groups, policy-focused approach to research concerning; interest groups, predicting types of; political parties, relationship with interest groups

interest groups, policy-focused approach to research concerning, 10–13, 13–14, 18, 20–23, 27, 34, 79–80, 81, 95, 262; and city policies, 82; usefulness of, 111

interest groups, predicting types of, 82–92; ethnic and racial minority organizations, 91; potential groups that have large, direct, and regular economic interests in city decisions concerning public service provision, 88–89; taxpayer groups, 91. *See also* businesses; unions

International City/County Management Association's (ICMA): Economic Development Survey of, 164, 165, 168, 169–70, 175, 176, 313n22; labor-management relations surveys of, 208; Municipal Form of Government (FOG) Survey of, 58, 70, 300n32; Police and Fire Personnel and Expenditure Surveys of, 207, 208

Jackson, Matt, 225, 226
Jackson, Mississippi, water crisis in, 264
Jensen, Nathan, 172, 173, 175, 176, 178
Johnson, Lloyd, 226

Kentucky, 98, 112, 130

labor councils, 85–86, 93, 94, 106
land use, 82, 110, 239, 241, 311n4, 315n55; and economic development, 151, 154; and the land-related costs of local policies, 149–50, 151; politics of, 53; unusual features of land use costs, 150. *See also* housing development

Law Enforcement Management and Administrative Statistics (LEMAS) data, 203, 208, 212–13, 232, 233, 234, 239;

LEMAS Body-Worn Camera Supplement, 235–36
Leech, Beth L., 35, 36, 294n58
legislatures, 6; legislature behavior, 276; and theories of Congress, 270
liberalism, 73
Libertarian Party, 306n9
Lightfoot, Lori, 133
lobbying, 20, 23–24, 27–28, 37, 39, 46, 81, 134, 206, 240, 270, 274, 302n9; body of literature concerning, 24; formal, 14, 15, 29, 56, 135; registered, 14, 28, 56; studies of, 35
Lobbying and Policy Change (Baumgartner et al.), 37
Logan, John, 53, 141
Lowery, David, 24–25

Macpherson, David, 89
Malesky, Edmund, 172, 173, 175, 178
mass publics, 9, 10, 31, 136–37, 160, 276; characteristics of, 181; influence of, 20, 157; mass publics, party, and ideology, 157–60; policy makers response to, 155; role of, 268–69
material interests/benefits: as essential to the emergence of "vested interests," 32; as a motivator for political action, 31–32
Mayhew, David, 130
memorandum of understanding (MOU), 272
mobility, 84; decreased, 1; of taxpaying residents and businesses, 5, 64
Moe, Terry, 31–32, 144, 147, 205, 207, 242–43, 318n26; on groups' resources, 292n28; on "vested interests," 290n10
Molotch, Harvey, 53, 141
Moraga, California, 55
Moraga-Orinda Fire District, 55
Mothers Against Police Brutality, 231

neighborhood associations: as active in city politics and policies, 87–88, 94, 95, 97, 100, 102, 141–42, 181–82, 188, 193–94, 221, 253–54; as an anti-growth force, 169, 197; leverage of, 199–200
New Haven, Connecticut, 59–60; analysis of key policy decisions in, 9–10

INDEX 333

New Orleans, politics of education reform in, 147
Newton, Massachusetts, 55
Next Generation Action Network, 231
Northland Investment Corporation, 55
Not in My Backyard (NIMBY), 142

Obama, Barack, 69, 130
Ohio, 98, 130; union activity in, 43; weakening of collective bargaining rights in, 42
Oliver, Eric, 29–30, 140, 299n19; collective action model of, 31
Olson, Mancur, 23–24, 25–26; collective action theory of, 84, 288n46
Oregon, 98
Orinda, California, 55

Palmer, Maxwell, 183–84
parks and recreation departments, 6, 215; spending on, *221*, 222, 299–300n22
partisanship, 5, 6, 68–69, 72, 143, 266–67, 271; Democratic, 111, 272; local, 106; measuring of at the local level, 158–60; national, 19, 159, 220; relationship of to city residents and total city spending, 216–17; theoretical case for, 178–79
Peterson, Paul, 29, 53, 64, 82, 138–40, 171, 199
Pierson, Paul, 22, 34, 39, 40
police brutality, 1, 152, 202
Police Reform Organizing Project, 230
police reform/reformers, 230–32, 237; organizations pushing reforms, 231; specific reforms, 231; and the switch from "command and control" to "de-escalation," 231
police unions, 17–18, 49, 91, 94–95, 96, 100, 102, 111, 137–38, 149, 203, 218, 232, 235, 237–39, 304n29; activity of in city politics, 96–97, 98, 109–10, 156, 208, 211–12, 223, 231, 236–37, 276; competition with other groups in the selection of political candidates, 123–34; electoral activity of, 255, 258, 261, 262; influence of on city spending on salaries, 209–10, 212, 220
policing, 3, 255, 287n36; community policing, 232–34, *233*; and the deployment and use of body cameras, 13, 18, 65, 137, 203, 230, 231–32, 235–37, *236*, 246;

law and order dimension of, 145. *See also* compensation, for police and fire protection; police reform/reformers; work rules, and the police
policy change, 12, 35, 37, 39, 42, 270
PolicyLink, 230
policy making, 37. *See also* cities, policy making of
political activities, 20; number of cities by interest group and political party activity, *125*; and policy focus, 50–51
political candidates: interest group contributions to candidates who also received contributions from political parties, 127–29, *128*, 301n42; recruitment of, 123–25. *See also* elections, local
political economy, 33, 142; local, 44, 45, 86, 138, 141, 241, 285–86n20; quantitative local political economy literature, 143, 285–86n20
political parties, in local politics, 114–16; political parties as coalitions of interest groups, 115; political parties in city elections, 116–18, *117*; why does political party activity vary across cities?, 129–33. *See also* political parties, relationship with interest groups
political parties, relationship with interest groups, 118–19, 133–34; campaign contributions by political parties (2015), *125*; interest groups may not need political parties, 122–26; national parties as a bad fit for local interest groups, 119–22; national party incentives to be involved in city elections, 126–29; number of cities by interest group and political party activity, *125*
political representation, 9, 45, 157, 267–69, 287–88n39; and research concerning mass publics, 155
politics, local/municipal, 1, 85, 106, 139, 202, 215, 263, 270, 271, 292n35; breakdown of the expenditures of, 6, 7; conflict in, 264–66; core functions of, 6–7; differences from national politics, 6, 7–8; dynamics of, 5; homeowner involvement in, 141–42; importance of, 4–5; in local school districts, 271–72; relationship between business and labor in local politics, 119–22, *121*; representation

politics, local/municipal (*continued*)
and influence in, 51–54; research concerning, 3, 153, 298n6; responsibilities of, 5, 6; similarity to national politics, 5–6. *See also* elections, local; interest group activity, in local politics; political parties, in local politics

politics, national, 4, 15, 122; legislature behavior in, 276; primary lobbying entities of, 81; research concerning, 275–76

politics, urban, 88, 181, 241, 266; research literature concerning, 53, 82, 89, 138, 141, 142, 143, 148, 184, 200, 239, 302n3

Politics in Time (Pierson), 40

population ecology, 26

"post-materialism," 293n47

power: debate concerning community power, 47; exercise of by preventing debate and blocking issues, 9–10; "first face" of, 9; power dynamics, 147; "second face" of, 10. *See also* power, and local interests

power, and local interests, 264–67; and interest groups, 269–75; and political representation, 267–69; and public policy, 275–77

Progressive Era, municipal reformers during, 114–15, 130

property development, 82, 99

public education, 5, 6, 51, 110, 215, 229–30, 287n33; role of teachers' unions in, 202, 215. *See also* New Orleans, politics of education reform in

public opinion, 21, 44, 46, 52, 137, 154–55, 157–60, 217, 218, 220, 268, 273, 287–88n39; lack of data concerning, 8; and policy, 295–96n88; public opinion data, 8–9, 10, 19, 52, 160, 267; public opinion influence, 155; public opinion polls, 8, 21, 267

public policy: and agenda-setting, 296n96; development of, 39; and the influence of interest groups, 12–13; and "policy subsystem" actors, 35; and power 275–77; what older case study-based research got right concerning, 35

public safety, 16, 149, 201–2, 255–58, 265; measuring local candidates' positions on public safety, 246–47; public safety provision as a staple of municipal government, 90

public-sector unions, 16, 17–18, 28, 42–43, 103, 106, 108–9, 138, 143–44, 208, 209, 215, 220, 240, 266, 268, 271, 274, 303n24; and collective bargaining, 28, 203, 205, 207, 247; influence of, 147, 202–3, 205–6, 216; policy interests of, 228–29; political science literature concerning, 144, 147, 148, 202, 228, 238; relationships between public-sector unions and elected officials, 145–46; union activity in city/local politics, *109*, 110, 111, 144–45, 238; union-management relations governed by state laws, 89; union membership and political activity of, *107*; weak and fragmented opposition to, 146–47

quantitative analysis, 10, 35–36, 37, 38, 182, 200

racial and ethnic minority groups, 91, 94, 106, 141–42, 143, 209–10, 220–21, 232, 134–35, 237, 256, 258

racial profiling, 246

racism, systemic, 1–2

Redwood City, California, pandemic-induced economic turndown in, 2–3

regime theory, 83, 308n11

Republican Party, 116–18, 119, 127–28, 130, 132, 145; coalitions of, 127

Republicans, 72, 77, 79, 105–6, 144, 195, 210, 217–18, 224

research, qualitative, 47

resources, 4, 8, 31, 37, 49, 62, 66, 81, 123, 246, 269, 292n28; business resources, 83–85; citizens' resources, 79; importance of, 11; inequality of, 27; interest groups' resources, 34, 48; political resources, 50, 136, 292n35, 297n101, 307n1

Rhode Island, 98, 112, 130

RightSize Newton, 55

roll-call votes, 35; analysis of, 36–37, 39

Romney, Mitt, 130

Saiz, Albert, 164, 186–87, 188–90, 191, 315n55

INDEX 335

Scanning, Analysis, Response, and Assessment (SARA), 234–35
Schattschneider, E. E., 31, 35
Seattle, Washington, efforts to reform the police department in, 2
Seattle Police Officers Guild (SPOG), 2
Shaghaghi, Venus, 176
Shang Ha, 29–30, 140, 299n19
Sierra Club organizations, 197, 274
Smoot-Hawley tariff, 35
South Carolina, 98, 250; campaign contributions to municipal elections in, 57, 74, 75; campaign finance data of, 125–26; cities in that lean Republican but have low union membership, 103; city campaign finance data in, 103–5, *104*; Democratic Party activity in, 126; labor groups in, *103*; percentage of construction workers that are unionized in, 86; percentage of government workers that are unionized in, 89; prohibition in against collective bargaining for government employees, 41–42; as a right-to-work state, 41
South Carolina State Ethics Commission's Public Disclosure and Accountability Reporting system, 74
status quo bias, 42–43
Stuart, Kenny, 2
Summers, Anita, 164, 186–87, 188–90, 191, 315n55

Tausanovitch, Chris, 69, 158, 159, 181, 216–17, 218
taxes/taxpayers/taxpayer groups, 91, 94, 95, 138, 170, 251, 255, 313n28; activity of taxpayer groups regarding housing development, 191; activity of taxpayer groups regarding police and firefighters' salaries, 209–10; difficulty of raising taxes, 146, 238; tax abatements, 17, 137, 148, 151, 164, 167, 172, 174, 175–76, *178*, 179, 180–81, *180*, 199–200, 280, 313–14n31, 314nn33–34; tax increment financing (TIF), 313n22. *See also* businesses, tax incentives for
Taylor, Breonna, 201
Taylor Ranch Neighborhood Association, 2
teachers, 90, 144–47, 152, 204, 229, 231,

273; self-interest as a political motivator of, 309n26. *See also* teachers' unions
teachers' unions, 21–22, 48, 90, 94–95, 235, 271, 274, 297n101; and collective bargaining, 229; influence on school board elections and decisions, 147, 242–43, 272; opposition to, 146; political activity of, 109–10, 145; research concerning, 144–45; role of in public education, 202, 215
Texas Chapter of the American Civil Liberties Union (ACLU), 231
Tiebout, Charles, 33
"traditional party organizations" (TPOs), 130, 131
Truman, David, 26

UCLA Theory of Parties, 118, 119, 122, 123
unions, 2, 24, 41, 81, 82, 103, 302n9, 303n24; building trade unions, 89, 94, 170, 252, 313n28; city employee unions, 89; labor unions, 2–3, 15, 102, 104, 106; "miscellaneous" unions, 90; municipal employee unions, 90–91; private-sector unions, 86, 89, 104, 120; stake of in city policies, 85–86; unionization as higher in the public versus the private sector, 89; union membership in Mississippi, 48, 296n99. *See also* firefighters' unions; police unions; public-sector unions; teachers' unions
Urban Fortunes (Logan and Molotch), 141
US Census Bureau's Building Permits Survey, 192
US Department of Justice (DOJ), 2

Volcker Rule, 21
voting/voters, 20, 178; economic voting, 140; linkage between elected officials and voters, 172; mobilizing voters, 123; the rational choice puzzle concerning, 26; research concerning, 26. *See also* roll-call votes, analysis of

Walker, Jack, 26
Warshaw, Christopher, 69, 158, 159, 181, 216–17, 218
Washington Public Disclosure Commission, 74

Washington State, 98, 129, 250, 306n13; campaign contributions in municipal elections in, 57, 74; campaign finance data of, 125–26; city campaign finance data in, 103–5, *104*; contested municipal races in, 120–21; Democratic Party activity in, 126; high level of union membership in, 103; labor groups in, *103*; percentage of construction workers that are unionized in, 86; percentage of government workers that are unionized in, 89, 90; percentage of police and firefighter that are unionized in, 90

West Contra Costa Unified School District (WCCUSD), 272–73

West Covina, California, 203, 238; collective bargaining between the city and the FFA, 225–26; fiscal pressure and fire protection in, 224–28; fiscal risk and near bankruptcy of, 227–28; and the funding and defunding of Engine 4, 224, 225, 226

West Covina Firefighters' Association (FFA), 224, 227

West Covina Police Officers Association, 226, 227

West Sacramento, California, 77, 78, *78*

Whithorn, Larry, 225

Who Governs? (Dahl), 47, 48, 59, 276

Wilson, James Q., 52

Wisconsin: union activity in, 43; weakening of collective bargaining rights in, 42

work rules, and the police, 228–37; causes and effects of work rules, 229; rules concerning contracts, 229; union influence on work rules and contracts, 229–30

Wu, Tony, 226

YIMBY (Yes in My Backyard) movement, 1

zoning, 29, 31, 99, 167, 185, 186, 299–300n22

Lightning Source UK Ltd.
Milton Keynes UK
UKHW052343170223
416949UK00014B/520